As Peter Elbow examines the prose of Gretel Ehrlich and Richard Selzer, he explores how we can account for the literary quality of voice in nonfiction and what this says about the nature of voice in general.

In Part III: Implications for Pedagogy, five contributors, including Jim W. Corder and Chris Anderson, show how the theories expressed in the earlier essays can be applied to the classroom. All of the contributors argue that literary nonfiction, by its nature, reveals the complexity, power, and rhetorical possibilities of language—and that this ought to be the unifying concern of rhetoric and composition as a discipline.

CHRIS ANDERSON is Assistant Professor of English and Composition Coordinator at Oregon State University. He is also the author of *Style as Argument: Contemporary American Nonfiction.*

Southern Illinois University Press
P.O. Box 3697
Carbondale, IL 62902-3697

Printed in the United States of America

D1300411

LITERARY NONFICTION

Theory, Criticism, Pedagogy

Edited by
Chris Anderson

Southern Illinois University Press
Carbondale and Edwardsville

Literary nonfiction

Printed in the United States of America
Edited by Lawrence Klepp
Designed by Jody Dyer Jasinski
Production supervised by Natalia Nadraga

91 90 89   4 3 2 1

Library of Congress Cataloging-in-Publication Data

Literary nonfiction : theory, criticism, pedagogy / edited by Chris
    Anderson.

    p.   cm.
    Includes bibliographies.
    ISBN 0-8093-1405-3
    1. American prose literature—20th century—History and criticism.
2. American prose literature—History and criticism—Theory, etc.
3. American prose literature—Study and teaching (Higher)
4. Reportage literature, American—History and criticism.
5. American essays—History and criticism.   6. Journalism—United
States.   I. Anderson, Chris. 1955–   .
PS366.R44L58 1989
818'.508'09—dc19   88-18726
                                                              CIP

CONTENTS

v

Contents

ACKNOWLEDGMENTS

Many people helped in the writing of this book. John Clifford, Robert DiYanni, Charles Schuster, Dennis Rygiel, and I collaborated on the panel discussion that started it, "Literary Nonfiction and Composition Studies," at the 1986 Conference on College Composition and Communication in New Orleans. Clifford was the first to suggest that the session might be the basis of a book—and he and DiYanni and Schuster made many useful suggestions after CCCC about the design of the collection as it was getting off the ground. Schuster read and commented on several of the chapters when I wasn't sure how to respond myself, as did my former colleague Walter Beale of the University of North Carolina at Greensboro. Lisa Ede, Suzanne Clark, and Lex Runciman of Oregon State helped me through innumerable drafts of my own chapter on Lewis Thomas. Linda Peterson of Yale University gave a very insightful reading of the first draft of the manuscript as a whole.

As an editor I was fortunate to have reasonable, conscientious contributors. Working with these people was a most rewarding experience for me—an experience of genuine scholarly community.

I was able to complete the introduction with the help of a research grant from the College of Liberal Arts at Oregon State. Arlene Garren, Margaret Kickert, and Anne Wilson of the English Department staff were very helpful with typing and the details of correspondence. My student workers, Jennifer Stenkamp and Robert Easterday, labored long and hard checking bibliography, footnotes, and quotations. My sister-in-law, Roberta Sabotka, did a wonderful job of proofreading.

Once again, Kenney Withers of Southern Illinois has been a pleasure to work with. And once again, Barb and the kids have been patient and understanding.

INTRODUCTION

Literary Nonfiction and Composition

Chris Anderson

Ronald Weber coined the term "literary nonfiction" in his important study of the New Journalism, *The Literature of Fact*.[1] For him it designates journalism that has some kind of intrinsic value exceeding its value as information, some value as language. The term is problematic because both words in it are problematic, as a number of essays in this collection argue. The word *literary* masks all kinds of ideological concerns, all kinds of values, and is finally more a way of looking at a text, a way of reading—most essays in this collection agree—than an inherent property of a text. The problem with *nonfiction* is that it's a negative term for something positive, implying that somehow nonfiction is less than fiction. More importantly, a number of contributors to the collection argue that it's difficult to tell the difference between the fictive and nonfictive, since we can never apprehend reality without bias.

We also need to distinguish between at least two kinds of writing that fit underneath the larger notion of literary nonfiction. Carl Klaus points out in this book that *essay* is a very slippery term historically and theoretically, but we might say in general, borrowing Walter Beale's taxonomy of discourse, that the essay is reflective and exploratory and essentially personal. Its pur-

1. For criticism of the New Journalism, see also John Hellman's *Fables of Fact: The New Journalism as New Fiction*, John Hollowell's *Fact and Fiction: The New Journalism and the Nonfiction Novel*, Mas'ud Zavarzadeh's *The Mythopoeic Reality: The Postwar American Nonfiction Novel*, and my *Style as Argument: Contemporary American Nonfiction*.

Introduction

pose is not to convey information, although it may do that as well, but rather to tell the story of the author's thinking and experience. Journalism, or the "New Journalism," is informative rather than reflective; its main purpose is to convey information, although it may certainly use autobiography as a perspective and device for conveying that information. There can certainly be essay writing or journalism that is not literary, but the kind of writing that concerns us here is literary in some way, however that is defined. In these terms, of the writers represented in this collection, Selzer, Orwell, and White, for example, are essayists; McPhee and Crane are journalists or informative writers; Didion fits both categories.

But even given these limitations and distinctions, *literary nonfiction* is still a useful phrase for describing what this book is about since it conveys the hybrid nature of the texts we study and thus their paradoxical, threshold, problematic nature. In particular *literary nonfiction* evokes the two different fields we have drawn on: literary criticism, and rhetoric and composition. The texts we study are a site where the methodologies and concerns of these two disciplines—which have always overlapped—come together in unique and provocative ways. Literary critics may read this book without regard for the composition issues. Rhetoricians may read it without regard for the literary theory. But ideally, we would like *Literary Nonfiction* to be read so that the literary and rhetorical issues are always spilling into and influencing each other.

The hybrid nature of our material and our inquiry is reflected in the structure of the book. It begins inductively with a section I've called "Readings." Each of the essays here approaches a particular nonfiction author from the standpoint of a particular critical methodology. Rather than putting these opening chapters in historical order, I've arranged them qualitatively, beginning with a comprehensive aesthetic analysis (Schuster), moving to linguistic, rhetorical, formalist, and psychoanalytical approaches (Rygiel, Filloy, Roundy, and Allister respectively), then concluding with a pair of poststructuralist readings, feminist (Clark) and deconstructionist (Frus). Taken

x

as a whole this section provides a grammar of critical approaches to nonfiction as well as a set of introductions to many of the major nonfiction writers of this century. The second section, "Generalizations and Definitions," examines the genre and theory questions raised by the readings, particularly problems of definition and boundary. How have essayists themselves conceived of the essay, and what can this tell us about the nature of the form (Klaus)? Can we discriminate between what we have called the essay and what we understand as narrative or story (Hesse)? How do fictional accounts operate in persuasive, nonliterary discourse, and what are the implications of this for understanding the relationship of the literary and the nonliterary (Dillon)? How can we account for the literary quality of "voice" in nonfiction, and what does this tell us about the nature of voice in general (Elbow)? What values does the essay form embody (Zeiger)?

These first two headings are both somewhat arbitrary. Essays under "Readings" make important theoretical claims, and essays under "Generalizations" include readings of particular works. The final section, "Implications for Pedagogy," is also a somewhat arbitrary designation, because a number of essays in the previous two sections allude to pedagogical questions, and all have important implications for teaching. But this is just the point. The contributors to this book are writing teachers who are also literature teachers, literary critics who also do work in composition, or vice versa, and their effort has been to see literary nonfiction as crossing genre and discipline boundaries. The underlying argument of the final section, and of the book as a whole, is that the theoretical and critical questions raised in the first two sections are not alien to the composition classroom. Clifford and Schilb apply poststructuralist theory to classroom settings; Hoy, Corder, and I explore both the positive and the subversive influences of the essay form on writing students.

Our effort to break down discipline barriers is reflected even in the style and structure of some of the essays—Corder's, for example, which is an essay itself about the implications of writing and teaching essays. All the authors in the collection, I think, have mirrored in their own prose some of the grace and concreteness and voice they celebrate in Orwell or Didion or White.

Critical Context

The book began in 1986 as a panel discussion at the Conference on College Composition and Communication in New Orleans, "Literary Nonfiction and Composition Studies," involving Dennis Rygiel, John Clifford, Charles Schuster, Robert DiYanni, and myself. We were all teachers of writing, all interested in nonfiction as something valuable in itself and important for composition. After the conference we began corresponding about the possibility of using our papers as seeds for a collection of essays; we contacted a number of scholars and critics from around the country; and the book began to evolve, take on a life of its own.

Our project, in part, was to respond to Rygiel's important call for criticism, "On the Neglect of Twentieth Century Nonfiction: A Writing Teacher's View," which argues clearly and commonsensically that because contemporary nonfiction fills our readers and is the model for so much of what our students write, we should better understand how it works. Very little research has been done on this kind of prose, Rygiel points out, in composition or literary theory, and it's time that composition teachers addressed the need.

First, a thorough criticism of Tom Wolfe, Joan Didion, John McPhee and other contemporary nonfiction writers will help us validate or revise our generalizations about contemporary prose style. "Just as descriptions of English grammar by modern linguists have awakened many of us from one type of dogmatic slumber," Rygiel says, "so rhetorical and stylistic descriptions of modern English prose will awaken us from another" (395). Second, a better understanding of the literary dimension of nonfiction can help make writing intrinsically interesting. If our students see the models in their readers only as models, if they see writing as merely utilitarian, composition will not "register consequentially" in their minds, Rygiel quotes from Corder, and thus we will even undercut our practical interests (397). Third, a better notion of contemporary nonfiction and how to teach it will help us impart "humanistic" values to our students. Though literary nonfiction can illustrate effective patterns of exposition and development, its qualities of voice and style can also demonstrate the value of personal engagement, concreteness, and the recognition of complexity. Fourth, a full body of criticism of nonfiction will help us develop "holistic" methods for dealing with various kinds of nonfiction in the classroom. Literary theory from the New Criticism to poststructuralism has provided such strategies for teaching the reading of fiction and poetry, but Rygiel notes that despite the sporadic efforts of a few composition scholars, we have no similar techniques for teaching contemporary nonfiction.

Rygiel's call for criticism was only the first indication of a resurgence of interest in nonfiction in rhetoric and composition. It was followed the next year by a series of articles in *College English*: William Zeiger's "The Exploratory Essay," an argument for the value of the open-ended forms of the reflective/exploratory essay for freshman writers; Charles Schuster's "Mikhail Bakhtin as Rhetorical Theorist," an application of Bakhtin's theory of the "dialogic" to rhetoric and to a reading of metaphor in McPhee's prose; and Phyllis McCord's (Phyllis Frus's) "Reading Nonfiction in Composition Courses," an application of poststructuralist literary theory to nonfiction prose. In the winter of 1987 my analysis of Tom Wolfe, Truman Capote, Norman Mailer, and Joan Didion, *Style as Argument: Contemporary American Nonfiction*, was published by Southern Illinois University Press; later that spring the Conference on College Composition and Communication in Atlanta featured another panel discussion on nonfiction, this time involving Donald McQuade, Peter Elbow, Charles Schuster, Pat Hoy and Robert DiYanni, as well as Richard Selzer and Gretel Ehrlich, two noted essayists. Our developing plans for a collection of essays were a natural outgrowth of this new interest in nonfiction, an effort to bring together the scholars and critics and teachers who have been writing about nonfiction over the last few years for a new, more sophisticated study of the essay and the New Journalism.

This is not to suggest that the book we've produced is without precedent. The study of nonfiction has an important, if limited, history in composition beginning well before Rygiel's article.[2] James Kinneavy's *A Theory of Discourse*, for example, established the relationship between aims and modes in discourse, arguing in the process that form carries value and that we ought to teach a variety of forms in the classroom, not privileging the referential or the persuasive over the expressive. Ross Winterowd's "The Grammar of Coherence" and "Disposition: The Concept of Form in Discourse" developed ways of looking at coherence beyond the sentence level as well as calling attention to the rhetorical power of form qua form in discourse. Howard Brasher's analysis of the familiar essay argued that the essay as a form is designed for aesthetic effect, not for clarity of idea or strength of proof. Richard Larson's "Towards a Linear Rhetoric of the Essay" presented an alternative to hierarchical models of how the essay works, while Frank D'Angelo's "A Generative Rhetoric of the Essay" argued that the order of an essay can be described with some precision as a set of necessary relationships. Edward Corbett provided a model for the rhetorical criticism of nonfiction prose that draws on common sense and the tradition of figures and topoi in classical rhetoric. Francis Christensen's work on the cumulative sentence has a great deal of bearing on the study of nonfiction prose, since the cumulative sentence is the stock in trade of contemporary stylists. In one of the most cited essays in the composition canon, "Form, Authority, and the Critical Essay," Keith Fort argued persuasively that our emphasis in

2. In this paragraph I am paraphrasing part of Jim Corder's original review essay, "Theoretical Analysis of Writing," in Gary Tate's *Teaching Composition: Ten Bibliographical Essays* (235–36). See also Richard Larson's "Structure and Form in Non-narrative Prose," Edward Corbett's "Approaches to the Study of Style," and Frank D'Angelo's "Aims, Forms, and Modes of Discourse" in the new Tate for further bibliographical material relevant to the study of literary nonfiction.

literature classes on the critical essay as developed by critics like Cleanth Brooks reflects totalitarian attitudes towards literature, forcing students to control and limit rather than explore a text.

For that matter, implicit notions about contemporary nonfiction have haunted much of the work in the last twenty years on the writing process. In "Different Products, Different Processes: A Theory About Writing," Maxine Hairston has recently noted that certain strategies of invention are best suited for certain kinds of writing. Tagmemics lends itself to analytical writing, for example. Historically it is significant that literary nonfiction has been linked, implicitly or explicitly, to much of the work in composition on the composing process. Janet Emig, after all, in *The Composing Processes of Twelfth Graders*, the seminal text on the study of process, repeatedly alludes to writers like Tom Wolfe, Norman Mailer, and Truman Capote as alternatives to the mechanical forms of the "fifty-star theme" (97). Their greater freedom and personality and spontaneity correspond on the level of the product to the greater freedom and personal involvement Emig argues for in the writing process itself. Indeed, her central insight is that the process of writing is conditioned by the writer's genre expectations. Students close themselves off from their surest instincts and innate competence because they are discouraged by their teachers' prescriptive and narrow conceptions of what the written product should look like.

In the same way Peter Elbow admits that freewriting, although it can serve the ends of expository writing, naturally leads in the direction of autobiographical prose, and several of the examples he uses for "collage writing" are drawn from the New Journalism (284, 150, 152). Indeed, all the qualities of voice celebrated by Elbow, Ken Macrorie, William Coles, and others in the authentic voice tradition are exemplified by the freer, more concrete forms of the New Journalism and the new essay. In this sense the New Journalism has been an integral, if unacknowledged, part of the New Rhetoric.

But despite occasional articles on the form and style of literary nonfiction, despite the implicit connections between process and a literary nonfiction product, the importance of literary nonfiction for composition studies has remained unacknowledged until recently. Our own paradigms have not allowed such a recognition. The emphasis in composition has been on the process, not on the product, whether literary or nonliterary. It has been easy to associate any concern with product with "current-traditional" pedagogies and dismiss it out of hand. The product is seen as static, a limitation rather than a help to invention. Much of the work on the sentence level has encouraged us, furthermore, to see the study of the written product as mechanistic, since the linguistic bias of these studies tends to atomize the whole essay, studying only small parts in isolation and then often from the perspective of quantitative methodologies. Perhaps most importantly, there has been an anxiety in composition about the use of examples from literary products. Literary examples, whether fiction or poetry or nonfiction, have often been regarded as too polished, elite, unattainable, and—the real issue—impractical to be of any real use in a composition classroom.

Some large questions are at stake here. As Robert Connors notes in his landmark essay, "Composition Studies and Science," many people in our field "yearn" for the power and prestige of fields like physics or biology, implicitly or explicitly adopting scientific paradigms in an attempt to establish composition as a scientific field—paradigms that exclude the kind of criticism this book undertakes. As Connors goes on to suggest, nothing published in rhetoric and composition since the revival of interest in writing in any way approximates the empirical verifiability of true scientific research, and there is reason to think it never can. The point is the yearning itself, the desire for scientific precision.

In a much more polemical article two years later, "Breaking Our Bonds and Reaffirming our Connections," Hairston explicitly opposes literature and composition. Rhetoric and composition, she proclaims, should rebel against literature, psychologically and even physically breaking away from the rest of the English Department. "I see us stunted in our growth because we are not able to free ourselves from needing the approval of the literature people," she says. "We've left home in many ways, but we haven't cut the cord. We still crave love" (274). She then takes to task those of us who try to link rhetorical and literary theory (we're simply trying to show that although we're forced to be composition teachers, our "hearts are still pure"), as well as those of us who try to combine rhetoric and composition with literary criticism in dissertations, books, and articles. This is merely an attempt at marketability, she claims, and it suggests our fear "that our discipline may not be scholarly and substantive enough" to stand by itself (274, 275).

Hairston's psychological analysis, it seems to me, is symptomatic of widespread attitudes in composition, attitudes that we are just now starting to overcome. At the heart of much composition research in the last twenty years has been an antiliterary bias—stemming from political as much as from theoretical issues—which has tended to marginalize any serious study of the relationship between literature and composition. As William Irmscher notes in a recent essay, the "positivistic" approach to research in composition initiated by Richard Braddock in the early sixties has prevailed in composition studies ever since, despite important counter-voices (82). It's time, Irmscher says, to reassess our identity as a discipline.

This is why we think that the essays collected here are significant. Like Irmscher, like Wayne Booth, Richard Lanham, Robert Scholes and the other contributors to Winifred Horner's *Composition and Literature: Bridging the Gap*, like a growing number of voices in the discipline, the contributors to this volume try to reconnect literature and composition, in both theory and practice, and thus establish a more comprehensive understanding of rhetoric and composition as a field of inquiry. "Composition theory and critical theory," Horner says, are "opposite sides of the same coin, and the 'teaching' of writing and the 'teaching' of literature are applications of theories that are closely connected, often inseparable, and always fundamental to the study of language" (2). Because

Introduction

literary nonfiction is a hybrid form, because it occupies the middle ground in the spectrum of discourse, it can test this generalization in particularly powerful ways.

Our Claims

We hope, then, that *Literary Nonfiction* will be a useful reference tool for upper division and graduate level courses in nonfiction prose, which are becoming increasingly popular across the country. At the same time we hope it will provide teachers of writing at all levels with new terms and models for talking about the kind of nonfiction they teach every day. But ultimately we hope the book will have a larger impact. We hope the book will constitute an argument for including the study of literary nonfiction in composition:

(1) The essays in this book attempt to be holistic in the sense Rygiel recommends. They see the act of reading not as static nor as a matter of dissection but as an experience, a drama to be acted out. As the book developed it became a series of essays applying a whole range of contemporary theoretical approaches to nonfiction: deconstruction, reader-response, stylistics, rhetorical criticism, feminist criticism, and so on. Some of these approaches are contemporary, some more traditional. I've put Schilb and Hoy side-by-side, for example, because they represent two radically different approaches to Didion, one deconstructionist, the other New Critical and symbolist. Yet however we might situate them in the critical debate, all of the critics in this collection approach the text in its whole context, and all see the reading of a text as dynamic, a process. John Clifford points out in his essay for this book that most objections to using nonfiction in the writing classroom "are less objections to the idea of using nonfiction in writing classes than to the limitations of a specific reading technique and its resulting pedagogy." In "our poststructural climate," Clifford says, "there are alternatives" to the formalist theories of reading and writing that have dominated composition classrooms for a generation, alternatives that emphasize the process of the reading experience (248). Indeed, as Joseph Comprone

xviii

explains in his contribution to the new *Teaching Composition: Twelve Bibliographical Essays*, contemporary literary and composition theory both "are coming together around research and theory into the processes of reading and writing, rather than around the results of those processes" (298). In this model, both writing and reading are seen as processes of making meaning, and this suggests in turn that teaching composition and teaching literature are not antithetical but ultimately versions of the same enterprise.

(2) Every form has value, makes an argument, qua form. The values of literary nonfiction, we are all saying, ought to be made an active part of composition studies and the teaching of writing. By *literary* most of us do not mean literature in the elitist sense of a set of texts we must admire, texts written by geniuses unlike us, an unattainable sacred canon. By literature we are talking about a way of looking at the world, a way of knowing, a form of inquiry—concrete, dramatic, grounded in a self—a way of knowing that we think ought to be taught to our students. Some authors in the collection, Schuster and Hoy, for example, imply that the "literary" or "aesthetic" is in some sense a quality inherent in a work, but their notion of this quality is not elitist or exclusive. We are all trying to ask the question: What should be the center of a composition course? What is it we are doing when we teach writing? What are the relationships between the practical and the less immediately practical, the less tangible? These are large questions, and we only answer them in part, but our answer, we think, is challenging: One thing we should do in the composition classroom is teach these interesting texts and ask our students to do similar kinds of writing.

(3) It is, in fact, hard to distinguish between the literary and nonliterary, between what Frus, borrowing from Benveniste, calls "discourse" and "history." On closer inspection, the boundaries between what Douglas Hesse calls the "story" and the "essay" don't hold. The traditional hierarchies of literary study are actually quite porous or fluid, and recognizing this, many of the essays in this book maintain, has the effect of opening things up, releasing new energies. Nonfiction is no

longer the bastard child, the second-class citizen; literature is no longer reified, mystified, unavailable. This is the contribution that poststructuralist theory has to make to an understanding of literary nonfiction, since poststructuralist theorists are primarily concerned with how we make meaning and secure authority for claims of meaning in language. Any text can be interpreted from a literary perspective, Scholes and Comley say in *Composition and Literature*—and furthermore, "all texts have secret/hidden/deeper meanings" (99). By the same token, literary nonfiction is ideal ground for testing poststructuralist theory, since it concerns directly and by definition the relationship between the real and the imaginary, the factual and the fictive. The effect on composition is dramatic: we can't relegate the questions this book considers to the realm of the "literary" and deem them irrelevant to our concerns in the classroom. As Lanham argues more generally in *Composition and Literature*, once we recognize that no prose style is truly "transparent," the problematic relationship between literature and composition "simply disappears." If no difference in kind exists between the literary and the "composition" text, "teaching literature and teaching composition form different parts of the same activity" (19).

(4) We ought not to give up our heritage as readers of texts. Composition is properly a multidisciplinary field; we ought to continue to work on process and invention, drawing as much as possible on science and social science for insight. But we ought to insist that one part of this patchwork field, one crucial part, is the reading of texts, and of certain kinds of texts—texts with style, voice, inherent worth as language. In defending the character of the cumulative sentence, Francis Christensen deplored the tyranny of what he called "exposition" and the "plain style." In his view, "both are a sign that we have sold our proper heritage for a pot of message. In permitting them, the English Department undercuts its own discipline" (347). *Literary Nonfiction*, in its styles and ways of approach, is making the same argument. To gain respect as a discipline, to find a "comfortable identity," Irmscher claims, "we need to work toward a model of inquiry appropriate to

our own discipline—composition as a part of English Studies—consistent with its values, supporting and enlightening it" (84). The essays in this collection perhaps offer one way of achieving this model.

(5) In fact, the essays in the collection have implications for the style and structure of the writing we do about composition. Our scholarship may well take the form of the New Journalism itself; that approach ought to be accepted as valid. The task in Irmscher's new conception of the discipline is to "present the fullness of the experience." As researchers we must "take pride in personal investigation, recognizing that it is necessarily limited, fallible, and selective"; we must "describe and narrate in such a way that the subjects are revealed as living things, not inanimate objects." In other words, whether we are writing about texts or about students and the dynamic of the classroom, we need to engage in a concreteness and self-dramatization much like that of literary nonfiction. The fictionalizing of Coles's *The Plural I* and the autobiographical grounding of Elbow's *Writing With Power* are "no less reliable than factual reportage" in Irmscher's view, and all the authors in this book, I think, would agree—there is "no reason why dissertations and scholarly articles need to be only 'barren factual statements' " (86–87).

(6) Thus *Literary Nonfiction* can have the effect of complicating and frustrating the teaching of writing. It argues that nonfiction is not immune from the troubling questions of contemporary literary theory. The Huns have arrived, to paraphrase Wolfe in his essay on the New Journalism. Nonfiction is not a stable set of texts easily and readily subordinate to our illustrations of rhetorical categories. Literary nonfiction opens up on a whole set of vexing, disturbing, frustrating epistemological and ontological questions. The breaking down of boundaries releases energy but also temporarily creates chaos, letting literary criticism finally invade the supposedly safer terrain of the classroom.

(7) Yet ultimately, and for the same reasons, the greater effect of *Literary Nonfiction* is to argue again, in a new and forceful way, that the teaching of writing is important and

interesting. From the perspective of the essays in this book what we do in the classroom is caught up in central questions of meaning and value, choice and vision, desire and symbol. As Winterowd has said of the value of theory, a discipline is defined by the quality of the questions it asks (*Contemporary Rhetoric* ix). This book asks some important questions. Theory, to put this another way, can be a morale booster, since it argues that what we are doing as we face a stack of papers is implicated in theoretical issues of the greatest interest.

Conclusion: Literary Nonfiction and the Rhetorical Tradition

None of this is to suggest that literary nonfiction is *the* answer, the central solution to what's so troubling in composition studies. Literary nonfiction is only one part of the picture, but it's an important part. It's important because it gives us access to the larger questions.

Despite the contemporary theoretical framework of many of the essays in the collection, *Literary Nonfiction* really participates in a very old debate about the province of rhetoric. After all, rhetoric and poetic have always overlapped.[3] Poetry serves Aristotle in the *Rhetoric* as a mine of illustrative material. There are frequent gaps in the *Poetics* where Aristotle seems to have been referring us to discussions in the *Rhetoric*—for example, in his discussion of how to arouse emotions in the audience of a drama. The main overlap is style. Aristotle notes that the early orators affected poetic diction because they realized how much of the poets' success was due to the beauty and elaboration of their language.

In other words, though rhetoric and poetry have different aims—one to persuade and move to action, the other to create objects for contemplation and intrinsic pleasure—they can have similar modes or ways of achieving those ends. They can

3. In my discussion of Aristotle I am following Friedrich Solmsen's introduction to the Modern Library version of the *Rhetoric* and the *Poetics*.

Introduction

also have similar secondary aims. Poetry can seek to persuade, rhetoric to be beautiful in itself. Even more importantly, rhetoric and poetry embody similar values. Both exist in the realm of the concrete and unprovable. Aristotle's job is to defend both from Platonic deconstruction. Both depend on the capacity to make knowledge felt, not just understood.

Those calling for a scientific paradigm in composition are oddly Platonic in that they want to transcend the messy and urgent and achieve the realm of the uncontingent. The real and the valuable for them is abstract, the proper methodology always dialectic. As Irmscher notes, "in their zeal to follow rigorous procedures, researchers frequently run counter to the act of composing or the act of teaching they are supposedly studying" (83). But the implicit argument of this collection is that the process of writing and the structure of discourse are inherently involved in the contingent. Rhetoric is by definition a form of language acknowledging feelings and values not provable or quantifiable in logical demonstration. Furthermore, in the tradition of rhetoric as a humane discipline, this provisional quality of rhetoric is something to celebrate. In the tradition of Isocrates, then Cicero, and more recently of Weaver, Perelman, Burke, Booth, and others, reality is defined not as ideal but as concrete. In this view what's important cannot be measured. For the rhetorician, the contingent, the debatable, and the unprovable encompass all that we value in our daily experience. "A dialectic takes place in vacuo," Richard Weaver says, but rhetoric "impinges on actuality. That is why rhetoric, with its passion for the actual, is more complete than mere dialectic with its dry understanding. It is more complete on the premise that man is a creature of passion who must live out that passion in the world" (77–78).

Even though literary nonfiction is only one part of a rhetoric that impinges on the actual, only one part of the passion we live out in the world, it points to the larger argument. It's not that we crave love, to return to Hairston. It's that we recognize the relevance of literary study for composition, the many overlaps historically and conceptually of the two areas, and the usefulness of literary study as a model for a discipline

Introduction

concerned with contingencies. We crave humanistic methodologies. Later Hairston claims that we should avoid "physics envy" and recognize that the field is a humanistic discipline; she urges us to seek connections with disciplines outside the field in linguistics, psychology, sociology, and so on (279). The contradiction is obvious. Only the discipline of literary study, with all its time-honored continuities with rhetorical tradition, is excluded from this drive for connection. And in the end Hairston, too, within the same paragraph where she declares the humanistic basis of composition, succumbs to the very physics envy she decries: We must carefully examine "the data that comes to us through language," she says; we must learn how to "control for bias" (279).

Hairston is exactly right that the data of composition studies comes to us through language. All we can finally know about the composing process is revealed in various kinds of written records of it, from snippets of freewriting to finished essay. But this is not "data"; it is discourse, and we learn to understand it and thus motivate and influence our students not by controlling for bias but by showing our students how the language we use is everywhere involved with desire. This is the argument of the essays in *Literary Nonfiction* taken as a whole: that literary nonfiction, by its nature, reveals to us the complexity and power and rhetorical possibilities of language—and that the complexity and power and possibility of language ought to be the unifying concern of rhetoric and composition as a discipline.

Works Cited

Anderson, Chris. *Style as Argument: Contemporary American Nonfiction.* Carbondale: Southern Illinois UP, 1987.
Beale, Walter. *A Pragmatic Theory of Rhetoric.* Carbondale: Southern Illinois UP, 1987.
Brashers, Howard. "Aesthetic Form in Familiar Essays." *College Composition and Communication* 22 (1971): 147–55.
Christensen, Francis. "A Generative Rhetoric of the Sentence." *Col-

Introduction

lege Composition and Communication 14 (1963): 155–61. Rpt. in *Contemporary Rhetoric: A Conceptual Background with Readings*. Ed. W. R. Winterowd. New York: Harcourt, 1975. 337–51.

Coles, William. *The Plural I: The Teaching of Writing*. New York: Holt, 1978.

Comprone, Joseph. "Literary Theory and Composition." *Teaching Composition: Twelve Bibliographical Essays*. 291–330.

Connors, Robert J. "Composition Studies and Science." *College English* 45 (1983): 1–20.

Corbett, Edward P. J. *Classical Rhetoric and the Modern Student*. New York: Oxford, 1971.

———. "Approaches to the Study of Style." *Teaching Composition: Twelve Bibliographical Essays*. 83–130.

Corder, Jim. "Rhetorical Analysis of Writing." *Teaching Composition: Ten Bibliographical Essays*. 223–40.

D'Angelo, Frank. "A Generative Rhetoric of the Essay." *College Composition and Communication* 25 (1974): 388–96.

———. "Aims, Modes, and Forms of Discourse." *Teaching Composition: Twelve Bibliographical Essays*. 111–36.

Elbow, Peter. *Writing with Power: Techniques for Mastering the Writing Process*. New York: Oxford, 1981.

Emig, Janet. *The Composing Processes of Twelfth Graders*. Urbana, Ill.: National Council of Teachers of English, 1971.

Fort, Keith. "Form, Authority, and the Critical Essay." *College English* 32 (1971): 629–39. Rpt. in *Contemporary Rhetoric*. 171–83.

Hairston, Maxine. "Breaking Our Bonds and Reaffirming Our Connections." *College Composition and Communication* 36 (1985): 277–82.

———. "Different Products, Different Processes: A Theory About Writing." *College Composition and Communication* 37 (1986): 442–52.

Hellman, John. *Fables of Fact: The New Journalism and the Nonfiction Novel*. Urbana: U of Illinois P. 1981.

Hollowell, John. *Fact and Fiction: The New Journalism and the Nonfiction Novel*. Chapel Hill: U of North Carolina P, 1977.

Horner, Winifred Bryan, ed. *Composition and Literature: Bridging the Gap*. Chicago: U of Chicago P, 1983.

Irmscher, William. "Finding a Comfortable Identity." *College Composition and Communication* 38 (1987): 81–88.

Kinneavy, James. *A Theory of Discourse*. Englewood Cliffs: Prentice-Hall, 1971.

Introduction

Lanham, Richard. "One, Two, Three." *Composition and Literature*. 14–29.

Larson, Richard. "Towards a Linear Rhetoric of the Essay." *College Composition and Communication* 22 (1971): 140–46.

———. "Structure and Form in Non-Narrative Prose." *Teaching Composition: Twelve Bibliographical Essays*. 39–82.

Macrorie, Ken. *Telling Writing*. Rochelle Park, N.J.: Hayden, 1970.

McCord, Phyllis. "Reading Nonfiction in Composition Courses: From Theory to Practice." *College English* 47 (1985): 747–62.

Rygiel, Dennis. "On the Neglect of Twentieth Century Nonfiction: A Writing Teacher's View." *College English* 46 (1984): 392–400.

Scholes, Robert, and Nancy Comley. "Literature, Composition, and the Structure of English." *Composition and Literature*. 96–109.

Schuster, Charles. "Mikhail Bakhtin as Rhetorical Theorist." *College English* 47 (1985): 594–607.

Solmsen, Friedrich. Introduction. *Aristotle's Rhetoric and Poetics*. Trans. W. Rhys Roberts and Ingram Bywater (respectively). New York: Random House, 1954.

Tate, Gary, ed. *Teaching Composition: Ten Bibliographical Essays*. Fort Worth: Texas Christian UP, 1976.

———, ed. *Teaching Composition: Twelve Bibliographical Essays*. Fort Worth: Texas Christian UP, 1987.

Weaver, Richard. *Language is Sermonic*. Baton Rouge: Louisiana State UP, 1970.

Weber, Ronald. *The Literature of Fact: Literary Nonfiction in American Writing*. Athens: Ohio UP, 1980.

Winterowd, Ross W., ed. *Contemporary Rhetoric: A Conceptual Background with Readings*. New York: Harcourt Brace Jovanovich 1975.

———. "The Grammar of Coherence." *College English* 31 (1970): 828–35. Rpt. in *Contemporary Rhetoric* 225–33.

———. "Disposition: The Concept of Form in Discourse." *College Composition and Communication* 32 (1971): 39–45. Rpt. as "Beyond Style" in *Contemporary Rhetoric*. 206–24.

Wolfe, Tom. "The New Journalism." In *The New Journalism*. Ed. Wolfe and E. W. Johnson. New York: Harper and Row, 1973. 3–52.

Zavarzadeh, Mas'ud. *The Mythopoeic Reality: The Postwar American Nonfiction Novel*. Urbana: U of Illinois P, 1976.

Zeiger, William. "The Exploratory Essay: Enfranchising the Spirit of Inquiry in College Composition." *College English* 47 (1985): 454–66.

PART ONE

Readings

1

THE NONFICTIONAL PROSE OF RICHARD SELZER

An Aesthetic Analysis

Charles I. Schuster

In "Surgeon as Priest," the second essay in *Mortal Lessons,* Richard Selzer describes the diagnostic abilities of Yeshi Dhonden, personal physician to the Dalai Lama. Unlike his American counterparts, Yeshi Dhonden peers at no X-rays, draws no blood. Instead, after two hours of bathing, fasting, and prayer, he enters the female patient's room and for a long time gazes at her. Then he takes her hand and feels her pulse, cradling her hand in his for thirty silent minutes. Finally, he pours a portion of her urine into a wooden bowl, whips the liquid until a foam is raised, and inhales the odor three times. He speaks no word to her, nor her to him, except for her "urgent and serene" calling of " 'Thank you, Doctor' " as he leaves to share his diagnosis with the physicians of the Yale School of Medicine (35). In the conference room, he speaks, his words translated by an interpreter:

> He speaks of winds coursing through the body of the woman, currents that break against barriers, eddying. These vortices are in her blood he says. The last spendings of an imperfect heart. Between the chambers of her heart, long, long before she was born, a wind had come and blown open a deep gate that must never be opened. Through it charge the full waters of her river, as the mountain stream cascades in the springtime, battering, knocking loose the land, and flooding her breath. Thus he speaks, and is silent.
>
> "May we now have the diagnosis?" a professor asks.

3

The host of these rounds, the man who knows, answers.
"Congenital heart disease," he says. "Interventricular sep-
tal defect, with resultant heart failure." (35)

I restate this story because it stands as a central paradigm
for Selzer's work. As Selzer makes clear, Dhonden is surgeon
as priest, a man so holy that his spirit can "enter" the body of
his patient. Dhonden is also lover, a physician who gives the
serene beauty of himself, so much so that Selzer declares he is
envious—not of Dhonden but of the patient: "I want to be
held like that, touched so, *received*" (34). Dhonden furthermore
possesses the humility necessary to all fine surgeons and stands
as a warning against what Selzer later will label "the gauleiter
mentality of some of the surgeons," that vulgar, meaty pride
which suffocates the sensibility (*Letters* 42). In typical fashion,
Selzer has yoked disparate concepts together here—the physical and the spiritual, Western analysis and Eastern intuition,
medicine and religion—and he has maintained them in, to use
one of his favorite terms, a resonance.[1] But I call attention to
this one episode for another reason. And that is to claim that
Selzer himself is Dhonden. Not in any literal way, of course,
for Yeshi Dhonden is no figment of Selzer's pen. Like Dhonden, however, Selzer makes of science an art. Like the Dalai
Lama's personal physician, Selzer elevates his craft, transforming the bloody drabness of the operating room into religious
ecstacy, poetic possibility. Under his gaze, blood and flesh
become sacrament; surgeon becomes Christ and Judas, healer
and murderer. It is this kind of unresolvable conflict and
tension that vitalizes Selzer's work.

Selzer seldom perceives object as object. He has instead a
poet's vision, the ability—even the compulsion—to transform
reality through image. In a recent interview, Selzer described

1. Selzer used the term repeatedly during my interview sessions with
him. For instance, in discussing "Tube Feeding" (*Confessions of a Knife*, 159–
66), he spoke of the narrator "resonating back and forth" between the husband
and wife. Shortly later he spoke of the relationships among characters and
narrator in "The Masked Marvel's Last Toehold" (*Confessions*, 149–55) as a
"kind of resonance in a way, where nothing is static." Richard Selzer, personal
interview, 11 August 1982.

his thinking during a breast operation: "I noted that her breasts reminded me of the blue and white china teapots on my grandmother's shelf. They were so fragile, that I was always afraid that I would break one, and here I was going to break one now" (Beppu 35). For Selzer, the breast and the teapot merge, and yet neither loses its identity in the other. Such thinking may not aid the surgeon, but it is of incalculable benefit to the artist. Like Baudelaire—and the French symbolists to whom he is greatly indebted—Selzer reorders reality, creating correspondences between the delicacy of a woman's veined breast and the rare, fragile china placed out of the careless reach of the child. This is the observation of the surgeon as priest, seer, and poet. Even more than Yeshi Dhonden, Selzer practices medicine through art and mystery, transforming objects into metaphor and symbol.

In Selzer, an object frequently becomes enriched with multiple associations. The surgeon's scalpel, for example, is called "the knife," a common synonym but one which nevertheless signals violence and potentially murderous intent. But this dead metaphor does not suffice. Within the first paragraph of his essay, "The Knife," Selzer creates an association of the scalpel with the bow of a cello, a tulip, a slender fish, and a "terrible steel-bellied thing" with which the surgeon conspires (*Mortal Lessons* 92). Each association creates interpretative possibilities. As cello bow, the scalpel is seen as an instrument that plays upon the strings of the human body, making music, creating art. The surgeon, concomitantly, becomes musician, artist. Sensitivity is required, a delicacy of drawing bow across strings of gut. The play of possibilities complements Selzer's themes of surgeon as artist and surgery as a fusing of surgeon and patient into one cooperative relationship of mutual dependency. As a tulip, the scalpel is transformed into an object of pure delight, frivolity, and delicacy. It is, as well, an object or token of love. And the tulip, I would wager, most commonly conjures up an image of a blood-red flower at the end of a long stem. This, too, is of a piece with the scalpel "drawing across the field of skin," leaving a trail of blood (92). Finally, the scalpel works silently beneath the surface of things

5

like a fish. And it travels quickly, almost swimmingly, across and inside the flesh, not only like a fish but like some sinister alien object, a "terrible steel-bellied thing." It is true that Selzer only names these associations, developing them slightly if at all in this opening paragraph, but that is part of his power as an artist. These associations are invitations to create contexts for terms left bare in Selzer's prose. The scalpel is not simply an instrument; it is an emblem, a mysterious totem, like a thyrsus or a crucifix, to which the reader can affix subjective interpretations.

Selzer continues to create multiple significance for the scalpel throughout "The Knife." An operation, writes Selzer, is "an entry into the body" (92), so that knife becomes sexual instrument in an act of physical penetration—it is penis honed to a razor-thin edge. This association of scalpel with sexual organ, of surgery with lovemaking, immediately gives way to religious imagery. The knife has become chalice, the operation a literal communion in which the body and blood are alto-gether body and blood: "Not surplice and cassock but mask and gown are your regalia. You hold no chalice, but a knife. There is no wine, no wafer. There are only the facts of blood and flesh" (94). The surgeon, moreover, is accorded a mystic vision of an ancient world. He becomes "a traveler in a danger-ous country" (94). But knife is more. It is also the dread double-headed axe, for the surgeon is "like an executioner who hears the cleric comforting the prisoner" (98). It is wild and fierce, untameable, an animal—"It grins. It is like a cat . . ." (100). It joins with the surgeon "like the Centaur—the knife, below, all equine energy, the surgeon, above, with his delicate art" (100–01). "In a moment it is like the long red fingernail of the Dragon Lady" (101). It is the peer among the instruments, the sneering lord.

But all these figurative attempts do not suffice; in the last section of the essay Selzer returns to the basic question: "What is it, then, this thing, the knife . . ." (102). His initial response is to find refuge in objectivity, in a brief discourse on the historical origins of the knife followed by the most objective and scientific description that yet appears in the essay. Why

place this dictionary-like attempt here at the end of an emotionally charged series of complex allusions and associations?
It is, I would argue, an example of rhetorical irony, of Selzer
indirectly claiming once more that the meaning of *knife* is not
conveyable in these terms. The scalpel's physical characteristics, the description it is given as handle and blade with "a
narrow notched prong" (104), appear ludicrous now after the
previous celebration of scalpel in all its power. Selzer himself
seems aware of this, for by the third sentence, art and association have once again intruded upon scientific detachment.
"Without the blade," Selzer explains, "the handle has a blind,
decapitated look. It is helpless as a trussed maniac" (104). The
reader is immediately thrust back into a more literary context,
a poetic rendering of this mysterious object. And Selzer's answer to "What is it, then, this thing, the knife" becomes in large
part a climactic restatement in slightly different terms—it is
knife, and beast, and penis, and death, and life:

> Now the scalpel sings along the flesh again, its brute run unim-
> peded by germs or other frictions. It is a slick slide home, a
> barracuda spurt, a rip of embedded talon. One listens, and
> almost hears the whine—nasal, high, delivered through that
> gleaming metallic snout. The flesh splits with its own kind of
> moan. It is like the penetration of rape.
> The breasts of women are cut off, arms and legs sliced to
> the bone to make ready for the saw, eyes freed from sockets,
> intestines lopped. The hand of the surgeon rebels. Tension
> boils through his pores, like sweat. The flesh of the patient
> retaliates with hemorrhage, and the blood chases the knife
> wherever it is withdrawn. (104)

Afterwards, like some brute animal it lies "spent, on its side,
the bloody meal smear-dried upon its flanks" (104). There can
be little doubt, I think, of the sexual suggestion of "spent," a
verb used frequently in eighteenth- and nineteenth-century
literature. Like a phallus, the knife here is exhausted but
capable of renewal.

What is remarkable in this essay, I think, is the profusion
of images and associations that are poured into a very few
pages. Nor is "The Knife" atypical. The essay that follows it

7

in *Mortal Lessons*, "Skin," opens by describing its subject as "baklava," "scabbard," an "instrument," a means by which we are "bagged and trussed," and a covering that "upholsters," all of which is followed by the "seamless body-stocking" image that opens the succeeding paragraph (105). Moreover the opening clause, "I sing of skin . . . ," evokes Virgil and sets up comic expectations that "Skin" belongs somewhere within the heroic tradition. Indeed, the language here is clearly mock-heroic with its comparison to the dawn and its highly descriptive, parallel phrases. The body itself is an item of furniture; the armpit is transformed into a "grotto." Our body becomes an interior landscape, each perforation "with its singular rim and curtain" (105).

That Selzer makes continuous recourse to images and allusions suggests two possibilities concerning his writing. First, it implies a limitation of expositional language, of the linear, denotative, explicative use of words. This explanatory mode simply will not suffice. Selzer's at times almost uncontrollable use of allusion and image suggests the lengths to which he is compelled to write in order to create a personal code, a meta-language that can express the center of his mystical, affective experience. Selzer pushes language to its limits. When accepted words of the English language are insufficient, he invents others: *siffling*, *apter*, and *slidder*.[2] He stretches syntactical boundaries by inverting his word order and piling phrases and Latinate constructions into his essays. (For example, in *Mortal Lessons*, "First from his fingertips did the rich blackness fade—to no mere cocoa or tan, but to such a white as matched the fairness of a Dane" [110]). He enriches his prose with a profusion of figurative tropes and stylistic usages—simile, metaphor, asyndeton, aposiopesis, hyperbole, anaphora. This is a writer who pushes rhetoric to its limits. It is thus fair to say that the profusion of images and allusions contributes to Selzer's overall attempt as an author to bypass

2. Selzer has stated that he creates neologisms "simply because out of sheer enthusiasm I just carry it one step too far. And that turns out to be just right somehow." Richard Selzer, personal interview, 11 August 1982.

conventional linguistic forms. Selzer's language strives for connotation, association, implication, signification beyond sign. This is not always the case, of course, for every writer must provide sufficient linear exposition to provide a context for the reader. But as the brief description of the scalpel at the end of "The Knife" illustrates, expositional prose frequently fails. Its explicit nature disallows hypothetical and imaginative responses on the part of the reader. Such language oversimplifies; it is too stipulative, too parched, too bare of the contradictory impulses that feed Selzer's work. The images and allusions represent, therefore, a deliberate and continuing attempt to signify the unsignifiable.

Second, I would suggest that the neologisms and seemingly random and grotesque images also contribute considerably to the impression Selzer's work gives of originating in dream and nightmare. When he first began writing professionally, Selzer composed between 1 A.M. and 3 A.M. and he acknowledges that he tapped his dream life as he wrote (personal interview, 11 August 1982). One can feel the tempo of dream in much of his work. Objects flower into vivid images: a slug is extolled as lover; a Civil War doctor looks into a peach orchard and sees a mortally wounded Pegasus collapsing to the earth; the young Selzer punches a young bully in the chest and then watches him first cough up meaty gobs of blood and, over the period of a year, succumb to a tubercular death. These are the images of dream and restless sleep. The profusion of them, moreover, is dictated in large part by association, just as are the symbols of dream. In "Virgil, Longfellow, and Me," for example, Selzer notes that one of his teachers "gorged us with Latin" (*Mortal Lessons* 201). The verb, apparently, triggers an association, for Selzer extends the metaphor: "We were geese being primed for pâté," and the image of students as geese continues until the teacher becomes Medea "slaying her children"—perhaps serving them up to a figurative Jason as pâté de fois gras. Back and forth career the tropes and associations like the subliminal events in a dream state. The effect in Selzer is to add a dimension of interpretive possibility: things in Selzer are not only themselves but, to use Freud's terms, "hieroglyphics, whose symbols must be translated, one by one, into the language of the dream-thoughts" (4:277–79). Nor is there a one-to-one ratio of image with meaning. Often Selzer's tropes are nonspecific; they are signs of an inchoate sensibility, images for which no fully specific language is available.

Selzer, in this respect, can be likened to Keats, a poet who has significantly influenced him. Keats, in a well-known passage from an 1817 letter to his brothers, George and Thomas, writes: "It struck me what quality went to form a Man of Achievement especially in Literature and which Shakespeare possessed so enormously—I mean *Negative Capability*, that is when man is capable of being in uncertainties, Mysteries, doubts, without any irritable reaching after fact and reason" (71). The poet must be able to sustain the ambiguity of dream, the confusion of a sensibility over-charged by experience. The literal, the unitary and isolatable event, is denied by such a writer in order that he may express the complications of an unresolvable world. In another well-known passage from his letters, Keats argues that the poetical character "has no self—it is everything and nothing—It has no character—it enjoys light and shade; it lives in gusto, be it foul or fair, high or low, rich or poor, mean or elevated—It has much delight in conceiving an Iago as an Imogen. What shocks the virtuous philosopher, delights the camelion Poet" (226–27). Selzer, too, is a "camelion Poet" to whom no action or event is so terrible as to be unreportable. His words and images pluck slices out of the profusion of life played out about him. That they are contrastive, contradictory, and at times wholly created by the occasion of the prose is part of Selzer's expression of his negative capability.

Out of this binary impulse both to reach beyond the literal and tap the subliminal power of dream, Selzer has introduced into his work a particular kind of figurative trope which has, to my knowledge, never been fully characterized in critical study. It has its roots, I am convinced, in the work of Poe, Dickens, the romantics, and the French symbolists, within which the evocation of dream and the desire to capture affective, ineffable experience are as strong as they are in Selzer. What characterizes this trope is the conjoining of two independent and distinct entities which are then bound and held together by one shared feature while simultaneously maintaining all their difference. In other writers, this kind of comparison takes the form of simile, metaphor, or analogy. But Selzer yokes the two terms together without the use of explicit "like" or "as" and without extending the vehicle. My term for this kind of trope is "fusion" or "fused image," and it appears frequently in Selzer's work.

For example, in "Down From Troy," Selzer writes humorously and lovingly about his boyhood in Troy, New York, and about his relationship with his general practitioner father (*Mortal Lessons* 177–91). After his expositional opening, he tells an Edgar Allen Poe tale of descending with his brother down the forbidden stairs into the cellar where they discover an old chest in the gray and moldy gloom. In typical fashion, Selzer describes this journey as a return to the mythic womb and an Orphean expedition, but these are mock-heroic allusions here for comic effect, not fused images. What the two boys find inside the chest are two skeletons "lying athwart each other in terrible disarray" (182). Immediately they convince themselves that these are the bones of two murder victims, patients, perhaps, of their father's haphazard practice. Swearing each other to secrecy, Selzer and his brother afterward "haunted the house like spectres . . . we failed to thrive, lost weight, became spidery and full of sighs" (184–85). The boys became skeletal. Selzer makes this identification explicit, stating "that in some subliminal way, far below the threshold of consciousness, those two skeletons had become us, that by some strange inconsistency of time, Billy and I had come face to face with our own mortal remains" (185). The two brothers have merged with the skeletons, and yet the skeletons remain skeletons, the brothers brothers. This is no simile, no metaphor, no allusion. It is a fusion of separate identities in which neither is lost.

The power of the fused image is that it locates itself ambiguously, between the literal and the figurative. It possesses no clear border, thus denying the reader any clear ground for response. In "The Belly," for instance, Selzer describes the effects of an overacidic stomach:

> Rubor, Tumor, Dolor, Calor (Redness, Swelling, Pain, Heat), the Four Horsemen of Peptic Apocalypse come riding hard, galloping across the midriff, pillaging, raping tissue, laying waste. On and on they stampede, unchecked by antacid, surcease, even sleep, their lust sated only by the triple calamities of Obstruction, Hemorrhage, and Perforation. (*Mortal Lessons* 121)

In this example of fusion, Selzer takes four physiological effects (Latinate terms and all) and personifies them into literary-biblical figures without losing the interpretive weight of either tenor or vehicle. The semantic tension makes itself felt in the words themselves: the phrase "laying waste," a dead metaphor, gains by the identification of waste with rot, excretion, and products of physical corruption. These horsemen not only "lay waste" in the sense of siege and destroy but also in the most literal sense of producing waste, brooding and hatching it out of the bowel. In the next sentence, the tenor and vehicle seesaw in somewhat the following manner:

Tenor (*physiological-scientific*)	Vehicle (*Four Horsemen-Literary*)
	On and on they stampede,
unchecked by antacid,	surcease,
even sleep,	their lust sated only by the
	triple calamities of
Obstruction, Hemorrhage, and Perforation	

The sentence pitches back and forth, with the three final terms coming full circle in the sense that they, like Rubor, Tumor, Dolor, and Calor, are both physical symptoms and literary personifications. Moreover, this description is, like the passage in Revelation from which it draws its inspiration, a prophetic vision except that this one ironically describes the problems of overacidity.

Placed as it is between two quite technical, scientific descriptions, this example of fusion suggests its own genetic roots. Selzer is a surgeon who is also a writer, but he is also a writer who practices surgery. (In fact, he is now a retired surgeon and a full-time writer.) He is a doctor and humanist, a man of science and of letters. He considers himself as a writer to be an artist seeking aesthetic effects, a surgeon explaining the delicate intricacies of his profession, a resident doctor teaching his students, a mystic who wants to turn our thoughts to soul and spirit, a devotee of Poe who seeks to immerse us all over again in the formless horrors of our childhood. These impulses make themselves apparent in the tables of contents of his books: he includes treatises on medical subjects, personal essays, excursions into the grotesque, anecdotes, didactic addresses to particular and public audiences. As an artist, Selzer is invigorated by a host of irreconcilable intentions which create irreconcilable effects in the writing. In "Belly," he develops a descriptive explanation of the effects of acidity, suddenly interrupting this mode with the fusion example of the four horsemen. And this fusion participates within the text as both exposition and metaphor, situating itself uneasily between the two, bridging the passage that precedes it with the one that follows, both of which are highly expositional. The fused image thus complicates the reading, heightens the effect without wholly giving way to the figurative, artistic, humanistic impulse. It mixes elements without blurring their identity. It captures the multiplicity of Selzer's mind and art, the irreconcilability of his contradictory interests and intentions. And by this very power and ambivalence, it creates powerful moments in the text.

Perhaps its most climactic usage is in "The Masked Marvel's Last Toehold," an account Selzer offers in *Confessions of a Knife* (149–55). This book, the successor to *Mortal Lessons*, blends fiction with nonfiction, so that the reader is at times unsure of the mode of a particular piece. But in the case of "The Masked Marvel," Selzer has made himself clear: this is nonfiction.[3] Selzer describes the experience in the first person,

3. Selzer was emphatic: "This is an absolutely true event.... Totally true.... This thing really happened. It was so uncanny. I would never have

13

Charles I. Schuster

as surgeon ministering to patient. And his patient in this case is Elihu Koontz, a seventy-five-year-old diabetic amputee who, as a young man, lumbered around the wrestling circuit as "The Masked Marvel."

Selzer opens the essay with a brilliantly impressionistic description of the gnomish old man who once basked in his physical, muscular power but who now sits in a hospital bed staring at the "collapsed leg of his pajamas" (149). This theme of strength and health amputated by time and disease echoes through the essay. Koontz is a man living backward, a refugee of popular culture still carrying his old clippings and photographs, celebrating his gloried past. He is a wrestler once and always, a point that Selzer returns to at the end of the narrative. Koontz's admission of his past identity pushes Selzer himself backward, to a night in Toronto's Maple Leaf Gardens where the featured wrestling match was "The Angel vs. The Masked Marvel." Typically, Selzer's narrative is vivid, filled with the violence of the action. Witness his description of The Angel:

> The shaved nape rises in twin columns to puff into the white hood of a sloped and bosselated skull that is too small. As though, strangled by the sinews of that neck, the skull had long since withered and shrunk. The thing about The Angel is the absence of any mystery in his body. It is simply *there*. A monosyllabic announcement. A grunt. One looks and knows everything at once, the fat thighs, the gigantic buttocks, the great spine from which hang knotted ropes and pale aprons of beef. And that prehistoric head. He is all of a single hideous piece, The Angel is. No detachables. (152)

Selzer's exaggerated terms make of the angel a mythic antagonist; he is a combination of Antaeus, *Tyrannosaurus rex,* and Moby Dick. And the Marvel, through nearly all the heroic battle, is victimized by this brainless, brutish power, especially by the Angel's use of the toehold, which twists his

written that story had this shocking coincidence not been true. It was an astonishing event." Interview with Richard Selzer, 11 August 1982, transcript of tape 2B, p. 20.

foot downward, straining bone and ligament to the cracking point. Selzer, the young boy, is horrified, but his uncle roars to the Angel, "Break it off! Tear off a leg and throw it up here!" (153). The uncle's shout reverberates through the story. It is the scream of a madman, a calling forth of the primeval urge for sacrifice and mutilation. Selzer's response is more plaintive, more civilized. "That's not fair," he states, as the Marvel's toes are twisted further. Selzer and uncle, in their opposing loyalties, mirror Marvel and Angel, even as the wrestlers themselves ironically participate in what Tom Wolfe calls single combat warfare (*The Right Stuff* 101–05). The wrestlers signify opposing forces, though not particularly of good and evil. If anything, the Angel suggests direct, open brutality while the Marvel, because of his mask and secret identity ("No one knows who The Masked Marvel really is!" [152]) implies mystery and the ominous unknown. Theirs is a highly ritualized struggle. Moreover, it is a parodic battle. Wrestling, in our culture, is strength and showmanship. It is theatre. There is within Selzer's depiction of this match the unstated irony of the play of it all, the sense that the whole affair has been scripted. The agony of the toehold is both real and totally false; the violence of the match is, for the contemporary reader, at best mock-heroic. But from within the point of view of the essay, the point of view of the young boy and his uncle in the Gardens, everything that unfolds is high melodrama and utterly credible. They are not watching a performance, but a gladiatorial fight to the finish. It is at this point, when the Marvel has been almost totally subjugated, that the Angel does something unspeakable: he turns, while maintaining the toehold, and begins to pull off the Marvel's mask. Young Selzer's response is instantaneous: he screams for someone to stop the Angel. In an instant it is over—the Marvel miraculously kicks free, pins the Angel, and arises victorious and mysterious still.

All this Selzer remembers, and it leads him to the climax of the essay where a complicated fusion contributes to the power of the narrative. I quote it here in its entirety:

15

Charles I. Schuster

> Once again, I am in the operating room. It is two years
> since I amputated the left leg of Elihu Koontz. Now it is his
> right leg which is gangrenous. I have already scrubbed. I stand
> to one side wearing my gown and gloves. And . . . I am masked.
> Upon the table lies Elihu Koontz, pinned in a fierce white light.
> Spinal anesthesia has been administered. One of his arms is
> taped to a board placed at a right angle to his body. Into this
> arm, a needle has been placed. Fluid drips here from a bottle
> overhead. With his other hand, Elihu Koontz beats feebly at
> the side of the operating table. His head rolls from side to side.
> His mouth is pulled into weeping. It seems to me that I have
> never seen such misery.
>
> An orderly stands at the foot of the table, holding Elihu
> Koontz's leg aloft by the toes so that the intern can scrub the
> limb with antiseptic solutions. The intern paints the foot, ankle,
> leg, and thigh, both front and back, three times. From a corner
> of the room where I wait, I look down as from an amphitheater.
> Then I think of Uncle Max yelling, "Tear off a leg. Throw it
> up here." And I think that forty years later I am making the
> catch.
>
> "It's not fair," I say aloud. But no one hears me. I step
> forward to break The Masked Marvel's last toehold. (154–55)

History has repeated itself with a merciless vengeance. Only
this time the outcome is not playfully mock-heroic. Koontz,
the wrestler, is wrestling still, held, "pinned," helpless. Just as
before, Selzer affirms that "It is not fair." Just as he had as a
boy, his response to Koontz's pain is "It seems to me that I
have never seen such misery" (154). The scene, the agony,
the action, the phrases repeat themselves like a twice-dreamt
nightmare, identical in theme if not in detail. Past and present
merge; the match in the Gardens has fused with the scene in
the operating room. Koontz's misery defies temporal boundaries. And Selzer himself has fused. He has become the
Masked Marvel victorious once again ("And . . . *I am masked*").
He has become the Angel, who at long last is obeying Uncle
Max's vehement demand. And he has even become his uncle,
now about to make the catch. Selzer, here, by tearing off the
Masked Marvel's leg, has most clearly allied himself with Angel
and uncle, yet he is the Marvel as well. Indeed, the line "No

16

one knows who the Masked Marvel really is" suggests that in some subliminal way the hooded wrestler is not Koontz at all. He is unknown, nameless, all of us, Selzer himself. What accounts for the Marvel's mythic proportion is not his strength or, like the "Angel," his neck and "bosselated skull," but his mysterious identity. He is a cipher, an etymological blank. He is the nameless, unrecognizable force inside us all. We are the Masked Marvel, in the same sense that we are all mysterious superheroes—Batman, the Lone Ranger, Spiderman. His strength and cunning, his ability to overcome the Angel's toe-hold, his final vulnerability and defeat make him a focus of our projected subconscious. In a very real sense, Selzer is looking down at the table as if into a mirror.

Selzer's use of fusion blurs lines of identity; boys become skeletons but remain boys; Selzer becomes Marvel and Angel and uncle while remaining altogether himself as surgeon. The reader, as emotional and imaginative participant in the text, experiences similar ambiguous relations between self and other. It is in this tension, this resonance between opposite and apposite, that Selzer's genius as a writer is particularly apparent. He is, in Mikhail Bakhtin's terms, a "dialogical" writer, with all the various textual manifestations that such an orientation necessarily produces. In coining the term *dialogical*, Bakhtin attempts to describe an authorial presence which deconstitutes itself. A dialogical text is an aesthetic creation in which plurality and polyphony replace a single, rigidly conceptualized voice or point of view. Dialogical texts are characterized by comingled voices, by open-ended ideological speculations submerged within a textual framework, by the presentation of consciousness as multiple and ceaselessly contrastive.[4] Selzer's use of fusion is one aspect of this dialogical

4. In "From the Preshistory of Novelistic Discourse," Bakhtin states: "Every type of intentional stylistic hybrid is more or less dialogized. This means that the languages that are crossed in it relate to each other as do rejoinders in a dialogue; there is an argument between languages, an argument between styles of language. But it is not a dialogue in the narrative sense, nor in the abstract sense; rather it is a dialogue between points of view, each with its own concrete language that cannot be translated into the other"

Charles I. Schuster

quality. Another aspect is the frequency with which he merges his authorial voice with that of characters, literary figures, subjects—simultaneously maintaining a voice or style with multiple accents, tones, and orientations. It is as if Selzer engages in the trope of fusion and then enlarges it to embrace an entire work.

Of all the irreconcilable impulses colliding within Selzer's work, however, perhaps the most significant from a formal point of view is his inability, his unwillingness, to separate the fictional from the nonfictional. His work, he claims, has "a central core of truth" even though he uses many "fictional techniques" to recover it (personal interview, 11 August 1982). For most readers the distinction between real and unreal modes of telling is a significant one. Human beings have created a phenomenologically divided world where experience is filtered through oppositions such as good and evil, up and down, in and out. In reading, this emphasis gets expressed as the question, "Is this true or not? Is this fiction or nonfiction?" The answer to that question allows most readers to gauge their responses to a work, to classify the experience of their reading as being of the world or of the imagination.

Selzer consistently confounds that expectation. It is as if he is engaging in dialogism ontologically, as it were, by refusing to accede to the conventional limitations of the fictional/nonfictional generic distinctions that guide most of us through experience. Although *Rituals of Surgery* is a collection of fiction, the stories contain a good bit of surgical and physiological fact. *Mortal Lessons*, a work of nonfiction, reveals Selzer using numerous fictional techniques, especially shifts in point of view, to achieve his ends. *Confessions, Letters to a Young Doctor* (1982), and *Taking the World in for Repairs* (1986) include both essays and short stories, at times in ways that make it difficult to perceive to which category a title should be assigned. Cast loose between two

(*Dialogic*, 76). Selzer, in his own hybridized literary language and melding of voices and modes, displays a similar dialogic quality. For a more extended discussion of parody, double-voiced discourse, and the dialogic, see *Problems of Dostoevsky's Poetics*, esp. ch. 5.

equally indistinct shores, readers must devise their own chart to steer by. They must become more willing to sustain doubt and ambiguity, more capable of supplying their own direction within the parameters established by the work itself. For no essay (story? narrative?) is this more true than "Pages of a Wound-Dresser's Diary," which, in fact, is a fusion of the nonfictional and fictional held in perfect tension.

"Pages" (*Confessions* 133–48) recreates the experience of a Civil War doctor-surgeon stationed aboard a steamboat plying the Mississippi from Pittsburgh Landing to St. Louis. It is less a story than a narration, a slice of experience which contains at its center a delicate tale of the love the doctor discovers for a young fifer who ultimately dies of his wounds. This sketchily drawn tale exemplifies Selzer's depiction of war: the doctor's passionate but concealed love represents a hopeful and healing prospect, while the boy's death is a small part of the fabric of wholesale death and dismemberment which the war weaves all around them. "Pages" is marked by features typical of Selzer's art: grisly depiction of wounds, illness, and medical treatment; short narrative scenes strung together without transition, a blending of reality with dream and nightmare; the use of neologisms and archaisms such as "musicked" (133), "clackety" (135), and "chunter" (145), which, along with the phrasing and frequently inverted word order, achieve a heightening of the style; a general lack of dialogue; and a substantial amount of direct and indirect allusion, such as the link of the doctor and the Mississippi to Charon on the Styx. But it is the story's uneasy relationship with the actuality of the Civil War that gives an added twist to its power. Written in the first person as a series of undated journal entries, "Pages" recreates the experience of a Civil War doctor. The names of ships and ports, the detailed descriptions of river and wounded soldiers, the felt language of the narrator as he recounts experiences and visions all combine to achieve a remarkable verisimilitude. Nor is this any accident. For at the center of this fictive account lies a series of actual letters written by a young Civil War doctor to his brother and sister while he was stationed aboard a steamboat on the Mississippi. Now housed in the Beinecke Library at Yale, these letters were offered to Selzer to read by his friend, Archie Hannah, the curator of the Americana Collection. Selzer's description of the experience of reading this material is informative: "I read about 300 of this man's letters. He wasn't a writer by any stretch of the imagination, but he was a letter writer and a recorder. Everything was written down in these letters. If something floated by in the river, he reported it in one of his letters. So that by reading them one was suddenly . . . well, they had an enormous power by themselves, even though he wasn't what we think of as a writer. After I had read 100 of them I totally identified with this man. He was 25 at the time, and I was then on that steamboat myself. It required absolutely no transformation, no transmutation. I felt myself to be in the position of that man, and I knew then that I would write something" (personal interview, 12 August 1982).

What Selzer wrote, however, did not just evolve out of a fusion of identity between a Civil War doctor and himself. He felt the need for an additional element to complicate the unfolding of the narrative. He found that element in the figure of Walt Whitman. According to Selzer's own admission:

> I wanted to write about the events that took place on this steamboat, and its effect on the doctor, his role. But I also wanted to use language. And I remembered that Walt Whitman had been a wound dresser during the Civil War . . . and in fact wrote a poem called "The Wound Dresser." So. Now I had it. I had the way to get into this material that would satisfy me as a writer. . . . I wrote it in the form of a diary, fragmented, using the language that approximates Whitman. In fact my character I describe from a photograph of Whitman as wound dresser. I use the word "wound dresser" as the title. I was making no secret of the fact that I was relying on Whitman's life experience and applying it, applying the poetry, applying the poetic sensibility to the events in this young doctor's life. (personal interview, 12 August 1982)

With his idealistic and explicit love for his fellow man, his poetic sensibility both horrified and enraptured by the experiences that washed over him, Whitman assumes an importance in the fusion equal to that of the historical doctor and Selzer himself. "Pages" blends the languages, experiences, perspectives, and points of view of all three individuals to produce a story which is neither fictional nor nonfictional but an indivisible fusion of both.[5]

Here, for example, is a short passage which functions as an independent section of the text: "Another dawn. I stand on the upper deck. A strange elation has seized me, so that I am unable to sleep, except fitfully. The *January* rocks at her pier to the rhythm of faroff Minnesota springs. It is a soothing, amniotic pulse. On the opposite shore, a great hairy cypress surmounts the stream, dangling tendrils in the water" (142). One can feel here Selzer's rhythm: the opening fragment, the rhythmic rise and fall of the following sentences as they settle into what may best be described as a rough, quantitative dactylic meter ("rocks at her pier to the rhythm of far-off Minn-e-sota springs"). But the language is not his alone; it is possessed, as well, by the doctor and Walt Whitman. The opening fragment recalls the journal form of the historical doctor. The terms used to describe the scene—the "soothing, amniotic pulse" and the "dangling tendrils"—forge a link between this writer and Selzer by creating a physiological personification of the natural scene. The "strange elation" he feels, however, is his Whitmanesque love for the young fifer, the image of the cypress being as naturalistic and evocative as one of Whitman's poetic figures. Throughout "Pages," the narrator writes in the elegiac tone of the continuously bereaved mother and father, mourning the death of so many children. The narrator emerges as a Whitmanesque persona who is himself like the cypress tree he describes, a tree associated since classical times with sorrow and death.

Later on, the narrator presents another scene which effects a stylistic identification of the doctor, Whitman, and Selzer.

5. Interestingly, Selzer himself was adamant about the "truth" of the story. During the interview, he stated emphatically, "But I mean to tell you that it ["Pages"] is in fact nonfiction. This is not fiction. I was representing

Charles I. Schuster

> One of the wounded is a Rebel lieutenant from Alabama. There is a sucking wound in the left side of his chest. With each inspiration, air is expelled through this ragged opening despite that I have plugged it with oiled lint. His fever rages. He is dying, certain. I sit with him during his final hour, and, all the while, he talks of the reasons for the war, why it is necessary.
>
> At the last, he tears a brass button from his gray coat and places it in my hand. There is that telltale "give," the taut arms gone limpsy, the onrush of silence that fills the space abandoned by labored breathing, moans; and I, visiting such new silences every hour. (146)

Again one hears the specificity of the historical doctor: the identification of the officer and his state, his desperately matter-of-fact statement about having "plugged it [the wound] with oiled lint," the somewhat old-fashioned use of "inspiration." The very phrasing of "despite that I have" syntactically reaches backward to the doctor's era. Yet the descriptions of the injury, the "sucking wound" and "ragged opening" suggest Selzer, particularly his love of horror and the grotesque. And the rhythms again are his, the use of the post-position adjective in "He is dying, certain." Yet "Whitman, the poet-narrator," is also present with his characteristic omission of conjunctions and transitions between sentences, and the poetic descriptions like "that telltale 'give' " and "the taut arms gone limpsy." And only a poet could offer that dramatic, evocative last phrase in which the "I," the loving and grieving poet-doctor, is left dangling, alone, modified by an expression of continuous and unending bereavement.

Even in so short an analysis, I think it is clear that the language here is hybrid. The narrator is anchored to this context of steamer, Mississippi, and Civil War in a way that transcends place names and incidental detail. His language has become an inscape to the historical-medical-poetic experience. The very presentation of the story as a series of fragmentary images, associations, conjectures, and evocations, transforms

actual material in fictional terms." Interview with Richard Selzer, 11 August 1982, transcript of tape 1B, p. 9.

it into a prose poem, one in which the reader must reconstitute the work by creating subjective interpretations that provide necessary interpretive connections. "Pages" is thus like an extended asyndeton; it is a work in which semantic ligature is minimized. Like a William Carlos Williams poem, its concentrated focus on the experiential and empirical implies a metaphysics without stating it. By focusing on the vividly palpable, the affective response to all this horror is implied but seldom offered. Description becomes image, metaphor, and symbol but always within a language that locates itself inside a particular and poetic rending of the event.

What "Pages" reveals about Selzer's language in dramatic fashion is what is more generally true of it. Selzer's language is dialogic in the sense that Mikhail Bakhtin describes in his theoretical work. Fusion is simply one instance of the dialogic impulse in Selzer's art. The introduction within Selzer's language of words and phrases from Keats, Longfellow, Virgil, Whitman, Poe, and others is another, more obvious (and thereby perhaps less successful) form of the dialogic. Dialogism cannot be introduced by overtly interrupting words with another's. It enters into the very accents of the words themselves. As Bakhtin describes it: "The word, directed toward its object, enters a dialogically agitated and tension-filled environment of alien words, value judgments and accents, weaves in and out of complex interrelationships, merges with some, recoils from others, intersects with yet a third group; and all this may crucially shape discourse, may leave a trace in all its semantic layers, may complicate its expression and influence its entire stylistic profile" (276). Selzer's aesthetic power draws heavily upon this dialogism, or rather, the dialogism contributes to the aesthetic qualities of his prose. Selzer fuses fiction with nonfiction, tenor with vehicle, the language of one social and normative reality with that of another. The work won't settle down comfortably into one genre or category. Not only from book to book or essay to essay, but even within individual phrases and clauses Selzer's language, at its best, continually interacts with other languages, literary languages, scientific languages, humanistic languages—and with the entire social,

Charles I. Schuster

ethical, and philosophical constructs which surround those languages.

The following paragraph from "Bone" illustrates this principle:

> But this man who thrust himself from the earth, who wore the stars of heaven in his hair, was guilty of overweening pride. In act most audacious, he had defied nothing less than the law of gravity. He was to pay dearly for such high imposture. The vertebrae, unused to their new columnar arrangement, slipped, buckled, and wore out. Next, the arches of the feet fell. The hip joints ground to a halt. Nor was payment extorted only from the skeletal system. The pooling of blood in the lower part of the body distended the fragile blood vessels beyond their limits. Thus bloomed the fruitage of hemorrhoids; thus are we varicose. Worse still, our soft underparts have given way. Under the sag of our guts, we bulge into hernia. We turn to soft lump. (*Mortal Lessons* 60)

The opening sentence situates itself in a sermonic mode; the speaker here has mounted a pulpit. The second sentence takes a step toward the melodramatic with the post-position adjective in its opening phrase, in its word choice ("audacious," "defied"), and its echoing the theme of *Paradise Lost*. There is a literary quality here—and throughout—of words put together for dramatic effect, of syntax straining for originality. Moreover, there is a mocking tone produced by a combination of over-statement and the insinuation into this voice of a posture of the overly-righteous, a kind of Chadbandian overearnestness. That tone emerges distinctly in the third sentence, with its frocked, haughty denunciation of "man" made in the high Victorian tones of commercial metaphor ("pay dearly"). The language then shifts quite radically to the scientific, with its description of the vertebrae, arches, and hip joints. But the language is in part colloquial as well ("wore out," "fell"), until it ultimately slips into cliche ("ground to a halt"), which escapes the charge of triteness by the very fact of its being, in this case, literally true. Through the remainder of the passage, Selzer interweaves the language of the medical-school classroom, commercial boardroom, poet's study, and neighborhood bar.

24

And yet it is all *his* language, his style, reflecting though it does the languages and styles of a wide spectrum of usages.

A second example illustrates a different kind of dialogical impulse at work in Selzer's prose. In "Longfellow, Virgil, and Me," Selzer confesses his love for these two particular poets and the important role they played in his literary development. Earlier, in "Bone," Selzer had imitated Longfellow's distinctive tetrameter verse with a ten-line poem followed by the declaration, "Homage to Longfellow! One now understands why he wrote this way. Once you start, you can't stop" (56). In "Longfellow, Virgil, and Me," he declares his debt even more directly: "Within my mind, there are two men to whom I remain belted by filaments of the imagination of such a tensile strength as to have withstood the distraction, the wear and tear of thirty years. These are Longfellow and Virgil (bacio mano)" (*Mortal Lessons* 198). Selzer's love for Longfellow has indeed become so internalized that his writing "can't stop" being influenced by the rhythms of that earlier poet. Here, in stanzaic form to illustrate my point, is the third paragraph of the essay:

And, ah, that intrepid youth
"who bore 'mid snow and ice,
a banner with the strange device, Excelsior."
Where, we died to know,
was he going?
What implacable fury
hounded him up that mountain
as the shades of night were falling fast?
What did it mean, Excelsior?
Was it the emblem of a promise given?
Some cryptic warning?
A terrible cri de coeur?
It did not matter.
The very syllables drove us mad with yearning.
We longed to climb with him,
side by side,
sharing his passion and his agony,
to take from his faltering arm that banner,
and to wrap ourselves in Excelsior. (199)

There can be no doubt that Selzer here is having fun with the rhythms and diction of Longfellow in his own prose. Those rhythms and that diction, however, have become internalized, so that at the end of the essay when he is concluding a delicate and humorous example of mistranslating Virgil, Selzer can write "Here was no mere gesture of gratitude, / but an exchange of the heart. / Between those two smiles / (0 measure them in quanta, / in light years) / a rainbow arced; / there was sealed a covenant, / a secret troth plighted" (205). Here is no imitation of Longfellow's irregular trimeter, but an internalization of the diction and rhythm so that it has become merged within Selzer's own style. The identical argument can be made in connection with other writers of prose and poetry, such as Virgil, Keats, Whitman, and Poe. Their distinctive words, phrases, and rhythms echo, at times consciously but more often dimly and indistinctly, in Selzer's prose.

This then is the dialogic element in Selzer's prose. Bakhtin describes the effect that this quality has on other forms and genres by claiming:

> They become more free and flexible, their language renews itself by incorporating extraliterary heteroglossia and the "novelistic" layers of literary language, they become dialogized, permeated with laughter, irony, humor, elements of self-parody and finally—this is the most important thing—the novel inserts into these other genres an indeterminacy, a certain semantic openendedness, a living contact with unfinished, still-evolving contemporary reality (the openended present). As we will see below, all these phenomena are explained by the transposition of other genres into this new and peculiar zone for structuring artistic models (a zone of contact with the present in all its openendedness), a zone that was first appropriated by the novel. (*Dialogic* 7)

For Bakhtin, *novel* is a term that transcends generic boundaries to include all literary forms concerned with "becoming," that is, with language in the process of stylistically creating itself out of the array of languages around it. Dostoevsky is a novelistic writer, according to Bakhtin, but so are Rabelais, Ibsen, and Byron. Selzer, I would claim, also can be characterized as a novelistic writer whose language is dialogized in the sense that Bakhtin claims for the most innovative and exceptional works of art. For this dialogic quality contributes substantially to the richness of interpretation, the "semantic open-endedness" that characterizes Selzer's prose.

Fusion and the dialogical are leaf and stem from the same root, and in a very real sense they sum up Selzer's art. In the beginning of this essay I suggested that Selzer is Yeshi Dhonden, that he makes of science an art. Selzer's gift as a writer is precisely this ability to fuse together disparate worlds of thought and experience. In his images, his words, his language, his conception of art, Selzer welds contrastive elements into a sculpted tension. His work is mercurial, unstable, unresolvable, ambiguous, ambivalent. It is ungraspable, like the song of Keats's nightingale—or like Keats's poetry itself. It is for this reason that I think Selzer's work will endure. At its best, it reflects the themes, languages, and traditions of literature and fashions them to its own vision of the world. The genius of Richard Selzer is not that he is a surgeon who is also a writer, but that he is an artist who also happens to practice surgery. And like his narratives, that opposition too is unresolvable.

Works Cited

Bakhtin, Mikhail. *The Dialogic Imagination.* Ed. Michael Holquist. Trans. Caryl Emerson and Michael Holquist. Austin: U of Texas, 1981.

———. *Problems of Dostoevsky's Poetics.* Ed. and trans. Caryl Emerson. *Theory and History of Literature* 8. Minneapolis: U of Minnesota, 1984.

Beppu, Keiko, and M. Teresa Tavormina. "The Healer's Art: An Interview with Richard Selzer." *Centennial Review* 25 (1981): 20–40.

Freud, Sigmund. Vol. 4 of *The Standard Edition of the Complete Psychological Works of Sigmund Freud.* Trans. and ed. James Strachey. London: The Hogarth Press, 1953, 1958.

Keats, John. *The Letters of John Keats.* Ed. Maurice Forman. 4th ed. London: Oxford, 1952.

Charles I. Schuster

Selzer, Richard. *Confessions of a Knife.* 1979. New York: Morrow, 1987.

———. *Letters to a Young Doctor.* New York: Simon and Schuster, 1982.

———. *Mortal Lessons.* New York: Simon and Schuster, 1977.

———. Personal interview. 11 August 1982.

———. *Rituals of Surgery.* 1974. New York: Morrow, 1987.

———. *Taking the World in for Repairs.* New York: Morrow, 1987.

Volosinov, V. N. *Marxism and the Philosophy of Language.* Trans. Ladislav Matejka and I. R. Titunik. New York: Seminar Press, 1973.

Wolfe, Tom. *The Right Stuff.* New York: Farrar, Straus and Giroux, 1979.

2

STYLISTICS AND THE STUDY OF TWENTIETH-CENTURY LITERARY NONFICTION

Dennis Rygiel

I want to argue in this essay for increased use of stylistics in the study of twentieth-century literary nonfiction, not only by those interested in nonfiction as literature but also by those interested in composition.[1] Broadly conceived as the application of linguistic approaches to literature, stylistics is a relatively new area, dating mainly from the 1950s. It is a huge, fast expanding territory with ill-defined and shifting boundaries.[2] Here, however, I want to concentrate on what I take to be the most valuable kind of stylistics, the kind that combines "careful attention to theory and method . . . with knowledge of contexts and with intuition" (Bennett, *Bibliography* 5).

A bridge between linguistics and literary criticism, such stylistics integrates aims and methods from both disciplines.[3] This is especially clear with practical (as opposed to theoretical) stylistics, the branch I want to focus on. From linguistics, the

---

1. That there hasn't been much criticism of style in recent nonfiction, let alone criticism based on stylistics, is evident from Rygiel, "Style."

2. For a good mapping of the territory 1967–83, see Bennett, *Bibliography*.

3. Here I can only outline the approach, sketching in essential features and leaving important but subsidiary features aside. For further discussion of many of the key points, see Leech and Short, the best single introduction to prose stylistics and a book I have been strongly influenced by in developing the approach described in the following pages. Two other, earlier models of analysis have also influenced my approach significantly: Corbett, "Method," and Bennett, *Prose Style* 224–31. To a large extent, the approach described represents a synthesis of these three models.

Dennis Rygiel

scientific study of language, practical stylistics derives its aim of systematic description of language use, i.e., of stylistic devices. In this context, "systematic description" means that the description is to be based on principled analysis rather than impressionistic response, so that "the conclusions can be *attested* and *retrieved* by another analyst working on the same data with the same method" (Carter 5–6). But description in practical stylistics, however detailed or carefully done, is rarely an end in itself; it is almost always done for the sake of literary interpretation. Thus the fundamental question in such stylistics is not what stylistic devices occur in a literary work or how often they occur, but what effects those devices produce and why they are sought—in other words, how style relates to the functions and meaning of the work. It is this ultimate concern with interpretive rather than descriptive questions that practical stylistics derives from literary criticism and that makes it a branch of literary criticism.

In methodology, practical stylistics is also a hybrid, combining objective analysis based on principles, concepts, and techniques derived from linguistics with intuitive strategies characteristic of literary criticism.What this means in practice is a demand for a balance between rigor and insight: objective evidence to substantiate stylistic intuitions, intuitions to guide and motivate the search for evidence. The evidence sought is linguistic and numerical: "The more a critic wishes to substantiate what he says about style, the more he will need to point to the linguistic evidence of texts; and linguistic evidence, to be firm, must be couched in terms of numerical frequency" (Leech and Short 47). But the equally strong concern for literary insight affects the kind of linguistic evidence and numerical data employed. Thus while use of linguistic evidence presupposes "*analytic* knowledge of the rules and conventions of normal linguistic communication" (Carter 5), stylistics does not operate solely with the descriptive categories—phonological, lexical, syntactic, semantic—of linguistic analysis. It may and often does use such categories: e.g., *proper noun, passive verb, subordinate clause*. But because individual linguistic features, whatever the level, "are likely to have a less significant effect than features in combination," stylistics also uses "special stylistic categories, derived, by abstraction and combination, from more basic linguistic categories" (Leech and Short 46). These distinctly stylistic categories are more complex but often less well defined than basic linguistic categories. Examples include *rhyme, Latinate diction, metaphor, parallelism.* Together the two kinds of categories, linguistic and stylistic, make up the set of stylistic devices.

Whatever their derivation, stylistic devices tend to be studied in quantitative terms in stylistics. However, the nature and extent of the quantitative study depends on the kind of device(s) being studied and the purpose the numerical evidence is to serve. Stylistic devices that occur relatively infrequently or that are not very well defined don't lend themselves to counts. And even with those that do, quantitative study does not necessarily mean rigorous statistical analysis: "Style is such a complicated phenomenon that it would be impractical to demand hard evidence for every observation made. It may be sufficient for many purposes just to enumerate textual examples of the feature under discussion. In many other cases, one may agree with Halliday that a 'rough indication of frequencies is often just what is needed. . . .' The essential point is that the use of numerical data should be adapted to the need" (Leech and Short 47–48).

Which stylistic devices to study, which to seek evidence for, is a matter of choice, choice informed and guided by both literary intuition and analytic awareness of linguistic and stylistic categories. Unlike linguistic description, which ultimately strives for relative completeness, stylistic description is inherently selective. Not all stylistic devices will be found in every work, and of those that are found, not all will be significant to the work's function and meaning. Identifying the devices that are significant and thus merit attention is largely a matter of literary intuition, developed by extensive careful reading and by literary training. Still, analytic awareness of what devices are likely to be significant can aid intuitive strategies, and so stylistics sometimes operates with a checklist of likely possibilities as a kind of heuristic. The most useful I know of is the one Leech and Short have developed for fiction, but which is, as they claim, also applicable to nonfiction (75–80, 6). This framework consists of four major types of categories: (1) lexical categories (general, nouns, adjectives, verbs, adverbs); (2) grammatical categories (sentence types, sentence complexity, clause types, clause structure, noun phrases, verb phrases, other phrase types, word classes); (3) figures of speech (grammatical and lexical schemes, phonological schemes, tropes); and (4) context and cohesion. Within each category there is a series of questions suggesting a range of potentially significant stylistic devices, as in the following section on sentence complexity:

> Do sentences on the whole have a simple or a complex structure? What is the average sentence length (in number of words)? What is the ratio of dependent to independent clauses? Does complexity vary strikingly from one sentence to another? Is complexity mainly due to (i) coordination, (ii) subordination, (iii) parataxis (juxtaposition of clauses or other equivalent structures)? In what parts of a sentence does complexity tend to occur? For instance, is there any notable occurrence of anticipatory structure (*e.g.,* of complex subjects preceding the verbs, of dependent clauses preceding the subject of a main clause)? (76–77)

Stylistics provides various models of style, each of which leads to a different emphasis in analysis. Though there have been refinements and developments over the past several years, the three major models Freeman singled out in 1970 remain important: "style as deviation from the norm, style as recurrence or convergence of textural pattern, and style as a particular exploitation of a grammar of possibilities" (4). All three are useful in certain respects; however, in this paper I will deal with just one, style as deviation, mainly because I want to call attention to some valuable information on nonfiction norms which does not seem to be as widely known or as much used as it should be.

When style is defined as a deviation from the norm, it is assumed that the linguistic code provides alternative expressions for essentially the same content—in other words, stylistic variants (e.g., "I came home and saw the open window" as opposed to "I came home; I saw the open window" or "When I came home, I saw the open window"); that each variant occurs with a certain frequency in the norm; and that, in order to accomplish his or her purposes, the writer chooses to deviate from the norm by using a particular stylistic variant (or device) significantly more or less frequently than one would expect. Well-known examples would be Hemingway's relatively frequent use of coordinators and relatively infrequent use of adjectives. Methodologically, the style-as-deviation approach works in this way: a sample from a text is chosen and then explicitly compared, with respect to a particular stylistic device or set of devices, to an appropriate norm or set of norms. If the focus is on pervasive stylistic devices, a representative sample is chosen, its representativeness being established by its meeting requirements of sufficient length (usually a minimum of 350–700 words) and of random selection.[4] If the focus is on local characteristics of style, a sample is chosen on the basis of literary interest or significance (essentially an intuitive matter). Whatever the nature of the sample, explicit comparison to a norm is crucial. Without such comparison it is impossible to tell what, if any, significance there is in the use of a particular stylistic device in the sample. For instance, the number of unsubordinated sentences is one measure of stylistic simplicity: the more such sentences, the simpler the style in this one dimension. But if one finds, as Cluett does (l45), that in samples of Hemingway's *Death in the Afternoon* the percentage of unsubordinated sentences is 40 percent, how does one know whether that 40 percent is a lot, a little, or "normal"? It is possible to appeal to an intuitive sense of the norm ("It seems like a lot to me"), and this is commonly done in literary criticism. But practical stylistics, in its insistence on a high degree of objectivity, is not satisfied with stylistic judgments based solely on intuited norms. Instead, a corpus is established to serve as a norm, and explicit comparison is made to it. Cluett's study is a good example. Using as a norm a corpus made

4. On sample length, see Cluett 16.

up of samples from sixteen other writers, Cluett finds that Hemingway's percentage of unsubordinated sentences makes him "rank very low on this measure of simplicity; indeed, only three other writers, all of whom could be considered very old-fashioned, rank lower" (143). So if Hemingway's style is simple, it is not because of frequent sentences without a subordinate clause.

The key to the style-as-deviation approach is to establish a norm that is appropriate as well as adequate in range and manageable in size. Appropriateness is largely a matter of similarity in context(s) between sample and norm—i.e., similarity in genre, period, dialect, field of discourse, medium, attitude (formality/informality), and/or authorship. The more contextually similar sample and norm are, the likelier it will be that any differences in style are to be attributed to particular characteristics of the author or work under study and not to other factors (e.g., differences in period, genre, subject). Adequacy in range and manageability in size exert pulls in different directions, so some compromise is always necessary, and usually it is manageability that wins out. However, as Leech and Short say, "a small sample for comparison is better than nothing at all" (52).

Up to this point in the discussion of methodology, I have been emphasizing description of stylistic devices and of the relatively objective analytic techniques for description that stylistics derives and adapts from linguistics. But as already mentioned, in practical stylistics even description is influenced by intuitive strategies associated with literary criticism, notably in determining which stylistic devices are selected for study. However, intuition is even more apparent and crucial in interpretation of style—the ultimate purpose of practical stylistics—i.e., in answering questions about why particular stylistic devices are being used, why with this or that frequency, why in this or that combination. And since the answers to these "why" questions may lie in any of several aspects of the text or context, practical stylistics is essentially holistic. In other words, style is seen as just one way into a literary work, just one aspect, which cannot be understood apart from all relevant contexts and all other aspects of the text. Thus practical stylistics takes into account, at least implicitly, the whole range of contexts (cultural, historical, biographical, literary, linguistic) as well as the writer's purpose, the content of the work, the structure, the voice and tone, and, of course, the style.

I would like to show how the kind of stylistics I have been describing might work in a study of local characteristics of style in literary nonfiction. For this purpose I have chosen the opening four paragraphs of E. B. White's essay "Once More to the Lake." In the analysis I will draw on a range of norms for comparison: various sorts of contemporary prose, student and professional; twentieth-century British and American literary nonfiction; and the first three paragraphs of White's essay "The Ring of Time."[5] The last makes a good point of comparison because it is nearly the same size (767 words vs. 741), structurally similar (the opening of an essay with a narrative frame), and thematically related (an exploration of one of White's favorite themes—the experience/belief/illusion of the circularity of time). Because of limits of space, and because the emphasis is on exemplification of an approach rather than exhaustive analysis, I will comment briefly on contexts and on aspects of the text other than style and then focus on just two representative categories of stylistic devices, one lexical and the other grammatical.

Contexts: Biographical, Historical, Cultural, Literary, Linguistic

"Once More" was written in August 1941 after a trip to a camp and lake associated with White's childhood.[6] This was not his first time back to "this unique, this holy spot," but now White, whose parents had died in the mid-1930s, returned as

5. References to "Once More" and "Ring" are to White, *Essays*.
6. Biographical information for "Once More" is derived from White, *Letters* 8–10, 214–16, and Elledge 3–37; for "Ring," from *Letters* 411–16 and Elledge 306–18.

a parent himself, having taken along his ten-year-old son, Joe.Though nationally and internationally 1941 was a troubled time, nothing of the larger cultural and historical context is mentioned. However, the desire to return to a special place of childhood and perhaps reexperience a time of simplicity and innocence would have resonated strongly in a nation which had gone through one world war and, after a Great Depression, was facing the prospect of another. "Ring" was written almost fifteen years after "Once More" and again involved a trip, in this case one White and his wife, Katherine, took in late February 1956 to Sarasota, Florida, a place associated with Katherine's late aunt, Caroline, who had helped rear Katherine and who had lived with the Whites during the year before her death in 1955. Moreover, when the Whites arrived in Sarasota, they received word of the death of White's best friend, Gus Lobrano, who had been gravely ill. While undoubtedly influenced by these circumstances, "Ring" (at least the part I am concerned with) is ostensibly an account of White's visit to the winter home of the Ringling circus. Thus it is about something as familiar and as much associated with childhood as the summer camp of "Once More." But in contrast to the "finished show" children see, White saw the circus in preparation, epitomized by a mother and daughter practicing their horse-riding act. Finally, both "Once More" and "Ring" are informal essays intended for a sophisticated, well-read audience: the former appeared first in *Harper's* in October 1941; the latter in the *New Yorker* in March 1956. The linguistic norm for both is written American English of the mid-twentieth century, a norm whose informal variety may seem closer to semiformal than informal to an audience now.

Purpose

White's primary purpose in "Once More" is to tell not simply what he and his son did when White returned to the summer camp of his childhood, but how the return affected him—what he felt and why he felt it. At the center of the account are "the creepy sensation" of merged identities—father, self, son—that White experienced and the highly emotional realization he came to about time, change, and mortality as affecting himself. The essay is thus primarily expressive in aim, but as one would expect in a *Harper's* essay of 1941 it has a strong literary function as well. The same two aims are important in "Ring," but the proportions seem reversed, so that the literary is primary, the expressive secondary. This is not surprising given what White says he is trying to do: "to recapture" a "mild spectacle" witnessed, a moment of enchantment felt, as the young girl took her ten-minute practice ride around the ring while her mother held the long rein of the horse and herself "stepped a tiny circumference" (142–43).

Content

"Once More" is an account of a powerful experience in which are implicit various aspects of the theme of the circularity of time: the experience of recapturing or even reliving the past; the powerful effect memory can have on one's sense of the present; the cyclical nature of human life as reflected in the linking of the generations; and the ultimate realization that, for the individual, time is not circular but linear, leading to change and finally death. But the emphasis in the essay is on the experience itself and not reflection on it. Thus the essay is composed essentially of description (involving past as well as present) of the lake and camp, of the activities there of White, his father, and his son, and of White's feelings during his stay. "Ring" is also an account of an experience, albeit a less powerful one, but it contains as much or more reflection on the experience as description of the experience itself. White develops his themes explicitly and at length: that through its various paradoxes (e.g., order out of disorder) "the circus comes as close to being the world in microcosm as anything I know; in a way, it puts all the rest of show business in the shade"; that "the circus is at its best before it has been put together," that "one ring is always bigger than three" (143); and that, though time may seem circular, it is not.

37

Dennis Rygiel

Structure

The first paragraph of "Once More" explains the motivation for the return to the lake. The second and third, while mentioning the journey there, center on White's wondering about how much the lake had changed and remembering how it had been in his youth. The fourth paragraph describes the central experience of the return: the feeling that White had gone back in time, that his son was he and he was his father. "Ring" begins with a paragraph describing the circus scene and its effect on White and other watchers ("hypnotic charm"). The second paragraph covers the girl's entrance, what she looked like, and the start of her practice ride. The third explains White's whimsical sense of his own role "as recording secretary" (143) and his notions about the circus, both finished and in preparation.

Voice and Tone

White's voice is similar in both essays. He seems to be an extremely acute observer, able to find surprising significance in everyday matters, the kind of things that touch us all. He appears modest and unassuming, a very natural person; candid about expressing his feelings but not aggressive; amiably tolerant but with a good-natured taste for the play of irony. In "Once More" White's tone is generally quiet and casual. At ease with himself and his audience, he tells of his return to the lake simply and naturally, the seriousness of the experience emerging only in the final paragraph of the essay. White's usual slightly ironic distance from his subject is not so apparent here; after all, White is not simply an observer—it is his own experience of time and mortality that he is talking about. In "Ring," however, White is a visitor to the South and to the circus grounds. Despite having paid his dollar for admission, he calls himself a kibitzer; and having observed mother and daughter in the practice ring, he decides to record "the mild spectacle" because he sees himself as "a writing man, or secre-

38

tary" "charged with the safekeeping of all unexpected items of worldly or unworldly enchantment" (143). The very consciousness of being an observer rather than the person directly involved and of the responsibility of recording what is observed creates a kind of distance between White and his subject and between White and his audience that is not found in "Once More." With the distance come more playfulness (e.g., the imagery of "recording secretary"), less informality, and a greater sense of literary artifice.

Style

Since stylistics involves a continual dialectic between intuition and analysis, one may begin stylistic study of a work with either: with intuitions about the stylistic effects sought, the devices used; or with an analytic checklist of stylistic devices of the sort Leech and Short offer. In the first case the emphasis is on substantiating, refining, or correcting stylistic intuitions; in the second, on discovering stylistic effects or devices that might otherwise be missed. With the "Once More" passage, for instance, one might begin by following up on hunches about what stylistic devices, alone or in combination, might be producing effects such as simplicity, directness, informality. For the effect of simplicity, some obvious things to look at would be the relative frequency of coordination versus subordination, of monosyllables versus polysyllabic words, of concrete versus abstract nouns, of common versus proper nouns (White leaves out the names of the summer camp, the lake, the district, and even his own son) as well as the relative infrequency of adjectives, passive verbs, and rhetorical schemes and tropes. Or, starting at the other end, one might begin by working through the categories of a checklist of stylistic devices, spending as much or as little time on each category as the work under study warrants. Because this latter approach is the less familiar of the two, I would like to use it here, but selectively, concentrating on one lexical category and one grammatical category as representative of the whole approach.

Adapting and adding to Leech and Short's "General" lexical category (75), I would suggest the following as potentially significant stylistic devices:

a. Word length: monosyllables; words of three syllables or more.
b. Etymology: native or borrowed; morphological categories (e.g., compounds, words with particular suffixes).
c. Status: common core or variety class (e.g., regional, social, field of discourse, medium, attitude, interference).[7]
d. Collocation and set.
e. Function/associations: literal/figurative; descriptive/evaluative; denotative/connotative; referential/emotive.

In contrasting his own vocabulary with S. J. Perelman's, White once wrote: "I have to get along with a vocabulary of fifteen hundred serviceable words that I just use over and over again, trying to rearrange them in an interesting way" (*Letters* 573). This exaggeration fits "Once More" far better than it does "Ring." For example, in terms of word length, the selection from the former has 76.5 percent monosyllables and 4.9 percent words of three syllables or more, making it Hemingway-like "Tough Talk" in this respect (Gibson 136); the selection from the latter has 69.1 percent monosyllables and 9.9 percent polysyllabic words, thereby edging toward the "Sweet Talk" of advertising (Gibson 136). The preponderance of monosyllables in "Once More" does two things. It fosters the impression of simplicity and directness, the sense of experience presented as lived rather than as thought about later. And it makes the polysyllabic words stand out a little more—not so much the eight Native words, like *afternoon, evening, summertime,* or the ten Romance words, like *suddenly* (2x) and *remember* (5x), but the eighteen Latinate words like *incessant, placidity, desolated,* and the set *illusion, transposition, sensation* (2x), *persisted,* and *existence,* used to describe the powerful feeling of merged iden-

7. The terminology is based on Quirk, Greenbaum, Leech, and Svartvik, the best description of contemporary English grammar.

tities.[8] The seventy-six polysyllabic words in the "Ring" passage may not have as plain a background to stand out against, but they tend to be foregrounded in other ways. Let me mention just one: etymology. Forty-five of the words are literary borrowings rather than (as with Romance words) borrowings from spoken language; forty are Latinate (e.g., in just the first paragraph, *desultory, apparent, radius, revolving, circumference, accommodate, maximum, conical, repetitious, exercise, exerted, invited, spectators, experiencing, expected, entitled*); and five are derived from Greek (*hypnotic, octagonal, microcosm, aroma, aerialist*). Such words suggest not experience itself but reflection on experience, in other words, something more intellectual than affective.

With respect to status, the words in both selections are, as one would expect with White, mostly common-core. Among these, however, are some that have strong associations with a particular subject matter. In "Once More" these are mainly the expected terms for talking about a summer camp, but a few pertain to ocean sailing (*salt-water, tides, sea water*) and two (*holy, cathedral*) suggest a religious context and thus are applied figuratively, and revealingly, to the lake and camp. In "Ring" White naturally uses many circus terms, but he also uses several terms associated with the timeless world of mathematics (*ring, radius, circle, center, circumference, maximum, conical, octagonal*) and a few associated with magic (*bedazzlement, enchantment, magic*). The most stylistically marked words in the two passages, however, are not related to field but to attitude. Some few words in the selection from "Once More" are formal-sounding, notably the Latinate polysyllables mentioned above, but these are more than counterbalanced by the several informal words and expressions: e.g., *along about, got, got back, a couple of, took along, you* (5x), *I guess, clearest of all, clear to the top, pretty much, cropping up, creepy*, and the contractions *that's* and *wasn't*. In contrast, the passage from "Ring" has few informal expres-

8. I follow Borroff's distinctions of Native, Romance, and Latinate words (37) and use the *Oxford Dictionary of English Etymology* as the authority for a word's history.

sions (*bunch, kibitzers, you, puts . . . in the shade*) and a great many formal-sounding words (most of the Latinate polysyllables) as well as several unusual and rather formal collocations. The latter include *one of those desultory treadmills of afternoon, in his dull career, the radius of their private circle, cleverly proportioned, a sort of quick distinction, this mild spectacle, items of worldly or unworldly enchantment, preliminary shabbiness,* and *its gaudy dream,* most of which are figurative expressions that draw attention to themselves. There is nothing quite comparable in "Once More."

At this point the checklist suggests a look at distinctions in the way words are used (e.g., literal/figurative, descriptive/evaluative). However, since these distinctions are accommodated in traditional literary study, it seems more useful to move on to something less familiar: quantitative study of sentence complexity. Again I find it useful to modify Leech and Short's category (see page 32) mainly to incorporate devices suggested by other sources. Here is what I propose (the sources in parentheses provide explanation of the devices and, in the case of those capitalized, quantitative norms for twentieth-century nonfiction as well):

a. Sentence length: average sentence length (Cluett 265; Hiatt 22); amount of variation—proportion of sentences with ten or more words over the average and with five or fewer words below the average (Corbett, *Classical Rhetoric* 450–51); frequency distribution of sentence lengths (Hiatt 23); average clause length (Hunt 56).

b. T-unit length: average T-unit length (Hunt 56; Christensen and Christensen 145); average number of words in base clauses and in free modifiers (Christensen and Christensen 145).

c. Subordination: frequency of unsubordinated sentences (Cluett 145); proportion of words in subordinate clauses and average length of subordinate clauses (Gibson 136); ratio of clauses per T-unit (Hunt 56); types of subordinate clauses.

d. Coordination: ratio of T-units per sentence (Hunt 56); coordination of dependent clauses, phrases, words.

e. Anticipatory versus trailing constituents (Leech and Short 225; Christensen and Christensen 68, 145).

In average sentence length the two passages are similar: 27.4 words for "Once More," 26.4 for "Ring."[9] What is striking about these figures is not just that they are a little higher than the norm of about 21–25 words for comparable essays (Hunt 56; Cluett 265; Hiatt 22), but that they are significantly higher than White's own average of 20.3 (Fuller 107). In the one case the reason is, as Fuller suggests (107), the lyrical nature of the essay; in the other, it is probably the result of the pull of meditative reflection, even if White does not take himself overly seriously. According to most indicators, sentence length variation is also similar in the two passages (the figures for "Once More" are given first): range (5–73 words; 6–53); proportion of sentences with ten or more words above the average (7, or 25.9 percent; 9, or 31 percent); proportion of sentences with five or more words below the average (12, or 44.4 percent; 14, or 48.3 percent). However, there is more clustering of sentence lengths in "Once More" than in "Ring." For example, with sentence lengths distributed in five-word increments, 18 of the 27 sentences (67 percent) fall between 6 and 25 words, compared to 14 of 29 (48 percent); 4 between 26 and 45 words (14.8 percent), compared to 14 of 29 (48 percent); and 5 over 46 words (18.5 percent), compared to 1 (3.4 percent). The clustering is a factor for simplicity, as is another factor not yet discussed—clause length. In the "Once More" passage, the average length of the 72 clauses is 10.3 words per clause, a figure somewhat below the 11.5 found by Hunt for his "superior adults" (56), and even further below the 12.0 average for the 64 clauses in "Ring."

Some differences as well as similarities in simplicity and

9. I recognize that counting procedures may vary from critic to critic; that counts and calculations, no matter how carefully done, are subject to error; and that there may well be a difference between results based on a sample of 700 words and results based on several thousand words. However, I believe that the value of numerical comparisons here is sufficient to warrant the potential risks.

directness between the two passages are also suggested by measures associated with T-unit analysis.[10] The "Once More" passage (17.2 words per T-unit) is well below what Hunt (56) and Christensen and Christensen (145) found for comparable essays, namely, 20.3 and 19.5 words, while the "Ring" passage is right between those norms (19.7 words per T-unit). Moreover, as the figures on words in base clauses and free modifiers show, the difference in the two passages is almost entirely in free modifiers, modifiers which add texture and a degree of complexity: the average number of words in base clauses is 13.0 in "Once More," 13.5 in "Ring," and 13.3 in the sample from Christensen and Christensen (145); the average number of words in free modifiers is 4.2, 6.2, and 6.2, respectively. Significant, too, is the placement of the free modifiers: in "Once More" 36.5 percent are initial, 5.0 percent medial, and 58.6 percent final; in "Ring" the figures are 21.6 percent, 7.5 percent, and 71.0 percent. Three things are noteworthy here. First, the distribution of initial free modifiers is such that they open only 5 of the 25 sentences (20.0 percent) in "Once More," compared to 9 to 27 sentences (33.3 percent) in "Ring," a figure above the norm of 24.4 percent in Christensen and Christensen's sample (68).[11] In fact, 20 of the sentences (80.0 percent) in "Once More" open with the subject, which in 13 cases is personal, compared to 16 subject openers (59.3 percent) in "Ring," only 6 of which are personal. In this respect, "Once More" is clearly simpler and more direct than "Ring." Second, neither passage has many medial free modifiers, the kind that interrupt the base clause and may seem relatively obtrusive, particularly if lengthy.

Third, final free modifiers predominate in both pas-

10. The raw figures are as follows: for "Once More," 43 T-units, 560 words in base clauses, 181 words in free modifiers (66 initial, 9 medial, 106 final); for "Ring," 39 T-units, 526 words in base clauses, 241 words in free modifiers (52 initial, 18 medial, 171 final).

11. Here I count only 25 sentences in "Once More" and 27 in "Ring," because Christensen and Christensen exclude questions and most sentences beginning with *it* or *there*.

sages—58.6 percent in "Once More," 71.0 percent in "Ring"
—which is just what one would expect from the norm of 55.6
percent in Christensen and Christensen (145). Such modifiers
are trailing as opposed to anticipatory constituents (initial or
medial free modifiers are anticipatory elements). As Leech
and Short explain, sentences in which trailing elements predominate suggest loose structure, and "the qualities associated
with loose structure are, not surprisingly, easiness, relaxation,
informality: the qualities one expects, in fact, in a fairly uncon-
sidered use of language" (229). Also in the category of trailing
constituents are noninitial coordinate constituents, whether
full independent clauses or clauses with elipted subjects (e.g.,
"The partitions in the camp were thin and did not extend
. . ."). Both passages have about the same number of such
clauses without subjects: 6 in "Once More," 5 in "Ring." More
telling is the difference in the ratio of T-units per sentence, a
measure of the amount of coordination of full independent
clauses. In the one passage the ratio is 1.6, which is almost
exactly what Hunt (56) found for fourth-graders (1.59), compared to 1.3 in the other, which is close to Hunt's finding of
1.23 for "superior adults." The openings of the two passages
make a good contrast—heavy use of trailing coordinate constituents (italicized), with some short anticipatory elements
within them, versus a balancing of anticipatory and trailing
constituents, all free modifiers:

One summer, along about 1904, my father rented a camp on
a lake in Maine *and took us all there for the month of August.* We
all got ringworm from some kittens *and had to rub Pond's Extract
on our arms and legs night and morning, and my father rolled over in
a canoe with all his clothes on; but outside of that the vacation was a
success and from then on none of us ever thought there was any place
in the world like that lake in Maine.* (197)

After the lions had returned to their cages, creeping angrily
through the chutes, a little bunch of us drifted away and into
an open doorway nearby, where we stood for a while in semi-
darkness, watching a big brown circus horse go harumphing
around the practice ring. (142)

Dennis Rygiel

Measures of subordination, in contrast, do not distinguish the passages from one another very much, and, as Cluett has shown more generally (143–49), such measures often do not tally with one's stylistic intuitions. For example, the passages have about the same proportion of unsubordinated sentences (33.3 percent and 37.9 percent), which would put them at the lower end of Cluett's twentieth-century samples, close to where that other master of the simple style, Ernest Hemingway, is also paradoxically found (145). The ratio of clauses per T-unit is virtually identical in the two passages—1.67 and 1.66, about the level (1.68) of Hunt's twelfth-graders (56). Actually, the passages differ only in the proportion of words in dependent clauses (42.4 percent vs. 32.2 percent) and in average length of dependent clauses (10.8 words vs. 9.9), with the difference just the reverse of what one would expect. In fact, the "Once More" passage thus meets two of Gibson's criteria for "Stuffy Talk" (136). There is one factor, though, that may at least partially reconcile these findings with one's stronger sense of stylistic simplicity in "Once More"—the relatively unobtrusive nature of most of the subordinate clauses. Of the 29 such clauses, 10 are nominal clauses functioning as direct object (6), subject complement (2), or complement of a noun (2); all but 2 of the 11 relative clauses are restrictive; and there are only 8 adverbial clauses (27.6 percent of the total). On the other hand, of the 25 clauses in "Ring" only 1 is a nominal; 3 of the 12 relative clauses are nonrestrictive; and there are 12 adverbial clauses (48 percent of the total). Finally, one other measure of subordination may be as significant as any in distinguishing the two passages—the number of reduced clauses. The "Once More" passage has only 12 verbals (5 infinitives, 4 participles, 3 gerunds), while the "Ring" passage has 20 (11 infinitives, 8 participles, 1 gerund).

At this point it might be useful to sum up the findings for the two categories studied in terms of stylistic effects and functions. The greater informality of "Once More" compared to "Ring" is due, in part, to the presence of more, and more markedly, informal words and expressions and to the relative infrequency of markedly formal diction (Latinate polysyllabic words, unusual figurative collocations). The sense of greater informality is a factor in the naturalness of White's voice and his relaxed tone in simply describing his experience of returning to the lake with his son and letting its meaning and emotional force be communicated in and through the experience itself. The greater simplicity and directness of "Once More" compared to "Ring" is related, in part, to the same devices that produce the sense of greater informality as well as to several other devices: the relative high frequency of monosyllables and Native words; the greater clustering of sentence lengths; the smaller average length of clauses and of T-units; the smaller amount of free modifiers (especially sentence openers), combined with the more frequent use of personal subjects to open sentences; the higher ratio of T-units per sentence (especially when combined with trailing coordinate structures); the preference for relatively unobtrusive kinds of subordinate clauses; and the lower number of reduced subordinate clauses. Moreover, with respect to several of these devices, "Ring" can be seen to be at or above the norm for twentieth-century essays (e.g., average length of clauses and T-units, percentage of free modifiers and sentence openers, ratio of T-units per sentence), thus confirming that "Once More" deviates in the ways shown from more general norms as well. What these deviations toward greater simplicity and directness do is to impart an air of authenticity to White's voice and an air of inevitability to his account, both of which lead one to identify with White's point of view and thus share his experience and the sharp sense of personal mortality it leads to. Of course there is a residue of findings that doesn't fit into this scheme: the similarity between the two passages in average sentence length, percentage of unsubordinated sentences, and ratio of clauses per T-unit, and the greater complexity of "Once More" with regard to the proportion of words in subordinate clauses and the average length of such clauses. But even these findings are useful, since they demonstrate that stylistic effects typically result from a combination of devices, and not necessarily the ones that would first come to mind.

Dennis Rygiel

I would like to conclude by commenting on what I take to be the chief values of the kind of approach to twentieth-century literary nonfiction that I am proposing. In doing so, I recognize that there is doubt among some critics about the general fit between stylistics and nonfiction, and that there is doubt among some composition specialists about the value of studying nonfiction in a writing course. However, to those interested in recent literary nonfiction, I would suggest that the approach described here or one similarly based in stylistics can be valuable in several ways. It pushes critics of nonfiction, student as well as professional, to substantiate their intuitions about style even as it provides workable and accessible means to do so. It offers a heuristic which helps critics discover things about style that they might well have missed or not fully appreciated. Since the emphasis is on communicability of methods as well as results, it allows critics to verify, refine, or correct their own work and that of others, thus providing for progress in the field. And it can demonstrate that literary nonfiction sustains and rewards close attention to language—not to the same degree as lyric poetry, but perhaps to a greater degree than is commonly thought.

To those interested in composition, I would suggest that this stylistics approach or one like it can also be valuable in the composition classroom. It can help develop in students the kind of understanding and appreciation of style that they so sorely lack and sorely need—style as an important aspect of nonfiction implicated in and related to all other aspects, as much a shaping influence as a means of expression. In its insistence on connecting stylistic effects to stylistic devices and vice versa, it can demystify terms like *simplicity*, *directness*, and *informality* and thus raise the whole level of discussion between teacher and student. For in giving students a language for analysis (and having students do counts teaches such language better than anything else I know), a stylistics approach makes students more observant of style—as Annie Dillard says in another context, "Seeing is of course very much a matter of verbalization" (32)—and it empowers them to analyze and productively discuss their own work and that of others,

48

whether students or professionals. In making students analyti-
cally aware of a broad range of stylistic devices and the effects
that those devices may produce alone or in combination, it can
at once inform students about possibilities hitherto unknown
and motivate students to try them in their own writing. A final
word. I used to be surprised at a comment routinely made by
students in the courses where I used a version of the approach
described here, an undergraduate course in Contemporary
Rhetoric and a graduate course in Stylistics: "In this course I
learned more about writing and improved my own writing
more than in any other course I've ever had, including writing
courses." I used to be surprised; I no longer am.

Works Cited

Bennett, James R. *Bibliography of Stylistics and Related Criticism, 1967–83*. New York: MLA, 1986.

———. *Prose Style: A Historical Approach Through Studies*. San Francisco: Chandler, 1971.

Borroff, Marie. "Robert Frost's New Testament: Language and the Poem." *Modern Philology* 69 (1971): 36–56.

Carter, Ronald. Introduction. *Language and Literature: An Introductory Reader in Stylistics*. Ed. Ronald Carter. London: Allen, 1982.

Christensen, Francis, and Bonniejean Christensen. *Notes Toward a New Rhetoric: 9 Essays for Teachers*. 2nd ed. New York: Harper and Row, 1978.

Cluett, Robert. *Prose Style and Critical Reading*. New York: Teachers CP, 1976.

Corbett, Edward P. J. *Classical Rhetoric for the Modern Student*. 2nd ed. New York: Oxford, 1971.

———. "A Method of Analyzing Prose Style with a Demonstration Analysis of Swift's *A Modest Proposal*." *Reflections on High School English: NDEA Institute Lectures 1965*. Ed. Gary Tate. U of Tulsa P, 1966. 106–24. Rpt. in *Contemporary Essays on Style: Rhetoric, Linguistics, Criticism*. Ed. Glen A. Love and Michael Payne. Glenview: Scott, 1969. 81–98.

Dillard, Annie. *Pilgrim at Tinker Creek*. Toronto: Bantam, 1975.

Elledge, Scott. *E. B. White: A Biography*. New York: Norton, 1984.

Freeman, Donald C. "Linguistic Approaches to Literature." *Linguis-*

Dennis Rygiel

tics and Literary Style. Ed. Donald C. Freeman. New York: Holt, 1970. 3–17.

Fuller, John Wesley. "Prose Styles in the Essays of E. B. White." Diss. U of Washington, 1959.

Gibson, Walker. *Tough, Sweet, and Stuffy: An Essay on Modern American Prose Styles.* Bloomington: Indiana UP, 1966.

Hiatt, Mary. *The Way Women Write.* New York: Teachers CP, 1977.

Hunt, Kellogg W. *Grammatical Structures Written at Three Grade Levels.* NCTE Research Report 3. Champaign:. NCTE, 1965.

Leech, Geoffrey N., and Michael H. Short. *Style in Fiction: A Linguistic Introduction to English Fictional Prose.* London: Longman, 1983.

The Oxford Dictionary of English Etymology. Ed. C. T. Onions. Oxford: Clarendon, 1966.

Quirk, Randolph, Sidney Greenbaum, Geoffrey Leech, and Jan Svartvik. *A Comprehensive Grammar of the English Language.* London: Longman, 1985.

Rygiel, Dennis. "Style in Twentieth-Century English Literary Nonfiction: An Annotated Bibliography of Criticism, 1960–1979." *Style* 15 (1981): 127–70.

White, E. B. *Essays of E. B. White.* New York: Harper and Row, 1977.

——— . *Letters of E. B. White.* Ed. Dorothy Lobrano Guth. New York: Harper and Row, 1976.

3

ORWELL'S POLITICAL PERSUASION

A Rhetoric of Personality

Richard Filloy

George Orwell's writing was a response to the immediate issues of the age he lived in; and those issues, as he saw them, demanded writing that was clearly rhetorical. In his 1946 essay, "Why I Write," Orwell commented "Every line of serious work that I have written since 1936 has been written, directly or indirectly, against totalitarianism and for democratic socialism. . ." (*Collected Essays* 1: 28). This commitment may seem to express an indifference to literary reputation, yet he also wrote that he wanted to "make political writing into an art" (*Collected Essays* 1: 28). To judge from his subsequent reputation, he succeeded. In doing so, he faced and overcame two obstacles which all political nonfiction faces in achieving an enduring literary reputation.

First, political writing is usually written for immediate effect rather than long-term scrutiny. If political writers are to be effective with their immediate audiences, they must be topical. But if they are topical, interest in their writing is likely to fade with the issue's urgency. The writer who is to be remembered must find a way to overcome this dilemma. Second, the writer of nonfiction has to make his writing interesting without the mediation of a fictional world. Novels like *A Passage to India* or *Darkness at Noon* are certainly political and have kept their appeal beyond the time of the immediate topics they address. But such books have the advantage of fictional plots and characters to maintain an audience's interest even when their topicality has gone. The political essayist has only the subject matter and a perspective on it.

Certainly Orwell's reputation rests partly on his novels, but this explanation for his reputation is not sufficient. Of course *Animal Farm* and *1984* continue to be widely read and admired, but Orwell's four other novels (*Burmese Days, A Clergyman's Daughter, Keep the Aspidistra Flying,* and *Coming Up for Air*) have never enjoyed a great vogue and are not well known. On the other hand, essays like "Marrakech" and "Shooting an Elephant" and his books *Homage to Catalonia* and *Down and Out in Paris and London* have often been reprinted and are widely praised. Reflection suggests that the growth in Orwell's reputation as a writer depends largely on the rediscovery of and increasing admiration for his nonfiction.

To some extent admiration for Orwell's writing is based on the lucid and economical style he developed according to the ideas he put forward in "Politics and the English Language." Orwell's struggle to write "less picturesquely and more exactly" resulted in an impressive stylistic accomplishment; yet even this, to his mind, was the result of his political intention (*Collected Essays* 1: 29). "And looking back through my work, I see that it is invariably where I lacked *political* purpose that I wrote lifeless books and was betrayed into purple passages, sentences without meaning, decorative adjectives and humbug generally" (*Collected Essays* 1: 30).

If political purpose was the force behind Orwell's best writing, two important critical consequences follow. First, if we read Orwell's work in the spirit in which it was intended, his achievement depends on the power of his writing to persuade audiences of the worth of his political ideals. Long after his immediate political ends have been achieved or outmoded, his writing must still make audiences feel their importance at some level. Even his style, admirable for its own sake, is designed to help gain the audience's agreement and results from his sense of that purpose. Second and most important for the purposes of this essay, an understanding of Orwell's success as a writer must be based on an account of the rhetoric of his political persuasion. On what is it based? How is it constructed?

Orwell's Political Persuasion

In proposing an answer to these questions, this essay focuses on Orwell's creation of an effective and enduring ethos in his writing. It argues that the character he created is different in important ways from the classical conception of an effective ethos for the rhetor and further that the creation of this character was not a natural outcome of Orwell's "real" personality but the result of expert rhetorical and literary craftsmanship. In fact, the most important conclusion this essay urges is that Orwell's "rhetoric of personality" is the artistic achievement most responsible for both Orwell's immediate success as a rhetor and his continuing popularity. In making these arguments, the essay aims at a clearer understanding not only of Orwell's political rhetoric but also of an important aspect of the rhetoric of nonfiction. In doing so, it proposes a revision of the classical theory of ethos, one which seems especially well suited, and perhaps limited, to the century of the common man.

This view can best be presented by returning to the question of the basis of Orwell's rhetoric. How did he go about persuading his audiences? To a great extent, he did it by seeming to be persuading himself first and foremost. Once again Orwell's words in "Why I Write" are illuminating. "I am not able, and I do not want, completely to abandon the world view that I acquired in childhood. . . . It is no use trying to suppress that side of myself. The job is to reconcile my ingrained likes and dislikes with the essentially public, non-individual activities that this age forces on all of us" (*Collected Essays* 1: 28).

Good political writing for Orwell began with individual thoughts and feelings which were then adjusted, altered, even abandoned, to fit political principles. But as any reader of Orwell knows, that sense of the individual, of the person struggling with political necessity and social justice, is never lost. In a dust-jacket comment for *The Collected Essays*, Orwell's boyhood friend Cyril Connolly said of him, "He was a man. . .whose personality shines out in everything he said or wrote." If we stop for a moment to consider those works of Orwell's which are best known, we will be forced to concur. In fact, Connolly's statement does not go far enough. Orwell's

53

personality does not simply shine out; it is, in an important sense, always the subject.

In *Homage to Catalonia*, we do not merely see the Spanish Civil War through Orwell's eyes; we read the story of his commitment to and subsequent disillusionment with the republican cause. *The Road to Wigan Pier* is not merely a sociological study of miners' and workers' lives, nor is it simply reportage with the reporter's direct experiences incorporated; it is the story of Orwell's discovery of his feelings and attitudes toward these people and the system which controlled their lives. It is a recipe for creating personal political purpose. Similarly, "Marrakech," "Shooting an Elephant," "Revenge Is Sour," *Down and Out in Paris and London,* and many other much-admired Orwell pieces are structured around a report of the narrator's personal feelings about his subject. Those feelings are not brought to the foreground for their own merits; they are there to serve Orwell's general purpose, political persuasion. Success or failure in that effort is proportionate to our ability to share those feelings. While Orwell seems to be self-absorbed, busily recounting his personal discoveries, changes, and conversions, he is also inviting the reader to partake of the same experiences and to change with him. The narrator's character thus becomes the chief means of persuasion.

The reliance on personal experience is even clearer if we pause to consider the basic arguments that Orwell advances in these cases. They are not new or startling. By themselves, they have little power to persuade most audiences. About the Spanish republicans he tells us that ends do not justify means which pervert those ends. About the British Raj he reports that empire is unjust and corrupts imperialists and subjects alike. Of the unemployed he says that they are not poor and dirty by choice but as the result of a system which forces those conditions upon them. Put in this way, it is easy to see why Orwell has no great reputation as an original political thinker. What makes these commonplaces of political argument appealing is the report of personal discovery. We see the reporter reconciling personal likes and dislikes with political necessity and social justice. We are persuaded insofar as we see that process validated and verified in Orwell's personal experience. The immediacy of experience is a kind of shorthand induction. One personal story well told may be more affecting than many a statistical sampling. It renders the commonplace generalization it supports not only believable but appealing.

Argument from ethos is hardly new or surprising in political discourse. What should surprise us is the great intellectual currency Orwell has managed to lend it. Ordinarily, such argument is not well-regarded. It is considered the province of demagogues, a form of appeal well-suited to the masses but hardly likely to impress the educated, much less to endure, even be cultivated, among them. What should we make of this phenomenon? Why is Orwell's ethical argument persuasive and enduring while that of so many others is repugnant and ultimately ephemeral?

Before attempting to answer those questions in Orwell's case, we might profitably pause to recall the origins and development of the doctrine of *ethos* as an ingredient in persuasion. In doing so, we will be better prepared to note Orwell's departure from it. Aristotle originated the term as a rhetorical concept, along with *pathos* and *logos*, as one of the three artificial proofs, indeed the most important one. For him, a successful ethos was founded on three qualities: virtue, good sense, and goodwill. The first two traits, *arete* and *phronesis* in Greek, are exceptional characteristics connoting valor, wisdom, and ability which set the speaker above the audience and thus made him a good guide for their opinions and actions. Aristotle did note that common people are often more persuasive than their more educated fellows by reason of their understanding of the audience's beliefs and ways of thinking; but there is little doubt that his successful rhetor was a naturally superior sort, able to gain the audience's assent partly through a display of his personal superiority. From its beginnings, then, ethos as a means of proof depended on the speaker's ability to seem a special sort of person.[1]

1. See Aristotle's *Art of Rhetoric*. The introduction of the three kinds of

Richard Filloy

This understanding was heightened during the rest of the classical period. In the Roman world, where orators were specially trained advocates in courts of law, the speaker's personality could be separated from the client's. Cicero emphasized that, whomever he represents, the orator must always appear to be a man of exceptional probity, civic-mindedness, and virtue (1: 327–29, see also 2: 23–29). Quintilian captured both the importance and the essence of the Roman concept of ethos in his definition of the orator as "a good man, skilled in speaking."[2] When Augustine translated the pagan doctrine of rhetoric into a Christian context, it was even more obvious and important that the speaker, who served as an example to other Christians, must be an especially virtuous person.[3] There is in all these writers some recognition of the value of the common touch; but generally in the Western tradition, the speaker's or writer's character persuades by being especially good.

From that belief, indeed, springs much of the suspicion of arguments resting on the speaker's character. It is simply too easy to seem to be something one is not, and history is full of hypocrites and charlatans. Worse, one may be a genuinely attractive person with poor arguments. Because we are all attracted to some people's characters and because such charac-

artificial proof and the claim that ethos is the most effective are at 1356a. The discussion of the constituents of ethos and their importance is at 1378a. The claim that the uneducated may be more persuasive than the educated is at 1395b. (References here and elsewhere in this essay are to the standard numbering of Bekker rather than to pages of an edition.)

2. This simple quotation from the *Institutio Oratorio* (4: 355), while it is the familiar epitome of Quintilian's view, does not begin to convey the personal superiority of his ideal orator. Consider this passage: "It is no hack-advocate, no hireling pleader. . .that I am seeking to form, but rather a man who to extraordinary natural gifts has added a thorough mastery of all the fairest branches of knowledge, a man sent by heaven to be the blessing of mankind, one to whom all history can find no parallel, uniquely perfect in every detail and utterly noble alike in thought and speech" (4: 369).

3. This comment from *On Christian Doctrine* gives a fair idea of Augustine's view of the importance of ethos, "However, the life of the speaker has greater weight in determining whether he is obediently heard than any grandness of eloquence" (164).

ters can be counterfeited, it has come to seem especially dangerous to be persuaded by the character of a speaker or writer. To be swayed by character is to be distracted from the real issues; it is to make oneself vulnerable to demagoguery. The aim of the careful reader is to avoid such persuasion.[4]

Even in the face of such attitudes, Orwell's character has managed to have a great appeal to sophisticated readers and to form the basis of his persuasion. Why? That question may not be wholly answerable, but Orwell himself provided what seems a valuable insight. "And yet it is also the truth," he wrote, "that one can write nothing readable unless one constantly struggles to efface one's own personality" (*Collected Essays* 1: 29). At first glance that statement is at odds with both the earlier quotation about retaining one's world-view and the whole thesis of this essay. What keeps that from being the final import of the statement is the realization that total effacement of personality is not possible. What these words suggest is not that personality should or even can be driven out of effective political writing, but that Orwell had a different use for ethos than that ordinarily associated with such appeals. Orwell persuaded not on the strength of an exceptional personality but on the ordinariness of a commonplace one. Self-effacement was an important persuasive strategy for Orwell. By making his reports those of an ordinary person rather than those of a great man, he allowed his audience to put themselves in his position without imagining the impossible. He made Aristotle's insight into the understanding common people have for their peers the basis for a different sort of argument from ethos. In the process of doing so, he turned the classical theory of ethos

---

4. This attitude can be found in many places. The following passage, drawn from a textbook coauthored by one of the most distinguished contemporary theorists of argumentation, provides an illustration. "Evidently an eloquent speaker or writer can dress up his arguments in all kinds of ways so as to conceal their defects and make them attractive to his audience. . . . But in most cases, it is possible to separate the features that give our arguments genuine 'rational merit' from those other rhetorical devices that have the effect of making them more attractive and persuasive than they deserve to be" (Toulmin, Rieke, & Janick 106).

Richard Filloy

on its head. By offering us a character who is ordinary, Orwell not only allows the reader to share the perceptions of the writer, he also disarms our suspicion of an ethos which is so good and so intelligent that our training tells us to mistrust it. After all, we are not in the presence of an especially superior person, merely another poor soul like ourselves.

This technique can best be seen in a series of examples. Consider Orwell's ethical appeal in "Shooting an Elephant."

> In the end. . . the insults hooted after me when I was at a safe distance, got badly on my nerves. . . . [My job] oppressed me with an intolerable sense of guilt. But I could get nothing into perspective. I was young and ill-educated and I had had to think out my problems in the utter silence that is imposed on every Englishman in the East. . . . Feelings like these are the normal by-products of imperialism; ask any Anglo-Indian official, if you can catch him off-duty. (*Collected Essays* 1: 265–66)

Quite clearly Orwell reports his own feelings to support his point about the effects of imperialism; but, just as clearly, he seeks to make those feelings average and ordinary. He belittles his own mental processes and makes his personal experience unexceptional. His feelings of guilt and oppression, he implies, were merely common decency. Any decent person in a similar situation would share them. Nor is Orwell's response to his feelings exceptional. He gives in to pressure and shoots the elephant because it is expected of him, even though he knows it is wrong. Feelings and responses like this are likely to be familiar to his audience, even though the specific experience is not. The audience is thus encouraged to identify with the author's attitude toward imperialism by having first identified with the ordinariness of his perceptions and actions. More importantly, the audience is invited to conclude that Orwell's failure to act rightly is not a personal failing but one imposed upon him by the imperialist system. If the readers find Orwell a person like themselves and can identify with his discomfort under the circumstances, they are very likely to conclude that the circumstances ought to be changed.

The reader's ability to identify with the writer is crucial to the function of Orwell's ethical argument. It is perhaps no surprise that his ethical argument, a kind suited especially well to the egalitarian ideals of our century, is based in identification, a term central to the rhetorical theory of Kenneth Burke, who has done so much to recast rhetorical theory into terms fitting the twentieth century. Burke proposes, in fact, "that our rhetoric be reduced to this term [identification]. . ." and further urges that rhetoric must often be thought of as "a general body of identifications." By proposing identification as a basic human ideal, Burke validates the basis of Orwell's approach. He explains that the writer's character, insofar as it is the means by which the reader and writer are shown to be "consubstantial," is basic to persuasion.[5]

The same process can be seen at work in this selection from "Such, Such Were the Joys," Orwell's memoir of his early schooling.

> Whenever one had the chance to suck up, one did suck up, and at the first smile one's hatred turned into a sort of cringing love. I was always tremendously proud when I succeeded in making Flip [the headmaster's wife] laugh. I have even, at her command, written *vers d'occasion*, comic verses to celebrate memorable events in the life of the school.
>
> I am anxious to make it clear that I was not a rebel, except by force of circumstances. I accepted the codes that I found in being. Once, towards the end of my time, I even sneaked to Brown about a suspected case of homosexuality. (*Collected Essays* 4: 401)

Orwell's point in this piece is that such schools used brutal psychological techniques to perpetuate a corrupt social order. Yet he makes this point not by showing himself as a strong-willed rebel but by stressing how easily he was influenced.

---

5. Burke's discussion of identification is extensive and cannot be given full consideration here. For the present purpose, it is important because Burke makes identification and the ethical appeals which come from it central to persuasion rather than a feature we can or would want to separate from the "rational merit" of a discourse. The quoted passages are from *A Rhetoric of Motives*, pp. 20, 26, 21.

Once again he makes his experience typical, demonstrating the vulnerability of the average, well-meaning, reasonable person in the face of strong social pressure. Once again the audience is encouraged to identify with Orwell's feelings, if not his precise experience, and to conclude that the system which imposes them is wrong.

A similar, but somewhat different, technique for rendering his own experience commonplace can be seen in this passage from "Revenge is Sour," where Orwell describes his feelings on seeing a Nazi war criminal abused by a Jewish captor.

> So the Nazi torturer of one's imagination, the monstrous figure against whom one had struggled for so many years, dwindled to this pitiful wretch, whose obvious need was not for punishment, but for some kind of psychological treatment. . . . Who would not have jumped for joy, in 1940, at the thought of seeing S.S. officers kicked and humiliated? But when the thing becomes possible, it is merely pathetic and disgusting. (*Collected Essays* 4: 20–21)

Here Orwell abandons the first person altogether as he uses the impersonal "one" and "who" to report his feelings. He has so far effaced his personality that his perceptions are not merely ordinary, they are not even individual. Yet few people were ever confronted directly with the situation Orwell reports and many who were did not find such abuse disgusting. In this passage, we are forced to agree not so much because Orwell's feelings are typical as because they are morally correct. Punishment, especially physical abuse, of "pitiful wretches" ought to be disgusting; and therefore most audiences will not dispute Orwell's statement. But to report such feelings in the first person is to risk self-righteousness. By making them merely a moral commonplace, Orwell gains agreement from anyone who recognizes that two wrongs don't make a right.

In *Homage to Catalonia* Orwell again employs this technique when he reports how he came to fight in the war.

> I had come to Spain with some notion of writing newspaper articles, but I joined the militia almost immediately, because at that time and in that atmosphere it seemed the only conceivable

thing to do. . . . When I came to Spain, and for some time afterwards, I was not only uninterested in the political situation but unaware of it. I knew there was a war on, but I had no notion what kind of a war. If you had asked me why I had joined the militia I should have answered: "To fight against Fascism," and if you had asked me what I was fighting *for*, I should have answered: "Common decency." (*Homage to Catalonia* 4, 46–47)

Of course, most writers who came to Spain conceived of other things to do than join the militia, and many soldiers had a less naïve attitude about what they were fighting for. But by making his actions, even when they were exceptional and courageous, seem ordinary and common, Orwell demands that his audience identify his actions with general moral standards. Who can oppose common decency, especially if it seems the only conceivable course of action?

The extent to which Orwell used the techniques of generalizing his feelings and experiences and belittling his own actions can be gauged by this series of short quotations from *Homage to Catalonia.*

1. A little while later, however, a bullet shot past my ear with a vicious crack and banged into the parados behind. Alas! I ducked. All my life I had sworn that I would not duck the first time a bullet passed over me; but the movement appears to be instinctive, and almost everybody does it at least once. (22)

Here we see Orwell's denial of any special bravery and an equation of his actions with those of "almost everybody." Whatever he did in the war, this early passages assures us, was the action of an ordinary soldier.

2. It was the first time that I had been properly speaking under fire, and to my humiliation I found that I was horribly frightened. You always, I notice, feel the same when you are under heavy fire—not so much afraid of being hit as afraid because you don't know where you will be hit. You are wondering all the while just *where* the bullet will nip you. . . . (44)

As in the preceding example Orwell reports his humiliation at finding himself no braver than average. Here he conveys his ordinariness by using "you" to describe his own experiences. The technique reflects a certain daring since former soldiers among his readers must be willing to accept his description of the feeling of being under fire.

> 3. The few Englishmen I was among were mostly I.L.P. members, with a few C.P. members among them, and most of them were much better educated politically than myself. (58)

Orwell here shows himself not only physically but intellectually undistinguished. As we read, we see him groping for a valid political understanding among men who must be his teachers as well as his fellow soldiers. Reading the book is thus designed to be a political education for us also, but one about which we are not made to feel inferior or patronized.

> 4. All this while I was lying on my side in the greasy mud, wrestling savagely with the pin of a bomb. The damned thing *would* not come out. Finally I realized that I was twisting it in the wrong direction. I got the pin out, rose to my knees, hurled the bomb, and threw myself down again. The bomb burst over to the right, outside the parapet; fright had spoiled my aim. (90)

This passage reflects a commonplace: the effect of fear on physical actions. By saving the reason for his poor performance until the end of the experience, Orwell makes his readers see the whole action, which at first seems merely wretched and comical, as the result of fear. Once again, of course, Orwell shows us that he is not a hero.

> 5. Of course at the time I was hardly conscious of the changes that were occurring in my own mind. Like everyone about me I was chiefly conscious of boredom, heat, cold, dirt, lice, privation, and occasional danger. (105)

Here again Orwell reassures us that he is not really an intellectual. He itches, fears, and is cold. The changes which he underwent and the political consciousness which resulted seem not the result of a superior mind or of hard thinking, they were almost imperceptible and natural to anyone who had these experiences.

6. Everyone who has made two visits, at intervals of months, to Barcelona during the war has remarked upon the extraordinary changes that took place in it. . . . in December . . . to me, fresh from England, it was liker to a workers' city than anything I had conceived possible. Now the tide had rolled back. (109)

Here Orwell casually reveals his naïveté upon arrival in Spain, but at the same time he makes his realization of this naïveté a thing which "everyone" who has had his experience notices.

7. And I remember feeling a vague horror and amazement that money could still be wasted upon such things in a hungry war-stricken country. But God forbid that I should pretend to any personal superiority. After several months of discomfort I had a ravenous desire for decent food and wine, cocktails, American cigarettes, and so forth, and I admit to having wallowed in every luxury that I had money to buy. (116)

Even after his experiences had changed him politically, Orwell insists, he was no saint, no self-denier. Being politically aware, he reminds us often, is not synonomous with giving up the personal desire for luxury.

It would be easy to double or triple the number of similar examples, but these should be sufficient to suggest the general point. By making his own actions and perceptions seem so ordinary, Orwell makes identification with his views easy.

If this interpretation of Orwell is correct, we may say that Orwell's literary persona persuades us by becoming a sort of hero, that is, he inspires admiration and agreement. Orwell's political persuasion is a rhetoric of personality in which the individual person is both the source of all political principles and the basis for persuasion to those principles. But clearly this persona is not a classical hero, a great spirit moved to great actions. Nor is it an antihero, an exponent of meaninglessness, of a senseless world where the individual is all that matters.

Orwell's hero is that sort of person his audience might be at their best: decent, caring, and basically good, but fragile under pressure; often wrong, selfish, and confused, but capable of sacrifice for the general good. In Burke's terms, Orwell surrounds himself with properties which establish his identity, an identity in which the audience wishes to share and believes it can share because Orwell has rendered it an ordinary one (Burke 23–24).

By presenting his admirable properties as the ordinary and believable actions of one individual, Orwell achieves another important effect of ethical argument. He makes those properties real to the audience. Aristotle remarked that metaphor is the most persuasive of linguistic devices because it sets things "before the eyes."[6] Another way to characterize the immediacy of experience described above as shorthand induction is to call Orwell's personal narratives metaphorical presentations of the abstract principles for which he was arguing. Perhaps a better way of conceiving of this effect is to say that Orwell's ethical argument makes his principles present to his audience. Chaim Perelman considered presence an "essential factor" of rhetoric and said that "one of the preoccupations of the speaker is to make present, by verbal magic alone, what is actually absent but what he considers important to his argument. . ." (Perelman and Olbrechts-Tyteca 116, 117). As we read Orwell's reports of his thoughts and actions, we are present at the formation of his principles and come to believe in their reality. Few sensations are more conducive to persuasion. But the critic must not confuse the feeling of reality, of "presence," with reality itself. Perelman warns us, "Presence, and efforts to increase the feeling of presence, must hence not be confused with fidelity to reality" (Perelman and Olbrechts-Tyteca 118). What is true about this ingredient or effect of ethos must also be understood about ethos generally.

6. Aristotle, *Art of Rhetoric*, 1405a & 1411b. Aristotle's discussion of the power to "set things before the eyes" turns on the concept of *energeia* (which Freese renders as "actuality," while Liddell & Scott offer "action, operation, energy") and is thus very close to Perelman's notion of presence. Aristotle

Orwell's Political Persuasion

We have observed that seeing Orwell as a person like his audience inspires a belief in the rightness of his goals and the possibility of their attainment in all kinds of people, not just the already committed or exceptional. Lionel Trilling noted this characteristic when he remarked in his introduction to *Homage to Catalonia*, "He is not a genius—what a relief! What an encouragement. For he communicates to us the sense that what he has done, any one of us could do" (*Homage to Catalonia* xi). While this observation is correct as far as it goes, it is important for the rhetorical critic of Orwell and of political discourse generally to go beyond it. Orwell's literary ethos must be recognized for what it is. Like the presence of his first-person reports, Orwell's ethos is a rhetorical construct, achieved deliberately and through craft, with the same purpose as Orwell's lucid style: political persuasion. Trilling must be understood to describe not the writer but his rhetorical creation.

The temptation to equate the historical Orwell with his literary persona is strong. Few writers have done more to experience what they wrote about, and Orwell's rhetoric of personality was greatly aided by his breadth of experience. Indeed Orwell the writer and Orwell the man can be exceedingly hard to separate. After Eric Blair adopted the pen-name George Orwell, he increasingly abandoned his original identity in favor of the invented one. His second wife, Sonia, uses Orwell as her surname and always refers to him in her writing as Orwell. She notes that although he never legally changed his name, "new friends and acquaintances knew him and addressed him as George Orwell" (*Collected Essays* 1: 20). Once he determined to become a writer, he seems to have lived his life largely for that purpose. Much of what he did was done in order to write about it, and still more was turned to literary account as an afterthought. Yet it is not these facts of time, place, and action nor the deliberate attempt to re-create himself as the political being whose experiences he reported that

also discusses the power and importance of metaphor in the *Poetics*, 1457b & 1459a.

mark Orwell's persona as a construct; it is the way in which they are reported. This essay has repeatedly pointed out that the pose of ordinariness is an effective persuasive strategy. Incidentally it has shown how unreal that pose was. Orwell was not the average Anglo-Indian official, schoolboy, soldier, or reporter. His feelings and actions are made to seem commonplace, but they were not. They were the result of an exceptionally astute and sensitive observer of wide experience bringing a sophisticated intellect to bear on his situation. His very determination to experience the "ordinary" lives of those he wrote about was exceptional—and sometimes mocked as an affectation. Those who knew Orwell and have remembered him in print, Cyril Connolly, Richard Rees, and Malcolm Muggeridge among others, do not recall an ordinary man but an extraordinary one who had exaggerated sensibilities and a morbid sense of class consciousness.[7] It took all of Orwell's literary craftsmanship to bury his Eton education and his intellectualism and to render his perceptions and thoughts ordinary.

The insistence that Orwell's appealing ethos be viewed as a rhetorical construct is not intended to demean him. On the contrary, it should enhance his literary reputation, for such an achievement bespeaks superb artistry. For this very reason, it is important not to accept Trilling's verdict at face value. If Orwell's ethos is not a genius, its creation may have been the work of one.

It is of further importance to insist on the artificiality of Orwell's character in his writing because it is only through recognizing and studying the art of such an achievement that we will come to understand its role in the rhetoric of nonfiction. If we recognize it for what it is, Orwell's peculiar genius in creating an ethos of only average abilities may shed some light on how enduring political nonfiction is written. The careful manipulation of character may be seen as an important

---

7. Connolly's memories of Orwell are contained in his book *Enemies of Promise*; Rees's in his book *George Orwell: Fugitive from the Camp of Victory*; Muggeridge comments on Orwell in an introduction to *Burmese Days*.

ingredient in the rhetoric of political writing. For such writing to survive the occasion which begets it, it needs an appeal which is not topical. The writer's character is just such an appeal: a good man is still admirable and interesting even when his specific context is gone. Such characters attract audiences by exemplifying values that transcend time and place: honesty, loyalty, empathy, and humility in Orwell's case. It is at this level that the writer can make an audience feel that long-gone political aims are still important: they are important because they are motivated by such transcendent values. Certainly not every writer will create a character like Orwell's; but Orwell's writing, at least, often depends, and perhaps survives, on his character's attractiveness.

The role of ethos in giving political nonfiction lasting appeal without sacrificing topicality seems worth further consideration. Writers from Edmund Burke to Joan Didion provide ample possibilities for further study; and the modern rhetorical theory of Burke and Perelman, among others, can provide both a basis and a vocabulary for undertaking such an investigation. This discussion of Orwell suggests that in modern writing the classical formula for an appealing ethos must be recast. A momentary reflection on Didion would seem to confirm that impression. One result of more extensive and historically varied investigation would be to discover to what extent an appealing ethos is a construct of particular historical circumstances.

The importance of the writer's ethos in creating lasting appeal in political writing also suggests an answer to the question of how the writer of nonfiction overcomes the novelist's advantage of a fictional world. Where the novelist creates interest in fictional characters and their story, the essayist may substitute his or her own character and personal experience. An author's perspective on a subject may be as interesting as a fictional character's—provided that the author can become as human and engaging. For, ironically, fiction often achieves greater presence than writing based in reality. Thus, in elevating political writing to an art, the writer of nonfiction may need to borrow something of the fiction writer's rhetoric. Indeed

Orwell's essays are often much like short stories narrated in the first person.

Following from the idea that the rhetorics of fiction and nonfiction need not be qualitatively very different is an intriguing possibility. Perhaps the basis of the distinction between fiction and nonfiction is best located in the audience's perception of the "ordinariness" of the writers of nonfiction as opposed to the imaginative specialness of fiction writers. In announcing that a piece of discourse is fictional, writers set themselves the problem of convincing the audience that the worlds they create are sufficiently believable to compel the reader's attention. Thus, every novel or short story is a kind of tour de force, a demonstration and a celebration of the writer's imaginative and persuasive powers in creating and sustaining illusion. Nonfiction, on the other hand, must usually be content with the cloak of reportage. The writer of nonfiction is "merely" reporting what is, not inventing new worlds. Writers of nonfiction are thus always comparatively "ordinary." Their subject matter, rather than their artistry, is always the focus. Yet the techniques of fiction and nonfiction may be very similar, and the craft required of the writers not very different.

This last point indicates how very fine the line between fiction and nonfiction or between political persuasion and literature may be. At the same time it shows why an avowedly political writer like Orwell may, without contradiction, be seen as a literary artist.

Works Cited

Aristotle. *Art of Rhetoric*. Trans. J. H. Freese. Cambridge: Harvard UP, 1926.

Augustine. *On Christian Doctrine*. Trans. D. W. Robertson. Indianapolis: Bobbs-Merrill, 1958.

Burke, Kenneth. *A Rhetoric of Motives*. 1950. Berkeley: Univ. of California P, 1969.

Cicero. *De Oratore*. Trans. E. W. Sutton and H. Rackham. 2 vols. Cambridge: Harvard UP, 1942.

Connolly, Cyril. *Enemies of Promise*. New York: Macmillan, 1938.

Muggeridge, Malcolm. Introduction. *Burmese Days*. By George Orwell. New York: Time, 1962.

Orwell, George. *Animal Farm*. London: Secker & Warburg, 1945.

―――. *Burmese Days*. New York: Harper Brothers, 1934.

―――. *A Clergymans's Daughter*. London: Victor Gollancz, 1936.

―――. *The Collected Essays, Journalism, and Letters of George Orwell*. Ed. Sonia Orwell and Ian Angus. 4 vols. 1968. Harmondsworth: Penguin, 1970.

―――. *Coming Up for Air*. London: Victor Gollancz, 1939.

―――. *Down and Out in Paris and London*. London: Victor Gollancz, 1933.

―――. *Homage to Catalonia*. 1938. New York: Harcourt, Brace & World, 1952.

―――. *Keep the Aspidistra Flying*. London: Victor Gollancz, 1936.

―――. *Nineteen Eighty-four*. London: Secker & Warburg, 1949.

―――. *The Road to Wigan Pier*. London: Victor Gollancz, 1937.

Perelman, Chaim, and L. Olbrechts-Tyteca. *The New Rhetoric: A Treatise on Argumentation*. Trans. John Wilkinson and Purcell Weaver. South Bend: Notre Dame UP, 1969.

Quintilian. *Institutio Oratoria*. Trans. H. E. Butler. 4 vols. Cambridge: Harvard UP, 1920.

Rees, Richard. *George Orwell: Fugitive from the Camp of Victory*. Carbondale: Southern Illinois UP, 1962.

Toulmin, Stephen, Richard Rieke, and Allan Janik. *An Introduction to Reasoning*. New York: Macmillan, 1979.

4

CRAFTING FACT

Formal Devices in
the Prose of John McPhee

Jack Roundy

E. J. Kahn, one of the men John McPhee has credited
with establishing a "framework" for the kind of nonfiction
prose he writes, tells a story in *About The New Yorker and Me*
that says a great deal about McPhee's philosophy of composition. As Kahn tells it, he and McPhee are having a rather
mundane conversation over lunch at the Harvard Club when
McPhee brings up "the Kahn Rule," which he says he has
"always tried faithfully to observe." Kahn is brought up short.
McPhee is talking about a rule he has forgotten he ever laid
down. McPhee refreshes his memory, reminding him that in
1963, the year McPhee first published in *The New Yorker*, he
advised the newcomer to "Always know what you're going to
do next" (251). McPhee, impressed, had made the Kahn Rule
a staple of his working method, though his mentor promptly
forgot what was clearly an offhand remark.

At first glance, the impression made on McPhee by the
Kahn Rule might seem rather surprising for one of *The New
Yorker*'s self-confessed "fact" writers. One might suppose that
his factual subjects would present him with simple, straightforward formal dictates, and that he would answer with straightforward narrative or exposition. Recounting a wilderness trip,
for example, he would construct a simple chronological account, or describing the brewing and distillation of scotch
whiskey, he would construct a simple explanation of how matters proceeded from the field to the bottle.

Prose of John McPhee

McPhee could, of course, proceed in just this way. But his nature, interests, and style lead him to a more eclectic, digressive approach. Indeed, it would be easy for McPhee's reader to sail through his entire corpus without ever getting an inkling of the Kahn Rule. So various are McPhee's materials, and so digressive is his presentation of them, the reader might easily be led to think that McPhee follows his nose through a subject, improvising as he goes along and taking whatever detours his subject and mood suggest. That this is precisely what McPhee does not do is an indication of the complexity of his formal planning, since the contrivance of such apparently artless organization requires a good deal more planning than a simple formal arrangement does. A large measure of McPhee's creative energy, in fact, goes into his observance of the Kahn Rule.

In the course of the present discussion, I will examine the means by which McPhee arranges diverse bodies of factual materials into artful, literary nonfiction. I will begin by considering the structural planning he does before writing a piece, paying particular attention to the way in which he incorporates the formal dictates of his facts into an overall design. Having established the care McPhee takes with structuring his pieces before he begins to write, I will then draw upon the observations of Kenneth Burke, as presented in *Counter-Statement*, to analyze the formal devices McPhee employs. In a sense, Burke will be thrust into the role of devil's advocate, since his discussion focuses on "literary" forms; indeed, he takes the position that "information" is inimical to literary form, a position of considerable interest to the student of fact writers like McPhee, whose work creates such a "literary" impression. Following a general discussion of Burke's forms and the ways in which McPhee's work can be seen embodying them, I will focus on McPhee's use of metaphor (one of Burke's "incidental" forms), showing how extensively it serves as a formal and thematic ligature in his work. I will conclude by examining one of McPhee's more formally interesting pieces, "Circling the River" from *Coming Into the Country*, bringing to bear the formal observations I have made.

Jack Roundy

First the Structure

In an interview with Stephen Singular, McPhee has ac-
knowledged his need for an outline before he begins to write:
"What's most absorbing is putting these stories together. I
know where I'm going from the start of a piece. It's my nature
to want to know" (50). Taking the Kahn Rule entirely to heart,
McPhee sets up a structure for the piece he intends to write
before he puts pen to paper. Oddly enough, however, he
doesn't see his preconceived structures as confining: "Because
I'm interested in structure, I must sound mechanistic. But it's
just the opposite. I want to get the structural problems out of
the way first, so I can get to what matters more. After they're
solved, the only thing left for me to do is tell the story as well
as possible" (50).

As his remarks to Singular suggest, McPhee sees the act
of composition in two distinct phases. The first phase is structural; in it, he sorts through his materials, decides on an appropriate form in which to present them, and then arranges them
in a sequence he intends to follow as he writes. The second
phase is governed by his instincts as a writer; within zones of
free play marked off by a structure he has already determined,
he improvises his presentation of his subject.

William Howarth has given a very detailed picture of the
first, structural phase of McPhee's method in his introduction
to *The John McPhee Reader,* and as Howarth has described it, it
does sound very "mechanistic" (xi–xvii). Having gathered a
great many notes, both from on-the-scene reporting and from
wide-ranging reading, McPhee puts them into a binder and
sits down to puzzle through them, playing with possible shapes
his story might assume. Certain patterns, such as the day-by-
day sequence of on-scene events, are suggested by the order
in which he has taken his notes. Others are suggested by what
might be called "natural" forms; if he wishes to detail the
growing cycle of the orange, for example, a "natural" approach would be to proceed from bud to blossom to fruit. Still
other patterns are suggested by the written forms in which he
finds many of his materials; though these materials are diverse

enough to include everything from instructions on how to build a canoe to the diary of a man living alone in the Alaskan wilderness, they all come with their own formal characters— canoe-building instructions are arranged step-by-step; a diary is organized by calendar dates. In a sense, all these patterns are "givens" with which McPhee must work when he structures a story. And in some cases—as, for example, in "The Search for Marvin Gardens" (*Pieces of the Frame* 75–89), which he structured around the board game *Monopoly*—he will use a "given" structure as the basis for his own.

But McPhee is rarely content to follow given patterns in his stories (nor, for that matter, could he), in part because he writes his pieces from such a variety of materials, each of which comes to him with a distinct formal identity, and in part because his basic concern in structuring a story is the exposition of theme, and theme, since it is inevitably the creature of the writer's mind, is given only in his realization of it.

In a conversation I had with McPhee in 1979, he seemed fascinated with formal questions and problems, and in particular with the challenge "given" structures, like chronology, posed for him.[1] At one point, he became especially animated as he talked about how he'd got over a troublesome hurdle in setting up his story on Thomas Hoving (*A Roomful of Hovings and Other Profiles* 1–64). The problem, he told me, was to find a way to get in and out of chronology as he explored Hoving's life and adventures as an art sleuth. Picking up a pencil, Mc-Phee sketched a "V" on a piece of paper, and from it he drew lines, at the end of which hung little circles. From an oblique angle, his diagram appeared to represent two clotheslines that met at one end; from the clotheslines his circles depended.

Having drawn the diagram, McPhee explained his solution to the Hoving problem. Each of the circles represented a vignette (the Hoving profile is arranged as a series of self-

1. What follows is distilled from a conversation I had with McPhee in July 1979. I still have the diagrams I mention in the discussion, as well as a sheaf of notes on McPhee's remarks. My notes on our discussion are sketchy, I'm sorry to say, but I think I have represented McPhee's remarks fairly.

contained vignettes) picturing Hoving. Some of the vignettes were basically biographical sketches, dealing with Hoving as a man; others showed Hoving learning to distinguish genuine artistic treasures from clever forgeries. Biographical vignettes hung from one "clothesline," while art sleuthing vignettes hung from the other. At the conclusion of the profile, the two clotheslines came together, as did the two tracks of the Hoving profile. McPhee had taken a problem created by a "given" structure and had overcome it by imposing his own. I gathered from the way he spoke about it that this solution to the Hoving problem was something of a breakthrough for him.

McPhee went on to draw other diagrams for me. The pattern for *The Curve of Binding Energy* was another "V." "Travels in Georgia" (*Pieces of the Frame* 3–57) was a kind of widening spiral. "The Encircled River" (*Coming Into the Country* 5–91) was a kind of circle. Each diagram, as McPhee drew it and talked about it, seemed to represent a strategy by which he could both integrate his various materials and honor the formal integrity of his subject (or, to put it another way, represent his subject organically). His diagrammatic representations were no doubt oversimplifications of his method, but they showed how carefully he applied the Kahn Rule to his materials before beginning to write.

McPhee and Kenneth Burke: Giving Information Form

Once he has settled on an overall structure, McPhee has many formal decisions to make, ranging from those which affect the shape of an entire piece to those which determine the smallest elements within it. Kenneth Burke has noted many of these forms in *Counter-Statement*, and has discussed the manner in which they arouse and fulfill the desires of an audience—his definition of form (157). Burke's analysis is of particular interest in the context of McPhee's work because of Burke's contention that literary form has as its nemesis information—content-referenced factual matter. He argues his case by comparing literature to music, which depends more completely on formal gratification because it has no content. Literature, on the other hand, always has a subject matter, and insofar as that subject matter is intrinsically interesting, it detracts from the formal satisfaction of the work in question.

Burke summarizes his argument in a simple phrase: "Atrophy of form follows hypertrophy of information" (183). Where a sonata by Beethoven, say, can give formal gratification through repeated auditions, a zoology textbook satisfies only once, in the delivery of its information; once the facts have been absorbed, the means of their delivery are of no further consequence. McPhee, a self-professed fact writer whose stock in trade is information, would seem to be formally doomed by his own materials if Burke's analysis is accepted. That McPhee's work does deliver formal gratification in spite of its subject matter is not so much a counter-argument to Burke as it is a demonstration that information, when reconstituted out of conventional contexts into new forms (perhaps one of those mentioned by Burke), can, as in metaphor, transcend its intrinsic referential interest. Though as a man McPhee is fascinated by the intrinsic interest of facts (why else would he be a fact writer?), as a writer he is equally fascinated by formally gratifying arrangements of his facts.

Burke identifies five aspects of form in *Counter-Statement*: progressive form (subdivided into syllogistic and qualitative progression), repetitive form, conventional form, and minor or incidental forms. Syllogistic progression is, as Burke puts it, "the form of a perfectly conducted argument, advancing step by step" (157). Though the form may not be itself an argument, in the literal sense, premises established in the beginning force the conclusion, "as in a story of ratiocination by Poe" (157). Qualitative progression is subtler. It depends for development on qualities of tone or mood, as in *Macbeth* where "the grotesque seriousness of the murder scene" prepares us for "the grotesque buffoonery of the porter scene" (158). Repetitive form is "the consistent maintaining of a principle under new guises," or "restatement of the same thing in different ways," as in *Gulliver's Travels*, where "each detail of Gulliv-

75

er's life among the Lilliputians is a new exemplification of the discrepancy in size between Gulliver and the Lilliputians" (159). Conventional form depends on "the appeal of form *as form*" (159), as in a sonnet where the form is not revealed in the reading but conditions the reading in advance. Minor or incidental forms, "such as metaphor, paradox, disclosure, reversal . . ." (161), are distinct formal episodes within a work which usually contribute to the formal development of the work as a whole but are formally complete in themselves, like a monologue in a play by Shakespeare.

Having discussed his five varieties of form, Burke goes on to make the obvious point that in any work they tend to overlap, and indeed that one formal event might well be seen fitting his definitions of more than one formal variety. As we shall see in analyzing McPhee's formal practice, this formal interrelation is characteristic of his work. Burke makes a further point, in discussing the priority of forms, that is of considerable interest in the appreciation of McPhee's formal play. Noting that "there are formal patterns which distinguish our experience," Burke claims that formal experience and expectation are "prior to the work of art exemplifying them" (179). While Burke makes this argument only in the context of the audience of a literary work, it can be extended to embrace the work's author and the world he creates in his text as well. Thus, just as the reader has formal experience prior to his reading, the author has formal experience before writing, and the subject about which he writes has one or several prior shapes: the shape his perception has given it, the shape his understanding of "natural" order has given it, and/or the shape it has been given by someone else in transcribing it into language. These are the "givens" with which writers must deal, and, as we have seen, McPhee has a good many to deal with in his fact writing.

Prior forms clearly condition both McPhee's and his reader's formal expectations. When he writes about his trip with Anita Harris (the geologist-protagonist of *In Suspect Terrain*), for instance, his given is the progressive form of his chronological on-scene account, and his reader shares it, expecting a "natural" sequence of events in the narrative. In employing flashbacks and flashforwards, and in breaking up his chronological account with excurses into other subjects, McPhee gives his story two formal devices—a prior form and a new, self-generated one. It is precisely because he habitually restructures the prior forms of his stories that McPhee can arouse and fulfill formal desires with his facts, at the same time that he reaps the benefits of their intrinsic interest; presented to the reader in an unexpected formal context (again, like metaphor), his facts transcend the status of mere information and become tiles in McPhee's mosaic.

Typically McPhee will structure a piece by playing a prior syllogistic progression (usually chronology) against syllogistic progressions and repetitive forms of his own. *Levels of the Game* provides an interesting example of this strategy. The prior form of the piece is progressive; McPhee bases his story on the crescendo of action in a tennis match between Clark Graebner and Arthur Ashe at the U.S. Open Championships. This is the kind of prior form with which McPhee often works; basing his stories on extended on-the-scene contact with his subjects, McPhee naturally has to contend with the given chronology of his reporting. In the case of *Levels of the Game*, he constructs his story using a screening of the tape of Graebner and Ashe's match, a screening the two competitors have attended and provided commentary for. For the "lead" to his story he uses an *in medias res* presentation of early moments in the match, formally promising movement toward its climactic conclusion.

The lead also promises another, thematic progression, one McPhee will play against his chronological one. The thematic lines of the piece are drawn in its sixth paragraph, where McPhee declares: "A person's tennis game begins with his nature and background and comes out through his motor mechanisms into shot patterns and characteristics of play" (6). Much of the rest of the story is given to filling out this thematic line; detailing the backgrounds, lifestyles, and personalities of Graebner and Ashe, McPhee reconstructs the tennis match as an agon pitting the conservative, mechanical power of

Jack Roundy

Graebner against the liberal, flamboyant grace of Ashe. Throughout the narrative McPhee moves back and forth between the given chronological progression and his own thematic one, and in the end they come together, interreflectively.

The two lines of progressive development in *Levels of the Game* are thematically apposite, as the conclusion reveals, but they are developed independently, and this is what gives the reader formal pleasure. As he moves through the text, he is invited to wonder both "who won?" and "who are these guys and why did the winner win?" Bits of the answers to both questions are given in both formal lines, successively and alternately, and the reader's formal pleasure is heightened as the dilemma of his expectations is progressively embellished. Burke's reservations about the effect of information on form are answered in this way; because the reader is led to transcend his interest in the mere facts of McPhee's story by virtue of their place in the formal play, he is open to the formal pleasure of which Burke speaks.

In the course of *Levels of the Game*, McPhee often digresses (if independent developments of the theme can be called digressions), writing set pieces on the backgrounds and lifestyles of the two players. Such set pieces are characteristic of McPhee's work, and they assume an interesting place in the formal design of the story. Seen from the perspective of the overall scheme, they take their place as components of progressive and repetitive form. They are progressive in the sense that they advance the theme (as we have already seen). They are repetitive in that they tend to compound a single perspective in several guises. Thus Arthur Ashe's background and lifestyle reinforce the view that he is a volatile person, a view he confirms on the tennis court.

Set pieces, by their very nature as adumbrations of independent subjects, take on forms independent of the larger scheme, however. Thus, in developing them, McPhee has to manage another set of formal givens within the context of the set piece itself, and has to decide whether to simply accept those givens or to play with them as well. Characteristically, he will play with them. Given the chronological line of Ashe's boyhood, for instance, he selects intriguing events and re-counts them in places where they are thematically apposite, flashing backward and forward and splicing anecdotes told by Ashe's father and elements of the larger narrative into his account. Because this formal play is consistent with the formal play of the piece as a whole, it has the curious effect of reinforc-ing the piece's character, and seems more natural to the piece than it otherwise might.

While progressive and repetitive forms are central to Mc-Phee's development both of whole pieces and of set pieces within them, qualitative progression is central to his manner of juxtaposing various materials. In *The Survival of the Bark Canoe*, for instance, McPhee wishes to set up a contrast between the horrific mood of James Dickey's *Deliverance*, a tale about a canoe trip that is fraught with danger, death, and sexual perversion, and the more placid reality of his own canoeing experience. To do so, he begins by giving the reader a thumb-nail account of Dickey's plot, saying it is "about four men on a canoe trip, one of whom is sexually abused at gunpoint by a stubbly-bearded mountain man" (66). He then recounts a potentially similar event during his trip, picturing himself and a companion emerging from the woods—the two of them look for all the world like Dickey's rapists—and descending on two startled canoers taking a shore break. McPhee and his friend, and the canoers they have surprised, momentarily appear caught in a recreation of the *Deliverance* story, but the mood evaporates when they begin to exchange pleasantries and ob-servations on the weather. McPhee's point in introducing Dickey into his account is in part to disarm the *Deliverance* mythos, and his strategy in this scene helps him to do so without making his commentary explicit. Dickey's dire fantasy retreats before McPhee's ordinary counter-tale.

This passage, like many others that bridge juxtapositions, depends as much for development on tone and mood as it does on analogy, and in that respect it exemplifies qualitative progression. As Burke points out, however, more than one formal definition can often be applied to a single literary event, and such is the case in these examples; while qualitative form

Jack Roundy

can be found in their tone, syllogistic form can be found in
their advancement of theme.

Metaphor: Not Merely an Incidental Form

McPhee makes use of a variety of incidental forms in his
pieces, but none is as important as metaphor in sustaining the
thematic development of his stories. This is not surprising,
really, since on the larger scale his strategy is to build theme
through analogy, and metaphor is an analogic construct. One
of the clearest examples of his use of metaphor to create
thematic linkage appears in *In Suspect Terrain*, where he sets
up a connection between his trip with Anita Harris and the
history of the Ice Age. Discussing the effects of the ice on
the American landscape, he looks over his shoulder through
metaphor at the road he is traveling with Harris: "The ice
sheets of the present era, in their successive spreadings over-
land, have borne immense *freight*—rock they pluck up, shear
off, rip from the country as they move. . . . When the ice melts,
it gives up its *cargo*, dumping it by the trillions of tons. . . .
When the last ice sheet set down its terminal moraine, it built
causeways from one ridge to another, on which Interstate 80
rides west" (8; italics mine). Terms like freight, cargo, and
causeways, metaphorical because they are torn from accustomed context and set in a new one on the basis of analogy,
suggest trucks and the roadways they travel on rather than
ice sheets. But applied as they are here, they reinforce the
contiguity of McPhee's trip and the geological history he sees
evidence of as he travels—ice sheets and the semitrailers that
pass him on the road blur together as he writes. Metaphor
weaves together the two elements of his narrative. McPhee
doesn't always use metaphor in this way, but this formal strategy suggests how analogue informs his writing.

Like most of McPhee's formal strategies, his use of metaphor serves to integrate materials he has collected on the scene
with the lore of his subject. One of the reasons he favors this
use of metaphor has to do with the kinds of subjects he writes
about. In a sense, McPhee is a popularizer, though that term,

80

with its suggestion of catering to public taste, is a bit misleading. His aim in writing fact pieces is nearly always to lead the reader to unfamiliar territory—the Pine Barrens of New Jersey, interior Alaska, nuclear physics, geology—whose mysteries he will then reveal. In order to make his unfamiliar subjects accessible, he offers himself in on-scene accounts as his reader's surrogate—the novice addressing an alien world—and weaves revelations about the lore of his subject into these accounts as answers to a novice's questions.

Because he wishes to take his reader to unfamiliar ground in his pieces, McPhee's use of figures (by which I mean metaphor, in all its forms) frequently transcends Burke's definition of metaphor as an "incidental," distinct formal "episode." Indeed, though McPhee's figures are formally complete in themselves, they often serve (as in the passage from *In Suspect Terrain*) as pieces of a "repetitive" formal strategy: to construct a bridge between the world familiar to his reader and the rather more alien world of his subject. In this sense, his use of figures is clearly tutelary, and it leads him to a further step, which we shall see presently; having made the alien world accessible to his reader, he will create a new set of figures using the vernacular of his subject, bridging back to familiar ground.

The following on-scene passage from *The Survival of the Bark Canoe*, in which McPhee describes the behavior of the common loon, displays his characteristic use of figural devices: "He *cruises* now with only his head and neck above the water—his *conning tower*. . . . His maximum *airspeed* is sixty miles an hour, and his *stall-out speed* must be fifty-nine. . . . *Takeoff* is a considerable problem for him. With, say, ten fish in him, he needs a *runway* at least a quarter of a mile long" (30; italics mine). McPhee has seen this loon in a wilderness he visited partly to escape the pressures of metropolitan life, but he recognizes as he describes it that his metropolitan *New Yorker* audience will find it easier to visualize if he couches his description in images from the world they know. The "common" loon, after all, is not a common feature of their world. Submarines and jetliners, on the other hand, will certainly call vivid images to his readers' minds, focusing his picture of the loon. The effect "conning towers" and "runways" have here is much like that of Wallace Stevens's jar, which "made the slovenly wilderness/ Surround" (249) the hill it sat on. To a *New Yorker* audience, the loon may be part of a slovenly and hard to focus wilderness, but figural lenses from their own world can clarify the image.

Throughout *Survival*, as in all his pieces, McPhee reinforces his role as surrogate for the reader by using figural terms from a common world to picture the unfamiliar one he is visiting. The following sampler of figures from *Survival* suggests how vividly McPhee recalls that common world in his wilderness observations:

The sky after dark was as clear as a *lens*. (28)

A shooting star burst with almost frightening brightness, illuminating our faces, lighting the sky like a *flare*. (29)

He appears relaxed in the stern of his canoe—leaning back, looking for wildlife, his paddle in motion like a *wire whisk*. (34)

For thirty-odd years, I have been hearing tales of this lake and how it is a whistling groove whose waves stand up like the *teeth of a saw*. (75)

What lies between them [shores of the lake] looks like *broken glass*. (77)

Then, like a *siren*, the wind goes high. (78)

Warren, like a *tractor*, pulls the canoe. (85)

On the last stretch of lake before us, the surface suddenly appears scratched, like *rubber prepared for a patch*. (92)

Warren . . . hauls the canoe up the *freeways* he has made. (99)

. . . ten loons . . . *taxiing* in long half-flying runs. (109)

The lake becomes still, smooth, a *corridor of glass*. (113; italics mine)

The common world McPhee's text predicates is, upon reflection, a rather strange one. Freeways, runways, taxis, and tractors dominate the landscape. Sirens scream and flares illuminate the sky. Wire whisks whirr and broken glass lies scattered about. Saw teeth jut up, ready to cut, and inner tubes lie waiting for patches.

Considering McPhee's subject in *Survival*, these figural images are strange indeed, for they picture an almost entirely artificial world. Like the advertisements flanking McPhee's stories in their first appearance in *The New Yorker*, his figures invite identification with man-made things. In so doing, they suggest that the natural world, from which writers have so often drawn their figures in the past, has become an alien one to McPhee's reader. This fact partly explains a startling aspect of many of McPhee's stories, stories that take place in wilderness or semiwilderness settings. When McPhee describes, say, the head and neck of a loon as a "conning tower," his description has the jarring effect one feels when, looking along the shores of a pristine lake, one's eyes fall on a discarded beer can. However odd, it is an effect McPhee seeks, because the presence of that familiar object composes the scene. For better or worse, his figures are ground to the prescription of contemporary eyes, and they succeed in framing for the reader the unfamiliar world of his subject.

If, as we have seen, McPhee uses figures to take Mohammed to the mountain, he finds other means to bring the mountain to Mohammed. Observing quite literally his own injunction that once a subject has interested you, "you will have to deal with it on its own terms" (Singular 50), McPhee characteristically immerses himself in the vernacular of his subject so as to be able to write his story in its terms. In several of his pieces, in fact, he recounts his own first experiences with the vernacular of a subject as a way of introducing it to the reader.

One such account appears in *The Pine Barrens*, McPhee's story about a wild corner of New Jersey: "The vernacular language of the pines is splendidly metaphorical. An outsider needs a glossary to follow simple directions—for example, 'Go down here about a mile and turn left at the fingerboard.' A fingerboard is a place where several roads come together. A point is where a road forks. When highway workers do anything to a road, they are said to be sciencing it. One day while I was driving along with Fred Brown, he said, 'I didn't know this road was oiled all the way to here.' The road was covered with pavement" (59). For the moment, McPhee's subject has changed; he is now writing not only about the Pines but also about the language of the Pines. Mentioning "an outsider," which he was when he went to the scene of his story, he provides the reader with a surrogate. The reader, presumed to be himself an outsider, "needs a glossary" to follow the directions of the "pineys'" language, and McPhee takes this opportunity to give him one. Once the glossary is provided, the reader, like McPhee, will be able to address the Pines on their own terms.

A like passage appears in *Basin and Range*, the first of McPhee's two geology pieces: "I used to sit in class and listen to the terms come floating down the room like paper airplanes. Geology was called a descriptive science, and with its pitted outwash plains and drowned rivers, its hanging tributaries and starved coastlines, it was nothing if not descriptive. It was a fountain of metaphor—of isostatic adjustments and degraded channels, of angular unconformities and shifting divides, of rootless mountains and bitter lakes" (24). Here McPhee again takes his subject's terms as his subject, again provides the reader a surrogate (this time a student in his first geology class) through whom to encounter for the first time a presumably alien vernacular.

Having predicated in passages like this a reader unfamiliar with the vernacular of his subject, McPhee proceeds to make it intelligible in language the reader can understand, at the same time giving it specific applications. That he knows what he is about, and knows how difficult it is, is apparent in the following passage from *In Suspect Terrain*, where he tries to explain an aspect of the geology of Manhattan (geology one might assume would interest a *New Yorker* audience):

> When she [Anita Harris] goes up Fifth Avenue—as she did with me that summer day—she addresses Fifth Avenue as the axis of the trough of a syncline. . . . The structure of Manhattan is one of those paradoxes in spatial relations which give geolo-

gists especial delight and are about as intelligible to everyone else as punch lines delivered in Latin. There is a passage in the oeuvre of William F. Buckley, Jr., in which he remarks that no writer in the history of the world has ever successfully made clear to the layman the principles of celestial navigation. Then Buckley announces that celestial navigation is dead simple, and that he will pause in the development of his present narrative to redress forever the failure of the literary class to elucidate this abecedarian technology. There and then—and with intrepid, awesome courage—he begins his explication; and before he is through, the oceans are in orbit, the barren shoals are bright with shipwrecked stars. With that preamble, I wish to announce that I am about to make perfectly clear how Fifth Avenue, which runs along the high middle of a loaf of rock that lies between two rivers, runs also up the center of the trough of a syncline. (33–34)

McPhee's task is doubly difficult, as this passage acknowledges, because he is at once embroiled in explaining what the trough of a syncline is and in explaining how Manhattan can be seen embodying one.

As his explanation begins, his language at once becomes metaphorical: "Where rock is compressed and folded (like linen pushed together on a table), the folds are anticlines and synclines. They are much like the components of the letter S. Roll an S forward on its nose and you have to the left a syncline and to the right an anticline. . . . A carrot sliced the long way and set flat side up is composed of a synclinal fold. Manhattan, embarrassingly referred to as the Big Apple, might at least instructively be called the Big Carrot. River to river, erosion has worn down the sides, and given the island its superficial camber" (34). Using comparisons that range from fully compressed metaphor ("nose") to fully extended analogy ("They are very much like . . ."), McPhee uses the technique we have seen in his figures to introduce the reader to the alien world of geology's lexicon; he invokes the familiar world to help the reader see an unfamiliar one.

Once he has made the lexicon of his subject intelligible to the reader, he will let his subject speak through it. Typically, the vernacular he has glossed will provide him with the literal terminology for his explication of a subject; thus, the geologist's view of the "annals of the former world," which is his subject in the geology pieces, will be expressed in geologists' language. But he never entirely dismantles the analogical bridge by which he has taken his reader to an understanding of the vernacular. Using either compressed analogies as expressed in figures or more extended ones woven into the narrative on a larger formal scale, he will move forward and backward over the analogical bridge that connects the reader's familiar world and the world of his subject, expressed in its own terms. The following passage, from *In Suspect Terrain*, exemplifies this movement:

> Taiwan, at this writing, is evidently on its way to the Chinese mainland. Taiwan is the vanguard of a lithospheric microplate and consists of pieces of island arc preceded by an accretionary wedge of materials coming off the China Plate and materials shedding forward from the island's rising mountains. As the plate edges buckle before it, the island has plowed up so much stuff that it has filled in all the space between the accretionary wedge and the volcanic arc, and thus its components make an integral island. It is in motion northwest. For the mainland government in Peking to be wooing the Taiwanese to join the People's Republic of China is the ultimate inscrutable irony. Not only will Taiwan inexorably become one with Red China. It will hit into China like a fist in a belly. It will knock up big mountains from Hong Kong to Shanghai. It is only a question of time. (137)

Marrying his "lithospheric plates" and "accretionary wedges" (which he has already explained in earlier passages) to a political situation with which most reasonably aware readers will be familiar, McPhee explains one aspect of the theory of plate tectonics. The geological dynamics and political dynamics he brings together are not strictly analogous, but he capitalizes on the superficial promise of analogy to construct his bridge. And playing with familiar features of Chinese politics (inscrutability and hostility), he makes a geological phenomenon accessible, clinching his explication with a figure ("like a fist in a belly") that links in one phrase the antagonisms of the two Chinas and the geological dynamics of his subject.

Given McPhee's method for making the unfamiliar accessible through figures and extended analogy, it is not surprising that he will occasionally bridge backward from the vernacular to the familiar once he has made the language of his subject clear to the reader. In such cases, which are most visible in his figural play, the literal terms of the comparison become the familiar world of the reader, while the figurative terms become the vernacular of his subject. The following selection of figures from *Basin and Range* and *In Suspect Terrain* suggest the curious effect this reversal of technique has:

It is up to Deffeyes [a geology teacher] to interest them [his students] . . . or his department goes into a *subduction zone*. (*Basin and Range*, 60)

Hutton [a pioneer of geologic theory] had . . . an *oolitic* forehead. (*Basin and Range*, 99)

They [geologists] see the thin band in which are the all but indiscernable *stratifications* of Cro-Magnon, Moses, Leonardo, now. (*Basin and Range*, 128)

But just as metamorphism will turn shale into slate . . . Hutton had turned words into *pumice*. (*Basin and Range*, 139)

. . . and beyond them [the spires of Wall Street] the midtown *massif*. (*In Suspect Terrain*, 21)

She [Anita Harris] was impressed by a house of gabbro, as anyone would be who had spent a childhood emplaced like a *fossil* in Triassic sand. (*In Suspect Terrain*, 35)

Seeing that [Anita Harris's official status], [the postmaster] would develop a security clearance in the lower *strata* of his frown, and with solemnity accept the rocks. (*In Suspect Terrain*, 118)

They [geologists] debate in a language *exotic* in itself. (*In Suspect Terrain*, 144; italics mine)

87

The latter of these examples is wonderfully suggestive of the narrative capital McPhee derives from using the geological vernacular for his figurative terms. Taken out of context, "exotic" does not seem figurative here. But McPhee has explained in earlier passages that geologists refer to microplates (which to the tectonic theoretician are smaller plates whose movements may explain certain anomalies in his mapping of the effects of larger plates) as "exotic terrains." This explanation informs his use of "exotic" as a figure, drawing to the reader's mind not only the literal meaning of the word ("coming from elsewhere") but also a picture of microplates bumping into unsuspecting continents. It is an apt figure, suggesting as it does collisions of the microplates of geologic terminology with the continent of English. It is also apt in the larger sense that it reinforces the bridge McPhee has been constructing between his reader's familiar world and the "exotic terrain" of his subject. Having taken his reader to that terrain by analogy with features of his own world, McPhee then leads him back with a duffel of images through which to see his familiar world afresh.

Thus the formal promise of McPhee's lively sense of analogue allows him to transcend the formally distinct and episodic nature of metaphor as described by Burke. For McPhee, figural devices become ligatures tying his materials together, fundamental pieces in a repetitive formal strategy.

Circling the River

One of the most formally interesting pieces McPhee has written is "The Encircled River" (Part I of *Coming Into the Country*). In it, both the prior chronological form of his on-scene account (a given "syllogistic" form, as Burke would have it) and the formal strategy by which he has transformed it are clearly visible. On its face, "The Encircled River" is a straightforward account of McPhee's trip with five companions down a wild Alaskan river, the Salmon. McPhee invites the reader into the story *in medias res*, but apart from that circumstance and the fact that the story is related in the present tense (to give it greater dramatic immediacy, no doubt), the reader is at first given no reason to think that McPhee is not hewing to his prior chronological form, breaking it only briefly and occasionally for a digression into, say, the habits of certain wildlife or the cultural practices of inland Eskimos who live nearby.

Roughly halfway through the narrative, however, McPhee arrives at the chronological conclusion of his trip, as he recounts the group's return to the Eskimo village of Kiana, their point of departure, and mentions the plane that will come to fly them out. At this point, McPhee constructs a segue into a past-tense account of his setting out on the trip, and as the reader follows him to the story's conclusion, he discovers that the account ends where it began, in the middle of the trip. Strictly speaking, the account doesn't end with a chronological conclusion; rather, it points to its beginning, swallowing its own tail. This is the first hint of a reason for its title, "The Encircled River."

Superficially, McPhee's restructuring of his account may seem precious, or at least capricious. But under closer scrutiny, compelling narrative and thematic reasons for this reconstruction become clear. The dramatic high points of the piece are McPhee's meetings with grizzly bears. For McPhee, these bears are preeminent symbols of the country he is traveling through: "This was his [the bear's] country, clearly enough. To be there was to be incorporated, in however small a measure, into its substance—his country, and if you wanted to visit it you had better knock" (68). Because he felt most deeply in the country when he met the bears, and because these meetings were the most dramatic moments of the trip (representing at once what was most attractive and most repellent about the wilderness— its very wildness), McPhee faces a real problem in setting up the narrative curve of his story if he knuckles under to his syllogistic givens; his meetings with the bears happened early in the trip, and if he were to tell the story as it happened, a considerable portion of it would be denouement.

What he does instead is narratively ingenious. Opening the story as he will close it, with the bandanna that circles his forehead (one of many circles that are to come in "The Encircled River"), he sets the scene, briefly introducing his companions, their environs, their activities. At the close of the opening scene, he pictures his group in a conversation about bears, a conversation that ends with a decree by the trip leader, Pat Pourchot—"No more bear stories" (13)—and with Mc-Phee's admission of a mild nervousness about the propinquity of the grizzly. From this point forward, until after he has begun his past-tense narrative of the early part of the trip, he heeds Pourchot's decree, telling no more bear stories. Just halfway through his account, he almost unobtrusively begins to splice brief mentions of bears into the narrative, and then, abruptly, begins the account of his first close-up encounter with a grizzly (mirroring in prose the abruptness of that encounter). Once embarked on the subject of bears, McPhee focuses his story more completely on the grizzly than on any other feature of his experience, and he concludes the narrative with his nearest encounter, at which point he closes the circle of the tale with his bandanna.

If his reordering is narratively advantageous in setting up an attractive dramatic curve, it is also thematically advantageous in establishing a formal analogue to the many circles (or cycles) he will identify as characteristic of Alaska's cultural and natural life. As is the case with bears, McPhee introduces the cyclical theme early in the narrative: "Plants and animals are living on margin, in cycles that are always vulnerable to change" (6). Thereafter, cycles recur with great frequency as the story moves forward, and they recur in many guises. Typically, McPhee begins his loops by digressing into set pieces of various lengths, set pieces he moves into by virtue of contiguity. For example, he moves into a set piece (or, more accurately, part of a set piece that is spliced into several sections of the narrative) dealing with Eskimos by setting a scene on the Kobuk River, noting that Eskimos live on the Kobuk, and then discussing how they live. Once embarked on the set piece, he reverts to the cycle theme: "For thousands of years, to extents that have varied with cycles of plenty, the woodland Eskimos have fished here" (23).

Occasionally he will fill out such set pieces with accounts that mirror the cycle, as he does when he describes the seasonal living patterns of bears and Eskimos. But whether or not the set piece reflects the cycle theme formally, it will nearly always bear the imprint of the circle.

Cycles show up in many forms. They show up in the story's overall shape, in accounts of the seasonal lives of Eskimos and bears. They also show up in subsections of McPhee's on-scene account, as, for example, in the cycle of a day or, more pointedly, in the record of the hike on which McPhee saw his first bear (he calls the hike a "loop"). They show up in his discussions of the migratory patterns of caribou and Dall sheep, in his discussion of Alaskan political history, in his discussion of geological phenomena. They show up in his formal arrangement of paragraphs, as, for example, when he opens a passage speaking of wilderness paths, digresses to discuss various Alaskan fauna, digresses again to discuss tundra flora, and then returns to the path he and his companions are following—a path made by Alaskan fauna through tundra flora. They show up in several of his sentences which, though inevitably linear, are constructed to suggest cycles: "Past to present, present reflecting past, the cycles compose this segment of the earth" (16). And they show up in his metaphors, which, like the following, connect men's attitudes to the cycles of the wilderness: "Kauffmann, among Alaskans, represented only a small arc or two in a wheel of attitudes toward the land" (79).

In one of his more elegiac moments in "The Encircled River," McPhee says that the Alaskan wilderness "has a beauty of nowhere else, composed in turning circles" (89). Seeing his subject this way, he must feel that his own circular composition is more appropriate to it, more legitimately a treatment of it "on its own terms" than a linear one would be. Still the purveyor of a story that has the powerful matter of fact beneath it, he has merely addressed the problem of form and information identified by Kenneth Burke and surmounted it by crafting his facts. In this sense, "The Encircled River" is an apotheosis of the Kahn Rule, which he has "always tried faithfully to observe"; planning so ingeniously "where [he is] going from

Jack Roundy

the start of a piece," he offers the reader both the satisfaction of his appetite for facts and the formal pleasure of a well-planned itinerary in traveling through them.

Works Cited

Burke, Kenneth. *Counter-Statement*. New York: Harcourt, Brace, 1931.
Howarth, William. Introduction. *The John McPhee Reader*. Ed. William Howarth. New York: Random House, 1977. vii–xxiii.
Kahn, E. J. *About The New Yorker and Me*. New York: Putnam's, 1979.
McPhee, John. *Basin and Range*. New York: Farrar, Straus and Giroux, 1980, 1981.
———. *Coming Into the Country*. 1977. New York: Bantam, 1979.
———. *In Suspect Terrain*. New York: Farrar, Straus and Giroux, 1983.
———. *Levels of the Game*. New York: Farrar, Straus and Giroux, 1969.
———. *Pieces of the Frame*. New York: Farrar, Straus and Giroux, 1975.
———. *The Pine Barrens*. New York: Farrar, Straus and Giroux, 1968.
———. *A Roomful of Hovings and Other Profiles*. New York: Farrar, Straus and Giroux, 1968.
———. *The Survival of the Bark Canoe*. 1975. New York: Warner Books, 1975.
Singular, Stephen. "Talk with John McPhee." *The New York Times Book Review* 27 Nov. 1977: 1, 50–51.
Stevens, Wallace. "Anecdote of the Jar." *The Norton Anthology of Modern Poetry*. Ed. Richard Ellman and Robert O'Clair. New York: W. W. Norton, 1973. 249.

5

WRITING DOCUMENTARY AS A THERAPEUTIC ACT

Bill Barich's *Laughing in the Hills*

Mark Allister

Bill Barich's *Laughing in the Hills* is both a documentary of horse racing and the drama of his search for a form and language that will enable him to make sense of a senseless world.[1] "We tell ourselves stories in order to live," Joan Didion writes in *The White Album,* and Barich—whose mother's death from cancer has pitched him into despair—needs to create such a life-giving story. Mourning her, Barich begins to see around him a corresponding cancer: in the world of subdivisions and shopping malls, where the individual is lost in the mass; in man-made lakes and Johnny Carson, symbols to him of a society that values illusion over substance. Horse racing, Barich believes, stands in opposition to this cancerous world, and so he looks to the racetrack to find a re-vision of his trauma—to use its life to get past the sadness of death.

Thoreau's famous explanation of why he went to the

---

1. I use frequently, in this essay, the terms *documentary* and *autobiography,* realizing that while we don't all agree on what fits under such labels, they are nevertheless the best ones available. By *documentary,* I mean a "factual" account of a subject in which the writer takes the stance that he or she is "absent" from the work and is not using "imagination" to present the material. I do recognize, of course, the philosophical and literary problems such a definition raises. *Autobiography* literally means "self writing life," but it need not have a view of "life" as lifetime, as biography generally does. Autobiography, says Georges Gusdorf, is not a recapitulation of the past; rather, it is "the attempt and drama of a man struggling to reassemble himself in his own likeness at a certain moment of his history" (43). I use autobiography in Gusdorf's sense.

woods—"because I wished to live deliberately, to front only the essential facts of life, and see if I could not learn what it had to teach"—could serve as epigraph for Barich, who chooses a far different "arena" than Walden Pond but with a similar intent: at the racetrack he can front the essential facts of life. Like the pond for Thoreau, the racing world serves Barich as a closed, ritualized system, wherein he can learn about and understand metaphorically the larger universe, and himself. Barich must look outside to heal the inside; immersion in and writing about a public environment become essential to his private re-creation of self.

Barich is not alone in writing documentary that becomes a healing autobiography. In *The Snow Leopard,* Peter Matthiessen describes his arduous, dangerous trek across the Himalayas to the Crystal Mountain, a journey prompted by his despondency over his wife's death. His observations of both human and animal life, in this most forbidding of scenes, are fused with the story of his pilgrimage to integrate mind and spirit—and therefore end grieving. In *Blue Highways,* William Least Heat Moon chronicles his trip around America's backroads, a journey begun after he loses both wife and job. His book describes forgotten people with small dreams, people "who knew about stumbling . . . from having stumbled." Their stories can show him "the power to see again and revise."[2] *Laughing in the Hills, The Snow Leopard, Blue Highways*—all are books of mourning. Each begins with the writer recounting a recent trauma and declaring despair and uninterest in life, yet resolved to amend solipsistic impulses and move toward others. The determination to establish community produces the documentary. The intentional weaving of the mourning process into the documentary creates autobiography.

In my essay I do not intend, however, to describe a sub-

2. Numerous recent books are related to these three, in that their structures are a fusing of "nonfiction" genres that becomes a kind of autobiography: Robert Pirsig's *Zen and the Art of Motorcycle Maintenance;* Peter Jenkins's *A Walk Across America;* Michael Herr's *Dispatches;* Anne Morrow Lindbergh's *A Gift from the Sea;* Sue Hubbell's *A Country Year;* Alice Koller's *An Unknown Woman;* Annie Dillard's *Holy the Firm*—among others.

genre of contemporary nonfiction, but rather to demonstrate how a writer gains metaphorical understanding of self by shaping in language the other. I will focus on *Laughing in the Hills* to show how writing documentary can become a therapeutic act. Barich discovers at the racetrack a way of "reading" the world that will teach him to re-see and rewrite his past, so that in the future he can lead a life worth living. To conclude my essay, I will suggest the implications such a text has for the teaching of writing.

II

Barich opens his book with the event that precipitates his trauma: "For me it did not begin with the horses. They came later, after a phone call and a simple statement of fact: Your mother has cancer" (1). As he flies to New York, Barich begins to have a "sense of slippage," which is accentuated when he sees his mother, now "an old woman with bright eyes," ravaged by disease. To escape this image, to return to a time when she was vital, not dying, he wanders his old neighborhood, longing "for innocence, for breath." Out of emotional desperation, he begins playing the horses, where "anything might happen, could happen, probably would happen." The unpredictability of the horse races becomes a stay against the certainty of death, and soon the entire family begins playing, including the mother, who hears "in the track announcer's call a little pulse of life."

Barich flies back to California, where he falls "into a lingering sadness" and where the rest of his life comes apart. Other relatives get cancer. His wife is operated on for a brain tumor, which turns out not to exist. He argues with her and she with him. Barich wakes at night "to my mother's face or the memory of my wife lying in her hospital bed," and cancer becomes for him the disease of America, becomes all technological progress, a killer raging rampant without sensitivity or taste. He knows his anger has become excessive, out of control, when he flies into a rage upon seeing bulldozers or sewer pipes or even surveyors. Longing for "an escape into orderliness,"

Barich decides "with the same hapless logic that governed all my actions then," to leave home and spend the rest of the spring at Golden Gate Fields, a thoroughbred track near San Francisco. He is convinced that there is something special about racing, in part because "the track seemed circumscribed and manageable, especially when compared to the complex filigree of nature, hydrogen intertwined with embryos and tumors."

After thus laying out his fragile emotional condition, Barich gradually alters the style of his book to include the reportorial: discussions of thoroughbreds, jockeys and trainers, parimutuel betting, and even the geology of California—all intermingled, not insignificantly, with the Renaissance philosophy he is reading while at the track. These discussions are fascinating in their own right, but their importance in the narrative lies in their therapeutic effect for Barich as he uses them to indirectly work through his trauma.

The autobiographical text that weaves through this documentary, dealing as it does with conflict and change, lends itself particularly to psychoanalytic theory. Analysts agree that analysis must teach a patient that his or her disturbed past continues to be, unconsciously, the disturbing and disturbed present. A "cure" becomes dependent, therefore, upon the patient's ability to fashion, after examining the past life, a certain kind of story based on key recollected events. That story must be a history that heals instead of paralyzes. Analysts disagree, however, on the role that the patient must or even can assume—both in "recovering" or understanding the past, and in living the present.

Freud, as always, lays the foundation of this argument. In order to "resolve the symptoms" of neurotics, he says in his *Introductory Lectures on Psychoanalysis*, "we must go back as far as their origin, we must renew the conflict from which they arose, and, with the help of motive forces which were not at the patient's disposal in the past, we must guide it to a different outcome" (454). In this and many similar passages, Freud implies that patients in analysis can recover the past, which has been heretofore buried under layers of defenses, and then present it to themselves and their analysts for modification. The analyst, as Freud was fond of saying, becomes an archaeologist sifting through memories and desires, careful to keep what is of value.

The "analyst as archaeologist" assumes that patients' memories of their life always contain "historical truth," always tap into an actual happening of the past.[3] And yet Freud himself demonstrated, in his famous "Wolf Man" case, for example, that if we cannot recover the past, we can create it in order to make sense out of later symptoms. Freud showed, that is, the persuasive power of a coherent narrative. One's personal past does not have to be—cannot be—remembered precisely as it happened, but it can be constructed. Roy Schafer, though a Freudian psychoanalyst, simply accepts as a given rule that all life histories are a fiction. Psychoanalysis, he writes in *Language and Insight*, "consists of the construction of a personal past . . . merely a history of a certain kind" (8). For a "cure" the patient and psychoanalyst need to make a "narrative truth" that is coherent and consistent, that satisfies because it makes sense of something confusing. The analyst functions more as novelist than as archaeologist.

Schafer counters Freud's view that one is helped by recapturing memories and repetitively reworking them. Because patients have been shaped by language and can use it in turn to create new meanings, Schafer argues, they must, in essence, rewrite old events in new terms: rewrite in such a way that the past creates a healthy present. Schafer teaches the patient to become a "life-historian" and "world-maker," author of his or her own interpretation of past events and author of significant future events. From such a view of psychoanalysis, it is a short—but radical—step to what Barich attempts, which is not to address directly his present problems at all, but instead to

3. The term *historical truth* is Donald Pond Spence's, as is another term that I use later: *narrative truth*. Spence's critique of the psychoanalytic process is particularly helpful to me in that Spence stresses the therapeutic importance of making a story—rather than stressing free associating that digs into past memories.

immerse himself in a different "arena" in order to escape his memory's sustained probing of past actions and feelings. Of late, analysts are calling such a move "working through in the metaphor," a displacement which allows the person to move the conflict from his current life into an arena which takes on a metaphorical function.[4] Using the "distance of the metaphor," he works through the conflict unconsciously without needing to confront in a direct, cognitive way the issues in his real life.

Barich nearly sidesteps the past altogether. Only by constructing a new, present narrative—about his season at the racetrack—can he understand how even to begin rewriting his life-history. *Laughing in the Hills* exemplifies a situation in which the patient becomes, in a figurative sense, his own analyst through the act of writing. Barich's "cure" reminds us of Schafer's insistence that all an analyst can accomplish is to construct with his or her patient an explanatory story: a narrative, functioning as a metaphor, that gives new meaning to the disturbing and disturbed present.

III

For someone who is mourning, the importance of constructing metaphors can hardly be overemphasized. Humans think tropologically, and so metaphor is not simply embellishment—a matter of style—but a reflection of how the writer perceives self and other.[5] A metaphor "redescribes reality," Paul Ricouer claims: as a comparing of something unknown to something known, or as the intuitive perception of similarity between two things of a different order, a metaphor produces a new order "by creating rifts in an old order" (22–23). What

4. My discussion here, and the concept "working through in the metaphor," are indebted to my conversations with Dr. Donald Rosenblitt, a training psychoanalyst at the University of North Carolina-Duke University Psychoanalytic Institute.

5. For more on tropes and their relation to human thought, see Kenneth Burke's *A Grammar of Motives* and Hayden White's *Tropics of Discourse*.

a mourner sees as death-in-life, one way that things are related, must be turned into life, the opposite relation. Ricoeur, reviving Aristotle's use of the verb *metaphorize*, stresses predication over denomination, emphasizing the mental process and making of it an act of the constitutive imagination. The cancer that Barich sees in everything around him must be reimagined in terms other than cancerous, and metaphorizing is central to this re-vision.

Barich escapes to the racetrack, and immerses himself in its fabric, because he sees it as a world that retains causal laws, as a world that is free from death, confusion, randomness. He also goes to the track because it is "circumscribed and manageable," a place in which he hopes to assert a kind of control. To gain control, Barich believes, he must relearn what he has felt unable to do since his mother died—to construct for himself explanatory stories "modeled on notions of symmetry and coherence," stories, that is, that give order and purpose to life. His obsession with the art of handicapping becomes, therefore, more than a desire to win money by betting. Handicapping a race accurately is the proof that it is possible, even on the smallest scale, for him to construct such stories.

At the track, however, Barich fails to assert the control he desires, fails to create the winning narratives. He is devastated when, because horses don't run to form, the races imitate the chaos of the larger world. And even though he learns more about thoroughbreds, the behind-the-scenes business of the backstretch, and the various players in the racing theater, he is still unable to turn chaos into coherence. Barich has not discovered how to make of the racing world a healing metaphor.

What hinders Barich is his reluctance to give up one version of the past: the story of a precancerous, Edenic world he creates of old memories and mementoes, "shards of a human past that was being scraped from the edges of consciousness." But reconstituting the past with a collection of tangible and imagined relics—psychological retrenchment against technological progress—becomes mere nostalgia for Barich, never obtaining the significance of metaphor. What helps him move beyond nostalgia toward the construction of a healing metaphor is his reading in Renaissance philosophy. His fascination with the Italian Renaissance, he tells us, had begun fifteen years earlier when he spent a college semester abroad in Florence. He had left America for Italy after two desultory years in school, disillusioned with college and with America's intervention in Vietnam, disillusioned with himself. Florence was to become the symbol of something magical and worthwhile, sustaining him for years after. Florence and the Italian Renaissance were to become a useable past.

It is not surprising, then, that Barich sets out for Golden Gate Fields with books about the Renaissance—Florentines, he says, knew about death and liked to gamble. Barich is particularly drawn to Pico della Mirandola, who argued that a person's position in the universal scheme is not fixed but fluid, and that one can practice a "natural philosophy" by understanding the ways all things in the world are connected. The Renaissance becomes Barich's arena within an arena, helping him to understand the racing world. He interprets the track in terms of Florentine life. He observes that the track's backstretch is "as intricately nepotistic as the Medicis' Florence." Watching a groom work, he recalls the young apprentices who did "a hundred menial tasks so that Pollaiuolo or Verrocchio or some other master could step up, brush in hand, and apply the final strokes unencumbered" (109). When a horse breaks loose in the shedrow, knocking him down, Barich opens his next section, "Horses kept breaking loose in Florence, too, all the time, barreling riderless over the cobbles. . . ." This kind of transition becomes more insistent as the book proceeds: Barich revolving endlessly in two worlds, trying to understand one from the other through the double vision of metaphor.

IV

Going every day to the racetrack, reading about the Renaissance, Barich finds comfort but only partial understanding. He has been unable to create metaphorical stories that will fuse the Renaissance, the self-enclosed system of the track, the larger world consumed by cancer. A crucial turn in Barich's eventual recovery comes when he discovers, after learning more about how the track works and immersing himself in the Renaissance, that those worlds have an ugliness corresponding to the one he has fled. Losing his idealism, he gains a distance from which he learns what will be therapeutic for him.

Being more critical, Barich comes to an insight that begins to show him how the racing world will help him past the sadness of death. "I still believed something special was going on at the track," he writes, "but I was starting to suspect it had more to do with nesting birds than with money, speed, or class" (127–28). Understanding and feeling part of procreation, the continuity of generations, is crucial, not betting and performance. This revelation prompts Barich to pursue a subject— the thoroughbred itself, not the racing world—that eventually leads him down that path toward wellness.

"All horses are descended from the so-called dawn horse," Barich begins his commentary on the evolution of the thoroughbred. His research—into bloodlines and breeding, into stories of owners and breeders who have been fascinated with horses—helps him confirm "suspicions about thoroughbreds" he'd held from the beginning: "I thought their attraction was deeply mystical, deriving from some long-standing though lately violated bond between humans and animals, but the traditional view of racing—that it was a gambler's sport dependent on greenbacks for its survival—was at odds with this perception and kept confusing me. . . . Gambling was no doubt central to the racetrack scheme, but the sort of wager being made had a double nature and was of a different order than generally supposed" (203). The wager's "different order," transcending mere betting for money, is akin to the devotion of mystical faith. The "gambler" bets on renewing a crucial, though perhaps unarticulatable, relationship between man and thoroughbred.

The thoroughbred finally attains, for Barich, the status of a totem. As such, it helps show him the unity and continuity

he has longed for, not simply the continuity of human generations, but man's position in a universe not divided into self
and other. "The human race," writes Freud in *Totem and Taboo*,
"have in the course of ages developed three [unified] systems
of thought—three great pictures of the universe: animistic (or
mythological), religious and scientific. Of these, animism, the
first to be created, is perhaps the one which is most consistent
and exhaustive and which gives a truly complete explanation
of the nature of the universe" (77). Animism, for primitive
man, came unthinkingly—all animals and plants had souls and
a place in the natural order. But Barich, like many modern
persons, is self-conscious, creating thereby both an assertion
of separate identity and a desperate loneliness. While rejecting
science and technology, he finds no replacement. And so,
while not turning to myth, he does turn to the idea of a
unified universe, of which man's relation to the thoroughbred
becomes the symbol.

Disparate elements are finally beginning to cohere, Barich
says. One night, he attains an acceptance that has previously
eluded him. He thinks about how, when he is "in touch" at the
track, running thoroughbreds fire every neuron in his body,
"transforming me into one long synapse, bits of energy blowing apart." These moments can be subsequently renewing
for him in memory, retrospective occurrences when he feels
consonant with all things—like the Wordsworthian spots of
time. Barich recognizes his need for a less-controlled life: the
impossibility of predicting a horse race provides excitement,
provides spirit, in an overly structured world.

Though he had fled to the racetrack because it seemed
circumscribed and manageable in comparison to the larger
world, Barich discovers, ironically, that it is less so, that the
chaos he has seen at the track, its "awesome randomness,"
prevents him from creating the order he desires. In the end,
Barich accepts that events and feelings of a life are also beyond
the control that the writer brings to his narrative. He understands, however, that the flux which brings change and cancer
also brings life. The very wildness that he sees in thoroughbreds becomes their way of retaining dignity and being beauti-

ful. Once Barich discards the need to make a pattern, he reorganizes his vision of the future. "All connections," he says, are "ever tenuous." But since "nothing abides," there is "no cause for alarm." It's not a revelatory belief, simplified as it is to a shorthand which stands for all of the experiences that gave birth to it; but when born out of the struggle and believed, it heals. He thinks of hooking a steelhead, landing it after a tremendous fight, and then being amazed at the flimsiness of the line, at the tiny, fragile knot. "All connections ever tenuous," he repeats. "I knew what was happening then. I was letting go of the sadness, letting go of my mother. Living and dying, winning and losing" (219). Barich had originally begun playing the horses in order to get past the sadness of death. And finally, though in a way he hadn't imagined, he is successful, feeling "restored if not renewed": "In my mind the dying and the cancer had become separated, almost discrete, the one a natural process of organic decay, the other a cultural hastening of that process" (225).

Most significant in his healing process is not any single insight or the recovery of any specific memory, but rather a gradual "working through" of his conflicts, a working through that eventually reveals connections between self and other, self and nature. The thoroughbred itself, not the racetrack, has taught Barich what he needs to know, has become a healing symbol in the way that symbols have functioned since romanticism: fusing subject and object, the universal and the particular, order and spontaneity. Not simply the product of a linguistic act, perhaps not even the product of a conscious act, a symbol—the thoroughbred—becomes understandable only by intuition and feeling, not rational thinking, and therefore for an individual in a unique way.

"The most important wager I'd made had paid off," Barich writes, at last completing the mourning cycle. He closes his book with a passage from Christopher Columbus's journal, describing Columbus's first vision of a new, fertile, and beautiful continent. "Just this then," Barich tells himself, "to make every world the New World, to approach it with an explorer's sense of wonder." Barich has come to view his present story

103

in a way that makes us realize how, after he leaves the self-enclosed system of the racetrack, he will be able to rewrite his past story. That personal history will become, we speculate, a narrative that can be described by Schafer's terms of a successful analysis: a comprehensive but modified version of the past, a version "less fragmented, confining, anguished, and self-destructive" (18). *Laughing in the Hills* begins with cancer and ends with a New World, with a documentary on horse racing in between—a documentary that makes possible Barich's rebirth.

V

Barich's healing narrative holds the voices and experiences of not only himself but others, living and dead. Through his Renaissance reading and his interaction with racetrack people, Barich constitutes a "different" self, and this self is enabled, at the end of the story, to lead a life worth living. That is, by placing himself into unfamiliar environments, Barich learns and subsequently uses the "languages"—the vocabulary, feelings, ideas—of the Renaissance and of horse racing, which ultimately helps him construct his own language that allows a new kind of perceiving.

As writing teachers, we can learn a lesson from Barich. *Laughing in the Hills* exemplifies our maxim about "writing as discovery," writing that helps students understand their world and themselves. We should ask for essays that experiment with "languages" not readily at hand for students, even if the efforts to use such languages are clumsy. We should encourage essays that see the unfamiliar in terms of the familiar, that are extended metaphors, because students who do so must extend their minds intellectually and their writing stylistically. We should welcome essays that come to only tentative conclusions—or no conclusions at all, but only raise questions. Such essays often reflect a dynamic model of self-understanding, because the writers enact the recognition that knowledge of themselves in relation to their world is ever-changing and perhaps even illusory. In all cases, we should give students the opportunity to write fewer but longer essays, to live with a subject for many weeks and write about it in a variety of ways.[6] Comprehending something complex, and then discovering a means to portray that comprehension, takes time that we often don't give our students.

Barich's book implicitly suggests that we should consider stressing the therapeutic nature of writing. We rarely do so in writing courses: perhaps we fear encouraging solipsism, or we don't know how to evaluate or respond to such personal writing, or maybe we simply want students to learn how to present facts, how to marshal evidence. But there is much to be gained by surpassing those fears. Asking students to fuse documentary and autobiography—to write essays that impart information imaginatively and clearly, while demonstrating that something is at stake for the writer—can lead to the kind of writing we desire: engaged, reflective prose.

As I talk about engaged writing, or giving students longer and more challenging essay assignments, I am, in one sense, simply talking in code about developing "selfhood"—about students discovering that writing is something other than putting together commonplaces to make a "coherent" essay. "New ways of seeing can disclose new things," Least Heat Moon says at the beginning of his trip, but "do new things make for new ways of seeing?" (17). The answer for Barich after living at the racetrack, just as for Least Heat Moon after 13,000 miles of driving, is yes. The new things—whether people, landscapes, or philosophical views—show them how to see the world afresh. Our students may have no trauma to motivate them, or no opportunity to take to the road when they do have, but a student who visits a retirement home and talks to the people there—absorbing a different world view and a different vocabulary to explain that view—might begin to understand how knowledge of others gives self-knowledge. *Laughing in the Hills* and *Blue Highways* are indeed rich tapes-

---

6. A number of writing teachers already do this, of course, when they have students write a linked set of assignments that explore a subject in increasingly complex ways. William Coles dramatizes such a rhetorical sequence in *The Plural I*.

tries of documentary and autobiography, woven together by the glistening threads of philosophy. Our students can also make such weavings.

Works Cited

Barich, Bill. *Laughing in the Hills.* New York: Penguin, 1981.

Burke, Kenneth. *A Grammar of Motives.* Berkeley: U of California P, 1969.

Coles, William. *The Plural I.* New York: Holt, Rinehart and Winston, 1978.

Didion, Joan. *The White Album.* New York: Pocket Books, 1979.

Dillard, Annie. *Holy the Firm.* New York: Harper, 1977.

Freud, Sigmund. *Introductory Lectures on Psychoanalysis.* New York: Norton, 1966.

———. *Totem and Taboo.* New York: Norton, 1950.

Gusdorf, Georges. "Conditions and Limits of Autobiography," *Autobiography.* Ed. James Olney. Princeton: Princeton UP, 1980.

Herr, Michael. *Dispatches.* New York: Avon Books, 1978.

Hubbell, Sue. *A Country Year.* New York: Random House, 1986.

Jenkins, Peter. *A Walk Across America.* New York: Morrow, 1979.

Koller, Alice. *An Unknown Woman.* New York: Knopf, 1981.

Least Heat Moon, William. *Blue Highways.* Boston: Little, Brown, 1982.

Lindbergh, Anne Morrow. *Gift from the Sea.* New York: Vintage, 1978.

Matthiessen, Peter. *The Snow Leopard.* New York: Bantam, 1979.

Pirsig, Robert. *Zen and the Art of Motorcycle Maintenance.* New York: Bantam, 1975.

Ricouer, Paul. *The Rule of Metaphor.* Trans. Robert Czerny. Toronto: U of Toronto P, 1977.

Schafer, Roy. *Language and Insight.* New Haven: Yale UP, 1978.

Spence, Donald Pond. *Narrative Truth and Historical Truth.* New York: Norton, 1982.

Thoreau, Henry David. *Walden.* New York: NAL, 1960.

White, Hayden. *Tropics of Discourse.* Baltimore: Johns Hopkins UP, 1978.

6

ANNIE DILLARD

The Woman in Nature and
the Subject of Nonfiction

Suzanne Clark

Who is speaking? Who is looking at this place, this Tinker Creek or Puget Sound or Galapagos or Ecuadorian village, which seems to be a place we all inhabit, a real world, a nonfiction? Annie Dillard is the author, but who discovers the nature which we as readers find in the text; who is the seer, and who the teller? Does her work produce the figure of a woman as its subject? But women—like nature—have seemed the object of knowing, not the author.[1]

When we read Annie Dillard, we don't know who is writing. There is a silence in the place where there might be an image of the social self—of personality, character, or ego. There is little mention of her sex or her work or her success, or even—until later works—of the color of her hair. The voice of realistic fiction and the objective voice of fact are commonly anonymous and faceless in the service of giving us the illusion of nonbias. But this lack of self in Dillard is not a lack of subjective bias. Indeed, her prose style enacts a stylistics of bias, writing out the very gesture of perception as a kind of poetics. This "poetics" makes perception and self-identity

---

1. See Carolyn Merchant, *The Death of Nature: Women, Ecology, and the Scientific Revolution*. Her study shows the mutual implication of scientific knowing and the repression of women: seeming closer to nature than men, women in the Renaissance came to be viewed as untrustworthy, incapable of mastering objective knowledge, themselves the object rather than the source of knowledge.

figurative. At the very place of lack, there appears a figure of self-consciousness. Women writers commonly find themselves caught in a discourse which excludes the woman as author, even if the author is a woman.[2] Is it possible that Dillard has produced the figure of woman as object *and* author of knowing? Such a figure seems contradictory, hard to imagine.

The difficulties with calling Dillard's voice a woman's voice have not, in truth, seemed especially visible to other readers. In spite of the fact that Dillard's narrator does not call attention to her gender, and in spite of the striking absence of female detail, Dillard's writing has already drawn attention as woman's writing. But is this because we know Dillard to be a woman writer, or because she writes like a woman in some ways we can specify?[3] Vera Norwood argues that Dillard represents a woman's point of view, and that Dillard's celebration of wildness has specific, liberating implications for women, emphasizing nature over culture.[4]

Norwood's suggestive observations are extremely attractive. They seem, however, to leave unanswered questions. If

2. For example, in her examination of women who made important contributions to ecology, "Women of the Progressive Conservation Movement: 1900–1916," Carolyn Merchant finds that "this enterprise ultimately rested on the self-interested preservation of their own middle-class life styles and was legitimated by the separate male/female spheres ideology of the nineteenth century aimed at conserving 'true womanhood,' the home, and the child" (57).

3. For example, William Scheick's essay on Dillard for the *Contemporary American Women Writers* anthology, "Narrative Fringe," calls attention to the liminal in Dillard but connects contradictions and marginality not with her womanhood, but with the position of the artist and the mystic. Of course, the very inclusion of the essay in a book on women suggests connections, but Scheick avoids making them out loud much as Dillard's work itself does. (The woman speaks, but is not spoken?)

4. Norwood says that Dillard "frees women from safe, cultivated gardens, playing out their burden of guilt for destroying Eden" (51). Thus Dillard, Norwood argues, together with other women writers about the environment, emphasizes nature over culture: "Nature is: before culture there was nature, after culture there will continue to be nature. Their cultural drama is not one of successful challenge, nature overcome, but of full recognition, nature comprehended" (52).

Dillard is self-conscious, does that mean she creates an individual identity in her speaker? How do we know her? If nature wins over culture, that must silence the writer altogether—who, after all, practices a version of culture. The problem is that the speaker in Dillard's work, to be "she," must be problematic, producing a perspective which will make us question our knowing and evade our oppositional categories: male/female, nature/culture.

Dillard herself has called attention to the epistemological consequences of questioning the speaking subject. Though she has not connected her criticism to the problem of the woman writer, Dillard has advocated the problematic speaker as it appears in modern fiction. In an essay called "Is Art All There Is?" she argues that when you begin to wonder about the perspective of the witness, you are being drawn into the important debate about knowing itself: "Related to the theme of art, but actually grounded in metaphysics, is the modernist attention to the relationship between a tale and its teller. . . . Clearly fictions that have a biased narrator, or many biased narrators, deal in part with perceptual bias as a theme. . . . But perceptual bias is not limited to cranky characters. It is every artist's stock in trade. It is every perceiver's stock in trade" (63).

Perhaps Dillard is writing about her own practice here. Her work gives us a multiple answer to the question of who is writing, and the vulnerability of her narrator to changing contexts introduces a kind of bias into her observations, a bias like the fictional bias she is calling modernist. Furthermore, this subject of literature, the place of the writer, has seemed "feminine" to a long history of observers, up to the present.[5]

But Dillard is not writing fiction. She is writing nonfiction. When the speaker of her prose seems as problematic as a

5. See, for example, Frank Lentricchia's argument that Wallace Stevens writes poetry out of a "feminine" position, while his work in the insurance business inscribes him in the masculine economy, and the responses from Donald Pease, and from Sandra Gilbert and Susan Gubar. This debate appears in the Summer 1987 and Winter 1988 *Critical Inquiry.*

fictional speaker, she crosses the boundaries between fiction and nonfiction, raising questions about the status of both. Her liminality has implications for the way we might read text into context, context into text, for border crossings.

Dillard argues that the modernist interest in persona and point of view has implications beyond the boundaries of art, because the unstable, limited subject is all we have—we are all decentered, uncertain.[6]

In *Living by Fiction*, Dillard talks about the special status of the mystic, the poet, the madman, the child. These are figures whose perceptions are not reduced to the expected normal, who see a tree of light when the rest of us just see a tree. And, indeed, the observer in Dillard seems at times to see things like a mystic or poet or child or even like a madman. She oscillates between the writer of conventional exposition and the writer of a more singular text, in a repeated gesture of ordinary perception swerving to the extraordinary. Her writing seems itself to exemplify the paradox of living by fiction, for her style reworks a conventional reporting of what she experiences into something new and strange. The ordinary becomes metaphorical; the unquestioned observer becomes figurative, a figure of bias and difference.

Again and again she gives us what appears to be the natural, real world of experience and breaks it open, to expose its forgotten figurativeness. Take, for example, this passage from *Pilgrim at Tinker Creek:* "Now the blackness is in the east; everything is half in shadow, half in sun, every clod, tree, mountain, and hedge. I can't see Tinker Mountain through the line of hemlock, till it comes on like a streetlight, ping, *ex nihilo*. Its sandstone cliffs pink and swell. Suddenly the light goes; the cliffs recede as if pushed. The sun hits a clump of

6. Dillard writes, in "Is Art All There Is?": "Absolutely diagnostic as a theme of contemporary modernist fiction is this: many works, granting the uncertainty of any knowledge, treat the world in a new way, as a series of imaginative possibilities. Anything may happen. . . . Writers and artists of this century many well ascribe to their work a new and real importance. If art is the creation of contexts, *and so is everything else*, how false or trivial can art be?" (66).

110

sycamores between me and the mountains; the sycamore arms light up, and *I can't see the cliffs*. They're gone" (21). This interference with our habitual ways of looking at the world makes us question the perceiver, makes the artist visible.

This figure-making style which turns life into literature has much to do with the aspect of the speaker which Dillard does not talk about, the woman. "She" is the unspoken subject. By that I do not mean to suggest that Dillard is writing as a feminist or an advocate of women in any straightforward way. I mean that what subverts the coherent character presented as a speaker, what undoes the convention and makes the non-fiction literary, is the unspoken "she," a recurring strangeness, or estrangement, which acts as a counterpoint to the traditional and literal authority of the (male) observer—the naturalists, adventurers, and other writers whom Dillard cites. Dillard is/is not an author among them; she does/ does not participate in the authority and mastery over nature of scientific discourse. Her prose is not transparent; it is metaphorical. The speaker is in question, and, as Dillard suggests, that raises the question of knowledge itself.

Dillard does not represent herself as a woman narrator; she does not, as a speaker, solidify into any figure of certain identity, not even female identity. Instead, the female undermines the very principle of identity. Dillard does not let us off the hook by giving us herself as a cranky character, the artist, either, whose subjectivity is responsible for the distortions in "nature." Identity is a metaphor. Nature also writes on her, through her, making a sometimes bloody inscription.

This speaker's voice admits the painful sacrifice of self involved in the pursuit of knowing: "I am an explorer, then, and I am also a stalker, or the instrument of the hunt itself. . . . I am the arrow shaft, carved along my length by unexpected lights and gashes from the very sky, and this book is the straying trail of blood" (13).

II

If we look at the cover of *Pilgrim at Tinker Creek*, we find pictured there a very blond young woman, dressed in brown outdoor gear with sturdy shoes for walking, who is nonetheless somewhat ethereal, her build slight, the light making a halo of her long, fair hair. She is sitting at her ease in a rocky place filled with twisting tree roots and twiggy, rough tree trunks, also illuminated by the play of light. It could be winter; the tops of the trees are cut out of the picture. There is no green, no sign of other life; everything is brown shadow and luminous gold, dark and light. She is at the center of the picture. She looks directly at the camera, or at the reader. Even though her clothing is functional, ungendered, she is most definitely a she. It is a photograph. Therefore, though its play of light and dark seems almost symbolic, an appeal to imagination, we take the image as "real." Annie Dillard represents herself, the image of her proper person, as, presumably, she does in the voice of the text. The conventions of "real perception," not verisimilitude, will govern our reading of both photograph and text: this will seem to be a book about the experience of a real person, looking by herself, speaking for herself. As "natural" readers, we are not expected to think critically about the narrator; we will not read her as a character, a fictive creation who constructs her own subjectivity by the point of view she takes as she speaks. Rather, we will try to read her world as if it were a photograph. We will read according to the conventions of realism.

However, the cover of *Pilgrim at Tinker Creek* also promises, in words written under the title, "A mystical excursion into the natural world." And on the back: "Mystery, Death, Beauty, Violence." If the photograph on the front seemed to promise a faithful and objective transcription of someone's real experience, its play of bright and shadow, dark and light suggest the symbolism of good and evil associated with another kind of knowing, with mysticism. In Dillard, the special, unreasonable knowledge of the lover, the child, the poet, and the mystic is spoken by the voice of a female subject. A differing from rational order thus comes to be represented by the figure of a woman. She is not so much the subject of knowing, as subjected to it.

A nature that she later calls necessity—powerful, animal,

sensual—overwhelms each of Dillard's beginnings. And each of them violates ideas of the self in nature that the reader might expect to find. "Mystery, Death, Beauty, Violence" make the moment ambiguously like rape—or rapture.

Pilgrim opens with the scene of a repeated awakening: her "old fighting tom" cat, "stinking of urine and blood," would leave her "body covered with paw prints in blood." These stains, signs, markings write on her flesh messages which she cannot decipher: "What blood was this, and what roses? It could have been the rose of union, the blood of murder, or the rose of beauty bare and the blood of some unspeakable sacrifice or birth. The sign on my body could have been an emblem or a stain, the keys to the kingdom or the mark of Cain. I never knew" (PTC 2).

The writer begins, in other words, with a sense of strangeness, not a knowing but "mystery." What is mysterious is the self's encounter with signs of otherness—a violation, known only by its bloody traces. The meaning is untranslatable. This scene brings together two codes which violate each other: if this writing is about brute nature, the facts are what we're after, and it's shocking for her to describe these details and conclude "I never knew." But if the writing is about the mystery of good and evil, heaven and hell, the bloody messages and the suggestive scene are an animal intrusion into spirituality, bestial grounds for meditation. The metaphor of identity resembles the site of erotic violation, the scene of a rape. The only signs of gender suggest a horror of feminine sexuality— the passive body of the speaking subject is "kneaded" by the tom cat, "as if sharpening his claws, or pummeling a mother for milk." Here there is no trace in the narrator of the post-Enlightenment man of reason, no sense of mastery over nature, or of the world as body, and self as knowing mind. In this scene of blood roses, this writer speaks from unknowing, not momentary but a condition of existence ("I never knew"); here she is no more authoritative than the common people whose lack of mastery is signaled by their grammatical lapses: " 'Seem like we're just set down here,' a woman said to me recently, 'and don't nobody know why.' " At this beginning,

113

quoting the folk in their anonymity, the writer speaks as one of them, also anonymous, without ego. She records on her flesh, unresisting, the tracks of the old fighting tom, like film taking the print of the photographed image. The writer is defined—she is written by something else, something strange.

Dillard's voice in this beginning signals difference—but is it the difference of the woman, or of the poet? The madman or the mystic? Are they mutually overlapping? Dillard associates the poet with the madman, the mystic, and the child in *Living by Fiction*, but not with woman. Jacques Derrida, on the other hand, has suggested that the place of woman in language *is* displacement, difference.[7] And Susan Griffin, who says she was influenced by Annie Dillard, has presented a record of the displacement of woman and nature in *Woman and Nature: The Roaring Inside Her*. A sacrificial and alienated identity, from the point of view of literary traditions, might remind us of the poet—victim, at least since Rimbaud, of the visionary illumination in which "*je est un autre*"; witness, especially since Hopkins, to a beauty which is flawed and even violent.

On the other hand, this receptivity—this abjection— might remind us, from the point of view of a nonliterary tradition, of the passivity Freud associated both with the feminine and with the religious, a position Julia Kristeva explores in *The Powers of Horror*. This sacrificial posture of a self which is neither subject nor object is what she calls the *abject*. For Kristeva, it is a subjective position associated with the woman and the mystic. As in Dillard, the abject opens to both horror and ecstasy. There are other kinds of voices in *Pilgrim*, other moments when Dillard does not take on the attitudes of the abject. Dillard again and again speaks, in fact, with the cumulative voice of mankind: she quotes the natural historian, like Teale; the scientist, like Jeans; the explorer, like Scott, Peary, Byrd; Pascal, Einstein, Thoreau, Xerxes, King David, Rim-

7. For example, in "Choreographies," an interview between Derrida and Christie McDonald, in which he reflects on other places in his work where he has said the woman has no place, is not implicated in the discourses of essentialism.

baud—a citing of the male subject to provide the facts of expertise and the context of culture. Again and again Dillard evokes this male culture, these male conventions, and then works them at a bias, calling up and undoing their cumulative hold.[8]

Marius von Senden, for example, provides Dillard with the histories of sight restored to cataract patients. Then, in a sort of dialectic, Dillard provides the estrangement, adopting a falling away from the familiarity of the seeing culture into the metaphor of new sight—the world as patches of color and shadows, the contradictions of death and revolting fecundity: "So shadows define the real. If I no longer see shadows as 'dark marks,' as do the newly sighted, then I see them as making some sort of sense of the light. . . . This is the blue strip running through creation, the icy roadside stream on whose banks the mantis mates, in whose unweighed waters the giant water bug sips frogs. Shadow Creek is the blue subterranean stream" (PTC 64).

The perceiving teller of Dillard's narrations moves again and again from the realistic detail provided by observation and citation, what we might associate with the cultural mastery of the natural world, to a being overwhelmed, rape as rapture—the female version of the fortunate fall.

On the idea of being surrounded by locusts, she writes: "I cannot ask for more than to be so wholly acted upon, flown at, and lighted on in throngs, probed, knocked, even bitten . . . being so in the clustering thick of things, rapt and enwrapped in the rising and falling real world" (PTC 226). The "I" is grammatical subject here, but the very syntax is a passive construction. The subject is the object of the "real world," and we are far from the powerful speaker of western discourse about nature, and far from the objective style of scientific prose. Her observations are on the margins of what we can take without being appalled—her words close to the appalling

8. For a thorough review of the conventions associated with the representation of nature and of pastoral topoi, see Ernst Robert Curtius, *European Literature and the Latin Middle Ages.*

Suzanne Clark

natural fecundity she sees in the mantis laying eggs, clothes moths, rock barnacles, parasite: "the world as an intricate texture of a bizarre variety of forms" (PTC 183). What can she get away with? She works the mixing of texts, risking the moment when the reader drops away with revulsion at the uncanny recall of the female: "You are an ichneumon. You mated and your eggs are fertile. If you can't find a caterpillar on which to lay your eggs, your young will starve. When the eggs hatch, the young will eat any body in which they find themselves, so if you don't kill them by emitting them broad-cast over the landscape, they'll eat you alive. . . . Not that the ichneumon is making any conscious choice. If she were, her dilemma would be truly the stuff of tragedy; Aeschylus need have looked no further than the ichneumon" (PTC 174). The strangeness comes from a speaking subject which is vulnerable to being overwhelmed by a loss of borders, and the catastrophe of a violated self. But the strangeness is mixed with another perspective, the absurdity of regarding the ichneumon as the stuff of tragedy. Perception itself is nothing but receptivity: "For that forty minutes last night I was purely sensitive and mute as a photographic plate" (PTC 201).

These moments need the context of the cultural citing to keep the dialectic of voices. The male tradition gives distance, authority, a framework of conventions that mediate abjection and make female creativity less physical, more metaphorical and a matter of art.

But Dillard takes the bodily powers of metaphor seriously. For example, Dillard gives us an image of the wind as impreg-nating her: "A wind like this does my breathing for me; it engenders something quick and kicking in my lungs. Pliny believed the mares of the Portuguese used to raise their tails to the wind, 'and turn them full against it, and so conceive that genital air instead of natural seed. . . .' Soon something perfect is born. Something wholly new rides the wind, something fleet and fleeting I'm likely to miss" (54). She can understand Pliny's assumptions. The conceit is a concept, conceived in the brain like a child in the body. Dillard's conceit is also epistemologically ambitious—she is talking about herself, real experience, the perceiver's metaphor being all we have of knowledge. And the knowledge she is talking about is physical, of the flesh, not from imaginings or cognitions or spiritual insights or textual conventions alone. In the paradox of living by fiction, emphasis is on the living as well as the fiction. She sees by Pliny, and conventions of the maternal are written into perception, into the flesh.

Interestingly enough, the dialectic of male and female subjectivity seems most pronounced in *Pilgrim*, where it is also most metaphorical. The author there never appears in her own proper person, as a woman—never reveals her gender by any detail of appearance or activity. There is no cultural feminine in the book. The later works, in contrast, portray the speaker as a woman in certain ways, and yet give us portrayals of her that are much less attached to images of female sexuality, to reproduction and physicality. The shattering of codes takes a different direction. Furthermore, even though Dillard's work opens again and again on a scene of abjection, there are important differences in these inaugural scenes.

The beginning of *Holy the Firm* seems much more clearly in the tradition of religious meditation than *Pilgrim*. What seizes her is not the cat, but the holy. At the same time, the erotic quality of the scene is strong enough that we can't be sure if the god is a metaphor for human lovemaking or the flesh a metaphor for the god: "I wake in a god. I wake in arms holding my quilt, holding me as best they can inside my quilt. Someone is kissing me—already. . . . Today's god rises, his long eyes flecked in clouds. He flings his arms, spreading colors; he arches, cupping sky in his belly; he vaults, vaulting and spread, holding all and spread on me like skin" (HF 11–12). What can she mean? This is not fantasy: "The day is real." Yet it seems that the things of the world are of a more manageable demeanor than they were in *Pilgrim*: this cat is "a gold cat, who sleeps on my legs, named Small." As it turns out, the metaphors of identity here, too, will connect both to femininity and to writing, but somehow in a more controlled

117

way. Here, too, there is violence and sacrifice. "There is a spider, too, in the bathroom, with whom I keep a sort of company. Her little outfit always reminds me of a certain moth I helped to kill" (HF 13). Here, too, there will be an alienation of the writer from herself, made vivid by the flaming death of the moth, emblem of the writer. Then the story of "Julie Norwich," a young girl whose face is burned in a plane crash, invokes the image of Julian of Norwich—woman, and mystic.

Even without Frederich Buechner's note on the back cover, most of us would think of Virginia Woolf as we read Dillard's narrative of the moth flying into the candle. Here the literary and mystical connections are made out loud: "She burned for two hours without changing, without bending or leaning—only glowing within, like a building fire glimpsed through silhouetted walls, like a hollow saint, like a flame-face virgin gone to God, while I read by her light, kindled, while Rimbaud in Paris burnt out his brains in a thousand poems, while night pooled wetly at my feet" (HF 17). And here the ambition becomes quite visible: to overlap differences associated with male and female subjectivity, to make the analogy of the artist and the mystic extend into the "natural" experience of a real woman, who was camping out in the world of the moment when this happened. To colonize natural history for art. The most everyday ordinary perceiver of our common lives could see and say the same things, she implies. Gender *seems* not really intrinsically related—though the moth is a "she," and so is the camper, and so is the writer, and so is the other writer about the figure of the moth as the artist, Woolf. And, behind all, stands the female figure of Julian of Norwich.

But is it possible that a woman needs to stand at this place, to draw together the artist, the saint, and the overwhelmed witness out in the woods? For literature and nonliterature have been strictly segregated, and this is the issue: can the speaker of a writing about the nonliterary universe allow himself to be unknowing, passive, overwhelmed, and consumed? Can nonfiction have any authority without the mastery of understanding, since Bacon? Dillard's mind refuses to exercise authority over the nature of things. Her witnessing offers testimony to the powers of horror as well as to the powers of awe, in the tradition of Emily Dickinson. Thus she violates the codes of understanding itself.

One might ordinarily think that *Teaching a Stone to Talk* should not be considered a third book in a series, but rather another genre, a looser collection of essays. But Dillard urges us to think again, and further provokes the question of herself as speaker (Conventionally male? Writing as a woman?) in an "Author's Note" which refers to a writer with a male pronoun: ". . . this is not a collection of occasional pieces, such as a writer brings out to supplement his real work; instead this is my real work, such as it is" (TS 8). Is she distinguishing herself from a writer (in the male tradition) whose "real work" has some kind of centrality? Is her "real work," resembling the supplement, to be distinguished as some other (nonmale) kind of genre, marked by the quality of the "occasional" (a trait sometimes found in women writers)? But the words have a postmodern resonance: *occasional, supplement.*

The first essay, "Living Like Weasels," does not open with any "I" represented, but with a questioning "who." The question is: "A weasel is wild. Who knows what he thinks?" (TS 11) It is several pages before Dillard as narrator enters the picture with a narrative of her own experience, the encounter with the weasel. But that meeting represents the greatest violation of all boundaries, a wildness that exceeds language, a mutual gaze that eliminates separate selfhood altogether: "Our eyes locked, and someone threw away the key. Our look was as if two lovers, or deadly enemies, met unexpectedly on an overgrown path when each had been thinking of something else: a clearing blow to the gut. It was also a bright blow to the brain, or a sudden beating of brains, with all the charge and intimate grate of rubbed balloons. It emptied our lungs. It felled the forest, moved the fields, and drained the pond; the world dismantled and tumbled into that black hole of eyes" (TS 14). When Rilke wrote, in the Eighth of the *Duino Elegies,* of the exchange

119

with an animal gaze, he thought that we never see purely like the animal does:

> *With full gaze the animal sees the open.*
> *Only our eyes, as if reversed, are like snares*
> *set around it, block the freedom of its going.*
> *Only from the face of the beast do we know*
> *what is outside. . . (v. 1–5)*

Dillard writes within this symbolist tradition, though she is not writing poetry. (Look at her diction—it's parodic, hyperbolic, comic: "Our eyes locked, and someone threw away the key.") What she is talking about in the scene with the weasel, this "bright blow to the brain," defines the power that seizes the writer again and again—something not visionary or utopian or of the imagination, not the poet's power, but radically other: something other than subjectivity and prior to it, Rilke's "what *is* outside," to which the writer becomes abject. What the weasel's gaze teaches is before words: "I might learn something of mindlessness, something of the purity of living in the physical senses and the dignity of living without bias or motive. The weasel lives in necessity and we live in choice, hating necessity and dying at the last ignoble in its talons. I would like to live as I should, as the weasel lives as he should" (TS 15). That is, she gives us not freedom, but necessity—not mastery, but submission. Though their gaze is like "two lovers," she and the weasel are not about human love or desire, but about the intimacy with necessity that determines the animal self. She is looking at a subject that is undivided into speech, at "mindlessness," unknowing.

The experience of the speaker that in *Pilgrim* seemed almost like the scene of a rape has lost most of its extreme physicality—its urine and blood. Nevertheless, Dillard's metaphor here has her abandoning the tame and human self to mate with the weasel: "I could very calmly go wild. I could live two days in the den, curled, leaning on mouse fur, sniffing bird bones, blinking, licking, breathing musk, my hair tangled in the roots of grasses. Down is out, out of your ever-loving mind and back to your careless senses" (TS 15). This Dillard, a bit fantastic, like the heroine of a children's story or Alice in Wonderland, does not quite threaten our imaginations with the horror of bestiality—but the scene is lined and edged with the bones and musk of an animal experience. And she connects this encounter with the weasel both to the descent into the animal senses and to a mystical path, the "way down and out." There is something, a little, of the romantic and Gothic about this tale: the woman runs away with her demon lover, the weasel. But this story takes place outside the conventions of sexuality. The speaker is at once wild like the weasel and overtaken by its mindlessness. Can it be imagined the other way around—could the speaker here as easily be a man? Perhaps—if he identifies with the weasel, with nature as opposed to culture. This loss of ego and cultural identity is where the female subject intersects with the poet and the mystic; with Rilke, for example. The boundaries of the speaker are in flux, the identity of the self is neither human nor animal. And when she solidifies into an "I," the subject of a spoken word, it is with a sense of regret and belatedness and separation: "I remember muteness as a prolonged and giddy fast, where every moment is a feast of utterance received. Time and events are merely poured, unremarked, and ingested directly, like blood pulsed into my gut through a jugular vein" (TS 16).

Language mediates; the writer breaks silence and stops the flow of lifeblood. Like what Geoffrey Hartman once called the "unmediated vision" of poets like Wordsworth, Hopkins, Yeats, Rilke, and Valery, Dillard's is the paradoxical subject explored by symbolist and modernist poetics: the one who breaks the cultural traditions coded by language, who opens up imprisoning conventionality. What kind of utterance might break the hold of the expected phrase? How can wildness and the reader, mute, encounter one another's look?

The obvious metaphoricity of Dillard's work could seem *merely* figurative and not "real," not saying anything about nature or the world beyond the purview of creative writing. If the persona who speaks seems to be literary, she may cease being dangerous—or interesting—for the power of nonfiction is that language is *not* just appealing for its own sake, that style functions to make an argument, as Chris Anderson has put it. Dillard carries wildness out in a work that works to violate the very boundaries of the literary; her nonfiction carries fiction into living, poetics into the wild, invention into natural history, female subjectivity into language. In this, I want to designate her as postmodern.

The techniques of discovery are at work on the medium of language, like the poetics of modernism, but Dillard violates the well-guarded modernist barrier between literature and ordinary language. If her style takes up the impersonal stance of the modernist poet, it also opens up to the multiple voices of ordinary people. The logic is contradictory, the poetic itself violated by the unpoetic.

The paradox of a literary inquiry into nonfiction style arises from its self-destructive longing to prove that there is no such genre, and that reality is a fiction created by writing. In Dillard, the symbolist revolution of poetic language extends into nonfiction. However, Annie Dillard gives us a poetics which shapes not the seen but the seer. She gives us perception—Tinker Creek, Puget Sound—as a form of meditation. And thus she defines by her style not the weasel but the gaze that seizes it, the persona of an ecological knowing. She reveals, on the one hand, its debt to the spiritual exercises that helped define the poetics of the lyric from Donne to Stevens, and its place in the pastoral conventions.

And, on the other hand, she outlines the ecstatic impersonality of a female subject. This female self is impersonal because without power. The speaker is not the ego, not created by conquering the body of nature. If the object of her pilgrimage is the real world, still it is an object which is known by its action upon the subject—we read together with the gesture of her responsiveness the signs of an otherwise blank mystery, of an untranslatable real. And Dillard's real world makes itself known by messages violently counter to our desires, against even our desire for life itself. The messages come like the bloody tracks of her cat on her flesh. Nature limits and refutes the experience of will, enforces abjection. It takes a poetics, the subversion of language, to define vision. And yet ecstasy comes with the recognition of powerlessness: that she neither wills nor creates the creek, the bay, the cat, the crash, the weasel. Though she may write the terms of her encounter, her writing itself opens to the inscription of otherness, with the receptivity of a female author-ity.

Works Cited

Anderson, Chris. *Style as Argument: Contemporary American Nonfiction*. Carbondale: Southern Illinois UP, 1987.

Curtius, Ernst Robert. *European Literature and the Latin Middle Ages*. Trans. Willard R. Trask. New York: Bollingen, 1953.

Derrida, Jacques, and Christie V. McDonald. "Interview: Choreographies." *Diacritics* 12 (Summer 1982): 66–76.

Dillard, Annie. *Encounters with Chinese Writers*. Middletown: Wesleyan UP, 1984.

———. "Is Art All There Is?" *Harper's* 261 (August 1980): 61–66.

———. *Holy the Firm*. New York: Harper and Row, 1977.

———. *Living by Fiction*. New York: Harper and Row, 1982.

———. *Pilgrim at Tinker Creek*. New York: Harper's Magazine Press, 1974.

———. *Teaching a Stone to Talk*. New York: Harper and Row, 1982.

Griffin, Susan. *Woman and Nature: The Roaring Inside Her*. New York: Harper and Row, 1978.

Empson, William. *Some Versions of Pastoral*. New York: New Directions, 1974.

Kolodny, Annette. *The Lay of the Land: Metaphor as Experience in American Life and Letters*. Chapel Hill: U of North Carolina P, 1975.

Kristeva, Julia. *Powers of Horror: An Essay on Abjection*. Trans. Leon S. Roudiez. New York: Columbia UP, 1982.

———. *Revolution in Poetic Language*. Trans. Margaret Waller. Intro. Leon S. Roudiez. New York: Columbia UP, 1984.

Lentricchia, Frank. "Patriarchy Against Itself—The Young Manhood of Wallace Stevens." *Critical Inquiry* 13 (Summer 1987): 742–86.

Martz, Louis. *The Poetry of Meditation: A Study in English Religious Literature of the Seventeenth Century*. Revised Edition. New Haven: Yale UP, 1962.

Merchant, Carolyn. *The Death of Nature: Women, Ecology, and the Scientific Revolution*. San Francisco: Harper and Row, 1980.

———. "Women of the Progressive Conservation Movement: 1900-1916." *Environmental Review* 8.1 (Spring, 1984): 57–85.

Moi, Toril. *Sexual/Textual Politics: Feminist Literary Theory.* London and New York: Methuen, 1985.

Monk, Janice. "Approaches to the Study of Women and Landscape." *Environmental Review* 8.1 (Spring 1984): 23–33.

Norwood, Vera L. "Heroines of Nature: Four Women Respond to the American Landscape." *Environmental Review* 8.1 (Spring 1984): 34–56.

Ortner, Sherry B. "Is Female to Male as Nature is to Culture?" *Woman, Culture and Society.* Ed. Michelle Zimbalist Rosaldo and Louise Lamphere. Stanford: Stanford UP, 1974: 67–87.

Rilke, Rainier Maria. *Duino Elegies.* Trans. C.F. MacIntyre. Berkeley: U of California P, 1968.

Scheick, William J. "Annie Dillard." *Contemporary American Women Writers: Narrative Strategies.* Ed. Catherine Rainwater and William J. Scheick. Lexington: UP of Kentucky, 1985.

Thompson, Kenneth. *Beliefs and Ideology.* London and New York: Tavistock, 1986.

Yeats, W. B. "Leda and the Swan." *Collected Poems.* New York: Macmillan, 1956: 211.

7

TWO TALES "INTENDED TO BE AFTER THE FACT"

"Stephen Crane's Own Story" and "The Open Boat"

Phyllis Frus

It is a commonplace of American literary history that journalism was the incubator for fictional realism.[1] In this view, expressed most recently by Shelley Fishkin, novelists from Twain to Hemingway honed their documentary skills in journalism and then applied them to invented characters and to subjects with a broader appeal. A corollary assumption is that novelists historically have felt hampered by the factual constraints of journalism and have turned to fiction because of the freedom it offered.[2] Writers encourage this interpretation with pronouncements that their journalism is second-rate; Hemingway, for example, insisted that "the newspaper stuff I have written . . . has nothing to do with the other" and "no one has any right to dig [it] up and use it against the stuff you have written to write the best you can" (xi).

This version of literary history reinforces the high status that the novel holds in comparison with journalism in literary studies, thus obscuring the many similarities between the two

1. The author wishes to thank the Vanderbilt University Research Council for grant support during the preparation of this article.

2. Hofstadter notes, "With few exceptions the makers of American realism . . . were men who had training in journalistic observation" (197). Michael Schudson lists Dreiser, London, Crane, Norris, and Cather as novelists of this period who wrote in a "self-conscious realistic vein growing out of their experience as newspaper reporters" (73).

Phyllis Frus

forms and perpetuating the myth of journalism as the transcription of reality rather than an interpretation of events. A more accurate version of the relationship between journalism and fiction can be constructed by starting with the premise that both discourses are equally constituting structures, and that American journalism and the realistic novel are similar at the beginning of the twentieth century because both were responding to the positivism of the world-view prevalent at that time, namely its concern with "objective observation, analysis, and classification of human life" (Carter 102). As Corkin has shown, not only novels and journalism but the emerging film medium at the turn of the century show similar formal characteristics (invisible narration, privileging of the visual) and similar behaviorist attitudes toward their subjects and audiences (human beings are shown as mere objects among many others). The similarities among these forms dominated by realistic representation and a belief in objectivity may have been related to the ideology of developing industrial capitalism, whose positivistic assertion of the world as it appeared to be, disseminated in the journalism, literature, and cinema of the period, prepared readers and viewers to be subjects who would, as Althusser says, "work by themselves" (181).

If this thesis is correct, journalism and fiction may be more similar than we usually assume, despite efforts by writers like Hemingway to relegate the former to inferior status. William White points out that "not only did Hemingway use the very same material for both news accounts and short stories: he took pieces he first filed with magazines and newspapers and published them with virtually no change in his own books as short stories" (Hemingway xi).[3] This substitution works be-

3. Similarly, because the twentieth-century critic comes armed with the attitude that journalism is an inferior form, Crane's efforts in this medium are usually denigrated in favor of his fiction. The editors of *The War Dispatches of Stephen Crane* insist, however, that he was "not the failure as a journalist that almost every critic has labelled him," and they call him "a star reporter." This high quality makes the work seem all of a piece, and in compiling the collection they found it difficult to decide whether to label a given Crane narrative a newspaper sketch or a short story (Stallman and Hagemann 109, 108).

cause journalism is composed of narrative, not of events themselves, just as fictional texts do not refer to an absolute reality
but to a system of signs; both are therefore autonomous literary structures and are on the same narrative plane. Not only
do the separate categories into which we put short stories and
journalism—usually fiction and nonfiction, or literature and
"other"—affect the way we perceive them, but these perceived
differences affect our evaluation of each. We are nevertheless
likely to attribute these differences to objective qualities inherent in each genre, rather than to various reading, writing, and
framing conventions which predispose us to regard them in
different ways.

In order to demonstrate how these reified conventions
and common reader expectations affect not only our categories of literature and nonliterary genres but our interpretations, I will compare two narratives which exist in similar
relationship to the events which gave rise to them—two narratives by Stephen Crane which resulted from the same event,
and which were published only five months apart. These are
the justifiably famous story "The Open Boat," and a related
journalistic account, "Stephen Crane's Own Story." ("Stephen
Crane's Own Story" appeared on the front page of the New
York *Press* on January 6, 1897, while "The Open Boat" ran in
Scribner's Magazine that June.)[4] Both treat of events surrounding the wreck of the *Commodore*, a ship which was filibustering,
or carrying weapons and munitions to Cuba to aid the rebels
in the insurrection against Spain. Crane was on board as a
crew member in order to get to Cuba to cover the insurrection
for the Bacheller-Johnson syndicate. (Reporters were banned
from such expeditions because the U.S. was officially neutral.)

4. Both have been reprinted in two paperbound books, Katz—whose
page references are given in parentheses—and McQuade and Atwan. Crane
also used the experience as the basis of a highly invented story that appeared
in *McClure's Magazine* in August 1897. "Flanagan and His Short Filibustering
Adventure" is a narrative about a successful gun-running expedition; the
central character is the captain of the *Foundling*, which capsizes in a squall
only after it has delivered the weapons and men and fought off an attack by
a Spanish gunboat. Since this story was largely invented, its literariness is not
questioned and so it is not relevant here. It is collected in Katz.

Phyllis Frus

In "Stephen Crane's Own Story," Crane narrates events (in the first person) from the time he went aboard the *Commodore* in Jacksonville, Florida, on New Year's Eve to the ship's sinking (possibly as a result of sabotage) the next day, an event which he and three comrades watched from their precarious perch in a ten-foot dinghy. As a crew member, Crane had first joined in fighting a fire in the engine room and then in bailing efforts for a total of nearly twelve hours before the ship was finally abandoned. The story "The Open Boat" derives from the thirty hours Crane spent in the tiny lifeboat with the oiler, cook, and captain of the *Commodore* as they fought the Atlantic swells and steered for the Florida coast. When no one on shore spotted them to send a rescue craft out, they swam for the beach; three of them made it safely, but the oiler was drowned.

When we test these two narratives against the usual criteria for defining literature—fictional invention and aesthetic language—they do not fall into the literary and "other" categories so easily (Wellek and Warren 24–25; Wellek 19–21; Todorov, "Notion"). "The Open Boat" is not more fictional or invented than "Stephen Crane's Own Story." Both narratives follow the historical sequence of events surrounding the *Commodore* disaster as verified in contemporary newspaper reports, the ship's log and other shipping records, and accounts by witnesses (see Stallman chs. 14–15; apps. 5–7). Both proceed chronologically, with some digressions and foreshadowing. However, the news story telescopes the outcome, merely mentioning in the final two paragraphs the thirty hours "in an open boat," the bravery of the *Commodore*'s captain and the oiler, Billy Higgins, and Higgins's death. Thus the later narrative, "The Open Boat," for all practical purposes picks up where the detailed journalism leaves off, with the four men in the boat in heavy seas. Neither story invents facts or characters, although both narratives inevitably proceed by invention—in the rhetorical sense of producing the subject matter according to previous literary models while appearing to copy from nature or reality ("Invention").

A closely related way of contrasting such examples—saying that the news feature is limited to particular factual events while the short story works on a higher plane of universals (Cady 151)—does not seem valid in this case. There are few journalistic particulars in Crane's newspaper version after the ship gets under way (it is, after all, a "sidebar" story, a piece ancillary to the main news story, which gives more of the facts as pieced together from different sources). We don't know from Crane's front-page account, for example, how many men were on the ship and how many were lost. There are also several mysteries in "Stephen Crane's Own Story." We never find out how the captain's arm came to be in a sling or who took two huge valises into the first lifeboat (or what was in them, although we infer a connection with the filibusters). The journalist tells us that he and the cook discussed their contingency plans, but we do not hear what they have decided to do.

In "Stephen Crane's Own Story" most of the participants are named: Captain Murphy; Tom Smith, the old seaman who is going to quit filibustering after this trip; and the first rescuer into the sea: "John Kitchell of Daytona came running down the beach and as he ran the air was filled with clothes. If he had pulled a single lever and undressed, even as the fire horses harness, he could not seem to me to have stripped with more speed" (342). But Billy Higgins (spelled "Billie" in "The Open Boat") is named in both stories (he is the only character of the five in "The Open Boat" who is); and in both some figures are called only by their roles: in the newspaper account we have "the cook," "the Cuban leader," and "the chief engineer"; the short story includes "the captain," "the cook," and "the correspondent."

With regard to the second important way by which we usually define literature—its aesthetic qualities or use of fore-grounded language[5]—"Stephen Crane's Own Story" is not less literary. The analogy that Crane uses to describe the survivors'

5. "It is thus quantitatively that literary language is first of all to be differentiated from the varied uses of every day. The resources of language are exploited much more deliberately and systematically" (Wellek and Warren 24).

Phyllis Frus

first rescuer (quoted above) is a case in point: it is vivid and extended, and it contains a second comparison within, which gives it the effect of an epic simile, all showing the attention to detail paid by a drowning man even as he catches sight of a potential lifesaver. Crane is as amazed by the pattern of the clothes filling the air as he is at the idea of rescue, and the reader is as likely to notice the virtuosity of the figure of speech as the dexterity of the rescuer. In "The Open Boat," the narrator divides the description into three sentences, and it is toned down, almost flattened; the effect is to center the reader's attention on the rescuer instead of calling attention to the perceptions of the man needing aid. The style is more transparent because we see through the language rather than noticing it: "Presently he saw a man running along the shore. He was undressing with most remarkable speed. Coat, trousers, shirt, everything flew magically off him" (385). A tropological inventory of each narrative does show different *patterns* of figures. The number of similes far exceeds that of metaphors in the news feature, for example, whereas these are about evenly divided in "The Open Boat." This emphasis on simile in the front-page newspaper story is not surprising, because comparisons probably come to mind more readily as similes (with "like" or "as") to writers under deadline pressure, whereas it takes time to develop succinct metaphors, and Crane had at least six weeks in which to write the story.[6] It may also be that Crane was striving for a more transparent style of description in the later version, and attention-getting similes would interfere with this purpose.

Irony is a frequent trope in both stories, too, but it works differently in each. For example, the narrator of "Stephen Crane's Own Story"—the implied journalist speaking in the first person—is the source of all the information in that narrative. The irony in this voice reveals itself as understatement and incongruity, and in expressions which mean the opposite

6. William Rondel says that Crane must have finished "The Open Boat" about the middle of February, for his agent said *Scribner's* wanted to see it on the twenty-fifth. It was accepted on March 5 (364).

130

of what they say, as when he speaks of "the physical delights of holding one's self in bed" (when the *Commodore* is pitching in high seas—334), or describes the men's reaction to the captain's announcement that their little lifeboat will stay by the ship until it sinks as "fill[ing] us all with glee" (because the wake of the sinking could easily have capsized the small craft— 339). Situations as well as language may be ironic, but the origin of the irony in this first-person version is almost always the journalist-narrator, the recognizable source of the story.

In contrast, the irony in "The Open Boat" is distributed among several discourses, situations, and events, and because the dominant narrator is not the single source of the story, the irony is pervasive at the level of text rather than specifiable in a certain voice. We are frequently unsure as to whether certain statements are meant ironically at all, as when the correspondent's excessive detachment during the final swim through the surf is commented on with the remark, "Perhaps an individual must consider his own death to be the final phenomenon of nature" (384). Later he says, "An overturned boat in the surf is not a plaything to a swimming man" (385). Jonathan Culler calls such asides and understatements "violations of register, which one tends to assume are ironic; but it is extremely difficult to locate any covert assertion that they make" (158). The uncertainty about how to take many such statements is one of the factors which makes reading this story a complex experience, but this is not the same as saying that the narrator of "The Open Boat" utilizes irony while the journalist does not; we are not able to distinguish which narrative is more "literary" on the basis of the number of figures of speech, or the comparative degree of rhetorical patterning.

Matthew Arnold is reputed to have described journalism as "literature in a hurry," and so perhaps the published tale is literary merely because it is written "after the fact," when Crane had had time to reflect and consider, to digest the experience. But if the time lapse between these two narratives is indeed a factor in its literariness, then there ought to be changes in the text of "The Open Boat" that encourage our different perception of it. What we must not do is attribute these effects to an increase in qualities such as rhetoricity or fictionality, for as we have seen, "Stephen Crane's Own Story" is also literary on these grounds. Literature cannot be separated from other kinds of texts according to the numbers of rhetorical figures or invented characters, or, indeed, by making literariness an inherent property of the writing. (Texts do have qualities, but literariness is not one of them.)

There are changes in "The Open Boat" which we associate with our reading of fiction: besides the illusion of realism there are the conventions of closure and a complex system of narration (see Belsey 70ff.). In contrast to these features, "Stephen Crane's Own Story" follows the conventions of a particular kind of journalism, the survivor account, with its chronological story line (interrupted by foreshadowing and use of the pathetic fallacy), an account of the emotions produced by the escape from a tragedy that claimed others, and the dominant theme of blind luck or chance determining the outcome of events.

We are more apt to associate these conventions with journalism, but they are also likely to be adopted by a writer who is inventing his or her characters and setting; in that case, we would acknowledge their contribution to the verisimilitude of the story without confusing it with journalism. Similarly, when a journalist uses techniques we usually associate with fictional genres, such as naive narration, interior monologue, or extensive dialogue in a first-hand or eyewitness narrative, we may remark on the literariness of the writing without questioning its authenticity because it appears as a factual piece in a newspaper or other periodical.

Yet we may also read either example in such a way that the expectations which those conventions create are undercut or called into question, thus increasing the complexity, even tension, of the reading experience. For example, in "The Open Boat" we can note our inability to posit a specific persona as the source of the story, with the result that the "authority" of the whole is in doubt. Similarly, the journalist Stephen Crane who seems to be telling us "what really happened" to him as survivor of a shipwreck, but who leaves many gaps in the narrative and fails to explain the mystery surrounding the cause of the ship's foundering, raises nearly as many questions as he answers, a decidedly unjournalistic strategy. In short, if the differences in these two narratives are owing to conventions which we have reified into qualities of either journalism or fiction, we can change our hardened perception of them as two opposed categories of prose—and thus alter our interpretation—simply by noting the way the conventions undercut our expectations of journalism on the one hand, and a short story on the other.

Our first clue to what makes "The Open Boat" seem different from the journalistic narrative is the significant change from first person to third. This shift makes it possible for the implied author of the short story to vary the distance between the narrator and the character and events he is speaking about, and to mediate among the various discourses within the text. We can account for these effects by using descriptive linguistic categories developed by Emile Benveniste.

Benveniste makes a distinction between history (*histoire*) and discourse (*discours*) based on two systems of past tense for narrative in French (the simple past and the perfect) and on the corollary absence of the first and second persons in the simple past. Roland Barthes also has noted the effect of a distinctive past tense (with the accompanying use of third person) for written French texts (29–40). Although the distinction is not linguistically the same in English, the terms have also been used by contemporary theorists of narrative to distinguish between two types of narration: the story which seems to narrate itself without the intervention of a speaker, and the discourse of the narrator which implies a reader or listener and refers to the act of speaking (the enunciation) as such.

In Benveniste's explanation, in the system of historical narration (which uses primarily the simple past in the third person) "we can imagine the whole past of the world as being a continuous narration." The author remains "faithful to his historical purpose" and proscribes "everything that is alien to the narration (discourse, reflections, comparisons). As a matter of fact, there is then no longer even a narrator. The events are set forth chronologically, as they occurred. No one speaks here; the events seem to narrate themselves" (208).

In contrast, discourse assumes a speaker and a hearer and the speaker's "intention of influencing the other in some way." Obviously all kinds of oral discourse are intentional in this sense, and so are all the genres that derive from oral discourse, such as diaries, letters, autobiographical novels, "all the genres in which someone addresses himself to someone, proclaims himself as the speaker, and organizes what he says in the category of person" (208–9). The primary signals of discourse are either the first person or the perfect tense, but all tenses are possible, except the simple past, or aorist. When the simple past is used, the narration has shifted to *histoire*. Many such shifts are of course likely in any text, for pure historic narration cannot be maintained for very long; it is the dominance of one of these forms in a given genre or text that concerns us.

Despite the fact that English has no corollary literary tense, we can use the basic dichotomy of the two levels of narration (what Todorov in *The Poetics of Prose* calls the "two distinct levels of the speech-act") to explain our perception of two kinds of communication in realistic narratives, the transparent representation of "reality" (*histoire*) and the reference to the communication itself (discourse), which implies a speaker (a subject) and a listener. Todorov (*Poetics* 25) assures us that "each language possesses a certain number of elements which serve to inform us exclusively about the subject and the other elements of the speech-act and which effect the conversion of language into discourse; the others serve exclusively to 'present the phenomena which have occurred' [Benveniste's definition of *histoire*]."

It is this self-referential aspect of discourse that prevents the reader from regarding such prose as transparently "real," as Lionel Gossman emphasizes. "The tenses of [discourse] all maintain a relation to the present and direct attention to the subject, to the act of speaking (*l'énonciation*), and to the present relation between narrator or speaker and reader or listener, rather than exclusively to the events being narrated (*l'énoncé*)" (21).

"Stephen Crane's Own Story"

This description of discourse enables us to see why "Stephen Crane's Own Story" can be told chronologically, according to journalistic conventions, and yet achieve all the variety that shifting tenses makes possible. As Benveniste insists, the perfect is "the tense that will be chosen by whoever wishes to make the reported event ring vividly in our ears and to link it to the present" (210). This makes possible hindsight and foreshadowing, as when the three whistle blasts of the departing *Commodore* are remembered by the narrator as being impressively sad wails, and when the cook has premonitions of the ship's demise, even though he predicts that he and the narrator will meet again, "down at Coney Island, perhaps" (332, 335).

Another effect of the first-person narration, predominantly in the perfect, is that we know the source of the double view (of the past, from the platform of the present). It is always the journalist-narrator who speaks, even when he uses the simple past to relate events chronologically. The premonitions, interpretations of events, judgments, and so on, are always attributable to this voice, and it is also the source of the coherence of the narrative. Most importantly, the constant reminder of the speaker and his production of the story he tells so eloquently precludes our taking the events narrated to be the actuality. We are always aware that it is an interpretation, a version told from hindsight, although this realization does not detract from the narrative's vividness. The narrator does not assert "what actually happened," which is what we would expect twentieth-century "objective" journalism to claim,[7] but Crane's "own story," his subjective account.

When critics emphasize such features as the "tonal objectivity" of this report, in which Crane supposedly adopts a

---

7. For example, see the April 25, 1985, *New York Review of Books* cover featuring an essay which analyzes the shooting down of a Korean airliner over the USSR in 1983: "Murray Sayle Reveals *What Really Happened*" (italics added).

"reportorial stance" in order to suppress his emotions, particularly horror (Katz xvii), they seem to be ignoring its similarities to the short story he was to write in the next few weeks and the absence of the very journalistic conventions that would support their point. Indeed, they seem to locate in the newspaper account what their expectations of journalism lead them to find, for "Stephen Crane's Own Story" is not an example of the type of journalism which critics assert to be quite different from literature. It does not merely "present the phenomena which have occurred," as does so-called objective journalism, which is dominated by historic narration, but follows the traditions of late nineteenth-century personal reportage. Crane as narrator tells what he noticed (the chief engineer rushes to inform the captain that something bad has happened in the engine room), and how it impressed him (he was "affected" by the heat and hard work in the fireroom), but he does all this after the fact, and since it is not "what really happened" but only how it seemed to one person, he also gives us some means by which to evaluate it. He acknowledges the hindsight that may be influencing him, and assumes we know the facts from the main story, so that he can merely refer to incidents without explaining their significance. (We never find out, for example, what was wrong in the engine room, only that the men were forced to form bucket brigades to bail it and the fireroom; nor do we have any idea how long any of this lasted before the decision to abandon ship was made and everyone gotten off.)

The narrative's reliance on inference and its vagueness of reference have another effect, however. We realize that Crane is signifying the absence of meaning, of a determinate commonsense explanation, by his style: the lack of transitions, of time and place markers, and of explanations of various events. He conveys instead the confusion of being on the verge of an imminent disaster which no one will explain or even acknowledge. (Amidst talk of lowering the lifeboats, for example, an "unknown" man suggests sending up a flare to the mate, who replies, "What the hell do we want to send up a rocket for? The ship is all right" [337].) Crane has only fragmented knowledge of the crisis, and that is how it comes to us, piecemeal, instead of completed, filled out, explained and interpreted. This is not because the journalist is writing in a rush, unable to take the time to fill in details of what he knows; it is a conscious stylistic choice, for his account of going down the river toward the Atlantic is leisurely enough, and he gives quite full descriptions of natural phenomena and of the scene in the engine room.

> As darkness came upon the waters, the *Commodore* was a broad, flaming path of blue and silver phosphorescence, and as her stout bow lunged at the great black waves she threw flashing, roaring cascades to either side. (334)

> The engine room, by the way, represented a scene at this time taken from the middle kitchen of hades. In the first place, it was insufferably warm, and the lights burned faintly in a way to cause mystic and grewsome [*sic*] shadows. There was a quantity of soapish sea water swirling and sweeping and swishing among machinery that roared and banged and clattered and steamed. (336)

Crane also takes the time to develop comparisons and convey the physical ordeal of bailing and wrestling with the lifeboat, which "weighed as much as a Broadway cable car. She might have been spiked to the deck. We could have pushed a little brick schoolhouse along a corduroy road as easily as we could have moved this boat" (337).

But beginning with the ship's arrival in open seas, after she has twice ignominiously run aground in the river below Jacksonville, there is a steady fading away of any outline of what is happening. The journalist is unable to sleep, and he has premonitory conversations with the cook ("the old ship is going to get it in the neck, I think") and with Smith, who announces that this is his last trip, "if I ever get back safe this time" (335). Most of the action during the emergency is mysterious, including a censored conversation Crane has with the chief engineer about the man in the first boat with the mysterious valises and something which looked "like an overcoat":

I remarked to him:
   "What do you think of that blank, blank, blank?"
   "Oh, he's a bird," said the old chief. (337)

The final section, telling of the doomed men whom the captain tries to coax off the *Commodore* and onto makeshift rafts before the ship goes down, is all the more horrifying for its restraint, and for the scene's eerie silence: "This scene in the gray light of morning impressed one as would a view into some place where ghosts move slowly. These seven men on the stern of the sinking *Commodore* were silent. Save the words of the mate to the captain there was no talk" (340). Only four of the men jump. "On board the *Commodore* three men strode, still in silence and with their faces turned toward us. One man had his arms folded and was leaning against the deckhouse. His feet were crossed so that the toe of his left foot pointed downward. There they stood gazing at us, and neither from the deck nor from the rafts was a voice raised. Still was there this silence" (340–41). The men in the dinghy try vainly to tow the first raft ("a tugboat would have [had] no light task in moving these rafts"), when they suddenly realize they are going backward, because the man on it is pulling the line hand over hand in a frenzied attempt to get aboard the tiny boat. But "we were four men in a ten-foot boat, and we knew that the touch of a hand on our gunwale doomed us. ... The cook let go of the line. We rowed around to see if we could not get a line from the chief engineer [on the other raft], and all this time, mind you, there were no shrieks, no groans, but silence, silence and silence, and then the *Commodore* sank." That is all the narrator says, echoing the silence of the scene. "And then by the men on the ten-foot dingy [*sic*] were words said that were still not words—something far beyond words" (341).

That is the end of this particular story. Crane adds two paragraphs summarizing the fate of the four men in the dinghy and alludes to a possible "sequel": "The history of life in an open boat for thirty hours would no doubt be instructive for the young, but none is to be told here now" (342).

Conceding that there is a lesson to be learned from the experience the survivors were soon to undergo is not the same as drawing a moral from the story already told, however. In "Stephen Crane's Own Story" there is no closure, no statement of significance, and no answers, only questions. Catherine Belsey says that "the classic realist text moves inevitably and irreversibly to an end, to the conclusion of an ordered series of events, to the disclosure of what has been concealed" (105). "Stephen Crane's Own Story" does seem headed toward the point where the whole will be intelligible and order will be reinstated (some of the men will reach shore safely); but this return to security is only hinted at in the antepenultimate paragraph: "The lighthouse of Mosquito Inlet stuck up above the horizon like the point of a pin. We turned our dingy toward the shore" (341). However, the text never reaches that "point," instead breaking off to summarize briefly what happened afterward.

"Stephen Crane's Own Story" is naturalistically related, including dialogue, description, and concrete details, but the gaps in the narrative and the lack of explicit cause-effect relations, owing to the absence of historical narration (especially apparent once the ship is away from the security of shore), make it difficult for readers to experience it as a short story or "represented action."[8] According to Ralph Rader's refinement of this concept of an action of the "realism-plot-judgment" sort, "the author pits our induced sense of what will happen to a character against our induced sense of what we want to happen to him, our hopes against our fears, in order to give the greatest pleasure appropriate to their resolution" (34). Because of our experience of reading nonfiction novels and autobiographical novels, we know that this definition can apply equally to texts with historical referents, and from our comparison of Crane's newspaper story and "The Open Boat" we know that both use correct historical details, even proper

8. As Rader (33–34 and 67 n.3) explains the R. S. Crane-Sheldon Sacks concept of represented action, characters about whom "we are made to care" are placed in states of disequilibrium which are complicated and then resolved.

names. Therefore a journalistic narrative might fit this definition of short story or "nonfiction fiction"; and yet "Stephen
Crane's Own Story" does not. This should make us look even
more closely at the effects of the shift to third-person narration
(with its apparently transparent representation of reality) on
our perception of "The Open Boat" as fictional or literary.
Because we know that many individual features can occur in
either fiction and nonfiction (e.g., third-person transparent
narration, first person, closure, depth characterization, rhetorical patterning), these individual characteristics cannot be determining. There must be a complex set of variables that influence a reader to perceive a narrative as fictional.

As we saw in Benveniste's description, historical narration (*histoire*) is not limited to history but is also common in
the novel. This is another reason for the similarities between
the conventions of factual and fictional narratives: because
the "literary" mode of the simple past or preterite is common
to both, a story thus narrated appears authentic to the
reader whether events unfolding have happened or are only
imagined. We accept their existence and their significance.
The resultant authenticity hints at an ideological implication
of the system of historical, or impersonal, narration. As
Barthes suggests, when events are set down in sequence in
the preterite, they take on the appearance of being related
causally and of being ordered, even if they happen by
chance: "This is why it is the ideal instrument for every
construction of a world; it is the unreal time of cosmogonies,
myths, History and Novels. It presupposes a world which is
constructed, elaborated, self-sufficient, reduced to significant
lines, and not one which has been sent sprawling before us,
for us to take or leave" (30).

Now we can see the significance of the change to third-
person narration in "The Open Boat": it makes historical narration possible, and we have the introduction of a source which
becomes authoritative by hiding itself as discourse ("events
seem to narrate themselves"). It is an impersonal voice, not
attributable to the correspondent or any of the characters, or
even to the narrator of the discourse in other passages.

"The Open Boat"

The famous opening sentence of "The Open Boat"—"None of them knew the color of the sky"—is an apt example of this historical narration, which does not spring from a particular identifiable voice that calls attention to its status as discourse. So is the rest of the paragraph: "Their eyes glanced level, and were fastened upon the waves that swept toward them. These waves were of the hue of slate, save for the tops, which were of foaming white, and all of the men knew the colors of the sea. The horizon narrowed and widened, and dipped and rose, and at all times its edge was jagged with waves that seemed thrust up in points like rocks" (360). In the next paragraph the present-tense verb announces a shift to discourse, and we are aware of a narrator who is capable of reflection, comparison, and opinion: "Many a man ought to have a bath-tub larger than the boat which here rode upon the sea. These waves were most wrongfully and barbarously abrupt and tall, and each froth-top was a problem in small-boat navigation." This narrator is the source of the discourse spread throughout the text that expresses the gap between the way things ought to be and the way they are (certainly the boat is acting like a bathtub in holding water and "bathing" the men, but it "ought" not to). There are many examples of this particular discourse, such as this passage near the beginning: "A singular disadvantage of the sea lies in the fact that, after successfully surmounting one wave, you discover that there is another behind it, just as important and just as nervously anxious to do something effective in the way of swamping boats. In a ten-foot dinghy one can get an idea of the resources of the sea in the line of waves that is not probable to the average experience, which is never at sea in a dinghy" (361).

The third-person narration also makes it necessary to speak of the correspondent from the outside as one of four men in a small boat on the open sea (even though the narrator frequently has access to his thoughts), for the narrator here is not telling his "own story." This outside view occurs predominantly in the sections of historic narrative (as in paragraphs 3 to 5 that introduce the characters).

Although the narrator has regular access to only one of the men's minds, at times he is capable of surmising what the others are feeling. "As for the reflections of the men, there was a great deal of rage in them. Perchance they might be formulated thus: 'If I am going to be drowned—if I am going to be drowned—if I am going to be drowned, why, in the name of the seven mad gods who rule the sea, was I allowed to come thus far and contemplate sand and trees? Was I brought here merely to have my nose dragged away as I was about to nibble the sacred cheese of life?' " (369). When the sentiment recurs (at the end of part IV—374—and the beginning of part VI—377), it is not assigned to anyone, merely placed inside quotation marks. Is the narrator attributing the question to the correspondent, or to all the men?

This variation in point of view makes it possible to attribute a particular discourse to the correspondent or to the narrator. This is why careful attention must be paid to shifts in tense and to words that acknowledge the act of speaking like "then," "now," "at this time," and so on. Here is part of a paragraph which precedes the final run through the surf:

> The boat was headed for the beach. The correspondent wondered if none ever ascended the tall wind-tower, and if then they never looked seaward. This tower was a giant, standing with its back to the plight of the ants. It represented in a degree, to the correspondent, the serenity of nature amid the struggles of the individual—nature in the wind, and nature in the vision of men. She did not seem cruel to him then, nor beneficent, nor treacherous, nor wise. But she was indifferent, flatly indifferent. It is, perhaps, plausible that a man in this situation, impressed with the unconcern of the universe, should see the innumerable flaws of his life and have them taste wickedly in his mind and wish for another chance. A distinction between right and wrong seems absurdly clear to him, then, in this new ignorance of the grave-edge, and he understands that if he were given another opportunity he would mend his conduct and his words, and be better and brighter during an introduction or at a tea. (381)

The whole section beginning with "It is, perhaps, plausible
. . ." is the narrator's discourse (the "I" who speaks the
narrative as a whole, the subject of the enunciation); we
recognize it not only from the shift to present tense but
because we are by now (we are in part VII) beginning to
be familiar with the peculiar ironic attitude the narrator
takes toward the materials. It works much like the marginal
glosses in Coleridge's "Rime of the Ancient Mariner"—not
only to ensure our interpretation and focus the didactic
intention of the work itself, but to inflate the overt sentiments
and thus allow the internal, less pretentiously related actions
to become more acceptable because they seem more natural
and less subject to ironic treatment.

Distinctions among the discourses are important because,
as Barthes and others have pointed out, the historical narrative
becomes authoritative, the privileged "source of coherence"
of the whole, because it effaces itself as a discourse (Belsey 71–
72). In Barthes's words, as "the cornerstone of Narration," the
preterite (or in English the third-person "impersonal" narrator) "aims at maintaining a hierarchy in the realm of facts"
(30). In general, the use of the impersonal narration implies
that all accidents of chance or fate have meaning simply because they are told, explained in a story. In this particular text,
significance is imposed on a sequence of random, meaningless
occurrences by the very act of relating them in a coherent
pattern whose emptiness is not apparent unless the last sentence is read ironically: "When it came night, the white waves
paced to and fro in the moonlight, and the wind brought the
sound of the great sea's voice to the men on shore, and they
felt that they could then be interpreters" (386).

This is quite unlike Crane's newspaper version, his
"owned" story, which has an identifiable narrator (the persona
of Crane the journalist) who is responsible for the story. In
"The Open Boat," there is no responsibility taken for reporting events, and this absence of reference to the narrative situation in the historical narration, coupled with the illusion of
realistic representation and the tendency to reconcile the contradictory elements in a rounded-off ending, fixes the world

Phyllis Frus

the way it is depicted here, and the reader tends to accept it as presented (Belsey 70ff.).

It is because of these characteristics that readers designate (although they probably would say "recognize") a work like "The Open Boat" as fiction, whereas they are characteristics not limited to fiction—any realistic narrative can exhibit them.

Many histories are mimetic representations of a world they posit *a priori*; they use historic narration to affirm the existence of that external world and to "place" the other discourses they contain in order to reinforce that belief; and they aim for intelligibility of their materials, or closure. No matter how revolutionary the society being described or how much turmoil reigns in events at the end of a narrated sequence, when the text of almost any historical narrative comes to an end, *its* order is affirmed or reestablished according to its structuring conception, and its loose ends are tied up, usually in a "conclusion."

These characteristics—illusion of reality, closure, and a historical narration which orders the other discourses—doubtless produce the traditional interpretations of "The Open Boat," those that see the oiler's death as "redeem[ing] the significance of life," or the story as unified by Crane's "understanding of the indifference of Nature that comes to men through the comradeship of suffering, through the meaningless confusion of death" (Katz xviii; Going 82). The story is also generally regarded as an accurate re-creation of men's actions in adversity, revealing "just how it happened, and how [it] felt."[9] However, these readings may simply be a function of the reader's desire for coherence and satisfaction rather than being provided by the text, and this desire may be fulfilled by the very expectations of resolution and unity that we bring to texts designated as fiction or literature. In other words, reading a realistic narrative that has been presented as a short

9. These are supposedly Captain Murphy's words, assuring Crane that he had written "The Open Boat" accurately. He was overheard by journalist Ralph Paine, who recorded the incident in *Roads of Adventure*. (See Stallman 257.)

144

story, as literature, predisposes us to regard it as inherently significant and unified and as the representation of an intelligible world governed by causality and corresponding to the one we think we know.

Having discovered the characteristics of a classically realistic text in "The Open Boat," however, we do not have to accept the inevitability of these effects, for the unity of the text is encouraged primarily by the historic narration and by the closure it produces, and we can allow other elements present in the text to disrupt this level, open up the finality, and untie the unity. In an open reading, the traditional "meaning" is undermined by the contradictory elements within: primarily the pervasive irony of situation and of language commenting on itself, and secondarily the tropes of emptiness and absence. To make this truly "open 'Boat'" possible, we must be alert to the multiplicity of discourses and the possibility of reading them as contributing to the diversity and self-contradiction of the text. This will make the short story more like the newspaper version (in its avoidance of disclosure and certainty)—not less fictional, but less a text of high realism and with all the difference in ideology that an open, skeptical reading implies.

Because the historical narration does not call attention to itself as merely one version or interpretation but, by disguising its status, asserts the authority of what it indicates, in the traditional unified reading the illusion created by the realistic narration is asserted as the way the world objectively is, and the ending of the story resolves all the difficulties, even the death of the oiler, and re-establishes reason and order. The disruption of order revealed in the physical and emotional distress of the four men at sea in a pathetically vulnerable craft and the discord felt between the men in their plight and their ignorant fellows on shore who are oblivious of their predicament has been for a purpose: they have learned a lesson about brotherhood in the face of adversity. As this reading insists, although nature is "flatly indifferent" (as well as splendid and "serene amid the struggles of the individual"), those who have suffered but held together can be "interpreters." That is, they will mediate between the emptiness of a blank universe and their fellows who desire to understand, to know the meaning, although the only way to do this in a comforting way would be to be deceptive about what "the great sea's voice" said to them.

In this reading, the oiler's death is sacrificial, a propitiation of nature, which if not cruel, is at least cold and relentless. Evidence for this interpretation is the symbolism of the oiler's "thin little oar, . . . often ready to snap" (360), his being the only character given a "proper" name, his peacemaking (end of part I), his placid response to being inadvertently drenched (376), his selfless service to the others (emphasized by the repeated "Billie, will you spell me?" of the correspondent), as well as his savvy in boat handling and strength in leading the swim toward shore. All these virtues make his death even more ironic, and by the conventions of traditional realistic fiction, his death must mean something, especially considering the brotherhood that has arisen among the men (part III).

What contradicts this traditional interpretation is the pervasive undercutting of conventional sentiments, especially in the narrator's discourse, which emphasizes the contrast between the ridiculously inappropriate boat and the conditions surrounding it (360–62); and the frequent irony of language (as in the cook's reiterated "funny they don't see us"). There is also the reminder by the narrator of the absurd timing of disasters and of the fact that some men row for amusement, which seems a preposterous recreation to the correspondent now, as well it might (371). Then there is irony of situation: each hope turns out to be empty or meaningless, as the lighthouse they have aimed for marks no life-saving station, the house of refuge shows no signs of life, and no one comes from the seaside village to aid them. The helpless waifs can see potential rescuers on the beach, but their appearance to those on land is interpreted incorrectly—if they are noticed at all. A man waves his coat as if signaling to them, but the signal turns out to be meaningless to their situation, if indeed it *is* a signal. Perhaps he sees them but believes them to be out fishing or for other pleasure and mistakes their signal for a friendly wave.[10] Whatever their true significance, the man's motions turn out to be an empty sign to the men in the boat, a sign which infuriates by its very arbitrariness. Things *ought* to be what they seem.

> "I'd like to catch the chump who waved the coat. I feel like soaking him one, just for luck."
> "Why? What did he do?"
> "Oh, nothing, but then he seemed so damned cheerful."
> (374)

Critics have commented on the vividness of this dialogue among the four men as they first catch sight of the man, speculate about whether or not he sees them, contrive a signal to wave at him, soar with the hope that he is signing to them and that the object they can make out is a lifeboat on wheels rather than the omnibus it is, and then crash with the frustrated realization that they have not been seen and will have to "flounder out here all night," as one of them says. What is not usually noticed is that none of the fifty-three exchanges that form most of part IV is attributed to an individual speaker. This makes the men interchangeable, without individuality or uniqueness. We have no way of knowing who says what because they all talk alike. Because this works against depth of characterization and the assertion of individual identity, it is one more element that contradicts the certainty of the traditional reading.

Besides being a technical tour de force, this dialogue stands for the human propensity for attributing meaning to essentially arbitrary or even meaningless signs. When this tendency is elevated to a belief system, it becomes the basis for humanism. Like the narrator who says "they felt that they could then be interpreters," like the traditional readers of the story, like the men, we anthropomorphize natural forces,

---

10. One cannot help recalling two lines from Stevie Smith's poem "Not Waving but Drowning" (1957): "I was much farther out than you thought / And not waving but drowning."

attribute cause and effect to random events, and see meaning
where there is none in our desire for rescue from uncharted
oceans, for safety and security. Like us, the men strive to
interpret signs favorable to their cause, and they admit the
emptiness of gestures—their ludicrous and capricious qualities—only with terrible reluctance. Because the text does not
reward the tendency to assert meaning in the face of meaninglessness, we ought to question the sense of closure we experience on first reading.

Indeed, despite the many contradictions of certainty
within the text, the signs of absence or indifference in nature,
and the implication that there is no objective reality outside
that created by men, the narrative attempts an intelligible
ending with the assertion of a personified nature: the waves
pace and the sea has a voice of which the three survivors "can
then be interpreters." Because of the emptiness at the heart
of the text, however, we should wonder how they will repro-
duce for others what the sea says. How does one translate
nothingness? Perhaps this is the real significance of the ending,
that meaning is asserted but not demonstrated: the text ends
at the point where the interpretation should begin, perhaps
by showing the survivors accosting a wedding guest and holding him in thrall while they tell their tale. We might note that
this is also how "Stephen Crane's Own Story" ends: on the
verge of an interpretation and a lesson, which is then deferred.
Similarly, although the means are different, both narratives
avoid attributing significance to what is only difference, meaning to what is only a sign.

From these paired texts we see that the attribution of
superior, universal qualities to literary examples has consequences for our interpretations equal to the corollary devalua-
tion of nonliterary or factual genres. It is appropriate to consider "The Open Boat" one of the finest stories in American
literature, but regarding a short story as a masterpiece should
not keep us from questioning the certitude it seems to offer.
Perhaps Crane thought we would hear in the subtitle echoes
of "a tale . . . full of sound and fury, / Signifying nothing."
The reader is of course free to hear them whether intended

or not, in which case they further undercut the human tendency to give meaning to signs, and remind us of the "sound of the great sea's voice" that the wind brought to these men, who had already learned of the absence at the heart of nature's signifying system, the emptiness of natural signs. After all, "none of them knew the color of the sky."

But if changing our expectations of the "The Open Boat" affects our interpretation of it, the change in our attitude toward "Stephen Crane's Own Story" resulting from considering it as carefully as we do literary works is even greater. As we saw, its appeal to permanence and originality is made by the way it questions the reality of its own illusion and by the way it subverts the reader's expectation of journalism's "five W's" and requires us to fill in gaps left by incomplete explanation—which we are able to do from our experience of reading not only news accounts but other narratives, such as adventure stories. Although "Stephen Crane's Own Story" is no more tied to an empirical reality than is "The Open Boat," we tend to give it a very a different response the moment we recognize it as a journalistic account. And yet, all that is required to read journalism and all "true-life" texts as literary is a willingness to accept them as such, as a form of discourse not intrinsically different from other forms, and to pay attention to the particular conventions being either invoked or violated. Or we may simply disregard the journalistic context, which is easier to do when we read it in an anthology, and read it by adopting the conventions with which we read fiction.[11]

There is certainly room for both narratives in the Crane canon, and I would not teach the "The Open Boat" in any

11. The frame is also important in setting up expectations and giving us reading "instructions." In this regard it is interesting to consider the first publication of "The Open Boat." It was not the practice of *Scribner's* in 1897 to distinguish between fiction and nonfiction, and so nowhere in the June issue is there the label "a short story by Stephen Crane." Instead, after the title and by-line appears the subhead: "A Tale Intended To Be After the Fact: Being the Experience of Four Men from the Sunk Steamer *Commodore*." There is no distinguishing sign to enable the magazine's readers to regard the account as anything but factual narrative before they began to read.

Phyllis Frus

literature or writing course without also assigning the earlier, reportorial version. What this changed conception of literature might mean for our histories of American literature remains to be seen.

Works Cited

Althusser, Louis. "Ideology and Ideological State Apparatuses." *Lenin and Philosophy and Other Essays*. Trans. Ben Brewster. London: Monthly Review Press, 1971. 127–86.

Barthes, Roland. *Writing Degree Zero*. Trans. Annette Lavers and Colin Smith. New York: Hill and Wang, 1967.

Belsey, Catherine. *Critical Practice*. London: Methuen, 1980.

Benveniste, Emile. "The Correlations of Tense in the French Verb." *Problems in General Linguistics*. Trans. Mary Elizabeth Meek. Coral Gables: U of Miami P, 1971. 205–15.

Cady, Edwin H. *Stephen Crane*. Rev. ed. Boston: Twayne, 1980.

Carter, Everett. *Howells and the Age of Realism*. Philadelphia: Lippincott, 1954.

Corkin, Stanley. "Motion Pictures: Fixing a Definition of the Real." *ETC* 42:2 (Summer 1985): 170–75.

———. "Realism and Cultural Form." Diss. New York University, 1984.

Culler, Jonathan. *Structuralist Poetics*. Ithaca: Cornell UP, 1975.

Fishkin, Shelley Fisher. *From Fact to Fiction*. Baltimore: Johns Hopkins UP, 1985.

Going, William T. "William Higgins and Crane's 'The Open Boat': A Note about Fact and Fiction." *PLL* 1 (1965): 79–82.

Gossman, Lionel. "History and Literature." *The Writing of History*. Ed. Robert H. Canary and Henry Kozicki. Madison: U of Wisconsin P, 1978.

Hemingway, Ernest. *By-Line: Ernest Hemingway*. Ed. William White. New York: Scribner's, 1967.

Hofstadter, Richard. *The Age of Reform*. New York: Knopf, 1981.

"Invention." *Princeton Encyclopedia of Poetry and Poetics*. Ed. Alex Preminger. Princeton: Princeton UP, 1965.

Katz, Joseph. *The Portable Stephen Crane*. Ed. Joseph Katz. New York: Penguin, 1969.

McQuade, Donald, and Robert Atwan, eds. *Popular Writing in America*. 2nd ed. New York: Oxford, 1980.

Rader, Ralph. "Defoe, Richardson, Joyce and the Concept of Form in the Novel." *Autobiography, Biography and the Novel.* By William Matthews and Ralph Rader. Berkeley: U of California P, 1973.

Rondel, William. "From Slate to Emerald Green: More Light on Crane's Jacksonville Visit." *Nineteenth-Century Fiction* 19 (1965): 357–68.

Sacks, Sheldon. *Fiction and the Shape of Belief.* Berkeley: U of California P, 1964.

Schudson, Michael. *Discovering the News.* New York: Basic Books, 1978.

Stallman, R. W. *Stephen Crane: A Biography.* New York: Braziller, 1968.

———, and E. R. Hagemann, eds. *The War Dispatches of Stephen Crane.* New York: NYU Press, 1964.

Todorov, Tzvetan. "The Notion of Literature." *NLH* 5 (1973): 5–16.

———. *The Poetics of Prose.* Trans. Richard Howard. London: Blackwell, 1977.

Wellek, René. "What Is Literature?" *What Is Literature?* Ed. Paul Hernadi. Bloomington: Indiana UP, 1978.

———, and Austin Warren. *Theory of Literature.* 3rd ed. New York: Harcourt, 1962.

PART TWO

Generalizations and Definitions

8
ESSAYISTS ON THE ESSAY

Carl H. Klaus

Five years ago, I set out to design a graduate course on the nature of the essay, a course in which I hoped to engage students in a theoretical investigation of the form.[1] As a preliminary part of my planning, I went off to the library and the MLA Bibliography to compile a reading list, only to discover that I was venturing into territory that literary and rhetorical theorists had barely set foot on, much less explored in any systematic way. Oh yes, I found learned studies of Montaigne, Addison and Steele, Lamb, the eighteenth-century periodical essay, the Romantic personal essay, the modern essay. But the essay itself, the whole territory—its boundaries, its terrain, its deep interior—that was a place only a few scholars had chosen to visit. It remains almost as uncharted today, except for a lengthy review article by Chadbourne, documenting how little has been done not only in America, but also in England and on the Continent, to map the world of the essay and develop a theory of its form. So it is that I decided to consult the essayists themselves as an alternative source of commentary on the form.

At the beginning of my search, I already had on hand several passages and pieces about the essay, from Johnson's dictionary definition of it as "a loose sally of the mind" to White's celebration of it as the "excursion" of "a self-liberated man" (vii), so I had reason to hope that I might find several more. Since that time, I have collected material by some forty essayists, as varied as Montaigne, Bacon, Addison, Johnson,

1. This study was completed with the assistance of an Old Gold Summer Fellowship (1987), for which I am grateful to the University of Iowa.

Carl H. Klaus

Hazlitt, Lamb, Thoreau, Howells, Lukacs, Woolf, Priestley, Chesterton, Krutch, Daiches, Huxley, Adorno, Kazin, Hoagland, White, Thomas, Gass, and Hardwick. Some of their comments are as brief as Bacon's aphorisms, some as ample as the habitual digressions of Montaigne. Some of their remarks come in the form of prefaces, others in the form of reviews. But most of their commentary is to be found in essays entirely devoted to the essay. The essay on the essay, it would seem, is a subgenre itself, as Hilaire Belloc implied when he wrote "An Essay upon Essays upon Essays."

All in all, these self-reflexive statements and pieces engage a wide range of issues and problems concerning the purpose of the essay, the subject matter of the essay, the form of the essay, the length of the essay, the variety of the essay, the essay and other forms of writing, the style of the essayist, the voice of the essayist, the personality of the essayist, the mind of the essayist, the knowledge of the essayist, the composing process of the essayist, the essayist and the reader, the essayist and the culture, the essayist and the journalist, the essayist and the critic, the essayist and the scholar, the essayist and truth. Varied as the essayists are in the topics they discuss, the contexts of their discourse, and the backgrounds they bring to the discussion, they seem to me to hold surprisingly similar ideas about the essay—ideas strikingly at odds with notions of it that are purveyed by most literary guidebooks and composition textbooks.

The harmony I perceive in their thinking first caught my attention when I noticed a tendency among essayists from every period and culture to define the essay, or their own essayistic practice, by setting it off against highly conventionalized and systematized forms of writing, such as rhetorical, scholarly, or journalistic discourse. So, too, I repeatedly found them invoking images and metaphors suggestive of the essay's naturalness, openness, or looseness as opposed to the methodicality, regularity, and strictly ordered quality of conventional prose discourse.[2] Montaigne, of course, is the first to make

2. Of the essayists whose comments I have gathered thus far, only Thoreau does not concur in seeing the essay as a natural or open form of

such a contrast: "The scholars distinguish and mark off their ideas more specifically and in detail. I, who cannot see beyond what I have learned from experience, without any system, present my ideas in a general way, and tentatively. As in this: I speak my meaning in disjointed parts . . ." (824). Given Montaigne's well known commitment to follow "my natural and ordinary pace, however off the track it is," "to let myself go as I am" (297), to "seek out change indiscriminately" (761), it was hardly surprising to me that he should make such a contrast between the scholars and himself, between their "system" and his "disjointed parts." But Montaigne's "disjointed parts" also led me to think of the phrases that Bacon uses to describe his aphoristic essays—"dispersed meditations" (239) and "fragments of my conceites" (238)—phrases which suggest that at least in describing their essayistic practice these two might not be quite so different as they are often made out to be. Indeed, in *The Advancement of Learning,* Bacon concludes a brisk defense of aphoristic over methodical writing with a pithy antithesis which makes clear that for him, as for Montaigne, the essay is neither a mode of proof, nor of persuasion, but of inquiry: "And lastly, aphorisms, representing a knowledge broken, do invite men to inquire further; whereas methods, carrying the show of a total, do secure men, as if they were at furthest" (173). Montaigne, admittedly, is concerned with reflecting his own process of inquiry, whereas Bacon aims to provoke inquiry in others. Yet both essayists describe their practice in terms that emphatically distinguish essayistic form and purpose from the methodical discourse that dominated classical rhetoric and medieval scholasticism.

The persistence, indeed the codification, of this contrast can be seen in a surprising statement from one of Addison's *Spectator* papers: "Among my Daily-Papers, which I bestow on the Publick, there are some which are written with Regularity and Method, and others that run out into the Wildness of

---

writing, but his divergence is occasioned only by a preference for the even "more simple, less artful" way of communicating thoughts in his journal (III: 239).

those Compositions, which go by the Name of Essays" (IV: 186). When I first read this passage, I was struck by the sharpness with which Addison formulates the distinction between "Regularity and Method" on the one hand, and "Wildness" on the other, as well as by the detail with which he develops the contrast in the remainder of the piece. But a later reading led me to see that this brief passage also contains a notable revelation—that, contrary to prevailing descriptions of his work, Addison does not classify all of his *Spectator* papers as essays. Anything "written with Regularity and Method," as he indicates elsewhere, he considers to be "a Set Discourse" (II: 465); thus he only applies "the name of *Essays*" to papers that "run out into . . . Wildness." Addison's keen awareness of the differences in his two kinds of papers can be seen in the clear-cut contrast he draws between the composing processes he follows in each case: "As for the first, I have the whole Scheme of the Discourse in Mind, before I set Pen to Paper. In the other kind of Writing, it is sufficient that I have several Thoughts on a Subject, without troubling myself to range them in such order, that they may seem to grow out of one another, and be disposed under the proper Heads" (IV: 186). And to solidify the contrast, he identifies the precedents for each type: "*Seneca* and *Montaigne* are patterns of writing in this last Kind, as *Tully* and *Aristotle* excel in the other" (IV: 186). Indeed, given his neoclassical bias, Addison goes on to make a detailed case for "Methodical Discourse," arguing that in this form an author's "thoughts are more intelligible and better discover their Drift and Meaning . . . than when they are thrown together without Order and Connexion" (IV: 186). The firmness with which Addison distinguished between his two types of *Spectator* papers can be seen in an earlier formulation of virtually the same contrast: "When I make Choice of a Subject that has not been treated of by others, I throw together my Reflections on it without any Order or Method, so that they may appear rather in the Looseness and Freedom of an Essay than in the Regularity of a Set Discourse" (II: 465). Here, too, as in the other discussion of his composing process,

Addison reveals that despite his neoclassical allegiance to "Order or Method," he knows enough from his firsthand experience of writing to acknowledge that the essay allows him the "Freedom" to explore ideas, to engage material "that has not been treated of by others."

Having put together this small segment in a history of ideas of the essay, I realized that Johnson's well-known dictionary definition, though often cited as a striking invention, is actually an ingenious condensation of received ideas about its form. Johnson's complete definition, in fact, concludes with an antithesis that closely echoes Addison's version of the contrast, as well as Addison's neoclassical preference for methodical discourse: "an irregular, indigested piece, not a regular, orderly performance." But Johnson, too, is so widely experienced a writer that when he turns to thinking about the essay in detail, at the opening of a piece for *The Rambler,* he also recognizes the special advantages of the essay over methodical forms of writing:

> The writer of essays escapes many embarrassments to which a large work would have exposed him; he seldom harasses his reason with long trains of consequences, dims his eyes with the perusal of antiquated volumes, or burthens his memory with great accumulations of preparatory knowledge. A careless glance upon a favourite author, or transient survey of the varieties of life, is sufficient to supply the first hint or seminal idea, which enlarged by the gradual accretion of matter stored in the mind, is by the warmth of fancy easily expanded into flowers, and sometimes ripened into fruit. (201)

Indeed, as if to enact this stylized vision of an essay's accidental, easy and natural gestation—from a "careless glance" to a "seminal idea" to a "ripened . . . fruit"—Johnson expands his seminal idea about the essay into two paragraphs of reflection on the unpredictable and uncontrollable aspects of essay writing, which in turn lead into a meditative essay on the uncertainties of life.

By this point in my story, it might seem that the contrast itself has become so conventionalized as to be a mere commonplace, a convenient but largely formulaic way of writing about the essay or launching an essay upon some other subject. Yet, its persistence over so long a period of time—not only from Montaigne to Johnson, but from Johnson to the present—suggests that it must contain a significant element of truth, or belief, or value for those who invoke it.[3] In this case, it seems to be an inescapable, even imperative, way for these essayists to define and affirm what they also refer to as the "freedom" of the essay—its independence from the strictures and structures that govern other forms of discourse. Their preoccupation with this quality is reflected in the numerous synonyms and metaphors for freedom that pervade their comments. Howells, for example, refers to the essay's "essential liberty" (802), Chesterton to its "leisure and liberty" (2), Williams to its "infinite fracture" (323), Kazin to its "open form" (ix), Hoagland to its "extraordinary flexibility" (27), Lopate to its "wonderfully tolerant form" (1), Epstein to its "generous boundaries" (34), and Hardwick to its "open spaces" (xiv). By persistently invoking such expansive phrases along with such a sharp contrast, these essayists seem to be conceiving of the essay as a unique genre—a form of writing whose distinguishing characteristic is its freedom from any governing aspect of form. Strictly speaking, then, they seem to be portraying it as an antigenre, a rogue form of writing in the universe of discourse. Or as Adorno puts it, "the law of the innermost form of the essay is heresy" (171).

This conception of the essay, as antigenre, can also be seen in a very pointed contrast between the essay and the article that has dominated the thinking of essayists through-

3. The compelling appeal that this contrast has had for essayists may be seen in the shaping influence that it evidently had on Lamb's Elian persona, as he makes clear in "Imperfect Sympathies," when he distinguishes between "imperfect intellects (under which mine must be content to rank)" and "systematizers," between those whose "minds" are "suggestive" and those whose minds are "comprehensive," between those who "are content with fragments and scattered pieces of Truth" and those who strive for "ideas in perfect order and completeness" (Essays 69–70).

out the twentieth century. So pervasive is this distinction in their commentary that it seems to have the status for them of a self-evident truth. The earliest explicit use of it that I have been able to find occurs in a column by Howells, dating from 1902, in which he laments the time "when the essay began to confuse itself with the article, and to assume an obligation to premises and conclusions" (802). Though Howells does not venture to say when the change took place, he clearly contrasts the article's "premises and conclusions" with the essay's "wandering airs of thought" (802). This echoing of the persistent dichotomy between methodical and natural discourse, between strict and open form, can also be heard in more recent versions of the contrast between essay and article. Krutch, for example, calls the essay "man-made as opposed to the machine-made article" (19); Hoagland, in a similar spirit, asserts that "Essays don't usually boil down to a summary, as articles do, and the style of the writer has a 'nap' to it, a combination of personality and originality and energetic loose ends that stand up like the nap on a piece of wool and can't be brushed flat" (25–26). As these examples suggest, the contrast of essay and article is often defined in terms of a dichotomy between organic and mechanistic form, and by extension as an epitome of the conflict between humanistic and technological values.

The point of contrast that arouses modern essayists more than any other, however, is the distinction they make between the personal orientation of the essay and the factual orientation of the article. As Weeks puts it, the essay "does not deal in statistics or belabor an argument as does a magazine article. . . . The essay is an experience which you the reader share with the writer—you share his laughter, delight, or pity; you share a deepened understanding or a quickening of the spirit in a style that does not date" (81). In one form or another, this particular dichotomy is discussed more intensely and at greater length than any other issue they engage. Some of the intensity can be traced to the fact that modern essayists have perennially witnessed editors and readers being lured away

Carl H. Klaus

from the essay by the utilitarian appeal of the article.[4] Indeed, as early as 1881, Stephen considered "our magazines and journals" to be so "radically changed" that it was "easier to write about essay-writing than to write an essay oneself" (65). With the onset of World War I, and the numerous economic, political, and social upheavals that followed, magazine editors found themselves compelled to satisfy a persistent demand for highly informed articles about the most pressing and complex issues of the day. By the early 1930s, the changing editorial policies had become so widespread that essayists such as Gerould openly spoke out against "the spectacle of the old-line magazines forsaking their literary habit, and stuffing us month after month, with facts, figures, propaganda, and counter-propaganda . . ." (Information 393). By the early 1950s, Krutch considered the situation to be so far gone that "The very word essay . . . is avoided with horror, and anything which is not fiction is usually called either an 'article,' a 'story,' or just 'a piece' " (18).

The essayists' quarrel with the article, though obviously provoked in part by the competition for magazine space, seems to be rooted in their opposition to the fact-dominated conception of knowledge they perceive in the article. This opposition is reflected in their tendency to portray the article as being so heavily made up of "facts," "figures," and "statistics" that it allows no room for the personal experience, personal thought, or personal voice of the essayist. Given this extreme dichotomy, they depict the article, in turn, as being out of touch with human concerns. As Krutch puts it, "The magazines are full of articles dealing statistically with, for example, the alleged failure or success of marriage. Lawyers discuss the law, sociologists publish statistics, and psychologists discuss case histories,"

4. See Rucker for a highly detailed account of the essay's declining appeal during the first half of the twentieth century. Given her restricted historical orientation, she necessarily interprets the conflict between essay and article as a distinctly modern phenomenon, rather than as a twentieth century manifestation of a long-standing conflict between the essay and methodical discourse.

but "one man's 'familiar essay' on love and marriage might get closer to some all-important realities than any number of 'studies' could" (19). Krutch's remarks also reveal that their skepticism is aroused not so much by a scorn of facts per se as by a distrust of specialized "studies," whose heavy reliance on factual information they regard as symptomatic of an ill-placed confidence in the reliability of highly systematized—and thus highly impersonal—approaches to knowledge. Ultimately, then, they seem to be implying that the article embodies a naively positivistic approach to knowledge, an approach that fails to recognize the essentially problematical nature of things. Gass is especially emphatic on this score in his satiric portrait of the scholarly article: "It must appear complete and straightforward and footnoted and useful and certain and is very likely a veritable Michelin of misdirection; for the article pretends that everything is clear, that its argument is unassailable, that there are no soggy patches, no illicit inferences, no illegitimate connections . . ." (25). In keeping with his attack on the certitudes of the article, Gass portrays the essay by contrast as having a distinterested engagement in the play of ideas, and thus as making no special claims about the truth of its observations: "The essay is unhurried (although Bacon's aren't); it browses among books; it enjoys an idea like a fine wine; it thumbs through things. It turns round and round upon its topic, exposing this aspect and then that; proposing possibilities, reciting opinions, disposing of prejudice and even of the simple truth itself—as too undeveloped, not yet of an interesting age" (25). This conception of the essay, as embodying an inherently skeptical, and therefore antimethodical, approach to knowledge, is most fully developed by Adorno, who offers a seemingly inexhaustible set of variations on the theme of the essay's "heresy":

> Luck and play are essential to the essay (152). The essay does not obey the rules of the game of organized science . . . the essay does not strive for closed, deductive or inductive, construction (158). As the essay denies any primeval givens, so it refuses any definitions of its concepts (159). In the essay, concepts do not

Carl H. Klaus

> build a continuum of operations, thought does not advance in
> a single direction, rather the aspects of the argument inter-
> weave as in a carpet (160). The essay . . . proceeds so to speak
> methodically unmethodically (161). Discontinuity is essential to
> the essay (164).

Radical as these statements are in their rebellion against any systematized form of thought, they are, I think, no more extreme than Montaigne's contrast between the "system" of "the scholars" and his "disjointed parts," or than Johnson's contrast between the scholar's "long train of consequences" and the essayist's "fancy." Indeed, the continuity of their thought is reflected in Adorno's equation of "the neopositivists," whom he opposes, "with Scholasticism," to which Montaigne contrasted himself (160). Whereas both the neopositivists and scholastics adhere to "the traditional concept of method," the essay, according to Adorno, "takes the anti-systematic impulse into its own procedure" (160). So, the history of ideas of the essay comes full circle, and in doing so it calls attention, I believe, to the essayists' profound motive for persistently drawing so sharp a contrast between the essay and methodical prose discourse. By virtue of being free from the systematized form of such discourse, the essay offers a means of liberating the essayist from the systematized form of thinking imposed by such discourse. Thus, Montaigne declares "My Style and my mind alike go roaming" (761). So, too, Hoagland asserts that "because essays are directly concerned with the mind and the mind's idiosyncracy, the very freedom the mind possesses is bestowed on this branch of literature that does honor to it, and the fascination of the mind is the fascination of the essay" (27). Ultimately, then, the essayists seem to conceive of the essay as a place of intellectual refuge, a domain sacred to the freedom of the mind itself.

Given this conception, some readers, I imagine, must be wondering how essayists account for the formal essay—that type of prose in which "the author," according to Abrams, "writes as an authority, or at least as highly knowledgeable, and expounds the subject in an orderly way." Surprising as it

164

may be, this long-honored subgenre, which repeatedly turns up in literary handbooks, histories, and encyclopedias, does not seem to figure in the thinking of essayists, not even in the thinking of Hazlitt and Stephen, who survey the work of their predecessors and thus might be inclined to organize their surveys in terms of a distinction between it and the informal essay. In fact, this commonplace distinction is discussed only by Lopate, and he brings it up only to call it into question, noting that "it is difficult even now to draw a firm distinction between the two, because elements of one often turn up in the other, and because most of the great essayists were adept at both modes" (1). The closest that any of the others comes to making such a distinction is when Epstein mentions in passing that "there are formal essays and familiar essays" (27), or when Smith declares that "Bacon is the greatest of the serious and stately essayists—Montaigne the greatest of the garrulous and communicative" (40), or when Huxley distinguishes among three different kinds of essays—those that focus primarily on "the personal and the autobiographical," those that turn their attention outward to the "concrete-particular" aspects of "some literary or scientific or political theme," and those that "work in the world of high abstractions" (v–vi). But in elaborating their distinctions, neither Smith nor Huxley refers to the "formal" essay, or to any of the logical, systematic, and tightly organized qualities that are usually associated with it. Ultimately, most essayists simply do not recognize such a thing as the formal essay, presumably because it embodies the very antithesis of what they conceive an essay to be. They recognize, of course, that Bacon's manner is highly impersonal, and that he inclines to "work in the world of high abstractions," but they do not seem to think of him as having established a particular type of essay.

Most essayists, in fact, do not tend to classify essays at all, and the few who do make gestures in that direction offer little more than loose classificatory listings, such as Epstein's assertion that "there are literary essays, political essays, philosophical essays, and historical essays" (27), or Hardwick's observation that "most incline to a condition of unexpressed hyphenation: the critical essay, the autobiographical essay, the travel essay, the political—and so on and so on" (xiii). Classifications more rigorous than these would be inconsistent with the essayists' basic view of the essay as being deeply allied to the free play of thought and feeling. Accordingly, Epstein observes that "The essay is in large part defined by the general temperament of the essayist" (27). In keeping with this view, White playfully suggests the hopelessness of trying to classify essays, for, as he sees it, "There are as many kinds of essays as there are human attitudes or poses, as many essay flavors as there are Howard Johnson ice creams" (vii). In much the same spirit, Montaigne conveys the hopelessness of trying to classify human character and behavior: "I do not attempt to arrange this infinite variety of actions, so diverse and so disconnected, into certain types and categories, and distribute my lots and divisions distinctly into recognized classes and sections" (824). As these passages suggest, the antimethodical impulse of essay-ists probably also has something to do with their tendency to stay away from elaborate systems of classification.

Though they oppose methodical discourse, the essayists are careful to make clear that they consider the essay to be a highly disciplined form of writing. Indeed, their insistence on its freedom from conventionalized form and thought probably makes them all the more intent on dispelling any notion that the essay is a free-for-all form of writing. White is especially pointed on this issue: "And even the essayist's escape from discipline is only a partial escape: the essay, although a relaxed form, imposes its own disciplines, raises its own problems, and these disciplines and problems soon become apparent and (we all hope) act as a deterrent to anyone wielding a pen merely because he entertains random thoughts or is in a happy or wandering mood" (viii). Montaigne, "disjointed" though he professes himself to be, also sounds the same note of caution: "I go out of my way, but rather by license than carelessness. My ideas follow one another, but sometimes it is from a dis-tance, and look at each other, but with a sidelong glance" (761). Even Adorno makes a point of asserting that the essay "is not unlogical; rather it obeys logical criteria in so far as the totality of its sentences must fit together coherently" (169). Each of these passages clearly affirms a belief in coherence, but coherence of an unusual kind, as Montaigne suggests in his playful image of "ideas" that "follow one another . . . from a distance, and look at each other, but with a sidelong glance."

This view of coherence, as Montaigne implies, is based not on mere surface continuity from one statement to the next, but on a deep connection between ideas—on a cohesion so powerful that ideas seem to be animated by an awareness of their affinities to each other no matter how far apart, or how unrelated, they may seem to be. By personifying his ideas in this way, Montaigne is evidently trying to bear witness to the drama of thought itself—a drama in which ideas, like characters, often seem to assume a life of their own, and thus to develop and interact with each other in surprising and fascinating ways. Indeed, Montaigne apparently seeks to encourage just such developments—to "go out of my way, but rather by license than carelessness." In one sense, of course, this explicitly formulated intention may be seen as evidence of Montaigne's dedication to his role as essayist—that is, to essay, to test, to try out, to explore something, in this case his ideas. In another sense, these statements may be seen as confirmation of a desire to write in a way that authentically replicates the natural flow of his thoughts, as borne out by his assertion that "My style and my mind alike go roaming" (761). Yet his statement bespeaks so self-conscious, so deliberate, an intention to "go out of my way" as to be somewhat at odds with the genuinely purposeless or directionless movement implied by the activity of roaming—to be more in keeping with the spirit of Adorno's assertion that the essay "proceeds, so to speak, methodically unmethodically." In fact, in this same set of reflections on his writing, Montaigne reveals what may well be the ultimate motive behind his generally digressive behavior, when he exclaims, "Lord, what beauty there is in these lusty sallies and this variation, and more so the more casual and accidental they seem" (761). The clear implication of this statement, I think, is that Montaigne intends his "roaming," his "lusty sallies," to be seen as an elaborate fiction—as an

Carl H. Klaus

imitation, rather than an actual replication, of his mind in action. Indeed, in his very next statement, Montaigne declares that "It is the inattentive reader who loses my subject, not I. Some word about it will always be found off in a corner, which will not fail to be sufficient, though it takes little room" (761). So, it would appear that Montaigne is always in control of his thoughts, or aspires to be, letting them roam just enough so that they seem to be as "casual and accidental" as possible, yet keeping them sufficiently in check so that they do ultimately "follow one another" and "look at each other."

I have dwelt on these reflections of Montaigne because they embody a sophisticated conception of essayistic form that is echoed in various ways by subsequent essayists. According to this conception, the essay evidently calls for a delicate set of mental adjustments, attuned both to giving the mind a free rein and to reining it in, so that the form of the essay will appear to reflect the process of a mind in action, but a mind that is always in control of itself no matter how wayward it may seem to be. In other words, the essay is conceived as being based on an idea somewhat akin to the principles of organic form, yet also akin to the principle of artful artlessness. Addison hints at this complex quality when he says that in writing an essay "it is sufficient that I have several Thoughts on a Subject, without troubling my self to range them in such order, that they may seem to grow out of one another, and be disposed under the proper Heads" (IV:186). Gerould explicitly defines this complex principle when she asserts that "The basis of the essay is meditation, and it must in a measure admit the reader to the meditative process. . . . An essay, to some extent, thinks aloud; though not in the loose and pointless way to which the 'stream of consciousness' addicts have accustomed us" (Essay 412). Gass affirms the same principle when he speaks of Emerson as having "made the essay into the narrative disclosure of thought . . . but not of such thinking as had actually occurred. Real thought is gawky and ungracious" (34). Huxley redefines it as "Free association artistically controlled," in trying to account for the "paradoxical secret of Montaigne's best essays." And Adorno codifies the paradox in his idea of the essay's methodical unmethodicality.

Given this conception of essayistic form, the essayists, in turn, tend to see the meaning of an essay as residing not so much in any particular idea or point that it happens to affirm, as in its display of a mind engaging ideas. So, for example, Kazin claims, "In an essay, it is not the thought that counts but the experience we get of the writer's thought; not the self, but the self thinking" (xi). Hoagland similarly asserts that "through its tone and tumbling progression, it conveys the quality of the author's mind," and thus he concludes that "the fascination of the mind is the fascination of the essay" (27). And Gass declares that "the hero of the essay is its author in the act of thinking things out, feeling and finding a way; it is the mind in the marvels and miseries of its makings, in the *work* of the imagination, the search for form" (19–20). In each of these statements, as in others, the essayists focus so deliberately on the image of the author in the process of thinking that they tend to see the essay as embodying something very much like the drama of thought, or what Hardwick refers to as "thought itself in orbit" (xviii). Lopate, for example, asserts "that, in an essay, the track of a person's thoughts struggling to achieve some understanding of a problem is the plot, is the adventure" (1). Adorno shifts the dramatic focus from the essayist thinking to thought in action by asserting that "the thinker does not think, but rather transforms himself into an arena of intellectual experience, without simplifying it" (160–61). And Lukacs views the drama in such abstract terms that he does not even allude to the essayist, but conceives of the essay instead as enacting the experience of thought itself: "There are experiences, then, which cannot be expressed by any gesture and which long for expression. From all that has been said you will know what experiences I mean and of what kind they are. I mean intellectuality, conceptuality as sensed experience, as immediate reality, as spontaneous principle of existence . . ." (7). None of the essayists actually goes so far as to remove the essayist entirely from the scene of the essay, not even Lukacs, though his comments date from the pre-Marxist, idealist phase of his thought. Indeed, he explicitly notes that "The hero of the essay was once alive, and so his life must be given form; but this life, too, is as much inside the work as everything is in poetry" (11).

Most essayists, in fact, give special attention to the role of the essayist in the essay, and not only through their concern with the flow of an author's thoughts, but also through their preoccupation with an author's implied personality. The importance that they attribute to personality is reflected in the fact that almost all the essayists I have examined implicitly or explicitly make it a defining feature of the essay, and not just of the "familiar" essay. As Daiches puts it, "the essay, however serious and objective in intention, can be defined as a reasonably short prose discussion in which the personality of the author in some degree shapes the style and tone of the argument" (4). This emphasis on personality is reflected in a tendency, especially among the nineteenth-century essayists, to discuss their predecessors primarily in terms of the changing moods or aspects of personality that they find in their essays, and occasionally to judge them for what they deem to be an inappropriate manner, as Hazlitt does Johnson for being "always upon stilts" (101). Hazlitt's judgment in this case turns out to be reflective of norms that have prevailed throughout the nineteenth and twentieth centuries. The basic premise of these norms, as Stephen puts it, is that "no literary skill will make average readers take kindly to a man who does not attract by some amiable quality" (69). According to these norms, the essayist in Benson's view should have the "power of giving the sense of a good-humored, gracious and reasonable personality" (59). In keeping with these same norms, Woolf asserts that "the voice of the scold should never be heard in this narrow plot" (217), and Hardwick observes that "pompously self-righteous, lamely jocular forays offend because an air of immature certainty surrounds them" (xvii). As these remarks suggest, and as Gass makes clear, "this lack of fanaticism, this geniality in the thinker, this sense of the social proprieties involved (the essay can be polemical but never pushy) are evidence of how fully aware the author is of the proper etiquette for meeting minds. . . . If there is too much earnestness, too great a need to persuade, a want of correct convictions in the reader is implied, and therefore an *absence of community*" (24).

In view of their concern for engaging readers, "for meeting minds," it should come as no surprise that the essayists' conception of personality is on the whole as complex and delicately attuned as their overall conception of essayistic form. Woolf hints at the complexity when she speaks of personality as "the essayist's most proper but most dangerous and delicate tool" (222). A few sentences later she defines the complexity in the form of another paradox—"Never to be yourself and yet always—that is the problem" (222). This paradoxical conception of the essayist's persona as being at once an authentic reflection of personality and a fictionalized construction of personality can be traced in part to the practices of the periodical essayists, whom Hazlitt describes as having "assumed some fictitious and humorous disguise, which, however, in a great degree corresponded to their own peculiar habits and character" (95). In a similar fashion, Lamb's playful preface to his essays makes clear that what Elia "tells us, as of himself, was often true only (historically) of another." But even in the absence of self-evidently fictitious disguises, the essayists tend to discuss personality in terms that suggest they see it as involving a subtle combination of actual and fictional qualities. In an unpublished review of Hazlitt, for example, Lamb notes that "This assumption of a character, if it be not truly (as we are inclined to believe) his own, is that which gives force & life to his writing" (303). Similarly, Benson's previously cited remark that "the charm" of an essayist "depends upon his power of giving the sense of a good-humored, gracious and reasonable personality" seems to imply that such a personality is not a literal reflection of the essayist's own nature, but something that the essayist is capable of projecting, "of giving the sense of," in writing. Weeks likewise observes that "Style is at once the man himself and the shimmering costume of words which centers your attention" (81). This complex interplay between the essayist's authentic self and the self in "costume," between the actual and the fictional personality, is clearly delineated by White:

> The essayist arises in the morning, and, if he has work to do, selects his garb from an unusually extensive wardrobe: he can pull on any sort of shirt, be any sort of person, according to his mood or his subject matter—philosopher, scold, jester, raconteur, confidant, pundit, devil's advocate, enthusiast. . . . There is one thing the essayist cannot do, though—he cannot indulge himself in deceit or in concealment, for he will be found out in time. (vii–viii)

So it would seem that essayists explicitly recognize an intimate connection between role-playing and essay-writing, even as they affirm that the roles they play must be deeply in tune with their inherent nature.

It is one thing, however, to create the impression of a particular "sort of person"; it is quite another matter to do so at the same time that one is projecting the impression of a particular "meditative process." At first thought, of course, there might appear to be no problem here, since the two impressions presumably must be in harmony with each other—the personality giving direction to the meditative process, and the meditative process in turn revealing the most distinctive aspects of the personality. But as the essayists define personality, it seems to refer to a public aspect of self, something that one can put on as easily as if it were a "costume" or "garb," whereas a meditative process presumably involves the private aspect of one's self. Paradoxically, then, the essayists apparently conceive of the essay as somehow conveying a multistable impression of the self, an impression that projects the self in both its private and public aspects, in the process of thought and in the process of sharing thought with others. As Gerould puts it, "An essay, to some extent, thinks aloud." As Gass puts it, "The unity of each essay is a unity achieved by the speaker for his audience as well as for himself, a kind of reassociation of his sensibility and theirs" (35). As Hoagland puts it, "the artful 'I' of an essay can be as chameleon as any narrator in fiction" (26).

Essayists on the Essay

As the essayists see it, then, the essay, far from being a form of nonfiction, is a profoundly fictive kind of writing. It seeks to convey the sense of a human presence, a human presence that is indisputably related to its author's deepest sense of self, but that is also a complex illusion of that self—an enactment of it as if it were both in the process of thought and in the process of sharing the outcomes of that thought with others. Considered in this light, the essay, rather than being the clear-cut, straightforward, and transparent form of discourse that it is usually considered to be, is itself a very problematic kind of writing. So, it should not be confused either with article-writing and theme-writing, or with exploratory writing and expressive writing.[5] As Priestley says, "it is a pity that other types of prose composition which could easily be given such a title as 'theme,' 'thesis,' or 'article,' should bear the name [of essay]" (8). Given the essayists' view of it, the essay clearly calls for different ways of writing and different ways of reading from these other types of prose. It calls for using and understanding language as a symbolic form of action. To illustrate what this might entail is clearly beyond the scope of this piece—is presumably the purpose of other pieces in this book. For the moment, then, my only concern is to urge a rethinking of the essay, and to suggest that any rethinking of it might best begin with a consideration of what the essayists themselves have had to say about it.

Works Cited

Abrams, M.H. "Essay." *A Glossary of Literary Terms.* New York: Holt, Rinehart and Winston, 1981. 55–56.

5. Thus while I am in sympathy with Zeiger's desire to encourage "the spirit of inquiry in college composition," I consider his distinction between the "expository essay" and the "exploratory essay" to be potentially as misleading as the distinction between the "formal" and "informal" essay. Indeed, his conception of the "expository essay" is virtually identical to the methodical discourse that essayists have long opposed; and his conception of the "exploratory essay" does not seem to recognize any difference between the actual nature of mental exploration and the symbolic form of mental exploration that essayists attribute to the essay.

Carl H. Klaus

Adorno, T.W. "The Essay as Form." Trans. Bob Hullot-Kentor. *New German Critique* Spring-Summer 1984: 151–71.

Bacon, Francis. *The Advancement of Learning*. Ed. William Aldis Wright. London: Oxford, 1963.

———. *The Essays*. Ed. John Pitcher. New York: Viking Penguin, 1985.

Belloc, Hilaire. "An Essay upon Essays upon Essays." *One Thing and Another*. London: Hollis and Carter, 1955. 11–14.

Benson, Arthur Christopher. "The Art of the Essayist." In Vol. 4 of *Modern English Essays*. 5 vols. Ed. Ernest Rhys. London: Dent, 1922. 50–63.

Bond, Donald F. ed. *The Spectator*. 5 vols. London, Oxford, 1965.

Chadbourne, Richard. "A Puzzling Literary Genre: Comparative Views of the Essay." *Comparative Literature Studies* 20 (1983): 133–53.

Chesterton, G. K. "On Essays." *Come to Think of It*. London: Methuen, 1930. 1–5.

Daiches, David. "Reflections on the Essay." *A Century of the Essay*. New York: Harcourt, 1951. 1–8.

Epstein, Joseph. "Writing Essays." *The New Criterion* June 1984: 26–34.

Gass, William. "Emerson and the Essay." *Habitations of the Word* New York: Simon and Schuster, 1985. 9–49.

Gerould, Katharine Fullerton. "An Essay on Essays." *The North American Review*. December 1935: 409–18.

———. "Information, Please!" *The Saturday Review of Literature* 29 Dec. 1934: 393–95.

Hardwick, Elizabeth. Introduction. *The Best American Essays 1986*. Ed. Elizabeth Hardwick. New York: Ticknor & Fields, 1986. xiii–xxi.

Hazlitt, William. "On the Periodical Essayists." In Vol. 6 of *The Complete Works of William Hazlitt*. London: Dent, 1931. 91–105.

Hoagland, Edward. "What I Think, What I Am." *The Tugman's Passage*. New York: Random House, 1982. 24–27.

Howells, William Dean. "Editor's Easy Chair." *Harper's Magazine* October 1902: 802–03.

Huxley, Aldous. Preface. *Collected Essays*. New York: Harper and Row, 1960. v–ix. Johnson, Samuel. *A Dictionary of the English Language*. London: W. Strahan, 1755.

———. "Rambler No. 184." In Vol. 5 of *The Yale Edition of the Works of Samuel Johnson*. Ed. W.J. Bate and Albrecht B. Strauss.

New Haven: Yale UP, 1969. 200–04.

Kazin, Alfred. "The Essay as a Modern Form." *The Open Form: Essays for our Time*. New York: Harcourt, 1961. vii–xi.

Krutch, Joseph Wood. "No Essays, Please." *The Saturday Review of Literature* 10 March 1951: 18–19, 35.

Lamb, Charles. *The Essays of Elia*. London: Dent, 1929.

————. Unpublished Review of William Hazlitt's *Table Talk*. Lamb as Critic. Ed. Roy Park. Lincoln: U of Nebraska P, 1980. 299–307.

Lopate, Phillip. "The Essay Lives—In Disguise." *The New York Times Book Review* 18 Nov. 1984: 1, 47–49.

Lukacs, Georg. "On the Nature and Form of the Essay." *Soul and Form*. Trans. Anna Benstock. Cambridge: MIT, 1978. 1–18.

Montaigne. *The Complete Works*. Trans. Donald M. Frame. Stanford: Stanford UP, 1957.

Priestley, J.B. Introduction. *Essayists Past and Present*. New York: Dial Press, 1925. 7–32.

Rucker, Mary K. "The Literary Essay and the Modern Temper." *Publications in Language and Literature* 11 (1975): 317–35.

Smith, Alexander. "On the Writing of Essays." *Dreamthorp: A Book of Essays Written in the Country*. Portland, Maine: Thomas Bird Mosher, 1913. 23–46.

Stephen, Leslie. "The Essayists." *Men, Books, and Manners*. Minneapolis: U of Minnesota P, 1956. 45–73.

Thomas, Lewis. "Essays and Gaia." *The Youngest Science*. New York: Viking, 1983. 239–48.

Thoreau, Henry David. *The Journal of Henry David Thoreau*. 14 vols. Ed. Bradford Torrey and Francis H. Allen. Salt Lake City: Gibbs M. Smith, 1984.

Weeks, Edward. "The Peripatetic Reviewer." *Atlantic Monthly* Aug. 1954: 81–82.

White, E. B. Foreword. *Essays of E. B. White*. New York: Harper and Row, 1977. vii–ix.

Williams, William Carlos. "An Essay on Virginia." *Imaginations*. New York: New Directions, 1971. 321–24. Woolf, Virginia. "The Modern Essay." *The Common Reader*. New York: Harcourt, 1956. 216–27.

Zeiger, William. "The Exploratory Essay: Enfranchising the Spirit of Inquiry in College Composition." *College English* 47 (1985): 454–66.

9
STORIES IN ESSAYS, ESSAYS AS STORIES

Douglas Hesse

We make our world go round, it seems, by chasing our tales.

Ian Reid

"Narrative essays contain stories that illustrate or prove points, propositions stated or implied that tell the meaning of the story." Essentially, that has been the recent consensus of composition textbooks. In the virtual absence of theorizing about literary nonfiction, those textbooks have conveniently, if inaccurately, represented the wider-spread conventional wisdom regarding narrative in essays. But after carefully reading some 250 essays—by Steele, Addison, Goldsmith, Lamb, Hazlitt, De Quincey, Thackeray, Smith, Stevenson, Jefferies, Beerbohm, Forster, Woolf, Orwell, White, Eiseley, Selzer, Didion, Dillard, and Thomas—I concluded that what narrative actually does in essays is more complicated and interesting than what textbooks say it does. The following essay sketches some of the complications that appear most worth pursuing.[1]

1. For those who wish to compare textbook pronouncements with the "state" of essay theory, the following works describe its range: Bruno Berger, *Der Essay: Form und Geschichte.* Berne: Franke, 1964; Richard Chadbourne, "A Puzzling Genre: Comparative Views of the Essay." *Comparative Literature Studies* 20 (1983): 133–53; J. C. Guy Cherica, *A Literary Perspective of the Essay: A Study of its Genetic Principles and Their Bearing on Hermeneutic Theory.* Diss. South Carolina, 1982. Ann Arbor: UMI, 1985. 8220194; William J. Dawson and Coningsby W. Dawson. *The Great English Essayists.* New York: H. W. Wilson, 1932; Gerhard Haas, *Essay.* Stuttgart: J. B. Metzlersch Verlagsbuchandlung, 1969; Edward Hoaglund, "What I Think, What I Am." *The New York Times Book Review,* June 27, 1976; Douglas Hunt, "Introduction: About Essays and Essayists." *The Dolphin Reader.* Boston: Houghton Mifflin, 1986; Georg Lukacs, "The Nature and Form of the Essay." In *Soul and Form.* Trans. Anna Bostock. Cambridge: MIT UP, 1978; Robert Scholes and Carl Klaus. *Elements of the Essay.* New York: Oxford UP, 1969; Hugh Walker, *The English Essay and*

Stories in Essays

I will argue five main propositions. First, stories in essays do not prove points in the way that the conventional wisdom argues. Second, *story* in an essay is not equal to *narrative*. Third, borders between *story* and *not story* in essays are hazy and cannot be determined merely by the presence or absence of narrative. Fourth, narrative essays *make* points by giving propositions a place in story; propositions are events in the essay as story. Fifth, the persuasive force of narrative essays is less mimetic or ethical than formal. I'll locate these propositions in relation to several essays chosen purely because they lead to the points I wish to make.

Proposition One

Stories in essays do not "prove" points in the sense that the conventional wisdom argues.

The most direct way to understand the conventional position is to consider some of its representative pronouncements:

> Although a narrative may be written for its own sake—that is simply to recount events—in most college writing narration is used for a purpose, and a sequence of events is presented to prove a point. (Kirszner and Mandell 41)

> Here the writer uses narration to relate a sequence of events and to emphasize the thesis or central idea. (Raphael 33)

> Readers seek out the point of the story and use it as a mark of the story's success. (Wiener and Eisenberg 56)

Essayists. New York: J. M. Dent, 1915; Virginia Woolf, "The Modern Essay." In Vol. 2 of *Collected Essays.* New York: Harcourt Brace World, 1967; William Zeiger, "The Exploratory Essay: Enfranchising the Spirit of Inquiry in College Composition." *College English* 47 (1985): 454–66.

Such events as the recent symposia on the essay at Seton Hall University ("The Essay: Redefining a Genre for the Humanities," April 24–26 and June 19–29, 1987) provide some evidence that this fairly worn set of works is being dusted and expanded.

For a more thorough discussion of the tradition of narrative in essays, see Douglas D. Hesse, *The Story in the Essay.* Diss. Iowa, 1986.

> If you are to enjoy a narrative essay fully, you must understand that thesis, the point of the story, when you finish it. (Dobie and Hirt 32)

In all of them, stories are seen as furnishing evidence for the truth of a proposition. Whether point is extracted from incident or incident is supplied to verify an already-existing point, the two are presented as having an equationlike relationship, with story on one side of the equals sign and point on the other. In this view, the essential nature of an essay story is its compressibility into a thesis. Put another way, the story "stands for" the thesis, and in essays in which the thesis is implicit, the story stands alone. Put a third way, an essay story is light just before it passes through a magnifying lens. The story's "point," the dot that sets the leaf afire, consists of the story's "photons" focused beyond the glass—the writer.

But the formulation "point equals story" fails for a number of essays. Consider three of them, all very different in terms of the types of narrative they contain. In "Thoughts on Peace in an Air Raid," Virginia Woolf presents her thoughts as having taken place during a German bombing of London. Planes fly over, drop bombs, are shot at, then leave. This narrative serves primarily a structural function. Woolf plays back and forth between narrating the bombing and explaining why men are prone to fighting, before she finally calls upon women to "Help young Englishmen to root out from themselves the love of medals and decorations" (175). What's important is that the bombing account isn't "equivalent" to any "point" Woolf is trying to make. At most we can view it as proof that there are such things as wars and men who fight them. But we needn't be convinced of that. It makes no sense to ask, "What does the account of the air raid prove?" That is not to say the narrative demonstrates nothing. Woolf's description of the bombers' buzz as "a sound that interrupts cool and consecutive thinking about peace" (173) is enacted structurally by the interplay of narration and reflection in an essay that, ironically, is consecutive, if not cool. But Woolf's main argument less concerns the writer's craft than the resolution of war.

A second essay, "My Magical Metronome" by Lewis Thomas, better seems to fit the textbook model if for no other reason than that its story comes all in a chunk rather than being dispersed. That story, in which Thomas tells how he acquired his pacemaker, begins the essay. Following it are two pages of commentary about his vanity at having the device, his lack of curiosity about how it works, and his change of heart from being opposed to certain technologies to supporting them. Drawing upon the conventional wisdom, we assume, "Here is the point of the story." The meaning of the essay, the highest level abstraction that encompasses everything here, is something like, "I feel differently about medical technology now that I have a pacemaker." But Thomas's reflection doesn't furnish a point in the sense of a statement that has been proved by the story. If a story is reducible to its point or if a point can be extracted from a story, then that point has to be present somehow *in* the story; the photons at the focal point must be present in the light before it passes through the lens. But while the story in "My Magical Metronome" does trace a change in physical state (from pre-pacemaker days to post), it doesn't trace a change in Thomas's attitude, and that is the point of the essay. At best, the story leads to the point; it does not contain it. The point is something in addition to, not equal to, the story.

Let's try a more venerable example, Orwell's "Shooting an Elephant." Surely, *this* story exists to prove that "as I stood there with the rifle in my hands . . . I first grasped the hollowness, the futility of the white man's dominion in the East. . . . I perceived in this moment that when the white man turns tyrant it is his own freedom that he destroys" (285). In what sense, though, *does* the story prove it? In asking that, I'm after something more subtle than the skepticism with which we regard any proposition that relies for proof on the narration of an incident, a skepticism explained long ago by Aristotle's assessment of the relative inferiority of argument by example to argument by enthymeme. I'll discount as irrelevant the current suspicions that the incident described never happened. I'll even grant, with most readers, that Orwell's assertion is "convincing." But what is it that we're being convinced *of*? I believe it's something like this: Orwell. . . thinking this thought at this time is plausible. The story in "Shooting an Elephant" doesn't "mean" or "reduce to," "When the white man turns tyrant it is his own freedom that he destroys." Rather, the telling of these events creates a narrative moment in which such a thought can be expressed. What the story "proves" is that such a thought can exist.

In the three essays I have cited, the crucial issue is how propositions stand in relation to narrative. I've argued that the relationship is not one of equivalence, with "point" merely being a shorthand version for "story." In "Shooting an Elephant," the proposition that appears to be the best candidate for "point" is an event in the story. In Woolf's and Thomas's essays, by contrast, points appear to exist "in addition to" stories. The differences in these essays can be partly explained by the different degrees of narrative they contain.

Proposition Two

"Story" in an essay is not equal to "narrative."

Twenty years ago Scholes and Kellogg were able to answer the question "What is narrative?" fairly simply as "the presence of a story and a story teller" (4). But by 1986, Wallace Martin's review of narrative theory led him to confess that he couldn't finally define the term (190). He was able, however, to classify narrative theories into three viewpoints: narrative as a sequence of events, narrative as discourse produced by a narrator, and narrative as a type of verbal artifact organized and endowed with meaning by readers (82). Of these, the first has traditionally been the most popular, among both discourse theorists and textbook authors. James Kinneavy, for example, described narrative as that mode concerned with becoming rather than being, change, not stasis (36–37). But here is a problem. Isn't even a discursive essay that leads inductively to a final truth not stated at its outset "concerned with" becoming rather than being? One could address this challenge by re-stricting "changes" to changes in "nature"—in the world, not in the text or in the reader reading the text. Yet this implies that narrative is ultimately mimetic, and that, I will later show, is fraught with problems.

To push from this definitional quagmire, however, I suggest that Robert Scholes' definition of narrative is sensible: "A narration is the symbolic presentation of a sequence of events connected by subject matter and related by time" (209). The ambiguity of "changes" is preserved in the term "event," a concept that has beguiled and eluded narrative theorists; To-mashevsky offered "motif," Barthes "functional unit," and Chatman "narrative statement." Determining what counts as "event" will be pivotal in differentiating between narrative and exposition. But temporarily let's assume that "events" means "actions" as opposed to ideas about or interpretations or expla-nations of actions. Note that the very unsatisfactoriness of that definition, however temporary it is, indicates just how complicated the analysis of "narrative essays" should be.

It's no wonder, then, that textbook authors stumble badly when trying to define narrative. The customary gambit is to present *narrative* and *story* as interchangeable, which has re-sulted in such odd pronouncements as Michael Shugrue's no-tion that "narration tells a story or presents a sequence of events which occurred over a period of time. If the story is significant in itself, it is narration. If a story illustrates a point in exposition or argument, it may be called illustrative narra-tion. If a story outlines a process step-by-step, it is designated as expository narration" (3). To define *narrative* as *story* is to define a mode as a form. This is a slippery practice, like defin-ing prose as essays or leather as shoes. A better alternative is to recognize a distinction between the two. Once again Scholes is helpful: "A story is a narrative with a certain very specific syntactic shape (beginning-middle-end or situation-transfor-mation-situation) and with a subject matter which allows for or encourages the projection of human values upon this mate-rial" (210). As disappointingly simple as it is, this three-part structure has almost universally been accepted as the *sine qua non* of story, especially by story grammarians such as Gerald Prince or Tvetzan Todorov, who used the terms *equilibrium, disequilibrium,* and *new equilibrium* (111). Our cultural preference for this structure can be attributed either to centuries of conditioning or to its affinity with larger biological rhythms, birth and death and rebirth, as Frank Kermode, among others, has argued.

The upshot of these distinctions is that rather than broadly referring to "narrative essays," we should recognize three degrees of narrative in essays. There are essays with *narrative,* essays that contain narrative sections that do not themselves, however, take the shape of story. "Thoughts on Peace" is an example, as is "Control" by E. B. White (which I discuss below). There are also essays with *story,* such as "My Magical Metronome." In them, narrative has taken the shape of story, but this story is preceded, followed, or surrounded by text that is not narrative and therefore does not seem to be part of the story. Finally, there are essays *as* story, "Shooting an Elephant," for example, or "A Hanging," or Virginia Woolf's "Death of a Moth." In them every word is part of the story; story and essay have a one-to-one correspondence.

At this point a significant problem should be apparent. How does one determine what in an essay "belongs" to a story, for in each of these last three essays there are significant nonnarrative passages? Once these rocks start rolling, they avalanche even into works from my second category, essays with story. It does not take much, I'll argue, to see all of "My Magical Metronome" as a story.

Proposition Three

Borders between "story" and "not story" in essays are hazy and cannot be determined purely by the presence or absence of narrative.

Analyzing an essay to determine what in it is "of story" and what is not is such a vexed—and important—undertaking because essays contain two levels of exposition: exposition that "belongs" to the events of narrative (the exposition of action) and exposition that "belongs" to the essay (the exposition of ideas). The further complication is that stories consist of narrative *and* exposition, in various proportions to one another, as, for example, can be seen in a Hawthorne short story versus a Hemingway, and in various positions relative to one another. (The best discussion of these issues is Meir Sternberg's *Expositional Modes and Temporal Ordering in Fiction*, which presents a two-by-two matrix for the formal analysis of exposition: preliminary or delayed; concentrated or distributed.) What makes short stories stories (gives narrative the shape of story) is often exposition; only because Joyce tells us what the protagonist of "Araby" thinks before he visits the bazaar do we perceive the epiphany brought on by the visit. As a result of this natural mix of action, the exposition of action, and the exposition of ideas all in the same essay, there are frequently gray areas in which story-level and essay-level exposition are indistinguishable.

Consider "Shooting an Elephant." Is the opening exposition a part of the story that follows, or is it only part of the essay? The opening two paragraphs describe Orwell's situation in Burma, specifically, how he was the target of pranks and derision, which left him in an ambivalent position between hating the oppressors and the oppressed even though he intellectually opposed the former. All of this seems to be essay-level exposition, the background that helps us understand whatever he will later say about this situation. The story, accordingly, seems to begin in the third paragraph, with "One day something happened. . . ," a clear signal of narrative. But when the story starts, it starts with more exposition, "story exposition," we judge it, because it's "closer" somehow to the events. Yet I argue that what is happening is a movement from general to more specific exposition, and that clearly we would read the events of the story differently if the first two paragraphs of essay-level exposition were absent.

As a result it makes sense to read those opening paragraphs as "belonging to" the story. What I'm advocating is a shift in assumptions, from conceiving the events in "Shooting an Elephant" as existing to serve the essay that contains them (the essay level manifesting itself in the opening two paragraphs and in the "realization paragraph") to conceiving that the essay is *all* story, a story beginning with the first word of the essay. The "scenic norm," to use a term from Sternberg, of this essay-as-story begins in the third paragraph.

The same argument can be made, I believe, in essays that seem to have sharper borders between story and essay. As I've pointed out, that seems to be the case in Thomas's "My Magical Metronome." But a close reading of the last two pages of "commentary" reveals that most of the remarks there refer to the preceding events. By this I mean that they are labeled either as "after," that is, "as a result of" the story ("I would never have thought I had it in me, but now that I have it in me, ticking along soundlessly, flawlessly, I am subject to waves of pure vanity" [47]), or as "before" it ("I have written in the past about medicine's excessive dependence on technology in general. . . ." [48]). The former statements continue the story; the story's "events" have become thoughts. The latter constitute exposition transposed out of the "normal" position at the beginning. In this sense, "My Magical Metronome" is not far from "Shooting an Elephant" in being entirely story.

Unlike either of these essays, "Thoughts on Peace in an Air Raid" resists the collapse of essay-level and story-level exposition. The reason can be explained by the degree of narrative in this work. Earlier, I labeled it an essay with narrative and not an essay with story. This was because the events—the planes coming, dropping bombs, then going—do not make a story despite their three-partedness. The bombing seems instead to provide a ruler on which Woolf laid her thoughts. Is it possible then to say that there is a story in this essay? Yes. But that story is of Woolf's response to the situation represented by the bombing, her movement from agitation to analysis to uneasy peace at the end, having offered a "solution" to war. References to the bombing, then, are really signposts that alert us to the presence of story, to the fact that Woolf offers her thoughts in motion, following one another linearly in time and not just on the page as all words must.

Unless Woolf's essay is an anomaly, exposition in essays

with narrative does not function in the same ways as exposition in essays with or as story. In fact, in essays with narrative, narrative has primarily an expositional aim in the story that is the essay. When E. M. Forster opens "Me, Them, and You" with a visit to a museum, or Annie Dillard "On a Hill Far Away" with a short walk "late one January afternoon," we are drawn less by the expectation of meaning than we are by the promise that narrative will lead us somewhere worth going.

At the beginning of "Control," E. B. White finds two state agents in his barn, testing his cow. White doesn't turn this narrative into story in the sense of "finishing what happened." In terms of action, he leaves the scene open. Paragraph three is a turning point, the end of the narrative, and the beginning of a progression of ideas about the drawbacks of government control, the parts of the essay sharing that point in the same way that two ellipses might share the same epicenter. Narrative begins the story and brings it to a point at which discursive thought can complete it. The point is part of the story but not part of the narrative.

Proposition Four

Narrative essays don't prove points, they make them by giving propositions a place in story. Points are events in the essay as story.

With this proposition I am not arguing that we abandon the idea that stories prove points but that we understand proof as rooted in making, the bringing of points into plausible existence. Making a point is not "balancing an equation." I mean it more literally in the sense of establishing a juncture on the line of words that comprises the essay, a place at which the stating of propositions becomes possible, that place being either at the beginning, in the middle of, or, most frequently, at the end of the story. The point is a position that is usually but not always marked by a proposition. Stories with "implicit theses" are those that create a point but have not marked it with a sentence.

The broadest way of stating this is that narrative creates

a juncture in the reader's experience. Here let me be as plain as I can be. It is inconceivable that a writer can publish something as short as a sentence and have readers pay attention to it in the way that they pay attention to propositions argued in essays. A practical problem is how to provide propositions with a text of a conventional publishable length, one long enough to gain the reader's attention for a period of time. How this attention is gotten by stories might be explained in terms Susan Lohafer has used for short stories: "Short stories, unlike novels or poems, by their very nature, compete with the rhythms that keep us functioning as organisms. . . . [T]hey put us *through* something—reality warp is the shorthand for it—that happens to us with as much authority as a delayed meal or an overdue nap. Our minds adjust to a frequency" (159). Story shoves itself into our consciousness not by the substitution of a fictional world for the real one, but by enticing us into a familiar pattern. Once in them, readers view propositions they contain in relation to that pattern. A different appeal, not to psychology but to speech act theory, offers another explanation for our attention to stories. Stories are self-occasioning, inherently "tellable" and deemed by listeners as worth passing on. The reader's default mode for story is receptivity. Several textbook authors have even noted this:

> . . . telling a story is a particularly attractive mode of writing. Ours is a storytelling culture. (Bloom 35)

> In most cultures we find an exalted place for the story. . . . People delight in narratives. . . . (Wiener and Eisenberg 56)

> . . . narratives appeal to the reader's interest in following a story. (Raphael 33)

The opening narrative in "My Magical Metronome" creates a space, literally in the text, figuratively in the reader's mind, in which Thomas can introduce ideas about medical technology and not have them seem to come out of the blue. The point of the narrative is its end. That point is marked in the text by the stark transition: "Afterthought." In rather old-fashioned terms, the narrative occasions Thomas's reflections.

If we insist on asking what this story "proves," the best answer is that it proves Thomas's reflections have a right to exist because they have a place, "after the narrative, toward the end of the story."

Imagine Orwell wanting to declare that "the white man's dominion in the East is futile." He faces two problems: how to state it and how to prove it. Story solves both. Proof does not come from sufficient evidence but from the fact that if someone can reasonably place such a proposition within a story, then it has the status of being part of something beyond itself. It has the validity of connection. Orwell's realization of the oppressor's plight is an event in the story, one entailed by the events before it and the exposition against which they're told, one that leads to further events. That realization "solves" the ambivalent double hatred of the opening paragraph by explaining its source. But the horror of "Shooting an Elephant" is that this realization does not alter the course of events after it. He still pulls the trigger.

Perhaps the best way for me to illustrate propositions as event is with a very short essay by E. B. White, "The Age of Dust." The piece opens: "On a sunny morning last week, we set out and put up a swing for a little girl, age three, under an apple tree—the tree being much older than the girl, the sky being blue, the clouds white. We pushed the girl for a few minutes, then returned to the house and settled down to an article on death dust, or radiological warfare, in the July *Bulletin of the Atomic Scientists*, Volume VI, No. 7" (*Second Tree* 115). White summarizes the article, criticizing its detached tone and seemingly naive assertion that people can survive fallout by holding a wet handkerchief over their mouths. His third paragraph extends his comments and expresses a need for action. The fourth begins more specifically to tie the article to the girl, until at the end of it he returns to narrative: "We went outdoors again to push the swing some more for the little girl, who is always forgetting her handkerchief. At lunch we watched her try to fold her napkin. It seemed to take forever" (116). In the final paragraph White goes to bed thinking of the article, dreaming of the girl and other children walking north into unreality. A traditional way to describe the relation of narrative to essay here would be to invoke the concepts of introduction and conclusion. The girl is a device to get our attention and to create some pathetic appeal to boot. But the girl isn't merely tacked on. A better reading is to view "The Age of Dust" entirely as story, not as expositon framed by narrative. "We watched the girl swing, we read an article, and then we went to bed," would not be story but narrative. But the state of affairs at the end of the essay differs from that at the beginning. The opening precision, the oddly precise details of everything solidy in its place, is transformed to a world at the end that doesn't look nearly so secure, and that change is accounted for by the middle expository section. The ideas there are events in the story. The essay persuades not by offering propositions and formal proof but by moving us through narrative from one scene to another.

Essays like this one belong to a larger class of essays that move the reader toward a point, enacting the shape of thought rather than presenting it as already having arrived. By this, I don't mean literally that thought looks like these essays. Rather, the essayists have presented thought in the shape of story, the story of their own transformations as they wrote, our own as we read.

The argument that we should treat narrative in essays not as clumps of proof but as occasions for propositions and strategies of movement varies an idea that has existed some time. Several years ago Richard Larson argued for a "linear model" of rhetorical analysis to complement the prevailing hierarchical one. This model would view discourse as "a succession of events taken in a temporal sequence to achieve a goal" (141) following a "dynamic principle of forward motion" (144). How narrative in particular "moves" readers might best be investigated through theories like one offered by Ian Reid, who in writing about fiction has speculated that " 'action sequences' . . . are merely a sediment of transformations taking place at the rhetorical level, and *narrative may be most comprehensibly defined as the discursive mode that imparts an illusion of movement to its constituent figures*" (223). Narrative movement is more than Brownian motion; it is change polarized, as the writer brings us from some point to some other point. Particularly intriguing is Reid's concept of a "dynamic of troping" involving the processes of substitution and displacement (225). This movement is like that created by flipping a stack of cards on which the positions of cartoon characters have been drawn slightly different from one to the next to create, for example, the illusion of running.

The essence of narrative, then, is a writer's convincing us alternately to accept and abandon states of affairs, perhaps hundreds of times in a lengthy discourse, a for b, b for c, c for d, and so on to the end, each substitution growing out of the one preceding it. If Orwell's prisoner leaves his cell, he cannot be in his cell. If he climbs the gallows, he cannot be on the ground. If he dies he cannot be alive. If Orwell says he knows what it means to kill a healthy human being, it is not true that he says he doesn't know. The technique of narrative is worth trying to describe further and certainly in terms beyond those furnished by the conventional wisdom:

> Narration is a basic writing strategy for presenting action. (Axelrod and Cooper 386)

> The *narrative* mode, as its name indicates, is used by a writer basically to narrate or relate a series of events. . . . (Calderonello and Edwards 48)

> . . . the Writer uses narration to relate a sequence of events. . . . (Raphael 33)

These statements imply that there exist other ways of presenting action or sequences of events. But what might those be? Writers do not decide to report events then go shopping for the right technique to use, finally deciding on narrative. Rather, the very decision to relate a sequence of events is a decision for narrative. However, one *may* choose narrative as a rhetorical strategy as opposed, say, to deductive logic. The crucial question has to do with the "advantage" of arguing narratively, of storying readers to propositions.

189

Douglas Hesse

Proposition Five

The persuasive force of narrative essays is less mimetic or ethical than formal.

Textbooks cite the main advantage of narrative as mimetic, deriving its strength from vivid detail that recreates scenes so that readers can relive them as they happened. Some examples:

> Narrative serves to make your general feelings and ideas more concrete and specific. (Cavender and Weiss 79)

> A story has the tendency of making something much more vivid and real than a simple explanation might. (Ray, Olson, DeGeorge 18)

> Your purpose generally is to enable the audience to relive the event as you discovered it. (Gehle and Rollo 105)

The rationale seems to be that a close fit between words and events "as they happened" grants veracity to whatever may be said *about* those events. The appeal is ethical, in a sense, the reader believing that writers able convincingly to replicate reality can be trusted accurately to say what that reality means. But an advantage based on lifelikeness is problematic, and textbooks even reflect that. Nearly all of them cite the writer's flexibility in determining the order of presentation; the customary alternatives are using straight chronology versus starting in the middle, then flashing back or forward. But jumbled chronologies do not depict life as it happened. In fact, writing a story is a process of attributing order and meaning to events after the fact. Philosophers of history have long fretted over this, Louis Mink noting, for example, that, "The cognitive function of narrative form . . . is not just to relate a succession of events but to body forth an ensemble of relationships" (144). To their credit, some textbook writers recognize this as well: "[N]arration differs from life itself. . . . Life in itself has no clear purpose or meaning, at least none that we can be certain of except by faith" (Smith 281).

190

Stories in Essays

But if the value of stories is not mimetic, what is it? In *Actual Minds, Possible Worlds,* Jerome Bruner summarizes views of two cognitive modes that convince us of fundamentally different things. The first mode, the paradigmatic or logico-scientific, convinces us of truth through formal proof. The second mode, narrative, convinces us of lifelikeness (11). I agree with Bruner's distinction but would explain the second mode differently. Stories are convincing not because they're lifelike but because they're storylike. The power of narrative in essay comes not from the writer's ability to mirror reality, then state its meaning; rather, it comes from his or her offering us assertions in a shape attractive because it's so familiar. "Story" is a form of narrative argument in the way that "syllogism" is of logical argument.

Narrative is a means by which order is *constructed* rather than *represented.* The crucial offshoot is that in stories *the form claims truth.* An author who is able to present something well-formed persuades largely by allowing the reader easily to perceive form, just as the rhetor did by making clear the six parts of his oration. The power arcs between ethical appeal ("Here is someone who is able to form well, so what he says must be true") and the creation of something where there was nothing ("Here is a constellation. Without a competing version, why should I doubt its existence?"). Given the apparent primacy of story, what more compelling way to reveal form? What more alluring thing than to make propositions events in essays as stories when, as Knoblauch and Brannon put it, "The coherence of a text conveys a fiction about its certitude" (62) and a story *is* coherence? This is the same realization Joan Didion makes at the beginning of "The White Album," when she observes that "We tell ourselves stories in order to live. . . . We interpret what we see, select the most workable of the multiple choices. We live entirely, especially if we are writers, by the imposition of a narrative line upon disparate images, by the 'ideas' with which we have learned to freeze the shifting phantasmagoria which is our actual experience" (11).

Douglas Hesse

Implications for Analysis: A Demonstration

The value of the point I have reached—that we should regard narrative as a way of point-making that takes its rhetorical advantage from persuasiveness inherent in our acceptance of stories—can be most easily seen in the analysis of an essay far more complicated than those I've discussed so far, "Man in the Autumn Light," by Loren Eiseley. The difficulty of this essay is primarily a formal one. The work is highly discursive, almost aphoristic:

> The cosmos itself gives evidence, on an infinitely greater scale, of being just such a trick factory, a set of lights forever changing, and the actors themselves shape shifters. . . . (119)

> Man is no more natural than the world. (120)

> Some landscapes, one learns, refuse history; some efface it so completely it is never found; in others the thronging memories of the past subdue the living. (120)

> Man's urge toward transcendence manifests itself even in his outward inventions. (125)

Connections between propositions are almost nonexistent. Each comes with its own brief exposition—a reference to Cocteau, to a Brazilian two-lensed fish, to Thomas Love Peacock, to Ralph Waldo Emerson—and while the statements web thematically and imagistically, coherence in the essay seems spatial rather than causal or linear. One asks in reading, "What is the point?" not in the sense of "What does this finally add up to?" but "Where is this going? What is being entailed? What has started all this propositioning and what could possibly end it?" Seeing the story of this essay furnishes the best answers.

"Man in the Autumn Light" is divided into three sections. The first and third contain stories, the middle a discussion of the individual's reaction to his or her own mortality. The story in section one is of a hike Eiseley took in Wyoming when he was younger. He comes upon an old archaeological site where "time had no power" (121) and camps, waiting for a "message" that never comes, finally leaving to re-enter time, bearing "the

192

wound of a finite creature seeking to establish its own reality against eternity" (123). The story in section three is of another walk, on a winter night, in snow, to a man-made, junk-filled clearing where Eiseley, older now, pauses to reflect on past civilizations. That the second story echoes the first is obvious, but understanding how it does reveals the two stories as but scenes in the larger story, the essay.

As exposition, the intervening middle section explains the hollowness that Eiseley felt after the Wyoming hike, and it provides a richly complex context for the third section. There is narrative—second hand, anyway— even in this middle section with the summary of a story, "Twilight," the inclusion of which is itself a point-making strategy, one that clears a space for commentary. A thorough analysis of this middle section would involve examining how it moves readers "locally" to points as well as how the section as a whole moves readers "globally" to the point of the essay. What is required here is a sorting of layers—scene from story from essay as story, with exposition at each level—and an analysis of how they work in concert to bring us to points.

A brief discussion of the final section can sketch what's involved. In his observations on snow and light at the section's outset, Eiseley introduces the elements of the final story. But this exposition is thickened by his reference to prehistoric snows and to Cocteau, which appropriates the whole first section of the essay as exposition for the last. This allows him to do something with those earlier ideas: rethink them as events that occur on the walk as he pauses in the clearing. These thoughts have the status that Orwell's did in "Shooting an Elephant" or White's in "The Age of Dust." As the events of a particular time and place they carry a measure of credibility that pervades even broad propositions that otherwise demand proof: "Every civilization, born like an animal body, has just so much energy to expend" (132). What's important is what they entail. To what point do they lead? Out of the woods, home with a "still-green, everlasting" Christmas tree (134), Eiseley now somberly optimistic about the place of his civilization in the consciousness of those to follow. And we readers?

Douglas Hesse

Out of the essay, with a sense that this has been no aimless writer's stroll but a meaning-full succession of events. That belief derives from a final perception that we've just completed a story.

Conclusions

I've made my propositions stark enough that anyone who chooses to correct them should have clear aim at what I consider important about narrative in essays. There is certainly more to be added to what is here, the application of these ideas to more essays, of course, but also a refinement of the ideas themselves. If a number of essays can properly be analyzed as stories, their points as propositions to which the essayist moves readers, then it makes sense to sift through the current heaps of narrative theory. The rhetoric of much literary nonfiction may be best described by the conventions of storytelling, and those theories have certainly advanced beyond the conventional wisdom of textbooks. Until new theories emerge, we can make do with some of the existing textbook truisms— as long as we carefully define their terms. Consider three final quotations:

> In essay writing—unlike fiction—the story is primarily a means of portraying an idea. (Atwan and Vesterman, *Writing* 11)

> Writers in every field rely on narration to unfold a sequence of events. (Atwan and Vesterman, *Effective* xvii)

> In these two examples, the purpose of the paragraph is to get the reader from one event to another, to move the text from one point in the past to another point nearer the present. (Calderonello and Edwards 49)

If we define "portraying an idea" not as proving a point but as giving the shape of an idea, and if we define "events" in such a way to include propositions given a place in narrative time, then the idea of getting readers from one event to another, from one point to another is a fairly shrewd statement of the function of narrative in essays.

Works Cited

Aristotle, *Rhetorica*. Trans. W. Rhys Roberts. Vol. 11 of *Works*. Oxford: Oxford, 1924.

Atwan, Robert, and William Vesterman. *Effective Writing for the College Curriculum*. New York: McGraw-Hill, 1987.

——. *Writing Day-by-Day*. New York: Harper and Row, 1987.

Axelrod, Rise B., and Charles R. Cooper. *The St. Martin's Guide to Writing, Short Edition*. New York: St. Martin's, 1986.

Bloom, Lynn Z. *The Essay Connection*. Lexington: D. C. Heath, 1984.

Bruner, Jerome. *Actual Minds, Possible Worlds*. Cambridge: Harvard UP, 1986.

Calderonello, Alice Heim, and Bruce R. Edwards, Jr. *Roughdrafts: The Process of Writing*. Boston: Houghton Mifflin, 1986.

Cavender, Nancy, and Leonard Weiss. *Thinking/Writing*. Belmont: Wadsworth, 1987.

Chatman, Seymour. *Story and Discourse: Narrative Structure in Fiction and Film*. Ithaca: Cornell UP, 1978.

Didion, Joan. *The White Album*. New York: Simon and Schuster, 1979.

Dillard, Annie. *Teaching a Stone to Talk*. New York: Harper and Row, 1982.

Dobie, Ann B., and Andrew J. Hirt. *Comprehension and Composition: An Introduction to the Essay*. 2nd ed. New York: Macmillan, 1986.

Eiseley, Loren. "Man in the Autumn Light." *The Invisible Pyramid*. New York: Scribner's, 1970. 119–36.

Forster, E. M. *Abinger Harvest*. New York: Meridian, 1955.

Gehle, Quentin L., and Duncan J. Rollo. *Writing Essays: A Process Approach*. New York: St. Martin's, 1987.

Kermode, Frank. *The Sense of an Ending: Studies in the Theory of Fiction*. New York, 1967.

Kinneavy, James. *A Theory of Discourse*. New York: Norton, 1980.

Kirszner, Laurie G., and Stephen R. Mandell. *Patterns for College Writing: A Rhetorical Reader and Guide*. 3rd ed. New York: St. Martin's, 1986.

Knoblauch, C. E., and Lil Brannon. *Rhetorical Traditions and the Teaching of Writing*. Upper Montclair: Boynton/Cook, 1984.

Larson, Richard L. "Toward a Linear Rhetoric of the Essay." *CCC* 22 (1971): 140–46.

Lohafer, Susan. *Coming to Terms with the Short Story*. Baton Rouge: Louisiana State UP, 1983.

Martin, Wallace. *Recent Theories of Narrative*. Ithaca: Cornell UP, 1986.

Douglas Hesse

Mink, Louis O. "Narrative Form as a Cognitive Instrument." *The Writing of History: Literary Form and Historical Understanding.* Ed. Robert H. Canary and Henry Kozicki. Madison: U of Wisconsin P, 1978. 129–149.

Orwell, George. *Collected Essays.* London: Secker and Warburg, 1961.

Pratt, Mary Louise. *Toward a Speech Act Theory of Literary Discourse.* Bloomington: Indiana UP, 1977.

Raphael, Carolyn B. *The Writing Reader: Short Essays for Composition.* New York: Macmillan, 1986.

Ray, Richard E., Gary A. Olson, and James DeGeorge. *The Process Reader.* Englewood Cliffs: Prentice-Hall, 1986.

Reid, Ian. "Storypower: A Renewed Narratology?" *Southern Review* (Adelaide) 18 (1985): 215–31.

Scholes, Robert. "Language, Narrative, and Anti-Narrative." *Critical Inquiry* 7 (1981): 204–12.

—— and Robert Kellogg. *The Nature of Narrative.* New York: Oxford, 1966.

Shugrue, Michael. "Introduction." *The Essay.* New York: Macmillan, 1981. Smith, H. Wendell. *The Belmont Reader: Essays for Writers.* Belmont: Wadsworth, 1986.

Sternberg, Meir. *Expositional Modes and Temporal Ordering in Fiction.* Baltimore: Johns Hopkins UP, 1978.

Thomas, Lewis. *Late Night Thoughts on Listening to Mahler's Ninth Symphony.* New York: Bantam, 1983.

Todorov, Tzvetan. *The Poetics of Prose.* Trans. Richard Howard. Ithaca: Cornell UP, 1977.

White, E. B. *One Man's Meat.* New York: Harper and Row, 1983.

——. *The Second Tree from the Corner.* New York: Harper and Brothers, 1954.

Wiener, Harvey S., and Nora Eisenberg. *Great Writing: A Reader for Writers.* New York: McGraw-Hill, 1987.

Woolf, Virginia. "Thoughts on Peace in an Air Raid." In Vol. 4 of *Collected Essays.* New York: Harcourt Brace World, 1967. 173–77.

10
FICTION IN PERSUASION

Personal Experience as Evidence and as Art

George L. Dillon

Perhaps one of the most significant outcomes of a decade of theorizing about literature as a speech act (or activity, action, or discourse-type) is that an emphasis on it as a fictive or imitation speech act leads to the exclusion of rather substantial pieces of the traditional literary canon. Further, it seems to exclude from literature a good bit of contemporary writing that its readers feel is as rich and delightful and instructive as much that is in the canon—mainly reflective-exploratory, almost never persuasive, nonfiction prose. As long as we assume experience is being presented "for itself"—to be savored by the reader—the way that experience is presented, the style, tone, and voice in the passage, are proper foci for criticism. This is as it were an estheticizing move, though the work falls short of being pure fabulation, being committed to the factuality of the individuals and events it describes. But with persuasion, we enter the heartland of rhetoric, where style is not viewed as an end but as a means of achieving the main aim—as strategic—and voice leads one to ethos, another of the means of persuading. Assuming a persuasive purpose tends to narrow and simplify the critic's expectations about how the writing works: one is not looking for subtle exploration of the doing and undoing of language and representation. Language in persuasion is harnessed to the world; it is accountable to facts not of its own inventing; its descriptions and assertions can be assessed in the usual way for accuracy, truthfulness, and sincerity. The roles of style, tone, and voice are accordingly circumscribed. Criticism of persuasive writing often confines itself to listing various tactics and features of language that are appropriate for a purpose neither complicated nor problematic. I want to enter a plea here, however, that even very common devices of persuasive writing are not as simple or straightforward as they seem and hence can be deployed with various degrees of subtlety and skill. I will concentrate on one such device—the use of semifictionalized accounts of experience and events as *evidence*—in some contemporary persuasive writing ranging from advice for a popular audience to arguments designed for a more academic one.

When people take up the question of truth and fiction, they have generally been concerned with truthful or historical material appearing in the midst of fiction, or thinly veiled beneath it. In various places, however, we also find the opposite mixture—fiction, or something very like it, occurring in the midst of very real-world oriented persuasion. The writers of such mixtures often feel that some account of their practice is advisable, and it is these accounts, as much or more than the actual practice, that is of interest. I will focus on passages where certain writers state their claims for the fiction or truth of such things as case histories and dialogues, the passages where they themselves address the edge between modes of discourse. These discourses of the edge are in a sense the reverse of the fictional disclaimer—"all persons and events portrayed in this novel are fictitious, and any resemblance etc." The fictional disclaimer tries to purge the work of factuality; the discourses to be discussed try to purge certain passages of fictionality. I will first sketch an approach via John Searle's notion of fiction as nonassertion, which is basically an attempt to work out logical properties, specifically referentiality, and which leads to the conclusion that these passages do not give a logically consistent account of their fiction and truth; I will then look at them as rhetoric in the poststructuralist sense, that is, as writing that tries to accomplish as movement what cannot be maintained as logic.

Searle's account of fact and fiction can be found in his

article "The Logical Status of Fictional Discourse." He bases this distinction of fiction and serious assertion on the notion that in fiction, the speaker/writer is not committed to the truth or factuality of what he asserts. He suggests that various genres have conventions about which statements are to be taken as assertions of fact to which the writer is committed—"horizontal conventions" he calls them, which interrupt the normal "vertical" rules tying assertions to states of affairs in the world. He discusses two cases of nonfiction within fiction: first, when in the realistic novel statements are made about real places, and second, when general truths of the human condition are presented. The vertical conventions are different in each case. With descriptions of place, the vertical conventions link statements to facts in the public world accessible through experience or by means of maps or other descriptions. That is, the descriptions and paths of travel must be consistent with what is generally known about the places described. With general truths, the exact shape of the conventions has long been disputed by philosophers (how many and what kind of counterexamples would be necessary to refute them and so on). Let us simply assume that some vertical conventions can be settled on that can determine the truth value of generalizations and maxims. Horizontal conventions tell us which statements should be interpreted according to the vertical convention of factuality or truth. Equipped with the appropriate horizontal conventions, a reader could in effect read through a story with a highlighter, marking those statements to which the writer is committed as true. Consider one more example of a vertical convention for factual truth, this time for a truth of history. A description of actions, events, battles, and so on must square with already-written accounts enshrined as historical truth; if one wishes to offer a different description, considerable evidence must be furnished. The historical novel incorporates statements meant to be interpreted as historically true by means of certain horizontal conventions. Given these conventions, when Thackeray subjects George Osborne to the battle of Waterloo, his account of events, generals, battlefield, and what have you has to be consistent with what we generally know of that battle. With another set of horizontal conventions, he might not be so constrained.

Searle realizes that there is some play in this notion of convention: an author may innovate or establish special conventions with the reader, mixing true and fictional statements in unusual ways. However, in the absence of such negotiations with the reader, "default" assumptions will hold according to the genre: a reporter who writes a series of articles about the life and experiences of an individual who does not in fact exist is likely to have her Pulitzer prize taken away and to be sent to the mailroom for the rest of her career. Journalism is probably the most rigorously nonfictional of the genres, at least in regard to the identity of individuals, the factualness of events, and accuracy of quotation. Court challenges are obviously part of the reason these conventions are so thoroughly if not totally well-defined. Some scholarship is a little looser, allowing for exaggeration, even parody, especially in polemical uses. Even scientific writing allows for some fictionalizing, as Nigel Gilbert and Michael Mulkay show in regard to illustrations and diagrams in *Opening Pandora's Box*. Indeed, they show how illustrators attempt to assist readers in sorting out the factual and fictive in illustrations. In general, however, for all of these kinds of serious writing, individuals and events cited as evidence for hypotheses or theses should be carefully and accurately described.

This all seems quite reasonable and straightforward. Texts can contain stretches of factual discourse to be interpreted in the historical, geographical, moral, or cultural world we claim to share, and it can contain stretches of fictional discourse to be interpreted in a fictive world whose main standard is internal consistency. Horizontal conventions establish which stretches are which. We might note that the chief sources of fictitiousness are fictional places and individuals, and hence their experiences and actions—in most fiction, hemophilia is still an affliction only of men, and its not being so restricted in *Watt* is sufficiently atypical as to warrant a footnote by the author.

With this as a background, let us look now at a couple of

200

passages from advice books describing their use of personal experience and testimony. The first passage is from a diet book entitled *How to Get Thinner Once and For All:* "I will tell you some specific stories about real people with real problems whom I have treated in hospitals, at my Obesity and Nutrition Clinics of the New York City Department of Health, as well as in my private office" (14). The phrase *real people* is flagged with an asterisk; the asterisk leads to a footnote which reads: "The stories are all based on actual people and events. In order to avoid any identification, I have combined situations into composites, with fictitious names, ages, and occupations. Any similarity with one of my patients is absolute coincidence; any similarity with readers personally unknown to me is *not* unintended" (14n). What are we to make of this? The author, Morton Glenn, M.D., clearly means for his stories to be taken seriously as true, though the techniques he describes are those of the formation of a fictional character and incident. In fact, he deprives us of the very means by which we could check the truth of what he says: there may well be no actual, historical person who has been in the situation or had the experience he describes. If what Glenn reports to us are not facts, are his case histories fictions? That seems contrary to his intent also. The problem essentially is that we lack any vertical conventions for assessing the truth value of composite case histories.

Consider a second example, this from Manuel Smith's *When I Say No, I Feel Guilty,* a book which is fleshed out with many dialogues demonstrating assertive behavior: "Except for the specified training dialogues, all the assertive interactions offered in the following chapters are reports of real situations from learners using the systematic assertive skills out in the field. They were transcribed from notes, memory, tape recordings, and verbatim reports of students, patients, colleagues, acquaintances, and friends and were edited for purposes of confidentiality, brevity, clarity, and instruction" (133). Although Smith does not mention condensation into composites, the terms *brevity, clarity,* and *instruction* point to rather heavy editing, and the list of sources suggests some amalgamation. In addition, Smith has complicated matters by dramatizing rather than summarizing his sources, i.e., he uses directly quoted discourse (not "reported," despite what he says), which by convention is supposed to be closest to a speaker's exact words. That is to say, the vertical conventions for quoted speech involve a strong commitment to verbatim accuracy, and use of it forces the fiction/nonfiction issue: quoted speech is either factually accurate, or a dramatized fiction. Smith is not in fact claiming that the dialogues he gives actually occurred, or that the participants, if we could find them, would swear under oath that "that is what I said, to the best of my recollection." Elsewhere, in fact, he speaks of trying "to indicate [in the dialogue] the mood and emotional state of actual couples in therapy sessions," but he does want to make such a claim for the source or origin of the dialogues, however unavailable that may be for the reader's inspection. Again, are these dialogues truth, or fiction? What are the facts, the truth of which the writer is committed to? The problem is not with the presentation of generalized or typified statements per se, but the presentation of them as particular, concrete individual words and actions. To be sure, Smith and Glenn are trying to stipulate the proper conventions for interpreting their dialogues and composite case histories, but their accounts do not seem logically coherent. Indeed, they seem to be blurring the line between fact and fiction.

If then these passages don't make straightforward logical sense, what sense do they make? Whatever they are doing in the texts, they are not providing a coherent guide to truth claims, to sorting out the fiction and the nonfiction. To begin a rhetorical or functional approach, we may ask "why do these writers maintain that what they present is 'real' or 'actual'? What do they hope to gain by these muddled claims? Why don't they admit they are concocting fictional example to illustrate a type or mechanism?" It seems to me they want to offer the stories and dialogues as proofs that their analyses do touch empirical bases and their treatments do produce results in the real, tough, troubled world. Smith is quite clear about this. The passage cited continues: "Some of the dialogues are quite short, and, as you see, are examples of how some manipulation is rapidly extinguished. Others are quite long, and are left in their lengthy state to emphasize how persistent you need to be in some situations" (133). Glenn, the diet doctor, also wants to establish that his method does work with real cases off the streets of New York, but the last sentence of his footnote ("Any similarity with one of my patients is absolute coincidence; any similarity with readers personally unknown to me is *not* unintended.") suggests a second motive as well, namely that of promoting identification with the types and mechanisms of compulsive eating, perhaps on the assumption, widely promulgated by many writers, that people identify better with characters they assume are real, not make believe. Composite case histories fill the place of fiction for those who will not take responsibility for judging and evaluating the products of the imagination. If this analysis is right, the appeal of composite case histories and typical dialogues is founded squarely on a conceptual blur, a doubleness: they appear to introduce the evidence and testimony of actual persons, but are so idealized or typified that they cannot count as evidence, proof, support, verification, or what have you, only as illustration. They appear to be "experience speaking," but in fact they are an author's fictionalizing of his materials.

Glenn and Smith are unusually interested in trying to articulate their claims to truth, but basically they are not innovators in this regard; they simply make the conventions of "case history" explicit, though not logically coherent. It is worth looking now at two writers who address a more academic audience, writers who are somewhat innovative and considerably more sophisticated than our earnest advisors. These two authors, William Coles and Richard Mitchell, are writers writing about writing.

William Coles's *The Plural I* is an account of a composition class he taught at Case Institute of Technology some years ago, class by class, assignment by assignment. Coles's objective is to reenact the experience of change in that class, and for that purpose he develops what he calls a "novelistic account." Both Coles and the writer of the book's foreword, Richard Larson, are at some pains to articulate the exact truth claims and focus the engagement of the reader with the text. Here is Coles stipulating the horizontal conventions for reading *The Plural I:*

> Since certain readers will wonder, perhaps I should say here that in this fictionalized account of life in the classroom I have reproduced all the student papers we worked with and all the writing assignments for the course just as they were written. But it should go without saying that the dialogues of the book are not verbatim transcriptions of what was said in class. (Tape recordings of classrooms—aural, video, or both—have about the same relevance to the meaning of what goes on there as sex manuals do to what it means to make love.) I don't mean that I've simply made up the conversations; the student writing I reproduce should serve as proof that I haven't. The dialogues of the book have about the same relation to what went on in class as, say, van Gogh's *Sunflowers* does to sunflowers—when I am successful with them. When I am not successful with them, the relation doesn't matter. (4)

We could take out our highlighters, then, and mark all the assignments and papers as alleged historical fact. If Coles discussed a paper he does not cite, or didn't discuss one he does cite, he is falsifying the facts. Coles wants those papers to function as proofs—he cites earlier and later work by the same student to show improvement. Upon this basis of alleged fact, however, is erected the structure of dialogues mainly between him and the students about the writing, and in regard to these dialogues, the claims as to historicity are very carefully couched. Coles wants to claim a middle space between simply recorded and simply made up, which I suppose roughly translates into Searle's terms as simply asserted or simply pretend-asserted. To claim this space, he uses the two analogies of the sex manuals and the sunflowers, which make subtly different points. Sex manuals fail by not conveying the meaning of making love. Here the point is that for such mechanical records to be meaningful, they require interpretation. Any ethnographer would agree with that, and certainly maintain that no entanglement in fiction is necessarily entailed by the need for interpretation. The sunflowers, however, move us into the realm of intensity and subjectivity of perception, substituting "successfulness" for accuracy or meaningfulness. Does Coles's "successfulness" look back toward the original events (that is, "successful in recreating what was collectively experienced"?) or forward, toward the reader's experience of dramatic conflict and resolution? Is the standard of success historical accuracy or vivid insight? The kind of identification Coles seeks is not that of reader with a type of case history, but a complex involvement in a sustained drama—a concrete universal, an esthetic object, the experience of which is self-validating. Interestingly, Charles Altieri argues in *Act and Quality* that this is precisely the mode of knowledge to be obtained from literature.

The essence of Coles's account is a movement rather than a coherent logic. It begins with the appeal to real world origin and efficacy that we have seen in the case history books, but ends in an appeal to essentially esthetic criteria. The movement even tends to blur: on several readings, I have construed the sex manuals analogy as one based on intensity of realization of the experience, making it equivalent to the sunflowers. This is to miss its function linking fact to fiction. To see how delicate the effect is here, we have only to compare Richard Larson's paraphrase of this paragraph in his foreword: "The encounters between teacher and students, and between students and students, are recorded as they might have happened, or (to borrow Suzanne Langer's term for fictional creation) 'virtually' as they happened' (viii). This passage swings between the two poles we have been tracing, *recorded* on the one hand sounding like the reproduction of the real, but *might have happened* abruptly opening up another realm of reality pulling the discourse away from a merely verbatim account. "Set down as they might have happened"—yes, that's a frank acknowledgement of fiction; and on the other hand, "recorded in a somewhat schematized fashion"—yes, that's a reasonable claim to accuracy, but "recorded as they might have happened"—no, not within the same sentence. They need Coles's paragraph to allow them to blend.

Coles shares with Smith and Glenn a respect for the real

and the actual, since they all want to anchor the fictive parts of their texts to it as an origin. The last writer I will touch on, Richard Mitchell, does not respect the real materials and situations which he discusses. Mitchell's *Less Than Words Can Say* is a book about the decline of English, and he follows the rules of the genre in citing examples of bad writing that have actually been done, and signed, by persons who, though described, remain anonymous. These writings are the evidence—the signs of the the times—that English is in serious trouble. Mitchell balks at calling their writing *real*, though, because it fails to express anything meaningful. Mitchell is a sort of German idealist for whom the real is the rational, and only the rational is the real. There is indeed a strong current of fantasy in the book in which the unreality implicit in the writings comes to full realization. Bridging the real facts and the fantasies is a pervasive use of mythologizing, satiric exaggeration, and ironic mimicry which is not always clearly marked off from the seriously asserted parts. Even the actual incidents shade into parables in the telling. More than that, Mitchell constructs one chapter on the debasement of language leading to the debasement of culture by discussing the most primitive tribe known, the Jiukiukwe of the Orinoco basin. This sketch reads suspiciously like a compendium of traits of primitiveness amassed by anthropological linguists. As one reads this chapter, one may begin to suspect that it is violating what Richard Ohmann calls "perhaps the *only* serious condition of good faith that holds for literary works and their authors," which is "that the author not give out as fact what is fiction" (53). As my own hunch grows that chapter two is such a transgression—is an unannounced spoof—I seek confirmation that the Jiukiukwe do not exist. I scurry off to the reference librarian, who finds my request inconceivable: I want proof that no other information can be had about the Jiukiukwe. After twenty minutes of repeated explanation, we check through indices of the cultures and languages of South American. Eureka! I have not found them. The Jiukiukwe do not exist. The librarian does not understand my jubilation. She has failed, and offers to try to contact a friend at the Library of Congress.

Why am I pleased, as if I had just tracked down a case of plagiarism, though what I have tracked down is not the source but the nonsource. Why do I not feel indignant, deceived? Perhaps because Mitchell has made clear already that he does not court my good faith, but rather my ability to read, to tell the genuine from the fake, the real from the unreal without explicit stipulation of the horizontal conventions? I think so—both Mitchell and I are professors of English, and enjoy the reversals that arise from switching conventions. Especially I do not feel tricked because Mitchell is not claiming to prove his case or ground it on facts. Such a free trading back and forth would be disastrous for Coles or Smith or Glenn. I think we should conclude that in Mitchell's book, the distinction of fact and fiction is essentially neutralized: it carries no functional load. Or as Mitchell might say, his examples of the so-called real are less real than the Jiukiukwe.

Notice that with the Jiukiukwe, however, we are back again on the familiar, easier ground of public fact and have escaped the swampier terrain of true personal experience, composite and dramatized. That is, in the case of the Jiukiukwe, we know the vertical conventions for truth and can determine that, insofar as the chapter is asserted, it is asserted parabolically—it is fiction. But let us look back to Glenn, Smith, and Coles. It is not implausible to construe the passages cited as I have done, as instances of the setting of conventions with the reader governing the truth conditions of the various statements in the works. I think they would be totally unsatisfactory to a logician, however, and are better approached in terms of the desires of the authors to be taken as constituting serious evidence for their arguments. It is interesting that all of these passages pose the question in terms of the origin of the experience being presented, and are passages about writing, insofar as writing the experiences involves interpreting and reshaping the original materials, which are themselves only representations and traces of the experience itself. Only

Coles seems to glimpse the principle that such writing of experience inevitably involves deferral, that writing experience or dialogue always gives an experience different from its origin. Perhaps this is so because he undertakes to convey the most complex, particular experience, though even he wishes to insist on the factual and evidentiary nature of the dialogues. But conscious or not, even the most practical and unreflecting of writers cannot escape the problematic of writing that is now so much on our minds.

This piece has focused on writing as rhetorically strategic, and it has proved possible to appreciate intricacy, subtlety, and complexity (at times) as it goes about its job. I would like to conclude by locating this approach in relation to a basic struggle in the study of writing that just won't go away, both in composition studies and in prose analysis and criticism. In a recent piece called "Different Products, Different Processes: A Theory About Writing," Maxine Hairston describes a spectrum of kinds of writing which runs roughly from the purely ephemeral, instrumental kind destined for the circular file (Class I), through more complex tasks of organizing and presenting material for purposes more or less already defined (magazine feature articles, research reports, case studies) destined, as it were, for the office file (Class II), to original, exploratory, reflective pieces aspiring to an LC number and a place in the canon (Class III). Her point is that mid-scale practical writing is important in people's lives and that writing it well should be taught and valued as much as the production of pieces written with the "for itself" quality of art. Struggle as she will to redress the balance of value, she cannot resist the greater weight of Class III, and promotes to Class III judicial decisions, contingency plans, and position statements insofar as the writers are making meaning as they write (448). She concludes that the principle virtues of practical writing are clarity, smooth style, and solid competence. Such a conclusion reflects the conceptual impoverishment of "expository writing." Most of her examples of practical writing have a distinct persuasive point and can be praised or blamed for the relative skill and cunning they exhibit as arguments.

Fiction in Persuasion

A similar disregard, indeed, at times almost contempt, for the pedestrian, utilitarian, merely clear sort of plain prose is evident in the estheticizing school of prose criticism, the school that chooses to praise a nonfiction prose writer it likes for his or her *style*, where style can be measured by its distance from bland, ordinary good behavior. So Joseph Harris, in another recent piece, cites for praise William Coles (!), likening him to Roland Barthes and saying of them "Neither works much for that tone of lucid restraint that is the supposed ideal of scholarly prose, and neither settles for the numb workaday voicelessness that is its actual norm" (160). Elsewhere Harris praises the opacity of Coles's sentences, the way they force rereading. Similarly, Charles Schuster (in this volume) values Richard Selzer's style for its breathtaking departures from "linear exposition" with its excessive explicitness. Schuster's terms are eerily reminiscent of high New Critical valorization of the poetic image over discursive reason; Harris's are more poststructuralist in flavor; but they both valorize by pushing off against some workaday zero grade of prose devoid of esthetic interest, and therefore devoid of interest. In all fairness, I should add that some years ago when I wrote *Constructing Texts* I too described good writing in estheticizing terms like complexity, richness, and a significant ordering of experience. And I would still hold that such an approach is not wrong, but merely limited and likely to make the study of nonfiction prose an annex of literary criticism. We will discover a great deal of good writing when we can find ways of esteeming without estheticizing it. Certain of the poststructuralist insights into the working of written language extend beyond literature and can be illuminatingly applied to texts with clear practical purposes.

Works Cited

Altieri, Charles. *Act and Quality.* Amherst: Massachusets, 1981.
Coles, William. *The Plural I.* New York: Holt, Rinehart, and Winston, 1978.

Gilbert, Nigel and Michael Mulkay. *Opening Pandora's Box.* Cambridge: Cambridge, 1983.

Glenn, Morton, M.D. *How to Get Thinner Once and For All.* New York: Dutton, 1965.

Hairston, Maxine. "Different Products, Different Processes: A Theory About Writing." *College Composition and Communication 37* (1986): 442–52.

Harris, Joseph. "The Plural Text/The Plural Self: Roland Barthes and William Coles." *College English 49* (1987): 158–170.

Mitchell, Richard. *Less Than Words Can Say.* Boston: Little, Brown, 1979.

Ohmann, Richard. "Speech, Literature, and the Space Between." *New Literary History 4* (1972): 47–64.

Searle, John. "The Logical Status of Fictional Discourse." *New Literary History 6* (1975); reprinted in *Expression and Meaning*, Cambridge: Cambridge, 1979: 58–75.

Smith, Manual. *When I Say No, I Feel Guilty.* New York: Bantam Books, 1975.

11
THE PLEASURES OF VOICE
IN THE LITERARY ESSAY

Explorations in the Prose of
Gretel Ehrlich and Richard Selzer

Peter Elbow

We write not with the fingers but with the whole person.

Virginia Woolf, Orlando

It's hard not to talk about writing as though it were speech: in discussing silent texts we talk about the "voice" or "tone of voice"; also about the "speaker" and about what we "hear" a piece of writing "saying." Diverse critics even refer to a writer as having "found her voice."

Influential modern figures have rejected the psychological or metaphysical implications of voice and given us critical terms which seek to separate the "voice" or "character" or "ethos" in a text from the actual author or writer or self behind the text: Pound's "persona," Yeats's "mask," Booth's "implied author." Next come *post*moderns to insist that there is no such thing as a self or author behind the text—either to be revealed *or* concealed by the text. But when these critics kill off the author, they merely inject new life into voice: the text is nothing *but* voices. (Yet all discourse is "writing.")

Though voice has become more than ever an unclear and controversial notion, I will try to show that we need the term. Voice will become a useful critical concept for the study of texts once we build up a foundation of analysis and application—a foundation I seek to work on in this essay. I can make the term much more serviceable by distinguishing three kinds of voice: (1) *audible voice*: how much do we *hear* the text as we read it? (2) *dramatic voice*: what kind of speaker or writer is implied in the text (and how vividly)? (3) *one's own voice*: what is the relation of the text to the actual writer? I will illustrate these senses of voice with examples from Gretel Ehrlich and Richard Selzer.

(1) Audible Voice:
How Much Do We Hear the Text?

Robert Frost said that the distinguishing mark of good prose is "the speaking tone of voice somehow entangled in the words and fastened to the page for the ear of the imagination" (Introduction). Though texts are literally silent, some texts make us hear someone's voice. Admittedly, we can "sound out" any text and thus inject audible voice into it, but only some texts seem to make this sound for us. Texts with audible voice give us the sense of a sound coming up from the page by itself, and they seem to *give* us energy rather than requiring energy of us. I highlight here the uttered dimension of written language as opposed to the constructed or composed dimension: the aural and experienced-in-time dimension as opposed to the visual and experienced-in-space dimension.

Perhaps the best illustration of audible voice is the radical absence of it. The classic examples tend to come from government documents, army manual instructions, bureaucratic memos.[1] But garden-variety inaudible prose is all around us

---

1. From a letter from a stock company:

In connection with the Offer to Purchase for Cash All Outstanding Units of Beneficial Interest of American Royalty Trust (the 'Unit Offer') and the Offer to Purchase All Outstanding Shares of Common Stock, $3.33 Cumulative Convertible Preferred Stock, $2.28 Cumulative Preferred Stock and $1.65 Cumulative Preferred Stock (the 'Stock Offer') each dated August 7, 1986 by FPCO Inc., PETRO-LEWIS CORPORATION (the 'Company'), and, in the case of the Unit Offer, American Royalty Producing Company ('ARPCO') and PLC-ARPC, Inc. ('PLC-ARPC'), by letters dated August 7, 1986 (the 'Recommendation Letters'), have conveyed their recommendations regarding the Unit Offer and the Stock Offer.

in all the lifeless or tangled writing we cannot avoid having to read.

Because Selzer and Ehrlich are full of audible prose, they provide a good occasion for extended analysis of what turns out to be a rich question: where does this sound—or illusion of sound—come from?

The most obvious source is speech itself. I suspect research will bear me out in saying that written language is more likely to be *heard* if it uses the syntax, rhythms, and word choice characteristic of speech. For example, here's how Selzer begins an essay: "I heard the other day that Hugh Franciscus had died" (*Letters* 21). And here's how Ehrlich starts her book: "It's May and I've just awakened from a nap. . . . Winter lasts six months here" (*Solace* 1). These writers endow their prose with audible voice by using the syntax and diction of speech. (Admittedly, "awakened" is not something we usually say.)

But consider this passage from Selzer: "Not for me the festive air of the death bed. No, thanks. I can wait for the wonders of eternity. Wrap me not in tranquil joy. A shot of penicillin will do just fine" (*Letters* 146). Of course audibility comes from the little bursts of speechlike syntax and diction ("No thanks," "I can wait," "A shot of penicillin will do just fine"). But what interests me here is the audibility of the mannered and artificial sentences that we would never speak: "Not for me the festive air"; "Wrap me not in tranquil joy." Why do we hear these phrases? The term *sonorous* comes to hand, pointing literally at what we are investigating: sound. Rhythmic, iambic, pithy, poetic. Selzer loves cadences from Shakespeare and the King James translation of the Bible which our ears are accustomed to hearing sonorously declaimed from the stage and the pulpit.

Thus it's important to note that something completely different from speech can nevertheless be experienced as audible and have a strong "uttered" or existing-in-time quality—*if* it has the right kinds of rhythms, parallels, and echoes. I'm guessing that most readers would find the following example audible even though they'd never uttered or heard or spoken such a massively left-branching syntactic structure:

213

Peter Elbow

Because these men work with animals, not machines or numbers, because they live outside in landscapes of torrential
beauty, because they are confined to a place and a routine
embellished with awesome variables, because calves die in the
arms that pulled others into life, because they go to the mountains as if on a pilgrimage to find out what makes a herd of elk
tick, their strength is also a softness, their toughness, a rare
delicacy. (Ehrlich, *Solace* 52–53).

Musicians say that certain passages "lie under the fingers."
They mean that the notes are very playable. However un-
speechlike, that sentence by Ehrlich is very sayable.

For another source of audibility, consider next two versions of a passage about morning:

Morning. Blue air comes ringed with coyotes. The ewes
wake clearing their communal throats like old men. Lambs
shake their flop-eared heads at leaves of grass, negotiating the
blade. (Ehrlich, *Solace* 56)

In the morning when blue air comes ringed with coyotes,
the ewes wake clearing their communal throats like old men,
while the lambs shake their flop-eared heads at leaves of grass,
negotiating the blade. (My transformation)

I suspect most of us would hear Ehrlich's version more.
We could say that its short simple sentences are more speechlike than the long embedded sentence. Yet no one would ever
speak such poetic sentences, however short. It's my guess that
the real source of audibility is this: Ehrlich's simple sentences
give us an experience of mental activity *going on*—whereas the
single embedded sentence gives more of an experience of
a *completed* experience or thought. (Walter Ong relates oral
discourse to "language as event" and written discourse to "language as record.")

Think about sentence combining exercises which ask students to combine or embed simple sentences:

He stepped on the gas. The car surged forward.

becomes

After stepping on the gas, the car surged forward.

214

The Pleasures of Voice

Notice how this combining serves to undermine voice and energy and mental activity. We have changed thought-going-on into thought-having-gone-on.

Another source of audible voice in texts: textual cues that heighten our sense of a *person in there*—someone at home, someone making that language. For example: "Take Dom Pietro. Eighteen years in a monastery and he has remained a personage. I can see him carried across the Piazza San Marco . . . shedding benedictions on the crowd. Listen . . ." (and Selzer goes off on an illustrative anecdote) (*Repairs* 18). What interests me is "Take Dom Pietro" and "Listen." Yes, those two short sentences are speechlike, but more than that, they call attention to their status as *speech acts*.

Admittedly all discourse is a speech act—not just a *saying* but a *doing*; not just an assertion in the realm of meaning, but an acting in the realm of people. Speech act theory shows us that we haven't described discourse if we've just described the meaning or language itself; we've left something out till we've also described who is trying to do what to whom—and in what setting. Nevertheless, *writing*—especially poor writing—has a tendency to be remarkably effective at seeming to belie speech-act theory—that is, at *hiding* its status as an act. Writing often suffers from the sense that no one is trying to do anything to anyone, that there's no context, and thus that there's nothing but "language" sitting there asserting meaning under its own auspices.

The paradigmatic example of *non*-speech-act language is the grammar-book sentence—e.g., "The cat is on the mat." Notice how it becomes audible when we say, "I promise that the cat is on the mat." When prose calls attention to itself as a speech act—language doing, not just saying—it usually heightens our sense of audible voice.

Thus every time a writer writes, "Notice that . . ." or "What I'm arguing is . . ." or "Let me now turn to . . ." she is calling attention on the silent page to the speech act she's performing—thus heightening our sense of the writer's presence as a person acting on us. Usually this heightens the audible voice. This effect is stronger if she actually refers to herself or to the

215

reader. And stronger still if she uses first person for herself
and second person for the reader. Thus notice the progression
here:

Warm clothing will be needed for the trip.

The organizer urges participants to bring plenty of warm
clothing.

I urge you to bring plenty of warm clothing.

My subject here is not energy in general but voice in
particular—one kind of energy. But it's worth noting that
when a text has audible voice we experience the text as providing the energy to make a noise—the energy to make the meaning come up off the page. When words record thinking going
on rather than completed thought—or when words call attention to the speech act involved—then we experience the text
as having energy.

One of the strong sources of audibility in Ehrlich is her
fresh and interesting metaphors. For example:

A front is *pulling* the huge sky over me (1).

But why should sound be increased by metaphors (or at least
some metaphors)? Consider these two sentences:

The table is stationary.

The table lurks stationary.

Notice how "lurks" as a metaphor doesn't just animate the
table, it animates the writer. It heightens our sense of the
presence of an active consciousness at work in the text, exerting
a force on her material.

The principle here, then, is that audible voice is increased
by words which call attention to the presence of the person
writing. Thus the second sentence below will probably be
slightly more audible because of the mere change of one adjective—a change that signals the feelings of the writer:

The government food was distributed throughout the district.

The hateful food was distributed throughout the district.

216

And so when Ehrlich writes, "Winter lasts six months here," she is making her sentence more audible than if she had written, "Winter lasts six months in Wyoming." "Here" calls attention to a particular person writing from a particular place and situation. "Winter lasts six months in Wyoming" could be a sentence in an almanac—words, as it were, from nobody to nobody.

Though I'm obviously celebrating the pleasures of audible voice, I'm not saying it's enough by itself to make writing good. The following sentence may be full of audible voice, but if it were found in a serious essay about the causes of the French Revolution, it would have to be judged bad for not doing the task:

> I'm sitting here looking at the cursor on my screen. It's blinking at me as much as to say, "What *are* the causes of the French Revolution?"

(2) Dramatic Voice:
What Kind of Person Is Implied in the Text?

The sound of a spoken voice can tell us *who* is talking. Think of a phone call from a person we've not seen in years when we instantly recognize who it is. Voice prints are said to be more reliable than fingerprints. But more to the point here, the sound of a voice seems to tell us *what kind of person* is talking. That is, we often feel we can hear someone's character or personality in the way she speaks. Thus another species of pleasure in voice is the pleasure of sensing character in the text. This is voice as character, ethos, persona, mask, or implied author.[2]

The most obvious cues about this dramatic dimension of the text usually come from the audible voice or speech qualities. But even where there is no audible voice there is still this

2. For the sake of this analysis, I neglect the subtle but important distinctions between ethos, implied author, and persons. For a rich summary analysis of these terms, see Nan Johnson and Roger Cherry.

second dimension of voice as character. Wayne Booth uses the term *implied author* to stress that *every* text implies a character who produces those words. Just as there is no day without weather, however boring, so there is no text without implied author, however nondescript.

But even though we can infer an implied author in any text, it's important to note that not every text has an implied author or dramatic voice *to the same degree*. In some texts the ethos or implied author jumps out at us; the persona is vivid and dramatically realized (even if he is a quiet sort of person). In other texts we have to infer and indeed create that implied author.

Also, in some texts the implied author is consistent, whereas in others we may get mixed cues. Such inconsistency is characteristic of pieces by inexperienced writers or joint authors. Faint, inconsistent, or complex cues will make readers disagree more in their inferences about implied author.

And so, just as all texts can be sounded audibly but some seem to give us their sound, so too all texts can yield character or ethos but some seem to give the character. The terms *character*, *persona*, and *mask* all come from drama, and voice as character serves as the dramatic dimension of a text. When that dramatic dimension is strong—when we experience the implied author or persona as vivid and interesting and coherent—we tend to experience that as a virtue in the writing (though of course writing can be good without this virtue). Thus textbooks are characteristically dreary because they lack any strong implied author or persona or dramatic voice.

Perhaps we shouldn't use the term *voice* for this dimension of texts when we already have so many other terms to refer to the kind of person that a text implies. But even if we wanted to, we couldn't stamp out what is in fact the most common sense of voice when applied to texts. More positively, I find that one of the best ways to figure out the character of the implied author is to ask, "What kind of *voice* do you hear in there?" This question is especially helpful in teaching.

The Pleasures of Voice

Let's ask it then of Ehrlich. What kind of voice do we hear in the two following passages?

> It's May and I've just awakened from a nap, curled against sagebrush the way my dog taught me to sleep—sheltered from wind. A front is pulling the huge sky over me, and from the dark a hailstone has hit me on the head. I'm trailing a band of two thousand sheep across a stretch of Wyoming badlands, a fifty-mile trip that takes five days because sheep shade up in hot sun and won't budge until it's cool. Bunched together now, and excited into a run by the storm, they drift across dry land, tumbling into draws like water and surge out again onto the rugged, choppy plateaus that are the building blocks of this state. (*Solace* 1)
>
> To emerge from isolation can be disorienting. Everything looks bright, new, vivid. After I had been herding sheep for only three days, the sound of the camp tender's pickup flustered me. Longing for human company, I felt a foolish grin take over my face; yet I had to resist an urgent temptation to run and hide. (*Solace* 5)

I hear a somewhat flat voice; a bit tight-lipped; a refusal to be graceful; an insistence on somewhat muscularly shoving words together without much lubrication or comfortable rhythm. In describing people who live in Wyoming, Ehrlich happened to describe something of her own voice: "Sentence structure [here] is shortened to the skin and bones of a thought" (6). "People here feel pride because they live in such a harsh place . . . ." (3).

We hear something of the voice of Walker Gibson's "tough guy" (*Tough* 28–42). Here it's someone who lets us know she's been around, endured hard things we probably haven't endured, who is in fact interested in feelings but tends to avoid much direct talk or sustained attention to them. She doesn't seem to trust the traditional, graceful, and sonorous cadences that Selzer often uses. Her voice often seems stripped down where his sounds dressed up. Yet she lets in little blips of lyricism, and in the end there is considerable honest self-revelation. But where Selzer comes up close to us, as it were,

219

and puts his arm around our shoulder and speaks with an intonation of personal feeling, Ehrlich's personal revelations have a kind of flat, blurted, distant quality. It's as though she's saying, "I'll tell you about my inner life as long as you stay over there on the other side of the room. And I'm not going to tell it all at once. I'll only let it out in bits and pieces—and keep changing the subject."

The ordinary way to describe this rich voice is to say that we hear a complex character with many dimensions or sides— a voice that is moving in its complexity. But—taking a leaf from Bakhtin—we could designate these "sides" as, themselves, "voices" in a polyphonic self:

A laconic tough guy who refuses to name feelings.

sudden infusions of a deft lyrical voice.

Notes of a metaphysical, playfully intellectual voice such as in "negotiating the blade."

Occasional soundings of long periodic poetic voice—unsubtle, heavier.

(3) One's Own Voice: What Is the Relation of the Text to the Actual Writer?

This is slippery territory. I will explore a cluster of three phenomena *linked* to the phrase "one's own voice"—leaving open for now the question as to whether this is one entity or a family of three related ones: (a) One's own voice as a "distinctive, recognizable voice." (b) One's own voice as "having a voice" or "having the authority to speak." (c) One's own voice as "authentic voice" or "resonance."

(3a) *One's Own Voice as a Distinctive, Recognizable Voice*

Even the best critics sometimes speak of a writer "finding her own voice." (Helen Vendler says it of Sylvia Plath—describing how she went beyond sounding like Dylan Thomas

The Pleasures of Voice

["Intractable Metal" 131].) People use this common locution to mean that the writer has attained a distinctive style that sets her apart from others. One of the pleasures of reading is to get to know an author with her own voice—and to hear that voice again even in new and somewhat different material. "Having one's own voice" in this sense means, I suppose, that the writer creates a recognizable, consistent, and (usually) unique implied author—as I'd say that Ehrlich does in her book. Selzer in his many books shows more variation in voice. I'm not sure I'd say he has a single distinctive, recognizable voice. ("Distinctive, recognizable voice" is sometimes used in a narrower sense to mean that the writer's textual voice resembles her speaking voice.)

(3b) One's Own Voice as "Having a Voice" or "Having the Authority to Speak"

When a writer finds his own voice in the sense just used—finds a style that seems *his*—he often takes on a certain added assurance or authority. This relates to the fact that when we say someone "has a voice in something," we mean he has some power, "has a say," or can "speak out." In fact the phrase "having a voice" sometimes means explicitly "having a vote" or "having the official sanction to speak." The authority dimension of voice is most striking if we look at the negative case: people who somehow experience themselves as voiceless. "What's the matter? Cat got your tongue?" Notice that this classic jibe is always spoken by someone with authority to someone without—usually an adult to a child.

When someone has no voice in this sense, she may experience herself as having lots to say but unable to say it; or she may experience herself as empty. But when she "finds a voice" it's as though a cork were pulled out: she speaks up, speaks out, says her piece. She experiences herself as having lots to say. Sometimes she realizes in retrospect that she *did* have lots to say earlier even though she had experienced herself as empty. Adrienne Rich and Tillie Olson speak of women find-

Peter Elbow

ing themselves without voice. (See also Belenky et al. *Women's Ways of Knowing*.)

Voicelessness may stem from not getting enough respect and support. After all, it is hard to speak if you feel you will not be heard or taken seriously. People also experience themselves as voiceless because they don't "have the lingo"—don't know how to use the accepted voice or discourse of the community. But notice how undamaged children will speak out even if they don't know the lingo, and even if others are not really listening. It would seem that humans have a need to speak out and be heard. Thus in the end, this kind of voice depends on some kind of authority or trust *in oneself*.

The psychological merges into the political. Hannah Arendt was interested in what she called "action-and-speech": "finding the right words at the right moments, quite apart from the information or communication they may convey, is action" (*Human Condition* 26). Paolo Freire explores this dimension of voice as authority and action.

One of the pleasures of texts, then, is hearing a kind of assurance or solidity of voice. Many of our students undermine their writing by only tentatively proffering their discourse as though with a half-bent arm—as much as to ask the reader timidly, "Is this okay? Will you accept this?" This stance is not surprising when we reflect that students are not accustomed to writing to communicate what they know to someone who doesn't know it, but rather as a way to be tested for whether they know what the reader-teacher already knows.

Authority of voice comes naturally to Selzer—perhaps especially from his role as surgeon. He loves to celebrate his free violation of what is most deeply taboo— cutting into the human body—and clearly loves to make graphic what usually frightens or disgusts us. He titles one of his books *Letters to a Young Doctor*, permitting him to put his explorations for the general public in the form of advice from a seasoned professional to a green novice:

> The surgeon takes incorrigible delight in the immersion of his own body in that of another. It is a kind of love. But it

222

The Pleasures of Voice

is never to be confused with eroticism. Dwelling as he does
within his patient's body, when a surgeon makes an incision, it
is a self-inflicted wound.
    Poised above the patient the surgeon is like a priest guard-
ing and preserving fire. He takes strength from this closeness.
For the body of the patient is the sun, the whorl of light and
heat that radiates life into this room. It is the patient's heat that
foments this work, his light that makes it visible and possible.
(*Letters* 109)

    Authority of voice is most in question at the beginnings
of discourse. (How do we "gain the floor" when we haven't
spoken before?) If we look at the beginning of Ehrlich's book,
we see an interesting assertion of authority. ("It's May and I've
just awakened from a nap. . . .") She is faced with a problem:
she must establish herself as someone doing "man's work" in
"man's country" in the traditional male situation of solitary
explorer, yet she clearly wants to avoid the swagger and establish her credentials with quietness and understatement. She
pulls this off and establishes her own voice-as-authority;
though in this opening paragraph of the book I sense her, as
it were, *trying* to carry it off (needing *quickly* to demonstrate
her ability to survive the rigors) whereas later when she gets
rolling in the book she seems able to establish that authoritative
voice without trying—perhaps trusting herself more.

(3c) *One's Own Voice as "Authentic Voice" or "Resonance"*

    What is the relationship of the text to the real author?
This is the most controversial dimension of voice in texts. By
distinguishing three kinds of voice and dividing the third kind
into three, I've tried to "contain" most of the controversy about
voice here into 3c and thereby leave the other senses of voice
more solid and widely usable.
    To talk about the relationship of the text to the real author
is to violate the intentional fallacy. Let me pause a moment
and justify this practice on theoretical grounds.

223

Peter Elbow

Authentic Voice and the Intentional Fallacy: A Short Argument

Always there are two "authors" for any text: the implied author as it were *in* the text and the actual historical author as it were *behind* the text. (Even if the text is dry or jumbled, we can still infer an implied author; and if the text is generated by a committee or a computer, those are *are* real authors.) What's important to note is that we always have a choice about which "author" to emphasize, the real author or the implied author: which dimension of the text to attend to, the "behind-ness" or the "in-ness."

The New Critics tell us to emphasize the implied author, saying it is a fallacy even to try to talk about the real author at all because such talk is about something we can never know: we have contact only with what's *in* the text, we can never have contact with what's *behind* the text. (In truth, Wimsatt and Beardsley took a more moderate position in their original essay than what has come to be the doctrine of "the intentional fallacy." They allow written biographical material.)

But just because the real author and his or her intentions are invisible, that doesn't mean they are unknowable. It's a matter of where we put our attention. Think about Polanyi's example of a blind man using a cane. It's true that his hand has no contact with the street; only with the handle of the cane. Must we conclude that his inferences about the street represent an "extensional fallacy"? Obviously we can attend "through" something to what is beyond or behind it.

Thus our choice about whether to emphasize the implied author or the real author is really a choice where to attend—a choice about modes of reading. When we emphasize the implied author or "in-ness," we tend to treat the text as whole, integral, complete—to put a kind of frame around it. The New Critics show us how much this helps our reading: we make an act of faith that the text, even if it seems peculiar, is just as it ought to be, and our job is to find the rightness and coherence in that peculiarity. And correspondingly they show us how bad it is for our reading if we say, "Oh dear, Shakespeare seems to have been nodding here and didn't put down what he meant to say." Or, "This Anglo- Saxon text seems odd here so there must be a Papist interpolation."

When, on the other hand, we emphasize the real author or "behind-ness"—refraining from putting a frame around the text—we allow ourselves to think about a real person who wrote the text, allowing ourselves to make guesses about his or her intention. Thus we allow ourselves to think about the text as "damaged" or "incomplete" in the sense of not quite managing to say well or completely those things which (we infer from cues in the text) the writer was trying to say. In short, we allow ourselves to look at a text as showing "readable" signs of a writer's intention which lie behind the text.

The theory of the intentional fallacy grew out of work on established literary texts. Work on *student* texts compels us to look again at the theory. As teachers we have to permit ourselves, sometimes at least, to talk about "damaged" or "flawed" or "incomplete" texts—texts in which real authors did not achieve their intention but in which we, if we're good readers, can sense those intentions.

Yet teaching doesn't ask us simply to *deny* the intentional fallacy. We need *both* ways of reading texts. That is, we need to be able to play dumb with students about intentions or "behind-ness" and say, "Oh, did you really intend that? I had no idea. From what you actually wrote, I took your meaning to be———and your attitude to be———." Yet is there a good teacher who doesn't also play smart about intentions and "behind-ness" to read subtly and make good guesses—in order to detect faint or half-realized intentions in student writing? We can often help students realize their intentions better if we can see them. If we cannot see them most of our advice will be misguided. (And of course it's not just student writers who have intentions they are not aware of but which good readers can sometimes see.) Most good writing teachers are subtle readers who happily violate the intentional fallacy—listen for authentic and inauthentic voice—despite what they say in their literature classrooms. Example: a student drifts into a breezy or coy tone which we sense is false; we have a distinct impression that he has begun to be frightened by what he is on the brink of saying.

Both kinds of reading can fairly claim to be "careful reading." The New Critical emphasis on "in-ness" and implied author is careful by insisting on finding every scrap of meaning and coherence in the text *as it is*. This approach insists on figuring out how a text functions when posited to be a working organism. The other emphasis—on "behind-ness" and real author—is careful reading in a different way: it insists on looking at the text not only for what's there but also for cues about what's (in a sense) not there—or behind it. This latter approach is of course risky: how presumptuous of us to make these guesses, whether with proven artist or beginning student. We know we are often wrong. But good reading and good teaching depend on the ingrained human tendency to make these dangerous inferences.

Authentic Voice or Resonance in Selzer

If we want to give ourselves permission to talk about the relationship of a text to the actual author, literary essays like those by Ehrlich and Selzer are a good place to start. Both essayists write about their own reactions, experiences, and perceptions. They imply they are being honest, they engage in significant and striking self-revelations, and they convince me for the most part of their honesty. Yet they also clearly "perform" and adopt or create voices. Selzer in particular loves to dramatize himself and play with different voices and roles.

But when we've read enough of some writer, we sometimes sense that certain passages are particularly strong or "right"—have a reassuring resonance—because they are somehow in the right relationship to the writer. This is not a question of *sincerity*. When words are sincere, they fit only the writer's *conscious* intentions. We have all had the experience of hearing perfectly sincere words which nevertheless don't ring true or solid because they don't take account of important

The Pleasures of Voice

feelings or character-facets of which the speaker may be unaware. ("I just *know* I'm not angry." "I *promise* I'll have my paper in on time.") When words are resonant, they fit the whole person—including his unconscious. In a famous literary example, D. H. Lawrence claimed that Melville had a characteristic voice with a certain moral earnestness (a distinctive recognizable voice, as in 3a), but that this voice was nevertheless "false" because it left out a larger, deeper, amoral vision which Lawrence found central to Melville's best work.[3]

To illustrate resonance or authentic voice in Selzer, consider two passages which are both in a sense about the physical love of a patient's body. I've already provided the first passage a few pages back ("The surgeon takes incorrigible delight in the immersion of his own body in that of another . . ."). Compare that passage with this one:

> From the phone I see her [Ora Guilfoil, a nurse] approach the next patient. She takes out her bandage scissors as though to begin removing the dressing from the man's leg. All at once I see her move to the head of the bed. She bends to peer into the face of the man lying there. Suddenly, she flings herself upon his body. One knee on the bed, and she is aboard, her skirt hiked. Now she straddles the man and bends to clamp his mouth with her own. As though her tongue were a key that would unlock the secret that lay in his body if only she could find the right way to insert it. She beats his chest with her fists, and huffs, blowing into a grate to keep a meager ember alive. The whole bed rattles and slides.

3. "The artist was so *much* greater than the man. The man is rather a tiresome New Englander of the ethical mystical-transcendentalist sort: Emerson, Longfellow, Hawthorne, etc. So unrelieved, the solemn ass even in humour. So hopelessly *au grand serieux* you feel like saying: Good God, what does it matter? If life is a tragedy, or a farce, or a disaster, or anything else, what do I care! Let life be what it likes. Give me a drink, that's what I want just now.

For my part, life is so many things I don't care what it is. It's not my affair to sum it up. Just now it's a cup of tea. This morning it was wormwood and gall. Hand me the sugar.

One wearies of the *grand serieux*. There's something false about it. And that's Melville. Oh, dear, when the solemn ass brays! brays! brays!" (D. H. Lawrence, *Studies* 157–)

Such a passion would raise the dead. And so it did. Almost at once the man groans. A breath is taken. Another. Ora straightens, lifts her bruised purple lips away, pressing her mouth with the back of her hand, daring him to abandon her again. A minute later, Ora Guilfoyle has been replaced by the machinery of resuscitation. . . .

Ora and I resume our Rounds. I am suddenly shy, silent. I think to say something that will acknowledge this event. But I do not. I have seen this woman at her fiercest—wild and desperate. I have seen the rhythmic jounce of dead men's feet. It is best to keep silent. We finish our work and wheel the cart to the nurses' station. A woman is there. It is the man's wife. From the distance, she has watched the coupling of her husband with this nurse. The woman raises one hand as if to speak to Ora. Ora hesitates. But the woman, too, does not speak. There is a glance between them. Then they move apart, the one toward, and the other away from the bed where it took place. (82–3).

I hear more resonance or authentic voice in this tiny story than in the earlier passage about a surgeon's relationship with the body of the patient. Selzer himself puts his finger on the problem with the voice in the first passage: "Last week's letter was so full of cant and preacherei that I have been making up for it ever since by sinning all over the place" (*Letters* 92). That earlier voice somehow strained too hard in trying to be authoritative, avuncular, and poetic. And there is something self-regarding and stagey in the awareness of us, of his listener, of the language, and of himself doing it.

Am I saying that heightened, highly crafted language cannot be authentic? Not at all. The story of Ora Guilfoil and her patient has all those qualities. One might even call it "over written" or "purple"—but successfully or authentically so. The first passage has plenty of audible voice and plenty of dramatic voice. But somehow its voice isn't as *solid* as the voice in the second passage—it doesn't ring as true.

As English teachers and rhetoricians, we could find plenty of other ways to explain stylistic differences between these two highly written passages. But one of the advantages of voice as a critical concept is the very fact that we can make these distinctions by *ear*. As Polanyi points out, this kind of tacit, nonfocal awareness can be remarkably subtle and accurate. The ear is probably our most trustworthy organ of discrimination in writing.

There is an obvious objection to this analysis in terms of authentic or resonant voice. The objection would go as follows: Why mystify? Why complicate things? This resonance that you say results from the words fitting the author can be explained much more easily. The words resonate simply because they fit *you*: you *like* them. Why can't you just say you *don't like* Selzer's first passage—instead of saying it "lacks resonance"?

Obviously this objection reflects a simpler and more common sense model of reading. But haven't we all had the experience occasionally of reading something that we *don't* like—which is wrong for us (written perhaps by a personality we find repugnant)—but which we nevertheless experience as enormously powerful and resonant? Or reading something from a culture or speech community that is alien to us but nevertheless gradually experiencing great power and resonance in it? What happens when we experience power in what we don't like or what doesn't fit us?

Or think for a moment about what makes an editor or writing teacher genuinely good. Does she get the writer to make the writing fit just *her*—or even fit just the market? Surely not. Rather she helps the writer learn to produce what is right for that writer. She helps the writer move or grow in the direction that will bring out that writer's own potential gifts— even if the result doesn't fit her own tastes. Reading for authentic voice, then, is something subtle but natural that we all do with discourse, namely to sense not only how it fits us but to sense how it relates to the person producing it. Obviously we can only do this if we hear a lot of discourse by that person.

I have been implying here what some would call a "naïve psychological realism": implying that we live in a world of distinct selves; that we are able to know something of each other through language; that language or behavior can fit the self well or not so well; and that we can sometimes hear the difference as we listen for authentic voice or its absence.

229

Peter Elbow

Notice that I am not, however, implying a self that is simple, single, or wholly private and autonomous. A self that is deeply social—an entity made up largely of strands or voices from others and subject to powerful forces outside itself—can of course have identity and integrity, and thus authentic voice. To take a limiting case, even *committees* usually have identities and integrity. Even about committees, we can sometimes say, "That memo [action] certainly doesn't sound like the Curriculum Committee."[4]

Indeed I could have gone so far as to skip all mention of *selves* and *authors* and still have made most of my points about authentic voice. One could say that authentic voice is nothing but a matter of a text with highly consistent and integrated cues. Taking this line, inauthentic voice would not be a text out of sync with some alleged self or author but merely out of sync with *itself*: voices tend to sound fake when they give mixed signals. Nevertheless, despite some recent critical theory, I'm not yet convinced we should give up talking in terms of selves and authors.

Voice in Texts as It Relates to Teaching

I've been trying to rehabilitate a vexed and fuzzy critical concept and thus sought some precision by analysis or division into three parts. I have stressed complexities. But the applications of voice to teaching are relatively simple. I conclude by summarizing the three dimensions of voice as they relate to student writing.

Audible Voice

When student writing is tangled and dead and without audible voice, we can easily get the student to see the prob-

4. "One's own discourse and one's own voice, although born of another or dynamically stimulated by another, will sooner or later begin to liberate themselves from the authority of the other's discourse" (Bakhtin 348).

lem—or rather hear the problem—and break through to audible voice. If we get the student to *read the prose out loud*, he can usually hear the tangle with his ear or feel it with his mouth. Often he stumbles. Or we can read it out loud ourselves or have someone else read it. The student can usually hear the deadness with his ear. Then we can ask, "How would you *say* it? *Tell me* what you are getting at!" and usually he cuts through the tangle to clearer diction, stronger syntax, and often better thinking. (All this, note, without "teaching" or advice.)

Dramatic Voice

When another student uses an odd or offensive or contradictory stance in her writing, a problematic implied author, we can ask her what kind of voice she hears in there (or get her to ask her peer group to tell her who they hear in her writing). Or if we're writing comments, we can simply describe the problem in terms of voice: "You sound so timid here. [Or arrogant, or like two different people.] Did you mean to use that voice?" This kind of comment grants the student some safety through distance between herself and her text.

Authentic Voice

When writing is perfunctory and uninvested we can say, "I find myself doubting whether *you* even believe what you are saying." Or when, in contrast, the writing is desperately sincere but tinny and clichéd, we can say, "I believe you are sincere here, but somehow it seems as though you're *trying* too hard to *be* sincere. Why must you work at it so? In the end I don't quite trust the voice here." ("Methinks she doth protest. . . .") This is in fact a slightly evasive comment. I often suspect pressure from something the student may *not* be aware of, but I don't feel it's fair to say that. Or to put it more positively: I feel it's all right to comment on my sense of the language, but I'm reluctant to talk about inferences about inner dynamics. I try to make such comments tentatively—so the student can easily reject them. Most of all, I find it helpful to point to

231

contrasting passages and say, "I hear more resonance and solidity in these other spots." (They are usually spots where the student isn't breathing so hard or protesting so much— places where he or she is doing the work, producing a sound as it were from the diaphragm and not just from the throat.)

Authentic or resonant voice is especially important for teaching persuasive writing. As Aristotle points out in the *Rhetoric*, trustworthy *ethos* is a major source of persuasiveness. But he also notes that we are *not* persuaded if we sense that the "trustworthiness" is a matter of "conscious art." He clearly implies that we need to experience that trustworthiness as inhering *in* the actual writer. Indeed we *distrust* a writer to the extent that we sense him as a clever creator of personas.

Thus, even though there is not yet any critical consensus about voice, and even though the concept leads us into theoretical brambles, students quickly and easily understand talk about voice in texts. Talking about ineffective writing in terms of voice tends to bring about quicker improvements than talking in terms of, say, heavy nominalization, passive voice, or *ethos*.

Conclusion

Why do I care so much about voice? I think voice is one of the main forces that *draws* us into texts. We often give other explanations for what we like ("clarity," "style," "energy," "sublimity," "reach," even "truth"), but I think it's often one sort of voice or another. One way of saying this is that voice seems to overcome "writing" or textuality.

That is, speech seems to come *to* us as listener and the speaker seems to do the work of getting the meaning into our heads. In the case of writing, on the other hand, it's as though we as reader have to go to the text and do the work of getting the meaning. Speech seems to give us more sense of contact with the author.

To talk this way gets me in trouble with Derrida, of course: hopelessly phonocentric and a sucker for "presence." And I am a kind of "listening Tom" with a prurient interest in hearing voices in texts. But perhaps Derridians shouldn't be too quick on the trigger since I suspect my analysis might even aid their enterprise. For it could be said that I'm searching for what gives the *illusion* of presence. I'm trying to show how *some* texts give the sense of coming to the reader, of doing the work for the reader, and of producing genuine and direct contact with the reader—and others do not. After all, not much useful critical work gets done by grand epistemological and ontological arguments about whether *all* discourse is essentially speech or essentially "writing." What we need are tools to talk about *differences* among texts. I hope I've shown that voice is a crucial tool of this sort.

Works Cited

Arendt, Hannah. *The Human Condition.* Chicago: U of Chicago P, 1959.

Bakhtin, Mikhail. "Discourse in the Novel." *The Dialogic Imagination: Four Essays.* Trans. Caryl Emerson and Holquist. Ed. Michael Holquist. Slavic Series, no 1. Austin: U of Texas P, 1981.

Belenky, Mary, et al. *Women's Ways of Knowing: The Development of Self, Voices, and Mind.* New York: Basic Books, 1986.

Cherry, Roger. "*Ethos* vs. Persona: Self-Representation in Written Discourse." Unpublished MS.

Ehrlich, Gretel. *The Solace of Open Spaces.* New York: Viking, 1985.

Freire, Paolo. *The Pedagogy of the Oppressed.* Trans. Myra Bergman Ramos. New York: Herder and Herder, 1970.

Frost, Robert. *A Way Out.* New York: Seven Arts, 1917.

Gibson, Walker. *Tough, Sweet, and Stuffy: An Essay on Modern American Prose Styles.* Bloomington: Indiana UP, 1966.

Johnson, Nan. "*Ethos* and the Aims of Rhetoric." *Essays on Classical Rhetoric and Modern Discourse.* Ed. Robert J. Connors, Lisa S. Ede, and Andrea A. Lunsford. Carbondale: Southern Illinois UP, 1984.

Lawrence, D. H. *Studies in Classic American Literature.* New York: Doubleday, 1951.

Ong, Walter. *Orality and Literacy: The Technologizing of the Word.* New York: Methuen, 1982.

Peter Elbow

Polanyi, Michael. *Personal Knowledge: Towards a Post-Critical Philosophy.* Chicago: U of Chicago P, 1974.

Selzer, Richard. *Taking the World in for Repairs.* New York: Morrow, 1986.

———. Letters to a Young Doctor. New York: Simon and Schuster, 1982.

Vendler, Helen. "An Intractable Metal." *New Yorker* 15 Feb. 1982: 131.

Wimsatt, W. K., Jr., and Monroe C. Beardsley. "The Intentional Fallacy." *The Verbal Icon.* Lexington: U of Kentucky P, 1967.

12
THE PERSONAL ESSAY AND EGALITARIAN RHETORIC

William Zeiger

"Forms have their own kind of meaning," Keith Fort declares passionately (173): the standard critical essay form of thesis and support favors a hierarchical world view and resists the expression of other, less orthodox visions. Fort finds that thesis-proof essay structure asserts a claim to impersonal authority constituting a sort of "hidden omniscience" (178). Accepting the essay's argument means accepting not only the thesis, but also the tacit premise that the world of the essay may be mastered from a single point of view. Fort objects to this monistic assumption because it claims a false authority for the writer and because it excludes discussion of issues which may not admit of proved conclusions or which resist reduction to a single proposition. Alternate prose structures, Fort suggests, presume more liberal world views (182).

Although Fort describes at length the restrictiveness of thesis-proof structure, he only hints at the forms of essay that would accommodate freer world views—"conversational, exploratory essays" (175) in which "[t]he process of the writer's mind becomes the action of the work" (181). The "action of the work," presumably, would constitute a more open form than logical support for a thesis—a form which would privilege not an authoritarian, but an egalitarian universe.

Traditionally, the essay is described either as formal, employing the deductive or inductive hierarchy of logic, or informal, exhibiting a rambling, capricious structure of no definite shape, but exhibiting the idiosyncratic thoughts and feelings of the author. I believe that the informal or personal essay is the egalitarian medium which Fort desires: it is flexible enough to tolerate ambiguities, and, despite its egotism, unassuming enough to address the reader as an equal. The formal essay addresses both reader and subject with an intrusive rigidity. It establishes a premise, implicitly or explicitly, with which presumably the audience agrees, and then attempts to transmit the force of that agreement to a conclusion with which, presumably, the audience would not have agreed initially. Thus it rationally insists on a conclusion from which the audience, for nonrational reasons, may demur. This insistence exerts a painful force. It entails the presumption that logic should overrule the emotional and intuitive nature—a presumption which made no friends for Socrates among Gorgias's guests. The informal essay lays aside the critical essay's assumption of logical superiority. It is well known and much beloved for its egalitarian spirit—the congeniality and deference of the writer toward both the topic and the reader. The informal essay employs a variety of nonlogical forms of suasion, and these account for its flexibility in treating subjects which a rigorously rational treatment might distort.

Walter Fisher, analyzing public moral argument, also reacts to the restrictiveness of logical proof and the degree of authority it claims. Like Fort, Fisher finds that our exaggerated respect for deductive and inductive logic as the principal means of suasion obscures other arguments of considerable human value. He proposes a wider definition of rationality, a definition which recognizes other forms of proof equally and validates the range of proofs employed in the personal essay and other aesthetic forms.

In *Human Communication as Narration*, Fisher argues that conventional discourse is governed by a set of rational values which privilege experts and make most people seem incapable of judging. We have lived since Aristotle under the "rational world paradigm" (59–62), in which "the world is a set of logical puzzles which can be resolved through appropriate analysis and application of reason conceived as an argumentative construct" (59).

The means of communicating and making decisions in this world is by "clear-cut inferential or implicative structures"

(59). In such a world, public discussion is dominated by people who have acquired expertise in this form of argument, and the mass of people without technical expertise on a given matter are not qualified to comment on it. The world of ideas is a vast hierarchical structure, and higher position on this structure confers greater authority. Fisher proposes a more egalitarian alternative to this hierarchy in the "narrative paradigm" (62–69). Under the narrative paradigm, the world is conceived of as a set of stories, and people judge these stories in terms of "good reasons." By "stories," Fisher does not mean only fictions, but any "recounting" or "accounting for" human experience (62). "Good reasons" constitute a cooperative rather than a compulsory sort of suasion. Their effect is determined by "the nature of persons as narrative beings—their inherent awareness of *narrative probability*, what constitutes a coherent story, and their constant habit of testing *narrative fidelity*, whether or not the stories they experience ring true with the stories they know to be true in their lives" (64).

Because of the cultural universality of stories, anyone would be capable of making or judging a public statement. Speakers, whatever their expertise, would be heard as peers, not as wizards; they would speak from their full human experience, their special knowledge informing and informed by their general knowledge of life and the world. "[N]o form of discourse is privileged over others because its form is predominantly argumentative. No matter how strictly a case is argued— scientifically, philosophically, or legally—it will always be a story, an interpretation of some aspect of the world that is historically and culturally grounded and shaped by human personality" (49).

The narrative paradigm provides a context for expressing and validating ideas with a more realistic human range than rational argument. The chief difference between rational and narrative forms, I think, is that the former relies more on logos and the latter more on ethos and pathos. Rather than assert A because of its relationship to B and C, an egalitarian rhetoric asserts A for its own qualities. The personal essayist, rather than arguing for a concept, endows it with presence—

William Zeiger

relates a story imbued with sensations and appetites, perceptions and visions, personal relationships and the experience of everyday life. We all have this knowledge, of course, but the personal essayist, like the poet and novelist, articulates it well—takes the time to notice casual objects and events and to cultivate the habit of noticing. The personal essay does not "prove" ideas, but presents and amplifies them; it lacks the compulsory sense of the formal essay's enthymeme, and therefore represents not rational authority but more broadly human testimony.

To illustrate the use of nonauthoritarian "proofs" I would like to examine two forms of personal essay. The first I call the *story/comment* form, good examples of which come in a recent article by Chris Anderson. The second, which I call *mystical induction,* I illustrate in essays by Maxine Hong Kingston and Loren Eiseley. Each of these forms, I believe, represents the alternative genre of essay which Fort calls for. Both are conversational and exploratory; both, rather than proving a thesis logically, rely primarily for their suasion on appeals to the intuitive and physical senses.

Anderson describes a "dramatistic" essay form composed of the Burkean "representative anecdote" and "terministic screen." The writer dwells on the anecdote, dramatizing it and highlighting its most noteworthy facets with vivid description. The essay does not argue logically, but presents the writer's "thinking through of an experience" (37). Anderson illustrates this form in works by Ellen Goodman and Lewis Thomas. In "The Tucson Zoo," for example, Thomas recounts watching beavers and otters play in ponds whose glass sides permit him to see above and below the water. From this unusually intimate perspective, Thomas describes becoming so engrossed in the antics of the creatures that he begins to feel a kinship with them. He surmises that he and all humans must have a genetic coding for friendliness with beavers and otters, and with all nature, and that science often neglects such holistic vision. Anderson carefully explains that the anecdote and the author's reflection on it do not function as example and generalization. "The narrative is not subordinated to the arguments;

rather, the arguments grow out of the narrative" (35). Thomas's personal sense of kinship acts as a kind of generative fragment, or synecdoche, projecting from its terms and structure a larger, more elaborate whole. By dwelling on the anecdote, Thomas intensifies each of its important elements and savors and elaborates his pleasure in them, until his act of reflection has expanded the concrete incident to an abstraction of universal scope. The rhetorical power of the essay is "dramatistic," Anderson says, because this reflexive, inquisitive process imparts "presence" to the details of the anecdote and fixes the reader's attention so richly and intimately on it that it achieves the effect of "an event taking place here and now" (38). In "The Tucson Zoo," delight in the play of animals takes precedence over rational detachment because the writer lingers over his delight. He does not argue that this response is superior; he displays its inherent appeal. The relationship between story and comment, rather than supporting an idea with inductive or deductive reasoning, sets off an idea by clustering description and appreciative commentary around it. It is the application of the comment to the story, not a logical argument, or hierarchical pattern, that imparts value.

Another such essay, I believe, is Annie Dillard's "Living Like Weasels," in which Dillard momentarily finds herself staring into a weasel's eyes. This incident affects her so strongly that she inquires into and speculates on the nature of weasels, and from this speculation and her feeling of identity with the weasel she develops a principle of living-true-to-one's-strength.

Borrowing a concept from linguistics, I call this form of essay *story/comment* form because it closely resembles the "narratives of personal experience" (354) which sociolinguist William Labov collects and studies. In these narratives, all in black English vernacular, "the speaker becomes deeply involved in rehearsing or even reliving events of the past" (354). Labov identifies six characteristic formal features in the narratives he records, but the most prominent ones constitute "story" (orientation, complicating action, resolution) and "comment" (evaluation). The other two features, abstract and

William Zeiger

coda, bracket the act of telling (362–70). The function of "evaluation" is to call attention to what the narrator feels is remarkable or important about the story. Evaluation occurs both in a set of sentences at its own place in the narrative and throughout the text, in clauses, phrases, single words, and rhetorical devices; evaluation may participate to some extent at any level and any moment of the narrative (370–93). Thus the narrative as a whole is composed of a story and a comment on it, and the comment is subordinated to and intimately involved with the story, highlighting its drama. This narrative form is almost exactly the essay form which Anderson describes. Since stories are a cultural universal, it is likely that many essays besides the ones mentioned here take this shape. In terms of story/comment form, the universe is not a collection of theses to be defended and attacked, as in Fort's nightmare, but a collection of stories to be appreciated.

Essays of Maxine Hong Kingston and Loren Eiseley resemble an explosion of story/comment form, comprising not so much a single narrative as a set of fragments of narratives, incidents to be contemplated and savored. I like to call this form *mystical induction*, or *successive approximation*, because it consists of repeated attempts to capture an elusive idea. The writer seeks to define or express a concept which lurks just beyond the limits of articulate thought. The essay casts one loop after another to ensnare the fugitive. Each attempt falls short, but together they indicate directions and qualities from which the reader comprehends the nature of the quarry.

In "No Name Woman," Kingston, seeking a more lenient model of adult behavior than she finds in the terrifying and repressive story of her disgraced aunt, and hindered by her parents' grim silence following the single telling of this tale, sets out to re-create her aunt in imagination. In successive trials she conjures up "the lone romantic who gave up everything for sex," the obedient victim, the fanciful girl, the "wild woman" who "kept rollicking company," the seductress, the loyal wife, the fierce mother. Kingston struggles to evoke a sympathetic picture of her aunt through the negation and distortion of taboo and prejudice. Her effort to "see [my

240

aunt's] life branching into mine" (10) succeeds partially in elaborating an alternate concept of a woman's potential, conjuring up a cubistlike image, composed of shards, suggesting a number of possibilities rather than one distinct whole. Its ultimate success depends on the woman's ability to draw upon and live through the visions she has projected.

Like story/comment form above, this form assumes the contours given by the writer's mind pursuing a vision. Whatever deduction or logical inference Kingston uses is incidental to her experimental casting and recasting of possibilities. Her essay impresses the reader hypothetically. Virtually every paragraph combines conjecture about her aunt's behavior or feelings with inference on the repressive influences of social and familial conditions. Kingston speaks in three voices—the neutral voice of the historian, inferring and explaining her aunt's actions; the curious voice of a young woman seeking her own potential, caressing and embellishing with words her intuitive glimpses of the past; the stinging voice of a fellow sufferer, reviling the injustices that block her natural growth.

> Adultery is extravagance. Could people who hatch their own chicks and eat the embryos and the heads for delicacies and boil the feet in vinegar for party food, leaving only the gravel, eating even the gizzard lining—could such people engender a prodigal aunt? To be a woman, to have a daughter in starvation time was waste enough. My aunt could not have been the lone romantic who gave up everything for sex. Women in the old China did not choose. Some man had commanded her to lie with him and be his secret evil. I wonder whether he masked himself when he joined the raid on her family. (71)

Kingston embellishes the likelier of her visions at some length. She rejects the hypotheses of the "lone romantic" and the "wild woman" in a sentence or two; but the obedient victim and the fanciful girl get extended treatment:

> Perhaps she had encountered him in the fields or on the mountain where the daughters-in-law collected fuel. Or perhaps he first noticed her in the marketplace. He was not a stranger because the village housed no strangers. She had to have deal-

ings with him other than sex. Perhaps he worked an adjoining field, or he sold her the cloth for the dress she sewed and wore. His demand must have surprised, then terrified her. She obeyed him; she always did as she was told. (7)

But perhaps my aunt, my forerunner, caught in a slow life, let dreams grow and fade and after some months or years went toward what persisted. Fear at the enormities of the forbidden kept her desires delicate, wire and bone. She looked at a man because she liked the way the hair was tucked behind his ears, or she liked the question-mark line of a long torso curving at the shoulder and straight at the hip. (9)

Kingston does not make a rational argument for her liberation; but her evoking of scene after scene creates imaginary possibilities and endows them with palpable presence.

Kingston lavishes her greatest imaginative power on the aunt's giving birth, after the raid, in the yard. She drops almost completely her conjectural tone and describes the birthing as if she had witnessed it. "She got to her feet to fight better and remembered that old-fashioned women gave birth in their pigsties to fool the jealous, pain-dealing gods, who do not snatch piglets. Before the next spasms could stop her, she ran to the pigsty, each step a rushing out into emptiness. She climbed over the fence and knelt in the dirt. It was good to have a fence enclosing her, a tribal person alone" (16–17).

It is no longer a girl talking. The varieties of womanhood have extended in time as well as in kind. We realize that Kingston is writing as a mature woman and that, as she has grown, she has projected her aunt's experience before her. The series of imaginings have had at least some of their desired effect of providing the girl with an avenue out of her repressive conditioning. The reader, too, receives strong impressions of Kingston's visions and shares to a degree in her liberation of spirit. No rational demonstration, but a series of ardently invoked and intimately tendered images achieves this effect.

Two of Loren Eiseley's essays, "The Judgment of the Birds" and "The Brown Wasps," are similar in form. In "The Brown Wasps," Eiseley declares that every living creature needs a sense of a permanent home—a reassuring physical locale. He evokes this sense of a home with reference to derelicts who regularly sleep in the same unfrequented corner of a railway station; pigeons haunting an out-of-service elevated train platform, once a "food-bearing river" (232) to them; a field mouse, displaced by a construction project, burrowing in one of Eiseley's houseplants; himself, carrying in memory a tree which he and his father had planted together. Each of these scenes, lovingly and intricately detailed, conveys an urgency to be home, to have a familiar refuge. When at the end of the essay Eiseley impulsively returns to the site of the tree that he and his father had planted and finds it gone, he realizes that his "roots," like those of the other creatures he has described, "were all part of an elusive world that existed nowhere and yet everywhere" (235). On behalf of himself, a field mouse, several pigeons, and anonymous sleepers in a train depot, Eiseley's essay nominates the whole world as home and exile to all.

As in Kingston's essay, repeated attempts to capture a vision create an idea but do not attain the hoped-for reality. The series of examples might be said to demonstrate, inferentially, the need of every creature for a home; but the plain absence of the expected tree, the predicted tree, confounds this logic and asserts the spiritual power of the creature's longing mysteriously to summon, or supersede, its desired object.

The elements of the achievements of these essays are not enthymemes and examples but other tools of rhetoric, metaphor and diction, selection and arrangement of ideas. When Kingston, for example, imagines her aunt, in labor, struggling to the pigsty, "each step a rushing out into emptiness," this phrase strikes me as so true to its moment that it persuades me both that Kingston draws from her own deepest resources and that her instinct is reliable. The power of her prose builds, as Fisher's theory indicates, with accumulation of such deft strokes. In our efforts to speak as nearly as possible our truths, and to profit from each other's tellings, every choice and motion of our language participates in persuasion.

243

William Zeiger

I do not propose that the personal essay be elevated to the prominence that the formal essay has occupied. Better that both should assume the more humble station and the distinction between them blur. Each really represents, finally, only the authority of one voice talking. I do not mean to say that rational argument is a negligible quantity; it is a corner-stone of liberal education. If we learn better to use it as an element within a large field of persuasive techniques, well complemented with ethos and pathos, we open our minds to a fuller range of experience and dialogue. The personal essay reminds us of our own and others' humanity. Its egalitarian nature comes from its intention not to attempt to constrain its subject or to subdue its audience, but to render as truly as possible the confluence of impressions and reflections which shape one's thought.

Works Cited

Anderson, Chris. "Dramatism and Deliberation." *Rhetoric Review* 4:1 (Sept. 1985) 34–43.

Dillard, Annie. "Living Like Weasels." *Teaching a Stone to Talk*. New York: Harper and Row, 1982.

Eiseley, Loren. "The Brown Wasps." *Night Country*. New York: Scribner's, 1971.

————. "The Judgment of the Birds." *The Star Thrower*. San Diego: Harcourt Brace Jovanovich, 1978.

Fisher, Walter R. *Human Communication as Narration: Toward a Philosophy of Reason, Value, and Action*. Columbia: U of South Carolina P, 1987.

Fort, Keith. "Form, Authority, and the Critical Essay." In *Contemporary Rhetoric: A Conceptual Background with Readings*. Ed. W. R. Winterowd. New York: Harcourt Brace, 1975.

Kingston, Maxine Hong. "No Name Woman." *The Woman Warrior: Memoirs of a Girlhood Among Ghosts*. New York: Vintage, 1977.

Labov, William. *Language in the Inner City: Studies in the Black English Vernacular*. Philadelphia: U of Pennsylvania P, 1972.

PART THREE

Implications for Pedagogy

13
THE READER'S TEXT

Responding to Loren Eiseley's "The Running Man"

John Clifford

There is a growing urgency in English studies to develop more theoretically coherent ways for reading and writing to inform each other. Still, many writing teachers, perhaps in a lingering aversion to the long-standing misuse of literature in writing classes, remain suspicious of the value of using any literature, even literary nonfiction with their own students. For many of them, the reading they would wed to writing is more likely to include lucid models of good historical or sociological discourse than the polished prose of Joan Didion, Annie Dillard, or Loren Eiseley. The traditional strategy of assigning literary essays, discussing their themes and structure in class and then writing critiques, seems to many to constitute a flawed pedagogy. Dissenting instructors suggest that a mature literary style not only does not parallel the practical academic writing students will be required to produce, but also intimidates less accomplished writers, perhaps even undermining their understanding of the complex recursiveness of the composing process. Using literary nonfiction with a traditional pedagogy, their argument goes, focuses too insistently on the crafted linearity of discourse and thereby fails to demonstrate, for those who need to know, the inevitable and necessary behind-the-scene messiness and confusion of writing.

These are cogent arguments, especially given the pervasive influence formalist theories of reading and writing have had in composition classrooms for a generation. Nevertheless,

John Clifford

I believe they are less objections to the idea of using literary nonfiction in writing classes than to the limitations of a specific reading technique and its resulting pedagogy. In our post-structuralist climate, however, there are alternatives to those incompatable strategies developed during the hegemony of the New Criticism several decades ago. Several of these would be more congenial in a classroom environment that stresses process than an analytical close reading that situates meaning, form, persona, and coherence only in stable and unified texts. Students who, on the one hand, are encouraged to discover evolving meaning during the composing process, might right-fully inquire why, during the reading process, the locus of meaning suddenly shifts to the text. Why, they might wonder, does the pedagogical emphasis uncomfortably move from the synchronic in composing to an atemporal, objective analysis in reading? Why do we urge them to create meaning in writing and then merely uncover it in reading? Putting aside the ways writing might be encouraged and enhanced through reading, I want to suggest that such theoretical contradictions do not have to exist at all, that an active, process-oriented approach to studying texts is valid for both writing and reading, that the perceptions of readers matter greatly, that the making of meaning is as much a phenomenological and creative process in reading as it is in composing. The response-oriented theo-ries of Stanley Fish and Louise Rosenblatt, augmented with some insights from cultural criticism, can provide a flexible heuristic for reading nonfiction that is both theoretically and pedagogically coherent in either literature or composition classes.

In the brand of reader-response I am advocating, the focus of attention is not, as in Norman Holland's psychological variant, exclusively on the nature of the reader's identity. In-stead, the spotlight is on the nature of the interaction between reader and text, or more precisely, on the complex ways the reader's ideological baggage affects interpretive judgments. Early on, students are encouraged to write response state-ments that can prompt intellectual and emotional reactions to their reading experience. When students disagree with or are troubled by an idea in an essay, for example, I want them first to be clear about their position and then to try to interrogate the reasons for that response, that is, to "help them analyze the many influences—cultural, social, moral, historical, psychological" (Waller 17) that form the ground from which all readers understand texts. This critical sequence is a variation on Rosenblatt's long standing contention that since students bring to their reading "different personalities, different syntactical and semantic habits, different values and knowledge," they will fashion different syntheses, different texts under the text's "guidance and control" (122). Although that is true, and of seminal importance, I am also interested in the "interface" between the various texts produced by students and the cultural assumptions and expectations which generate these multiple readings.

Although I have for a long time been intellectually and emotionally committed to a range of contemporary nonfiction from Anne Dillard to Stephen Jay Gould, for a variety of personal reasons, reading Loren Eiseley's "The Running Man" is an especially rich experience for me. Apparently my experiences and values were engaged by Eiseley's text. Although I was half Eiseley's age when I first read the piece in 1977 and not nearly as melancholy or as haunted by the past, I was still strongly affected by Eiseley's anxiety over his identity, his strong sense of responsibility, and his rather circuitous but passionate need to confront repressed truths. His essay is for me a compelling portrait of a troubled mind hoping through writing to achieve personal peace. I wondered how my students, dramatically different from this famous scientist and writer, would respond to this chapter from Eiseley's haunting autobiography, *All the Strange Hours*.

My strategy was simple. After explaining and discussing the kind of active, personal, and cultural interaction I was after, I asked them to read the essay and to stop at key intervals to write a response statement. This move is influenced by Fish's belief that the mind needs to investigate its own activities, that critical attention is most profitably riveted on the sequence and flow of the reader's temporal experience. He wants to

John Clifford

"slow down" the actualization of the text so the mind of the reader is more clearly revealed to itself. I then asked them to read the essay again and answer four or five focused questions geared to jar them, perhaps to force them, into a confrontation with their own tacit cultural apparatus. After classroom discussions of their written and oral responses, I eventually assigned a more focused essay in which they developed one reaction to "The Running Man," trying to unpack their reasons for this particular reading. The rest of this paper is a comment on the earlier part of this assignment, an elaboration of what Rosenblatt calls a "coming-together, a compenetration of reader and a text" (12).

Here a summary of Eiseley's autobiographical essay is especially risky since my point is that there can be no substitute for the reading experience, not even vicariously; yet, it does seem necessary. Eiseley begins "The Running Man" with a surprisingly frank and bitter denunciation of his "paranoid, neurotic and unstable" (24) mother who had a gift, Eiseley sarcastically remarks, to make others suffer. However, he seems to quickly dismiss her significance by claiming "all the pain, all the anguish" were for nothing, adding that "It has taken me all my life to grasp this one fact" (25). At this point in the essay it appears as if we have no reason to doubt him. Such an assertion from a mature writer seems quite plausible. Eiseley's persona here, in fact, has been subtly created to seem spontaneously sincere and forthright, as if the truth were now suddenly pellucid after a long darkness. But after some meandering, the reader must wonder where Eiseley's essay is going. Then, realizing this need for a sense of direction and a tentative framework, he admits his narrative is faltering, "wandering out of time and place." But he tries to assure the reader with both a literary and a psychological explanation: "To tell the story of a life one is bound to linger about grave-stones where memory blurs and doors can be pushed ajar, but never opened." He then tells us that because he is "every man and no man" he must "tell the story as I may . . . . not for the nameless name upon the page," but because of "the loneliness of not knowing, not knowing at all." After our first reading of

250

this passage, we are still groping for what Rosenblatt calls a "guiding principle of organization" (54), and this enigmatic sentence does not initially clarify matters.

Apparently, after some five paragraphs, Eiseley is going to try to define who he is through a logical sequence, first locating himself in time and place, beginning with, "I was a child of the early century, American man . . . . " Then, after a brief reference to some traumatic midnight fights between his parents, Eiseley tries to define himself geographically, wondering how he could possibly have absorbed an ethical code to live by. But he abruptly concludes this fragmented attempt at locating his psychic roots: "So much for my mother, the mad Shepards, and the land," and then he mysteriously adds, "but this is not all, certainly not" (27).

Eschewing conventional transitions, Eiseley suddenly switches to a dinner at which W. H. Auden asks him quite innocently what was the first public event he can remember. Eiseley answers with three odd but seemingly plausible events. Then he fractures the narrative flow again with the unexpected confession that after the Auden dinner he had been glumly despondent for days: "For nights I lay sleepless in a New York hotel room and all my memories in one gigantic catharsis were bad, spewed out of hell's mouth, invoked by that one dinner, that one question" (29).

Apparently he has been repressing some deeply personal and painful truth. As readers we are bewildered once again, wondering if the anecdotes he has been telling us are true and if not, what is going on? But this time Eiseley appears to provide an answer, narrating once again several possible responses to the Auden inquiry, from playing dice against the universe in a deserted farm house to a fight with a neighborhood bully in which Eiseley admits he "went utterly mad." Surprisingly, after this event the reader is led back to Eiseley's mother, who was watching him wash his bloodied face. Finally, he writes a most revealing transitional sentence: "There was another thing I would not name to Auden" (33). At long last Eiseley tells the repressed tale: Once, when he was ten and playing with friends in a pasture at the edge of town, he was pursued by his mother, "behaving in the manner of a witch. She could not hear, she was violently gesticulating without dignity." Eiseley confesses that he laughed at her with his companions, then with his mother stumbling after, he ran, "Escape, escape, the first stirrings of the running man. Miles of escape." Using language reminiscent of ritual purgation, he admits he was "bitterly ashamed . . . ashamed at what he had done to his stone-deaf mother . . . ashamed at his own weakness. Ashamed, ashamed." The essay concludes: "That is what I could not tell Auden. Only an unutterable savagery, my savagery at myself, scrawls it once and once only on this page" (34).

This summary is static, an after-the-experience distillation. As such, it distorts and reifies the temporal phenomena, the lived-through experience of reading. As Fish notes in "Literature in the Reader," the real meaning of a text lies in the moment-to-moment experience of the reader attempting to organize and synthesize the simultaneous and multiple cognitive and emotional pulls involved in reading (36–37). From this perspective a summary of "The Running Man" seems especially anemic. The events narrated above surely tell what happens in Eiseley's work but only in the most superficially factual way. For what seems to me most dramatically significant about this essay, beyond the rich cultural suggestiveness of Eiseley's values and our response to them, is not what happens, but the reader's sense of mystery, curiosity, and heightened expectations about Eiseley's psychological evasiveness. The resulting sense of bewilderment that envelopes readers when they are encouraged to focus on the unfolding drama of their own reading experience is as much the meaning of the essay as the various interpretations of what Eiseley is running away from.

My students approached Eiseley's autobiographical essay with a rather narrow range of literary assumptions. Based largely on the experience of writing formal exposition, they conceived of the essay as a straightforward genre: propositions were made and developed, arguments put forth and defended. They trusted personas that seemed reasonable and sincere, and did not expect to be manipulated or tricked. Because of their limited literary training, they were simply not prepared to process fully an essay replete with false leads, fractured sequence, various levels of images, symbols, and gaps. Add a persona ladened with anxiety, repressed guilt, complex motives, and masked ideological values, and the reading experience becomes a richly challenging inquiry. In short, after experiencing such dislocations, they were ready to confront what Roland Barthes calls a crisis in their relation with language.

I doubt that this crisis was accidental or gratuitous. Although surely not completely aware of all his intentions, Eiseley has crafted a text that does defamiliarize the ordinary reader's sense of truth and identity. But it is more than that: the very experience of reading the essay illuminates and reinforces the implications of his running metaphor, allowing the reader to feel the fragility and elusiveness of reality and in discussion to experience the diverse situatedness of readers in our culture.

In response to my inquiry about what students noted most in their responses to "The Running Man," the predominant motif that emerged was Eiseley's tortured attitude toward his mother. A catalogue of their diverse reactions includes both surprise that an adult would still be concerned about what they largely saw as a distant incident and bewilderment over the point of this seemingly rambling narrative that begins with a maternal denunciation yet ends with a cry of agony and shame for his treatment of her. I specifically asked my students first what they thought of Eiseley's preoccupation with his mother, and then why they thought the incident had this particular effect on them. In response, some felt sympathy with Eiseley's frustration and resentment toward his mother; some felt he was excessively neurotic; others that such insensitivity to the plight of a outcast female called for the pain and guilt he suffered. But more important than these judgments of the narrator's sanity or lack of it were the reasons behind these assessments. I am as concerned here with *why* as with *what*, as interested in what they think as in why Eiseley's attitude would elicit both supportive and hostile reactions from readers raised in the same culture.

As a way to concretize the sources of their beliefs and attitudes in a "cultural text," I asked my students first to write narratives of comparable experiences they actually had with their own parents. We looked at these texts carefully and found predictably diverse family situations: mothers who were supportive and valued, fathers who intimated and wounded and whose value was thereby diminished. I thought of my class as a reasonable cross-section of American culture, admittedly overbalanced with positive experiences; nevertheless, there was enough rejection and bitterness for the class to approach the status of a collective representative anecdote. With their narratives now in the public domain, it was easy and natural to inquire about the meaning of these new texts. Do they reveal some truth about our culture that could help us understand Eiseley's dilemma? If we were anthropologists scrutinizing these personal accounts for wider significance about the culture that would produce such narratives, what might they reveal?

This then became the focus of our inquiry. And it is a crucial move in the kind of response-oriented reading that I am advocating. For in interpreting and discussing in a public forum their own narratives of family life, students can effortlessly be encouraged to make generalizations about their lives and thus be encouraged to uncover the cultural values, assumptions, and expectations that constitute all of us and are therefore tacitly understood by everyone in the room. These beliefs and attitudes form the cultural ideology that permeates their behavior, that informs and propels their thinking about families, mothers, and social identity. And by ideology I am thinking of a more general and less technical definition than, say, Louis Althusser's notion of an imaginary relationship to the real conditions of one's existence. That is an insight that is often useful, but for now I mean the "deeply ingrained sometimes only partly conscious, habits, beliefs, and lifestyles of a particular time and place" (McCormick 16). Eliciting these abstractions from the particulars of their early lives highlights two related ideas, both central to our understanding of how readers come to understand Eiseley's essay.

One is that we are not, cannot be, and probably should not want to be disinterested readers. The other is that during the process of reading we write texts in the same way our culture writes us: we judge, interpret, and find meaning in the values and behavior of real or imaginary people through cultural filters. Readers will tend to think Eiseley's initial bitterness toward his mother a cultural and psychological aberration if their experiences conform to the dominant ideology in America, one that urges respect for mothers in particular and authority figures in general. My reading of Eiseley's attitude as well as my students' was grounded in either our acceptance or rejection of certain cultural norms. That became demonstrably lucid when we looked at the class narratives and our interpretive notes about them. They indicated that we are always culturally situated; that we are unable to stand on neutral ground somehow metaphysically above our culture's ideological tenets. Since all criteria for judging the behavior and values of Eiseley as narrator or even the aesthetic of his fragmented essay cannot help but reflect some interpretive communities' version of what is proper or valuable or true, issues of subjectivity and faithfulness to the text soon lost their impact. We can find justification for this philosophical position as far back as C. S. Peirce, who argued that the "self is already embedded in a context, the community of interpretation or system of signs" (Michaels 199), or as current as Fish's assertion that "there is no single way of reading that is correct or natural, only 'ways of reading' that are extensions of community perspectives" (16).

It is axiomatic, then, that in a heterogeneous college classroom there will be multiple and irreconcilable readings, just as an analysis of any dominant cultural activity will reveal contradictory, oppositional values. If we allow a reading of a text that fully engages the diverse ways in which we are constituted as subjects by our society, then contradictions, multiplicity, and a struggle for dominance over the meaning of this word or that action will inevitably emerge. It is the dialectical richness of this struggle that enables students to appreciate how contextual complexity shapes meaning as the group responds to different dimensions of the text.

In an interactive classroom reading is not merely an elaborate Rorschact inkblot, mirroring individual psychological preoccupations. Of course in an academic setting where active response is valued, reading will bring personal and social concerns to the fore, but the primary movement in the class is not merely reporting what one sees and thinks about words and passages. Instead, the goal is always to be dialetical. The text does, however, remain an important focus during the responses and also in the readers' attempts to develop positions and comprehensive readings that will be consistent and reasonably developed in relation to the criteria of this particular community. But this does not mean we are working toward collaboration in Ken Bruffee's sense that groups should try for consensus. Oppositional views will and should exist. Often these divergent readings will seem puzzling to us, but that is usually because our previous literary experience valued analyses which were univocal not multivocal.

After reading Eiseley's text several times, writing and interpreting my own parallel narrative along with my students, and sharing in the discussions, I came to see more clearly than I did before that "The Running Man" existed for me on two important levels simultaneously: one, Eiseley's attempt in old age to exorcize the persistent ghost of his long-dead mother; the other, as a narrative of a divided and ultimately futile attempt to define himself by running away from internalized cultural values he had tried all his life to deny. As I now read the "The Running Man," it is dominated by the motif of escape and capture, an escape from the discontents of youth, but more insistently an attempt to escape ideology. This position might have been anticipated from reading my own narrative, since my own adolescence was also partly an existential struggle to assert values that went against the grain, coupled with a defiant need to move beyond the limiting ethical and cultural parameters of the urban working class. My own narrative is different from Eiseley's only in locale and specifics, the theme of struggle is the same. And so in the dramatic opening of the essay, when Eiseley stands above his mother's grave and claims, "It was all nothing. Nothing, do you understand? All the pain, all the anguish," my own ideological repertoire and experience strongly suggested to me that this protesting was, however sincerely intended, a posture. Eiseley as an intellectual and scientist would certainly wish that transcending such culturally conditioned emotions as obedience, respect, and love for one's mother were all that easy. But his insistence, coupled with the nihilistic chanting of "nothing" did not, for me, sufficiently mask his guilt and pain. For surely, if his memories were all "nothing," he would not, at seventy, be standing near his mother's grave on a remote prairie like an anguished romantic lover. Nor, in fact, would he be inscribing these assertions for all time, if he had made his separate peace. The evidence I selected belies his assertions: he does care, feels terrible about it, and wishes it were otherwise. Some of my students agreed, but most believed him, perhaps because their literary repertoire did not include looking beyond surface appearances or being suspicious of histrionic narrators, or perhaps they wanted to believe that Eiseley could obliterate his dark memories with an act of will.

Similarly, I read Eiseley's assertion that he is "every man and no man" as an unconscious realization that his values are at once a disturbing mix of those of the dominant ideology and those of the marginalized rebel. In this regard, the paragraph's concluding lament about his uncertain future is telling: "not for the confusion of where I was to go, or if I had a destiny recognizable by any star. No, in retrospect it was the loneliness of not knowing, not knowing at all" (25). Many students, no doubt under the influence of present cultural aspirations, focused on "destiny" and assumed that Eiseley was wondering if he was going to be famous. Since their reading strategies did not include a commitment to narrative conventions like coherence and unity, my undergraduate students tended to read this passage as not relevant to his earlier objection to "this mother-worshipping culture." But, because of both my literary and experiential background, I did read this as directly related to his question, "Why should I be embittered?" Against my students, I felt Eiseley was, almost certainly unconsciously, distraught over the staying power of ideology, its tendency to pull us back into the past. His "loneliness" is alienation, with a twist: in youth he agonized over whether or not he would ever become an individual in the traditional humanist sense of autonomous and unique and whether this battle would ever be won. The deconstructive irony here is that Eiseley is writing this passage in old age, now well aware that his earliest and his subsequent attempts both literally and metaphorically to run away from his mother were in vain. Even with abundant desire and uncommon intelligence Eiseley was, against his will, ideologically situated, first as a child "who begged for peace" and then at seventy as a man who can still "see his gesticulating mother and her distorted features cursing us." I could not help but think that his mother here is both a pathetic and effective symbol: like the fragmented and often oppressive culture we live in, his mother relentlessly pursues him into old age; distorted and irrational though she is, he cannot escape her as person or sign.

In retrospect, there are other signs of Eiseley's divided inner life. Phrases like "Listen, or do not listen, it is all the same" and "But then came the rage, the utter fury, summoned up from a thousand home repressions" add coherence to the essay's underlying motif of conflict, at least as I constructed the text. Although my students were perhaps impressed that I managed during discussions to find these bits of textual evidence to support my evolving interaction with the text, they could not "see" what I saw, could not write the same text. Given the explicit influence we allowed ideology to have on our readings, that was to be expected. It also, I hope, empowered them to value the texts they could write, and perhaps even inspire them to write richer ones.

The most prevalent of the multiple inscriptions I did receive from the class was one I, in turn, could not see—their lack of sympathy for Eiseley's narrator. They did not like or appreciate the fragmented organization, nor the idea that they had probably been manipulated into sharing a feeling they did not understand or respect. As I mentioned, there were oppositional voices, mine probably the most forceful, but most refused to see Eiseley as worthy of their support. Why such antagonism over a disturbed woman, why such obsessiveness over the past, why such deviousness, why the compulsive need for understanding and forgiveness? These questions were asked by students whose own narratives were filled with anecdotes reflecting acceptance of traditional values. In their discussions they evinced little sympathy for those who were frustrated by the limitations of a culturally approved identity. They had little interest in scrutinizing or debating the values they inherited. However, those whose lives and values were different, who did suffer and who did dream of other possibilities, were more tolerant of and more receptive to Eiseley. The matching of repertoires in these instances was perhaps more psychological than social or political, but their experiences were sufficiently at variance with the dominant culture to give them the confidence to assert themselves in class and to argue for the appropriateness of their perspectives. In just this way the struggle for meaning becomes grounded in real experiences, and the false opposition between classroom and society dissolves.

The urge for students to unify these responses, however, was not nearly as strong as mine. They were content to see coherence and structure less scrupulously than I. Since I was not trying to make them accept my standards, but rather to widen their literary and ideological horizons, I felt the community pressure would create its own reasonable criteria. Perhaps under the influence of what Rosenblatt calls the "synthesizing urge" (5), I did feel the need to "put the clues together," and so I found myself engaged in the self-ordering, self-corrective process of shaping my evocation of "The Running Man" into a resolution. The organizing principle here was not centered in the text, nor even in my learned desire for a final synthesis, but in my conscious weaving of the simultaneous literary, cultural, and emotional strands involved in my reading.

I must add that very little of this was clear to me after my first readings. In fact, the notes I took then reflect more

John Clifford

bewilderment than insight, more uncertainty than understanding. As Fish argues, the early "actualizing participation"
(28) of the reader should not be summarily dismissed when
discussing meaning. Traditionally critics usually report only a
polished and much revised version of their numerous readings, perhaps stretching over several years. The messy behind-
the-scenes process of how they came to these carefully constructed positions is often considered irrelevant. I would like
to hold on to my early bafflement with Eiseley's intentions, as
an important part of the reading experience of "The Running
Man." For surely, the reader as through a glass darkly, only
gradually begins to see and to understand what might be going
on with Eiseley's cycle of denial and admission. The actual
reading of the essay seems to recapitulate Eiseley's own process
of self-knowledge. So whatever conclusion readers finally ar-
rive at, this simulation is, in itself, reason enough for students
to grapple with the essay. In fact, it is not hard to see how this
process of reading could then be extended outward and used
by readers and writers as a heuristic for discoveries of all sorts.

Still, first readings do happen, and like Eiseley's youth
they cannot be undone. It makes sense, then, to integrate early
experiences and early readings into subsequent ones. The
lesson here for reader-response theory is crucial: the text is,
as Rosenblatt notes, "an event in time" (12). Potentially, reading has no end point, which suggests that it is a series of
decisions, not something given or natural. We can decide what
it is we want to pay attention to. And although we are certainly
not completely autonomous, we can choose to watch ourselves
and others read as "an especially fertile matrix for the study
of social and historical processes" (174).

After teaching "The Running Man" several times, I began
to see that the struggle among groups in the class for dominance over the meaning of certain passages was paralleled by
Eiseley's befuddlement over the struggle in his own divided
narrative. "So much for my mother," he avows, and immediately uncuts that with the anecdote of the Auden supper. "Why
should I be embittered? It is far too late," seems to dismiss
negative emotions, but in the very next paragraph he notes

that although he too is near death, he cannot be buried next to his mother: "neither of us then would rest." In this way the momentum of the essay can be seen to enact Eiseley's lifelong desire to be outside culture. His verbal assertions, however, give him only a brief respite. For example, in the first response to Auden's question about the first public event he can remember, Eiseley tells of a prisoner who escapes by blowing the gates with nitroglycerin, remarking that he had identified with the man. He then adds, my students thought enigmatically, " 'We never made it,' I repeated unconsciously" (28). Here Eiseley seems to me a modern Sisyphus, escaping again and again, only to realize he must escape anew. And perhaps that is ultimately what this essay hopes to do: to be his final ritual purgation of ideology, his last escape from that prison. What reader-response theory demonstrates is that this is only possible in an epistemological universe where culture exists outside of us as an objective reality. But if culture constitutes us, if as Emerson notes, "the soul is no traveller .... my giant goes with me where ever I go," then there can be no escape, not even through the desperate, distancing "scrawl" on the page. Perhaps Eiseley did, after all, understand this and structured his essay, crafted his persona to enlist the sympathy and forgiveness of his readers to free him of guilt, so that after his death, in the mind of his readers, at least, his elusive struggle to be free would finally come to pass.

Works Cited

Eiseley, Loren. *All The Strange Hours.* New York: Scribner's, 1975.

Fish, Stanley. *Is There a Text in This Class?* Cambridge: Harvard UP, 1980.

Michaels, Walter Benn. "The Interpreter's Self: Peirce on the Cartesian 'Subject.' " In *Reader-Response Criticism.* Ed. Jane P. Tompkins. Baltimore: Johns Hopkins UP, 1980.

Rosenblatt, Louise. *The Reader, The Text, The Poem.* Carbondale: Southern Illinois UP, 1978.

Walter, Gary, et al. *The Lexington Introduction to Literature.* Lexington: D.C. Heath, 1987.

14
DECONSTRUCTING DIDION

Poststructuralist Rhetorical Theory
in the Composition Class

John Schilb

Composition teachers wanting support for their interest in nonfiction can find it in the writings of poststructuralists. Consider, for example Derrida's analyses of philosophical texts, Foucault's genealogies of professional discourse, de Man's studies of Rousseau's hybrid genres, Barthes's essays on various sign-systems, and Fish's recent attention to legal theory. Moreover, the composition teacher concerned especially with the *rhetoric* of nonfiction might feel inspired by the many references to "rhetoric" made by deconstructive theorists. When a certain thinker declares that she teaches at an institution preoccupied with "rhetoric," this person isn't Maxine Hairston speaking about the University of Texas, but rather Shoshana Felman alluding to the Yale school of deconstruction (22). This group can be said to include Felman, Paul de Man, J. Hillis Miller, Barbara Johnson, Cynthia Chase, and Derrida himself. Whatever their differences, they all cite "rhetoric" as a major subject of their work.

Still, the composition teacher might feel acutely discomforted or even enraged by the definition of "rhetoric" that the Yale deconstructionists have in mind. Take, for example, the writings of J. Hillis Miller. Even though he's written three essays recognizing "rhetoric in the sense of persuasion" as well as "rhetoric in the sense of knowledge of the intricacies of tropes" ("The Two Rhetorics" 101), he's clearly bent on touting the latter. In his 1986 address as president of the Modern

Deconstructing Didion

Language Association, and in his new book *The Ethics of Reading*, he virtually equates rhetoric with tropology. Furthermore, Miller's analyses of how tropes operate in texts invariably conclude that "The text warns against the argument by tropes on which the text depends" ("The Two Rhetorics" 104). In other words, attention to the fundamental role of figuration in texts leads one to "see" how the text winds up subverting its main premises. With the possible exception of Derrida, each of the deconstructionists affiliated with Yale has shared Miller's notion of rhetoric.[1] De Man, for one, has asserted that "Considered as persuasion, rhetoric is performative but considered as a system of tropes, it deconstructs its own performance" (*Allegories* 131). According to him, "a more rhetorically aware reading of *The Birth of Tragedy*" would show "that all the authoritative claims that it seems to make can be undermined by statements provided by the text itself" (*Allegories* 131). In a recent article, Johnson suggests that rhetoric can be "defined as language that says one thing and means another" ("Apostrophe" 29). Felman claims that "Rhetorical constructions function, accomplish acts of language, in such a way that they end up unhinging the very epistemological foundations which they presuppose and postulate, and upon which they are built." Her blunt conclusion: "It is in the nature of rhetorical performance to pull the rug out from under its own feet" (27).

It's hard to imagine how one could voice sentiments like these in a composition classroom and not discourage the apprentice writers sitting there. If texts inevitably betray themselves, how can students find purpose in the act of writing? What sermons on motivation, what lessons in technique, what exercises in prewriting, what sessions of peer review could make sense to them if the deconstructionist view of rhetoric presided over the course? If, in analyzing model essays by

---

1. Derrida's notion of "rhetoric" is rather more complicated, largely because he sees terms like "metaphor" as being complicitous with the metaphysical tradition no matter what apparently subversive uses of them are possible. See his essay "White Mythology: Metaphor in the Text of Philosophy" (*Margins* 207–71).

professional writers, the instructor emphasized how the rhetorical performances of these texts pulled the rug out from under their own feet, why wouldn't the students resist the specter of humiliation by refusing to write or by transferring to another section of the course, taking their own rugs with them?

To pinpoint here what a poststructuralist approach to the rhetoric of nonfiction might involve, and to suggest how it might in fact prove fruitful in a composition class, I'll first explain how a certain essay by a professional writer might be deconstructed by a theorist working in private, and I'll then explain why and how the deconstruction might be carried over into the actual course.[2] The essay I've chosen is Joan Didion's "Some Dreamers of the Golden Dream," the first piece in her 1968 collection *Slouching Towards Bethlehem*. It's easy to envision this essay being used as a model text in a composition class, if only because Didion's works dot many freshman anthologies. This article appears in one of the most notable, Donald Hall's *The Contemporary Essay*. I'm personally interested in its deconstructive potential because years ago I taught it in an advanced composition class from what I now suppose was a traditional, "humanist" point of view: identifying its meaning as determinate, praising its detail as unflinchingly accurate, recognizing its author as conveying unproblematic truths. As a text that most readers would classify as reportage, the essay does evince the empiricist inclinations for which many people continue to admire Didion. I have in mind what Katherine Usher Henderson calls Didion's "uncompromisingly realistic portrayal of contemporary America" (viii), what Mark Royden

---

2. "Deconstruction" isn't, of course, to be equated with "poststructuralism," since the latter term has encompassed other schools of thought than "deconstruction." Deconstructive theorists, however, are the poststructuralists who have been drawn the most to the vocabulary of "rhetoric," and they're also the poststructuralists who are most seen as posing dramatic challenges to previous critical thinking, even if one may feel that it's ultimately possible to connect them to the mainstream of formalist criticism. For these reasons, I've chosen to focus on deconstruction in the composition classroom rather than some other body of thought within poststructuralism.

Winchell calls an "epistemology.... firmly rooted in the particular, the specific, the concrete" (30). These are, of course, the
sorts of claims that deconstructionists challenge.

"Some Dreamers of the Golden Dream" concerns the arrest, trials, and conviction of a woman named Lucille Miller
for the murder of her husband, Cork. While Didion examines
several twists in the case—including Lucille's adulterous affair
with a lawyer named Arthwell Hayton, the suspicious death
of Hayton's wife, Hayton's subsequent renunciation of Lucille,
and Lucille's pregnancy during the second trial—she seems
primarily determined to situate the events in the context of a
particular community. As the title indicates, she assumes that
Lucille Miller's life exemplifies the delusory quests of midwest-
ern immigrants to the San Bernardino Valley. The narrative
framework is basically synecdochic.

Didion's fleshing out of her thesis gains verisimilitude
through a number of techniques. For one thing, she dwells
on concrete details, ranging from large-scale features of the
landscape and crucial episodes in the Miller case to small aspects of people's appearances. Also, she presents increasingly
comprehensive versions of Lucille's actions up to the night of
Cork's death, as if approaching the true past. Moreover, Didion extensively quotes people involved in the case, thus creating the impression that she served as a human tape recorder.
The reality-effect of the essay is heightened as well by Didion's
withholding of information about her own activities as a reporter investigating what went on. Even though she doesn't
claim an omniscient point of view—and in fact suggests that
the minds of people she encountered were in some ways
opaque—her omission of data about when and how she herself
entered the scene as a particular interpreter of it enables Didion to establish a certain narrative authority.

In delineating how a deconstructive theorist might examine the essay, I don't wish to imply that all such theorists have
agreed upon a single, clear-cut procedure. Nevertheless, I
suspect that most would look closely at Didion's text, particularly its use of figuration; identify the oppositions apparently
at work in it; try to demonstrate how these oppositions can be

reversed and destabilized; and conclude that the meaning of the text is undecidable because of tensions (1) among the text's statements and/or (2) between what the text says and what it does. It's important to note that even though a deconstructive approach does usually seek to undermine the privileging of any one interpretation of the text, it comes to insist upon undecidability through a determinedly logical reading—what Barbara Johnson describes as "a careful teasing out of the conflicting forces of signification that are at work within the text itself" ("Teaching Deconstructively" 140–41). In other words, deconstruction isn't, as many critics of it declare, a merely nihilistic posture through which the theorist feels free to say just anything at all about a text. Whether the conclusion that a deconstructive reading leads to is ultimately tenable or not, the process of that reading exhibits an orderly pattern of thinking which appropriates the words on the page.

The oppositions most often cited by deconstructionists include referentiality and textuality, the literal and the figural, cause and effect, and inside and outside. In each instance, the deconstructionist holds that metaphysical thinking has privileged the first term of the pair over the second. This strikes me as being so when I consider oppositions in "Some Dreamers of the Golden Dream" from a deconstructive stance. Note the first sentence: "This is a story about love and death in the golden land, and begins with the country" (3). The word *story* is fundamentally ambiguous. It can denote both a series of undeniable events which an author simply transcribes and an interpretive construct which the author develops—in short, both a referent and a text. As her essay proceeds, Didion suggests that the real facts of the Miller case are hard to obtain, yet she doesn't present her initial hypothesis about the significance of the case as a vulnerable conjecture. Instead, she downplays the figurative aspect of "story" and presents her interpretation of the case as a literal truth. This strategy raises the issue of whether referentiality and textuality, the literal and the figural, can indeed be separated as much as Didion apparently wants them to be. Ambiguity operates in a related fashion with the word *begins*. On the one hand, it can denote an empirical origin or cause of events that an author might simply come along and discover. On the other hand, it can again denote an interpretive construct—something *given* conceptual and discursive priority by an author to generate and frame a text. And again, Didion doesn't proceed to reflect on the possibly figurative dimension of the "beginning" she posits for the Miller case. Rather, she continuously indicates that "the country" serves as the explanatory ground of it. In doing so, she obscures how her alleged "cause" might actually be an "effect" of her own retrospective thinking—how, to put the matter differently, she might really be engaging in that reversal of cause and effect which Paul de Man associates with the trope of metalepsis. At the very least, cause and effect can't perhaps be distinguished as much as Didion implies they can.

The first sentence is also notable in its omission of references to Didion herself as the creator or even the recorder of "the story." Using the words *This is* as subject and predicate helps convey the impression that the account which follows merely transcribes reality, with the author essentially being external to the rendition of events. As I've already suggested, the persuasiveness of the essay stems in part from Didion's not specifying the coordinates of her own role as investigator. Basically she maintains the voice of someone "outside" of incidents that she comes upon, the truth of the account's "inside" thereby seeming uncontaminated by authorial perspective. But if she *is* engaged in interpretation, she *is* in a sense "inside" the narrative, for it is in a sense *her* narrative. In making this claim, one isn't necessarily accusing her of utter fabrication; one is simply acknowledging her as the shaper of the text and the construction of reality it puts forth. The decision to seem primarily "outside" the account, being a choice made in relation to a whole repertoire of discursive moves, actually proceeds from the "insider" role that the author inevitably plays in unfolding a particular depiction of the world.

Infusing my deconstruction of Didion's essay so far are a certain sense of her overall intention and a certain assessment of it. I want to linger here over this matter of authorial intention, not only because some critics, including other deconstructionists, might disagree with my appraisal of Didion's aim, but also because deconstruction's treatment of intention has often been misunderstood. Despite concerns expressed by its foes, deconstruction doesn't reject the idea of intention in a text altogether. Elaborating his concept of citation, even the notorious Derrida states that "the category of intention will not disappear; it will have its place, but from this place it will no longer be able to govern the entire system of utterances" (*Margins* 326). In several of his analyses of leading Western thinkers, Derrida follows this principle by identifying what he considers to be their intentions and then by trying to demonstrate how statements in their texts reveal that they're trapped within the metaphysical tradition despite themselves. Similarly, in his essay "The Rhetoric of Blindness: Jacques Derrida's Reading of Rousseau," Paul de Man attributes particular aims to certain theorists and then emphasizes how they apparently undercut themselves: "To write critically about critics . . . becomes a way to reflect on the paradoxical effectiveness of a blinded vision that has to be rectified by means of insights that it unwittingly provides" (*Blindness* 106).

In my remarks so far about Didion's essay, I, too, have pointed to a combination of blindness and unwitting insight. More precisely, I've suggested and will continue to suggest that she aims to capture an empirical reality but is compromised in that ambition by certain discursive features of her text, which I feel she ought to reflect explicitly upon. But it should be noted that at least some deconstructive criticism regards the author as being thoroughly in possession of the deconstructionist's insight. J. Hillis Miller's exegeses of George Eliot's writings, for example, credit her with his sense of the indeterminate relation between trope and world. In the essay on Derrida and Rousseau that I've just quoted from, de Man faults Derrida for holding that Rousseau is blinded: "On the question of rhetoric, on the nature of figural language, Rousseau was not deluded and said what he meant to say" (*Blindness* 135). Following this line of thinking, some deconstructive critics might be more willing than I've been to give Didion the benefit of the doubt—in other words, to believe that she'd agree with them in finding the relation between text and reality in "Some Dreamers of the Golden Dream" uncertain, partly because she in effect supplies the materials by which the case for uncertainty can be made. In debate with such critics, I'd keep making the point that Didion doesn't conspicuously analyze the partiality of her own perspective in the essay, and instead clearly displays condescension toward the people she describes. At any rate, I and deconstructionists more hospitable to Didion would be alike in our tendency to quarry the article for evidence of indeterminacy. Moreover, we'd resemble each other in seeking to undermine the vision of Didion-as-realist espoused by the Hendersons and Winchells, who constitute a large segment of Didion's readership. Near the end of his essay, de Man declares that "There is no need to deconstruct Rousseau; the established tradition of Rousseau interpretation, however, stands in dire need of deconstruction" (*Blindness* 139). Just as de Man ultimately wants to challenge previous critics' blindness to Rousseau's sophistication about language, so deconstructionists approaching "Some Dreamers of the Golden Dream" would strive to counter the popular view of Didion as an author who validates an "epistemology . . . firmly rooted in the particular, the specific, the concrete," whether they believe she herself embraces that view or not.

To support my own approach to the essay further, I want to focus on two specific aspects of it: its invocation of a particular text and its arrangement of episodes in a certain order. Early in the essay, Didion writes the following: "This is the country in which a belief in the literal interpretation of Genesis has slipped imperceptibly into a belief in the literal interpretation of *Double Indemnity*, the country of the teased hair and the Capris and the girls for whom all life's promise comes down to a waltz length white wedding dress and the birth of a Kimberly or a Sherry or a Debbi and a Tijuana divorce and a return to hairdressers' school" (4). This is admittedly just one sentence, and Didion doesn't explicitly mention *Double Indemnity* again. Yet the theory of deconstruction encourages the critic to consider how an apparently marginal element of a text can actually bear a crucial relation to more

269

obviously central elements of it. And in this instance, Didion's allusion to *Double Indemnity* near the start of the essay implies that she considers it a relevant framework for the narrative that ensues.

The work can indeed be deemed analogous to the Miller case. Both deal with middle-class ambitions that manifest themselves in disturbing ways. Both concern an adulterous wife, with the adultery culminating in the betrayed husband's death (a definite murder in *Double Indemnity*, a probable one in the Miller case). Furthermore, in both the wife stands to gain from a double indemnity insurance policy.

Yet Didion's invocation of *Double Indemnity* warrants further study. When she observes that residents of the San Bernardino Valley believe "in the literal interpretation of Genesis" and of *Double Indemnity* as well, and when she then proceeds to mock the vision of "all life's promise" supposedly connected to these interpretations, Didion suggests that the community confuses the figural with the literal. She insinuates, too, that she herself has a greater ability to keep the figural and the literal apart. But while it's plausible that the residents believe "in the literal interpretation of Genesis," the contention that they also believe "in the literal interpretation of *Double Indemnity*" seems highly debatable. For one thing, many residents of the Valley probably haven't read the novel or seen the movie based on it. Neither the book nor the film would give Genesis much competition for audience, in the Valley or in countless other places. Moreover, would a literal interpretation of *Double Indemnity* actually entail behavior of the sort identified in the rest of the sentence? Lucille Miller may have engaged in adultery and murder, but the "girls" mentioned in the sentence apparently haven't. In fact, Didion signifies that Lucille's life is *atypical* of the Valley when she alludes to the writing of James M. Cain once more: "It was in the breakup that the affair ceased to be in the conventional mode and began to resemble instead the novels of James M. Cain, the movies of the late 1930's, all the dreams in which violence and threats and blackmail are made to seem commonplaces of middle-class life" (17). (Heightening the literal/figural confusion is the fact that

Didion probably has the date wrong here. If she's referring, as I think she is, to the tradition of *film noir* in general and to celebrated film versions of Cain's novels in particular, the correct time period would be no earlier than the mid-1940s. *Double Indemnity* was filmed in 1944, *Mildred Pierce* in 1945, *The Postman Always Rings Twice* in 1946.)

Besides, if a literal interpretation of *Double Indemnity* were possible in some sense of the term *literal*, surely that interpretation would have to encompass the entire plot of the work and recognize the moral lessons it evolves. To me, a literal interpretation of the work would more likely *dis*courage one from adultery and murder, given that it ends with the demise of the scheming couple. Perhaps Didion means something else by "literal interpretation" which would make her sentence credible. In other words, she might want to accuse me of taking the phrase "literal interpretation" *too* literally, or, then again, not literally *enough*. Yet any argument between us would probably wind up proving nothing more than that the literal and the figural are intertwined in Didion's statement about the community's relation to *Double Indemnity*.

Therefore, when Didion claims that the community's belief in the literal interpretation of Genesis has "slipped imperceptibly" into a belief in the literal interpretation of *Double Indemnity*, she herself "slips" from a declaration that seems literal to one that is far more problematic in its referential status—even if she wants to render the problem "imperceptible" in her attempt to put forth her interpretation of the Miller case as sound. And actually, one can argue that even the declaration about belief in Genesis isn't purely literal, since the Valley probably has a few people who aren't fundamentalist, and isn't purely figural, since the Valley probably has many people who are.

The instability of the literal/figural opposition in this part of the essay is of more than passing interest. As I've said, Didion is introducing here a text that presumably illuminates both the events in the Miller case and "the country" where the story "begins," so that indeterminacy between the literal and the figural here raises a question about the extent to which

271

John Schilb

Didion's narrative framework for the whole essay is *derived from* reality and the extent to which it's *imposed upon* reality. In particular, her effort to explain Lucille's behavior by linking it to the sentiments of the community could be undermined. Increasing this possibility is Lucille's individual background: as a Seventh-Day Adventist who apparently went on to betray and murder her husband, she uniquely could be said to have moved from belief in Genesis to some kind of belief in *Double Indemnity*. Didion therefore could be said to project the sordid aspects of Lucille's individual life *back* into her preliminary description of "the country," rather than really charting how Lucille's actions *emerged* from it.

In making these remarks about the *Double Indemnity* passage and what I see as implied by it, I don't wish to propose that "Some Dreamers of the Golden Dream" can never refer to reality at all. I register this disclaimer because deconstructionists are often accused of denying that anything exists outside of texts. What deconstruction actually denies is that the words in texts, and the relations among them, can transparently reveal the world. As Paul de Man puts it: "In a genuine semiology as well as in other linguistically oriented theories, the referential function of language is not being denied—far from it; what is in question is its authority as a model for natural or phenomenal cognition. Literature is fiction not because it somehow refuses to acknowledge 'reality,' but because it is not *a priori* certain that language functions according to principles which are those, or which are *like* those, of the phenomenal world. It is therefore not a priori certain that literature is a reliable source of information about anything but its own language" (*Resistance* 11). A deconstructive approach to Didion's attempt at placing Lucille's existence in context doesn't, then, automatically reject the idea that real cultural conditions may be at work. But it concentrates above all on how the text invokes such conditions *discursively* and how, in particular, the presentation of them seems to depend upon certain unstable oppositions which are characteristic of *linguistic* ordering and hence aren't necessarily infallible guides to a world outside of language. When the text makes use of another text, *Double*

Indemnity, in articulating explanatory principles supposedly operative in "the real world," the deconstructionist will be especially sensitive to how a certain instability or indeterminacy might be thereby occluded, whether by the author or her readers or both.

Didion's ordering of events in "Some Dreamers of the Golden Dream" raises a similar issue. One of her chief ideas in the essay is that Lucille Miller and other people in the San Bernardino Valley disregard the past, unfortunately choosing to learn nothing from it. Near the beginning of the essay, for example, Didion observes that "The future always looks good in the golden land, because no one remembers the past. Here is where the hot wind blows and the old ways do not seem relevant, where the divorce rate is double the national average and where one person in every thirty-eight lives in a trailer. Here is the last stop for all those who come from somewhere else, for all those who drifted away from the cold and the past and the old ways" (4). When later she notes that "there is some confusion in Lucille Miller's mind" (10) about the circumstances of her husband's death, Didion seems to be not only reporting a particular aspect of the case but also stressing the community's inability to get history straight. When, near the end of the essay, she ponders whether Arthwell Hayton suffered, she decides that "Perhaps he did not, for time past is not believed to have any bearing upon time present or future, not in the golden land where every day is born anew" (28). In mentioning, finally, the "illusion veil" (28) worn by Hayton's new bride, Didion emphasizes the bride's blindness to the case's revelations of character and intimates that the other people she's written about are blind as well.

Even though how Cork Miller died must remain a matter of conjecture, Didion seems to feel she can hold people guilty of neglecting a past that's ascertainable in some crucial sense. More specifically, she appears to criticize them for not taking seriously their own past actions and/or the past actions of others. But what is, in fact, the nature of the past as it emerges in the essay? Didion's sarcasm toward the people she describes, and the strong image of the "illusion veil" with which she

John Schilb

concludes the essay, lead me to think that she considers the past a literal reality, one that she can refer to in a morally assured way. But what if the past is more something that's *constructed* by people for various purposes? At the very least, such a possibility would make the nature of "*the* past" more indeterminate than Didion's sardonic language suggests.

To see how Didion's own narrative sequence points toward this possibility, note, to begin with, how key events she reports might be arranged chronologically:

coming of Mormons and then other immigrants to the San Bernardino Valley

life of Lucille Miller up to the night of October 7, 1964—including birth, college, marriage to Cork, decline of the marriage, affair with Hayton, death of Hayton's wife Elaine, breakup with Hayton

death of Cork in automobile fire on night of October 7

detectives' investigation of death scene at dawn of October 8

arrest of Lucille

Cork's funeral

detectives' attempt to find another man (eventually Hayton) in Lucille's life

Lucille's first trial, quickly ending in a mistrial

revelation of Lucille's pregnancy

Lucille's second trial

Consider next how Didion orders her presentation of events:

coming of Mormons and then other immigrants to the San Bernardino Valley

knowable actions of Lucille on the night of October 7

Cork's funeral

arrest of Lucille

life of Lucille up to the night of October 7—excluding affair with Hayton and excluding mention of the suspicious circumstances of Elaine's death

274

night of October 7 from Lucille's point of view, with new mention of her meeting with her lawyer

arrest of Lucille

detectives' investigation of death scene at dawn of October 8

detectives' attempt to find another man (eventually Hayton) in Lucille's life

Lucille's affair with Hayton, Elaine's suspicious death, breakup with Hayton

Lucille's second trial

Lucille's first trial, quickly ending in a mistrial

Lucille's second trial

revelation of Lucille's pregnancy

Lucille's second trial

I could pinpoint smaller moments in the essay that leap forward or backward in time, but I trust that juxtaposing the two columns shows that the discourse of the essay hardly matches chronology. If Didion wishes to impress "the past" upon her readers, she winds up having to present it in a nonlinear fashion. Evidently intending to jolt her audience into awareness of "the past," she abruptly mentions Lucille's arrest *after* mentioning Cork's funeral and suddenly reveals Lucille's pregnancy *after* beginning to describe the second trial. To grip her readers with the truth-disclosing intensity of a detective story, she traces Lucille's affair with Hayton and notes the suspiciousness of Elaine's death only when she reports the police's developing investigation.

The terminology of speech-act theory, so often deployed by deconstructionists to highlight conflicts between what a text says and what it does, might help me summarize my overall point here. To sensitize readers to "the past" that she feels Lucille and others ignore, Didion must, apparently, construct that "past" *performatively*—arranging episodes in an emotionally stimulating manner that can't be achieved through strict

275

chronology. But the fact of such arrangement, and the seeming need for its performative dimension, compromise the *constative* authority Didion apparently wants her invocation of "the past" to have. The tension between the performative and constative elements of her discourse ultimately makes unresolvable the issue of whether Didion's "past" is text or reality—despite her absolutist talk of "illusion veils."

According to deconstructive theorists, my attempt at deconstructing "Some Dreamers of the Golden Dream" could persist indefinitely. Parts of the text marginalized by my analysis could be brought to the fore in continued pursuit of indeterminacy. Furthermore, if Didion's essay can be deconstructed, there's no reason why my own study of it can't be, with the result being that oppositions of my own are reversed and destabilized and my own metaphysical proclivities exposed. Recognizing that in a sense deconstruction never stops, I nevertheless want to halt my deconstruction of Didion here and confront it with the exigencies of the composition classroom. How much of my analysis could remain intact there? In what ways might it have to be modified? How would I have to present it there so that it would move students to write with skill? In pointing out how a deconstructive approach can actually be of value in a composition class, I'll focus on four virtues of it: its ability to help students chart relations within texts; its emphasis on how writers make textualizing choices in negotiating reality; its pressure on writers and readers to examine how textual meaning is decided; and its encouragement of stimulating intellectual debate.

It's safe to assume that the more students can trace relations within texts, the better. Understanding the internal structures of discourse—or, more precisely, understanding the range of vocabularies with which these structures can be described—theoretically puts students in a stronger position to comprehend the power of other people's texts over them and to revise their own. It's also fair to say that when students enter the freshman composition class, they often come with a single, impoverished framework for the understanding of textual structures, one which was drilled into them during their high school English classes and may very well be drilled into them again in their college ones. I have in mind the traditional classification of discourse into distinct modes (for example, the personal essay, the expository essay, the persuasive paper, the research paper) and the traditional emphasis on thesis statements, topic sentences, and three or five paragraph "themes." A striking development in composition scholarship in recent years has been the attempt to pinpoint the organizational elements of discourse with greater exactitude, by such means as the study of lexical ties within and between sentences. Analysis of this sort has not only enabled researchers to distinguish better between poor writers and good writers, but has also provided a stronger foundation for composition teachers as they seek to make their students aware of how texts might be designed. I'd submit that deconstruction's attention to relations within texts can play a significant role in this effort. By stressing how texts might on the surface be organized through certain oppositions, and then by stressing how oppositions can be reversed and shown to be questionable—so that what looks like a cause and effect relation, for example, turns out to be an instance of metalepsis—a deconstructive approach to "Some Dreamers of the Golden Dream" can deepen composition students' awareness of how their own writing might be structured and described. By stressing how seemingly marginal elements of a text might support or undermine its apparently central components—so that what looks like a simple reference to *Double Indemnity*, for example, turns out to be a questionable hinge for Didion's overall narrative—a deconstructive approach to Didion's essay can make composition students more conscious of the possible relations between the marginal and the central in their own texts. By stressing the disjunction between the constative and performative dimensions of Didion's references to "the past," a deconstructive approach can lead composition students to be more cognizant of the relation between what their texts say and what they want their texts to do. By stressing how the relation between the literal and the figural in Didion's essay is actually quite complex, a deconstructive approach can help students see that fiction and nonfiction can coexist in discourse more than the traditional division into modes implies. This isn't to say that the terminology of deconstruction should drive out all other ways of talking about the organization of texts. Nor is it to say that the terminology of deconstruction can't be modified to come across as more accessible to students—although I, for one, think many could handle terms such as *metalepsis* and *synecdoche* if they're patiently defined and their use carefully demonstrated, and I, for one, consider terms like these important because they evoke discourse as an order of words.

The techniques of deconstruction can also be useful in a composition class in that they can help students question the authority of writers they might otherwise be tempted to deem as "realist" and can help them question what they might otherwise accept as "realist" aspects of their own writing. Even if one doesn't revel in indeterminacy, I think studying oppositions in Didion's essay does promote a healthy skepticism toward her treatment of the Miller case and toward her reputation in general—as well as toward the critics who've constructed that reputation. As a result of trying out a deconstructive approach toward "Some Dreamers of the Golden Dream," I for one have come to feel that Didion's stance toward Lucille Miller and the people of the San Bernardino Valley reflects class bias at least as much as it does empirical observation, that Old California (the Sacramento contingent) is looking down on New. At any rate, deconstruction's emphasis on questioning a text's apparent oppositions between referentiality and textuality, the literal and the figural, cause and effect, and inside and outside can lead students to develop a better sense of how a writer like Didion doesn't simply imitate the world but instead perceives, analyzes, and plots it through her own particular perspective and through the medium of language (which, to quote de Man again, shouldn't be automatically considered "a model for natural or phenomenal cognition"). And deconstruction can thereby help students ponder how they, as writers themselves, don't merely transcribe reality but instead make textualizing choices in their negotiation with it and their readers. With these aims in mind, I'd have students rewrite portions of "Some Dreamers of the Golden Dream" from different points of view and with different voices. They could write about the Miller case from Lucille's perspective, for example, or from Arthwell Hayton's, or from the police detectives'. They could write about it from the point of view of the author, but with a voice that suggests uncertainty about whether she's getting at the truth. They could write about it from the point of view of someone from the community who's watching Joan Didion investigate the case and evaluating her in a particular way. They could experiment with other narrative frameworks than the *Double Indemnity* one. They could rearrange the events in other orders than Didion's and explain the rationales for them. And then they could discuss what they've done in peer review groups, examining what their rewriting implies about Didion's stratagems and about the linguistic resources they draw upon in their own texts.

After studying Didion's essay in this manner, they could proceed to write essays of their own about, say, events in their hometowns, with the drafts being examined again in peer review groups alert to the possible repertoire of perspectives, devices, and structures from which the writers have selected. Moreover, given deconstruction's emphasis on how an utterly literal copying of the world is impossible and how authors necessarily resort to perspectives which are partial, language which mediates, the groups could then ponder in writing the criteria for deciding what does constitute a satisfactory interpretation for them of their hometowns. More specifically, they could compose responses to such questions as the following: If, as Didion does, they create plots for life in their towns, what might make one plot better than another? If, as Didion does, they inevitably look at their towns through particular filters and with particular voices, how might they decide which filter and which voice are most appropriate? If, as Didion does, they set up unstable oppositions in their writing about their towns, which oppositions might turn out to be persuasive, and under what discursive conditions? I'd submit that the opportunity to wrestle with questions like these is rare for many freshman composition students, given the tendency of their previous English teachers to focus such inquiry on belles-lettristic writing and discuss "nonfictional" prose in more mechanical, utilitarian ways. And if developmental studies of students entering college are to be believed, freshmen need assistance in moving from an absolutist mindset—one which looks to authorities for the one right view of the world—to greater consciousness of how a multiplicity of perspectives is possible (Perry). Of course, deconstruction isn't the only theory about texts that foregrounds relativism and the screening of reality through language. Various schools of rhetoric can claim such a focus, as can semiotics and certain strands of reader-response theory. What makes deconstruction special in this regard, I think, is its fundamental *insistence* on the ultimate indeterminacy of the relation between text and reality, along with its particular focus on working with linguistic terminology and probing the oppositions upon which the text depends.

At the outset, however, I suggested that composition students might react with considerable anxiety to the thwarting of the text's main premises that deconstruction seems to find inevitable. As I've already noted, deconstruction doesn't do away with the notion of authorial intention, although it's true that many exponents of deconstruction hold that the author's conscious purpose can't rule over all subsequent interpretations of the text. Yet even this tenet is hardly expressed by just deconstructive theorists. Paul Ricoeur, a leading contemporary philosopher of hermeneutics who has had reservations about poststructuralism, has himself declared that "the peculiarity of the literary work, and indeed of the work as such, is . . . to transcend its own psycho-sociological conditions of production and thereby to open itself to an unlimited series of readings, themselves situated in sociocultural contexts which are always different" (91). If composition students and composition teachers, for that matter, are frightened by the idea that authorial intention, as conceived by deconstructionists, can't pilot the text's voyage through the variety of contexts it may encounter, their fear may result in part from the failure of composition classes to circulate the texts written in it to various audiences and then to study what happens. The new emphasis in composition studies in writing for particular audiences may or may not prove helpful in this regard. If the composition student is asked to write for just one audience, no matter how particular, the shifts in textual interpretation that may occur with shifts in audience won't get addressed. If the composition student is able to see how different audiences react to the text he or she writes, influenced as they are by different contexts, valuable insights into the role of authorial interpretation may be achieved. The student would have the opportunity to see what about the text remains stable in its circulation, what about it is subject to different interpretations, what it is about particular contexts that leads to different interpretations, how the text might be written in the first place to limit as much as possible the extent to which interpretations might diverge from what the author intends, how much latitude in interpretation the author might be willing to accept, and what kinds of contexts might have to be established in order for the author's intention to persist. Student writing doesn't have to be circulated widely beyond the classroom in order for these questions to be confronted. The students right there in the classroom might be diverse enough to generate a distinct variety of audiences, and if they're not, they could assume the roles of readers with various backgrounds and interests. An essay such as "Some Dreamers of the Golden Dream" could be put through this exercise as a rehearsal for similar exercises dealing with the students' own papers.

Although more traditional versions of rhetoric might appear to offer more support than deconstruction for this endeavor, I'd contend that the opposite is true, and that the deconstructive approach I've taken to Didion's essay could actually be an encouraging instead of a traumatizing exemplar for students as they consider how interpretations of texts can change with contexts. As I've already indicated, deconstruction doesn't deny that a particular interpretation of a text may be satisfactory for certain pragmatic purposes, even if deconstruction would want to hold that in actuality, the meaning of the text is ultimately undecidable. To put the matter another way: deconstruction's emphasis on how texts are *epistemologically* indeterminate doesn't interfere with the notion that meaning can be at least *culturally* determinate, able to be tentatively stabilized through the semiotic systems operative in a culture at the moment and through the practical consequences of interpreting one way instead of another. Rather than make this point simply to deter criticism of deconstruction, though, I want to stress how it underscores one of deconstruction's strengths: the power to remind writers and readers that decisions about textual meaning are possible but are bound to be contextual and contingent, rather than being inexorably demanded by the realities of the text. Instead of merely disturbing composition students, deconstruction can vigorously attune them to the idea that writers and readers should closely study the situations and cultural predispositions through which analyses of texts are eventually foreclosed and decisions about their meaning established. A deconstructive reading of Didion's essay can impel students, more than other approaches can, to probe how interpretations are historically grounded and how texts can be reinterpreted in their transmission. If such probing can't ultimately guarantee students absolute control over their texts, it can nevertheless alert them to contexts they may be able to address in their composing, and it can more generally spur them to monitor how their texts are received. Note that I'm saying the deconstructive composition teacher shouldn't just rest with the ambiguities that Didion's essay can present. Instead, he or she should use them to open up for the students consideration of the *extrinsic* influences on the reception of texts—as well as to contest students' own particular interpretations if they start to get entrenched as the absolute truth.

Deconstructive theorists in philosophy and literature have, in fact, most often made their claims in response to claims by other theorists whom they've taken to be unduly hegemonic in their cognitive assurance. Henry Staten and Rodolphe Gasché have recently explained, for example, how Derrida's arguments need to be seen as a reaction to Hegel's, Husserl's, and Heidegger's visions of philosophy. In *Blindness and Insight* and the essays collected in *The Resistance to Theory*, de Man seems determined to counteract rival literary theories that have grown popular. Even J. Hillis Miller, who usually concentrates on microscopic readings of novels and poems, periodically acknowledges his desire to critique more traditional ways of studying literature. Because deconstructive criticism has so often surfaced as a reaction to other schools, composition students might be disoriented if they didn't encounter these positions along with it. Faculty members might know how deconstruction has arisen within, and contributed to, institutional debates, but students most likely wouldn't. Composition teachers might immediately resist the suggestion that they bring such debates into their courses, fearing that students wouldn't be mature enough to grasp them. But quite possibly students could follow theoretical controversy as it unfolded. And quite possibly a presentation of deconstructive and contending approaches to "Some Dreamers of the Golden Dream" could make them feel that the act of writing, and the discipline through which it's usually taught, are pervaded by intellectual excitement rather than simply being concerted attempts to put them through humiliating drudgery. English studies could emerge for them as not just a set of rules they have to obey and maxims they have to adopt—the image that many of them, I suspect, have acquired through their previous education—but instead as a center for vital questioning about the relations between mind, language, culture, and the world. Besides, as Gerald Graff has recently asserted, bringing a department's theoretical conflicts into its classrooms permits them to be more centrally addressed and provides the basis for a more achievable form of departmental coherence than traditional consensus models. Consider how a department might be pulled together by a debate between composition and literature faculty over the merits of a deconstructive stance toward Didion's essay. Consider how composition students watching the debate would not only be introduced to the possible dialectics between literary theory and composition theory, but would also be made increasingly conscious of how contemplating the act of writing might involve grappling with

John Schilb

philosophical issues germane to their own lives. Consider how these students might be encouraged to enter the debate themselves, through oral and written responses. And consider, finally, how these students might thereby come to regard their compositions as contributing to a dramatic exploration of the nature of knowing, even when their essays aren't explicitly about deconstruction and its opponents but instead concern a subject like their own golden dreams.

When I assert that deconstruction can provide leverage in the writing classroom for a stimulating debate between theories that too often nestle in separate corners of the English department, I'm suggesting that one doesn't have to subscribe fully to the principles of deconstruction in order to draw upon it in composition teaching. What would, indeed, be required at a minimum to launch the public controversy I've conjured up would be the teacher's recognition of the significant challenge deconstruction has posed to traditional theories, whether one ultimately accepts its concepts or not. Of course, it's more than just provisional tolerance of deconstruction that's driven my explanation of its other possible merits in the composition class, and my analysis of Didion's essay beforehand. Deconstruction is, for me, a highly illuminating way of looking at texts, not simply a disciplinary trend worth noting for its sociological import. Nevertheless, I'm unwilling to end on a note of brazen confidence about deconstruction's potential for writing classes—expressing what de Man himself himself derided as "a programmatically euphoric utopianism" (*Resistance* 12). In teaching as well as in writing, as in so many other things, there are no serviceable insurance policies, double indemnity or otherwise. But I do hope I've conveyed the impression that the definition of *rhetoric* from which deconstruction proceeds is potentially a great help, not a mere obstacle, to the teacher of writing. The rugs of students' texts may be crucially twitched; they may fear that the rugs will be snatched away completely. Yet improvement in writing ability probably can't occur if the rugs in composition classrooms simply remain in place. Hence, the advanced *dis*placement examinations carried out by deconstructive theorists may very well be of use there.

Works Cited

De Man, Paul. *Allegories of Reading: Figural Language in Rousseau, Nietzsche, Rilke, and Proust*. New Haven: Yale UP, 1979.
———. *Blindness and Insight: Essays in the Rhetoric of Contemporary Criticism*. 2nd ed. Minneapolis: U of Minnesota P, 1983.
———. *The Resistance to Theory*. Minneapolis: U of Minnesota P, 1986.
Derrida, Jacques. *Margins of Philosophy*. Trans. Alan Bass. Chicago: U of Chicago P, 1982.
Didion, Joan. *Slouching Towards Bethlehem*. New York: Farrar, Straus and Giroux, 1968.
Felman, Shoshana. *Writing and Madness: (Literature/Philosophy/Psychoanalysis)*. Trans. Martha Noel Evans and Felman. Ithaca: Cornell UP, 1985.
Gasché, Rodolphe. *The Tain of the Mirror: Derrida and the Philosophy of Reflection*. Cambridge: Harvard UP, 1986.
Graff, Gerald. *Professing Literature: An Institutional History*. Chicago: U of Chicago P, 1987.
Hall, Donald, ed. *The Contemporary Essay*. New York: St. Martin's. 1984.
Henderson, Katherine Usher. *Joan Didion*. New York: Frederick Ungar, 1981.
Johnson, Barbara. "Apostrophe, Animation, and Abortion." *Diacritics* 16 (1986): 29–47.
———. *The Critical Difference: Essays in the Contemporary Rhetoric of Reading*. Baltimore: Johns Hopkins UP, 1980.
———. "Teaching Deconstructively." *Writing and Reading Differently: Deconstruction and the Teaching of Composition and Literature*. Ed. G. Douglas Atkins and Michael L. Johnson. Lawrence: U of Kansas P, 1985. 140–48.
Miller, J. Hillis. *The Ethics of Reading*. New York: Columbia UP, 1986.
———. "The Function of Rhetorical Study at the Present Time." *ADE Bulletin* 62 (Sept.–Nov., 1979): 10–18.
———. "Presidential Address 1986. The Triumph of Theory, the Resistance to Reading, and the Question of the Material Base." *PMLA* 102 (1987): 281–91.

John Schilb

———. "The Two Rhetorics: George Eliot's Bestiary." In Atkins and Johnson. 101–14.

Perry, William. *Forms of Intellectual and Ethical Development in the College Years*. New York: Holt, Rinehart and Winston, 1970.

Ricoeur, Paul. *Hermeneutics and the Human Sciences*. Ed. and trans. John B. Thompson. New York: Cambridge UP, 1981.

Winchell, Mark Royden. *Joan Didion*. Boston: G. K. Hall, 1980.

15
STUDENTS AND TEACHERS UNDER THE INFLUENCE

Image and Idea in the Essay

Pat C. Hoy II

As I look for ways to get my students interested in the art of writing, I turn frequently to professional essayists for ideas. In their essays about writing, I find a common thread that loops together important notions about images, ideas, memory, imagination, and invention. Writing, whatever its form, grows out of a writer's intense personal experiences. Those experiences may be primary or secondary: the stuff of everyday living or the vicarious stuff of reading and reflecting. Those experiences shape our writing and inform our judgments. But because we do not normally write while we experience and because our judgments usually evolve over time, writing depends on memory, imagination, and invention. We must recall so that we can make sense; we must reconstruct and invent so that our texts are convincing and interesting. Our aim, of course, is to tell the truth as we understand it.

Students who come to my freshman composition classes have thought little about the truth as they understand it, and they are generally unaware of the value of their own experiences; they simply do not know how to mine those experiences, how to turn them into stimulating essays. So my task is to get them started, to move them from experience to essay, to help them discover ideas that will make their essays cohere. My starting point is often the image, the recollected picture of experience recalled from memory. Turning images into words, students discover imaginative possibilities; they discover their own ideas.

Pat C. Hoy II

Our vehicle is the exploratory essay. I choose that form over the more tightly organized classical oration—what we often call the five-paragraph essay—because I want my students to have more freedom to think within the form, want them to learn to care about language and the way they use it, want them to learn how to explore ideas before they develop tighter arguments. The terse five-paragraph overlay, imposed on young, inquiring minds, often subverts my developmental aims, putting form over content, leaving out the "I" that is the writer, substituting "proof" and linearity for exploration.

At the outset, I want my students to discover the rich complexity of their own images, and I want them to learn to identify and develop the ideas embedded in those images. Toni Morrison suggests that when she begins to think about certain people, "the images that float around them . . . . surface so vividly and so compellingly that I acknowledge them as my route to a reconstruction of a world, to an exploration of an interior life that was not written and to the revelation of a kind of truth." These images may be as "ineffable and as flexible as a dimly recalled figure, the corner of a room, a voice." Even an ear of corn sets off a chain of recollections for Morrison, and she goes on to "see corn on the cob," to move "from picture to meaning to text" ("Memory" 115–17). For Morrison, such tracking provides a beginning, a way from experience to literary texts. For students, such tracking can lead to compelling nonfiction essays that are coherent, crafted works of literature.

I think often of Matthew Arnold's "The Study of Poetry," of his high claims for literature. "The future of poetry is immense," he suggested in 1880, because "religion has materialised itself in the fact, in the supposed fact; it has attached its emotion to the fact, and now the fact is failing it." Arnold was telling his 1880 audience that poetry would offer "an ever surer and surer stay" in troubled times; it would do so because "for poetry the idea is everything. . . . Poetry attaches its emotion to the idea; the idea *is* the fact" (161). For Arnold, the poetic idea was supple. It could engender feeling and enjoyment. It could engage an audience. Poetry had not "material-ised" itself into dogma. The poetic idea was not fixed.

Concerned that even the poetic idea has become fixed in our time, I try to turn my students from a precise thesis to a supple idea. Doing so, I turn them away from overlay to exploration, to an idea that has not been denuded of emotion. The task is complex because I do not want from them mere expressive writing. I want writing that is grounded in their personal experience, yet I want writing that transcends the personal. Reading essays by E. B. White, Joan Didion, Loren Eiseley, Annie Dillard, and Gretel Ehrlich, I find those writers present in their essays, engaged and reflective. Behind their words, I find what Eliot discovered in Yeats's later poems: "a unique personality which makes one sit up in excitement and eagerness to learn more about the author's mind and feelings." Under Yeats's influence, Eliot, who for twenty years had called for "an extinction of personality," called instead for a poet "who, out of intense and personal experience, is able to express a general truth; retaining all the particularity of his experi-ence, to make of it a general symbol" ("Yeats" 250–51).

My aim is to move my students toward Eliot's mature discovery. Annie Dillard's essay "Living Like Weasels" gives them a sense of what the image might mean to a professional essayist and shows them how she turns a very personal experi-ence into a general truth. The central event Dillard recounts in her essay occurred when she encountered a weasel near Tinker Creek. She recreates for us the moment of that event, giving us a sense of what happened to her:

> He had two black eyes I didn't see, any more than you see a window.
>
> The weasel was stunned into stillness as he was emerging from beneath an enormous shaggy wild rose bush four feet away. I was stunned into stillness twisted backward on the tree trunk. Our eyes locked, and someone threw away the key.
>
> Our look was as if two lovers, or deadly enemies, met unexpectedly on an overgrown path when each had been think-ing of something else: a clearing blow to the gut. It was also a

bright blow to the brain, or a sudden beating of brains, with all the charge and intimate grate of rubbed balloons. It emptied our lungs. It felled the forest, moved the fields, and drained the pond; the world dismantled and tumbled into that black hole of eyes . . . . (13–14)

Dillard's personal experience with the weasel—the locking of eyes—must certainly have provided the occasion for this essay. That look seized her imagination, and she developed the idea she found embedded in the "black hole of eyes." What she found out about weasels through additional reading, she used to elaborate and enhance this central image.

In the introduction to the essay, Dillard gives us two instances of weasels in action. A weasel bit a naturalist, "socketed into his hand deeply as a rattlesnake"; the man could not pry him off; "he had to walk half a mile to water, the weasel dangling from his palm, and soak him off like a stubborn label" (11). Another weasel was found as a "dry skull . . . . fixed by the jaws to [an eagle's] throat." Dillard wonders about that weasel before his death, carried aloft as it was by the eagle. She wonders whether she could have seen the "whole weasel still attached to his feathered throat, a fur pendant" or whether the eagle gutted "the living weasel with his talons before his breast, bending his beak, cleaning the beautiful airborne bones" (12). She is obviously fascinated with this socketing image—with the weasel's instinctive action and his tenacity even in the face of death. Later in the essay when she regrets not going for the weasel's throat under the wild rose bush, we know what she has in mind. We understand more clearly the idea she is developing, the idea that we, like the weasel, ought to yield "at every moment to the perfect freedom of single necessity" and hold on for a "dearer life" (15–16).

Returning again and again to the socketing image through allusion as well as explanation, Dillard finally concludes her essay with a paean to the weasel as metaphorical image: "I think it would be well, and proper, and obedient, and pure, to grasp your one necessity and not let it go, to dangle from it limp wherever it takes you." Combining the two initial images from her introduction, she makes one last effort to put image and idea together for us as we are asked to imagine ourselves overcoming death even in the act of dying, being carried aloft, our eyes burning, our flesh falling off in shreds as our "very bones unhinge and scatter, loosened over fields, over fields and woods, lightly, thoughtless, from any height at all, from as high as eagles" (16). So from a very personal experience, Dillard develops an idea that goes far beyond a mere exchange of glances with a weasel. She exhorts us to be weasels, "to stalk [our] calling in a certain skilled and supple way, to locate the most tender and live spot and plug into that pulse" (16).

Taking an idea such as this one about image and idea and personal experience into the classroom, we need collaborators like Dillard who will show our students what they can do as writers. With the help of these collaborators, we can give student writers back to themselves, show them that all good essays take shape from their own personal experiences, that their personal values inform their judgments. I remind them of John Henry Newman's arguments against those who would view style as an *"addition from without."* Newman would call exploratory essays literature because they express "not objective truth . . . but subjective; not things, but thoughts" ("Literature" 230). Style, he argues, is a "thinking out into language," and literature, the product of that thinking, is "not . . . mere *words;* but thoughts expressed in language" (232). This special sense of style suggests more than the shape of one's sentences or one's penchant for various writing strategies; it suggests as well a writer's intimate connection with the words themselves. Because knowledge is, for Newman, "an acquired illumination . . . an inward endowment" ("Own End" 105), we can see why he considers a person's language "the faithful expression of his intense personality, attending on his own inward world of thought as its very shadow." Newman appreciated the "colouring derived from [the writer's] own mind," the coloring we do not find in objective, scientific writing ("Literature" 231). His is a subtle reminder that one's writing takes on character and complexity as one's education becomes more complete. Writ-

Pat C. Hoy II

ing is perhaps the clearest and most reliable index of the
quality of our education.

White, Didion, and Eiseley seem to have cut their eye
teeth on Eliot and Newman; they not only examine the idea
of personality as a subject of discourse, they also show us in
their essays how to keep the idea from being mired in the
particular; they show us how to make of the particular a general symbol. White, who is fond of tongue-in-cheek observations, reminds us that essay writers must be "congenitally self-
centered"; they have to sustain themselves "by the childish
belief that everything [they] think about, everything that happens to [them], is of general interest" (Foreword vii). When
he's in a more serious mood, White feels quite responsible
as the "writing man, or secretary" who is "charged with the
safekeeping of all unexpected items of worldly or unworldly
enchantment" ("Ring" 143). He feels a "duty to my society"
to "describe what is indescribable." Failing on occasion, he
reminds all of us who aspire to be good writers that we are
like acrobats who "must occasionally try a stunt that is too
much for [us]" (145).

Didion, echoing White, reminds us that "writing is the act
of saying *I*, of imposing oneself upon other people, of saying
listen to me, see it my way, change your mind" (2). Writing to find
out what she's thinking, she grapples with special images in
her mind that "shimmer around the edges." Those charged
images come to her with a "grammar" of their own, "the
grammar in the picture." She explains:

> Just as I meant 'shimmer' literally I mean 'grammar' literally.
> Grammar is a piano I play by ear, since I seem to have been
> out of school the year the rules were mentioned. All I know
> about grammar is its infinite power. . . . The arrangement of
> the words matters, and the arrangement you want can be
> found in the picture in your mind. The picture dictates the
> arrangement. The picture dictates whether this will be a
> sentence with or without clauses, a sentence that ends hard
> or a dying-fall sentence, long or short, active or passive.
> The picture tells you how to arrange the words and the

arrangement of the words tells you, or tells me, what's going
on in the picture. *Nota bene*:
    It tells you.
    You don't tell it. (2, 98)

Giving all of us new ideas about writing, Didion provides a
fascinating clue about the power that such pictures have over
us. The picture tells us; we don't tell it.

    Loren Eiseley also places primary importance on the pic-
tures in his mind. When he writes, he calls those images out
of his "artist's loft," retrieving them so that he can tell the story
about ordinary life that "already lies there" within the image.
Eiseley suggests that a fiction writer would invent "a human
story of equal proportions" to go with the image ("Willy" 155).
Embedded in that distinction between the essayist and the
storyteller is the notion that one kind of mind apprehends and
records, the other imposes. Eiseley's mind, the apprehending
one, discerns what lies behind the appearance of things, grasp-
ing the meaning that is already there in the image. He wrote
"concealed" essays, essays in which "personal anecdote [is]
allowed gently to bring under observation thoughts of a more
purely scientific nature." Those essays, he tells us, found their
evolutionary origins scattered from Montaigne to Emerson
("Ghost" 177–78).

    White's call for self-centeredness, Didion's pictorial gram-
mar, and Eiseley's concealed essays point beyond themselves
to a psychological notion that provides a bridge from theory
and pedagogy to product, to student essays themselves. James
Hillman, the archetypal psychologist, argues that in our time
we need to reexamine the metaphorical nature of soul, reminding ourselves that soul suggests "the imaginative possibility in our natures, the experiencing [of the world] through
reflective speculation, dream, image, and *fantasy*—that mode
which recognizes all realities as primarily symbolic or metaphorical" (*Archetypal* 16–17). Central to our discussion about
writing is the importance archetypal psychologists ascribe to
the image. Hillman agrees with Jung that "nothing can be
known unless it first appears as a psychic image." Becoming

conscious means becoming aware of images, becoming aware of their inherent poetic possibilities. Consciousness, Hillman argues, "refers to a process more to do with images than with will, with reflection rather than control, with reflective insight into, rather than manipulation of, 'objective reality' " (*Anima* 93–94). In other words, we perceive the world through images, but we do not create the images; they create us. They have a life of their own. They operate like the "original meaning of idea (from Greek *eidos* and *eidolon*): not only 'that which' one sees but that 'by means of which' one sees" (*Archetypal* 12). As Didion and Eiseley suggest, what we are looking for is in the image, in the picture, already. Our task as writers is to discover it, to let our imaginations work on the image. Images come to us encoded, and we have to get to know them imaginatively. Moving through image to idea, we move beyond the merely personal.

What then happens if we begin a remedial composition course with an excerpt from Virginia Woolf's "A Sketch of the Past" and give these theoretical notions to our students in a more palatable form? What if we simply remind them, using Woolf's words, that although life is made up primarily of routine, uneventful moments called "non-being" (70), there come to us other moments of such intensity that they seem to be accompanied by a "sledge-hammer force"? Those "exceptional moments" embed themselves in memory; they last. For Woolf the shock is always accompanied "by the desire to explain it." She senses behind the blow "a revelation of some order," and she wants to "make it real by putting it into words." She gets a great delight in putting the "severed parts together." "Perhaps," she says, "this is the strongest pleasure known to me. It is the rapture I get when in writing I seem to be discovering what belongs to what; making a scene come right; making a character come together." What Woolf discovers is a pattern behind the appearance of things, a pattern that binds the whole world together: "we are the words; we are the music; we are the thing itself," she says. "And I see this when I have a shock" (72).

Under the influence of Woolf, I asked my new remedial

students, students who had just failed freshman composition, to retrieve two images from their memory bank: the earliest they could recall, and the most profound. They too had read Woolf and had heard me talk about Didion and Eiseley's related ideas. The request did not seem strange to them, and it engendered a wide variety of responses including these from one student:

> Standing in a classroom learning to skip is as far as my memory reaches. The room was oddly shaped not resembling the typical rectangular shape of most classrooms. A large white circle took up a major portion of the room. I stood with my classmates around this circle and learned how to skip. We went around and around this circle many times. I skipped home because I was so proud of myself for learning this new mode of travel.
>
> My sister and I walked to school together very often at my early age of 7. This one day she must have learned the art of getting dizzy and decided to test this newly learned trick on me. She started to twirl me around and around in front of the neighbors house. I began to laugh and told her to stop, but her desire to see what would happen over came her. She laughed then lost control of me, and I had lost control of me long before she did. I fell and hit my head on the curb which didn't take half the damage I did. I didn't get stitches but I did get a headache.

When I heard this student read these short accounts, I wondered how he could have written the final exam that caused him to fail freshman composition the previous term. But as the course director, I had confirmed the failure. When I began to question him about these two memories, I made a significant discovery. He was unwilling to think. He recorded these memories but saw no relationship between them, saw no poetic possibilities. He was comfortable recording but uncomfortable with the formulation of ideas. All ten students in the room had the same initial problem.

Pressed by me and the other students (who were also being pressed), this young man finally wrote an interesting essay, exploring the idea that "practice is the most important

Pat C. Hoy II

part of learning." That essay developed out of the two memories, but he made use of neither as evidence; here is a revealing
paragraph:

> The hardest part of learning is practicing. I am a kayaker, and
> one of the most [pleasant]—and most dangerous—things about
> kayaking is the eskimo roll. The eskimo roll is an exercise where
> you flip upside down under water and then roll back up while
> in your kayak. The first time I did this roll, I saw my life flash
> before my eyes as water filled my nostrils. Even though I was
> scared to do it, I practiced more and more until I mastered the
> eskimo roll. My cousin knew this and took me to a whitewater
> river where we dedicated a whole day to whitewater kayaking.
> I flipped over once and easily flipped back up because I had
> practiced so much.

He framed this essay with a dream that focused on practice,
and he also considered implications of practice for learning
math and typing. His essay was far from perfect, but it showed
me that he could write coherently, that he could focus while
integrating disparate materials, and that he was beginning to
use his imagination to explore and to order experience. He
began to have fun with an idea.

Another student in a subsequent exercise told us what
happened to him while roaming around alone in the Arizona
desert during a family vacation; he had a harrowing experience with a javelina which wanted to protect its babies from
an intruder. After it had chased him up a mesquite tree, he
decided to make a run for the family campground. Here is his
account of what happened:

> I could hear her coming behind me as I grabbed the fence
> post and swung it around, striking her in the front quarters.
> All to my surprise, the mother went down, but jumped back
> up immediately and turned around to face me. I could see in
> her eyes that my original plan would not work. She was not
> going to leave me alone with her babies while she was alive.
> Somehow, I knew it was going to be me or her.
>
> She threw her pig like body at me again, and this time I
> hit her on the top of the head and caught part of her snout
> with the hitch, causing her to bleed profusely. She let out a

squeal of pain, but turned around to charge at me again. I ran again for the mesquite tree, but she was too close. I turned around and tried to hit her in the legs.

Her grey colored body came to a halt. I had missed her legs and had driven the shaft straight into her head for I heard the vertebrae breaking. Blood began to spill out of the mortal wound, and her [gray] body began to tremble and shake.

I stood there not knowing what to do. I had to kill her or she would have killed me. I could have gone for cover. I could have stayed in the tree. I could have [waited her out]. I could have, but I didn't.

The baby javelinas came out of their den and began to lick the blood off the motionless body of their mothers corpse. The runt turned towards me, and tears seemed to be running down its blood-covered face.

I do not need to suggest that this student is engaged. He is interested in his work. The essay from which this narrative account comes is entitled "The Greater Mother." It is a tribute to the javelina, a tribute that develops as he compares the javelina to a mother sea turtle, who having laid her eggs, leaves them and goes back to sea. By the time this student finished the various drafting stages for his essay, he was having minor problems with only a few difficult explanatory passages. But under the influence of White's "Death of a Pig," Orwell's "Shooting an Elephant," Hoagland's "The Courage of Turtles," and Ehrlich's "Friends, Foes, and Working Animals," he had developed his own essay about animals. Informing the entire project was the notion of the image and the embedded idea; he began his image work with his memory of the javelina savagely defending her babies. Searching, imagining, this student worked to discover meaning.

A final example from my remedial class points back to Hillman and suggests other imaginative possibilites for us as teachers. This student begins his essay by telling us about his obsession with the frogs that would emerge in his mind as "imaginary, nocturnal creatures possessing large fangs and sharp blade-like claws . . . . some were enormous and towered over [him] as skyscrappers tower over the skyline in the city." Because these images continue to interest him in his later life, he tries to account for their appearance in his dreams. He begins his exploration by trying to limit the image, by trying to pin it to a fixed idea from the world of "objective reality." First the frog represents the "white 'boogie man,' " the bill collector, but dissatisfied with that explanation, he turns to an image from Wright's *Native Son*, the image of "large, powerful [white] people." Having explored these possibilities, the student rejects them, remembering a conversation he had had years earlier with his father while they were watching tadpoles:

> "One day those suckers are going to be frogs."
> "Full grown ones, Dad?" I questioned.
> "Yep, full grown ones," he replied. "They'll be as big as that one over there."
> He pointed to a bull frog. I scanned the frog over closely. I noted its sharp claws and the balloon-like movements of its chest.
> This frog was my "goolie"! My imagination had made it some bigger-than-life object. It (the imagination) was making its initial entry out of my unconscious and had not yet determined what was real and what was fantasy. It, like the tadpoles, was going through a period of transition. . . .

This conclusion that frogs and his imagination go hand-in-hand keeps the image alive, establishes the basis for further inquiry into the imagination itself. And while this essay is not flawless, the student's exploration is interesting and logical, his inquiry is focused, and his personal development as a writer promising. His own imagination is so active that he cannot rob the image of its power by reducing it to a simplistic, fixed idea. He has begun to think and make connections. Under the influence of professional essayists, he has learned to see more clearly and to write more effectively.

My course eventually moves closer to purely analytical essays, essays that focus not on the student writer's images but on images in the essays of professional writers. I ask students to identify a single image in the work of a professional essayist and to show how that writer uses the image to create meaning. Preparing for this more difficult task, we look together at the way Gretel Ehrlich uses a number of images in "A Storm, The

Cornfield, and Elk" to develop an "exquisite" paradox about the beautiful sadness of autumn. It is an essay that develops almost entirely through images, the most interesting of which is very personal but deeply mythic. Having given us a clear sense of the changes that autumn brings to the Wyoming countryside, to the weather, to the animals, to the valley and mountains where she lives, Ehrlich tells us that when she dresses for the day, her "body, white and suddenly numb, looks like dead coral" (129). She too is full and ripe, acted on by the season; her life "is timbered, an unaccountably libidinous place: damp, overripe, and fading." Like Persephone, whom she does not mention, she is preparing for death, for an erotic closure, as she zizags "through the rows [of corn] as if they were city streets," wanting to "lie down in the muddy furrows, under the frictional sawing of stalks" (130). She becomes the earth—at once full, barren, contradictory, acted upon, changed and charged. She reels, finding beauty and sadness in the changing season. And we discover, through the medium of her own body as image, "that fruition is also death; that ripeness is a form of decay," that idea and image do indeed coalesce in fine essays.

After examining Ehrlich's cluster of autumnal images, we focus on Dillard's "socketing" image in "Living Like Weasels." Students must explain how Dillard uses the two images from her introduction to create meaning throughout the essay. The task is more difficult than the others in the course because it requires students to develop a conscious sense of how another mind makes use of personal images, how that mind puts idea and image together in the form of an exploratory essay. The student essay in this requirement must be tighter, must be a somewhat bounded exploration. But having made their earlier explorations, having discovered the importance of image and the excitement of idea, students are ready for a different kind of writing requirement. Their knowledge of images eases the transition into another form of discourse.

Under the influence of professional writers, students and teachers escape the inhibiting influence of fixed ideas about what can and cannot be done in composition classrooms. They learn especially that images generate ideas and that personal writing done in the context of what Hillman calls "image-work" "restores the original poetic sense to images, freeing them from serving a narrational context, having to tell a story with its linear, sequential, and causal implications that foster first-person reports . . ." (*Archetypal* 15). Discovering ideas in the images of their own experiences, students learn by exploring those ideas to see self in relation to others and to the world. Their essays become records of thought, discovery, and connection. Teachers learn that lively, interesting, outrageously good essays can indeed come out of freshman composition courses.

Works Cited

Arnold, Matthew. *English Literature and Irish Politics*. Vol. 9 of *Complete Prose Works of Matthew Arnold*. Ed. R. H. Super. 11 vols. Ann Arbor: U of Michigan P, 1960–77.

Didion, Joan. "Why I Write." *The New York Times* 5 Dec. 1976, sec. 7: 2, 98–99.

Dillard, Annie. *Teaching a Stone to Talk*. New York: Harper and Row, 1982.

Ehrlich, Gretel. *The Solace of Open Spaces*. New York: Viking Penguin, 1985.

Eiseley, Loren. *All The Strange Hours: The Excavation of a Life*. New York: Scribner's, 1975.

Eliot, T. S. *Selected Prose of T. S. Eliot*. Ed. Frank Kermode. New York: Harcourt Brace Jovanovich, 1975.

Hillman, James. *Anima: An Anatomy of a Personified Notion*. Dallas: Spring Publications, 1985.

———. *Archetypal Psychology: A Brief Account*. Dallas: Spring Publications, 1985.

Morrison, Toni. "The Site of Memory." *Inventing the Truth: The Art and Craft of Memoir*. Ed. William Zinsser. Boston: Houghton Mifflin, 1987. 101–24.

Newman, John Henry. *The Idea of a University*. Ed. I. T. Ker. London: Oxford, 1976.

White, E. B. *Essays of E. B. White*. New York: Harper and Row, 1977.

Woolf, Virginia. *Moments of Being* Ed. Jeanne Schulkind. New York: Harcourt Brace Jovanovich, 1976.

16
HOPING FOR ESSAYS

Jim W. Corder

As it happens, I often think of myself as an essayist. Given
the circumstances of the job I have held for all these years, it
would probably be better if I thought of myself as a rhetorician
or scholar. If I sometimes think of myself as an essayist, it's a
self-conferred title, for I am an unnoticed, though undis-
mayed, essayist. I'll report my credentials. Some years ago,
when I held a somewhat more exalted position than I do now,
the editor of the student newspaper invited me to write a
weekly column. I did so for two years, but no one seemed to
think that I should list those little essays on my vita. At the same
time, I wrote a column for the quarterly student magazine. I
like to think that they invited me for my own sweet self's sake,
but I rather suspect that it was because I was dean at the time.
Along the way I've also written a bunch of elegant trifles on
trivial topics for the alumni magazine. Then, too, I've published some thirty-five pieces here and there, mostly in little
magazines, pieces that one or two other people besides myself
might agree to call "essays." Some would say that the "scholarly" or "critical" papers I have published are essays, too, and
that's agreeable to me. Last year, *College English* published a
little piece, but put the heading "Opinion" above the title to
distinguish it from the real scholarship (see "Learning the
Text").

So. I'm a sometime, self-ordained essayist. Given that self-
induced quirkiness, when I see the new concern about nonfiction, I sometimes wonder what all the fuss is about—it's all just
writing, as novels and poems are just writing. A good piece of
writing of the kind we call *nonfiction* is worth at least as much
time and thought—I supposed everyone knew—as the

Jim W. Corder

speeches of a character in a novel, or a lyric poem, and can be studied in much the same way if one is of a mind to do so. On occasion, then, I haven't fully understood what all the fuss is about.

But then I remember two startling things.

The first is the peculiarity of my own recent talk about nonfiction. Not long ago, I was talking to a colleague about this book on the rhetoric of nonfiction. I do not remember exactly where our conversation had gone when I paused to wonder aloud to her, "I wonder if any of the contributors have ever written and published any nonfiction." When I heard myself say that, it brought me up short: I was obviously presuming some difference existed between scholarly and critical prose nonfiction on the one hand and, on the other, "imaginative" prose nonfiction, but just as obviously I did not know the nature of the difference or whether, in fact, there was a difference. I was talking about writing without knowing about writing.

The second startling thing is my own reaction to some extremes of reader-response and other new forms of criticism. They want, I find myself thinking, to take my own voice away from me and give such meaning as there might be over entirely to whomever might show up as an interpreter. They want me to die into oblivion if I should manage to publish something, never to be reborn in a voice for some reader, but to vanish before that reader's construction of the small thing I leave as a text waiting to become a text.

When I remember such oddities as these, then I think we ought to fuss a little about nonfiction prose and essays, and mostly unanswered questions swirl around me, about literature and nonfiction and essays in general and familiar or personal essays of whatever length. Less than my academic career ago, I might have been content with older sources and conventional accounts of nonfiction and of essays. When I was in graduate school, in the later Middle Ages, I was never, as best I can recall, held to account for any nonfiction except the *Tatler*, the *Spectator*, and the *Rambler*, which were chiefly treated as historical documents, and *Walden*, which was discussed at length by a professor who loved to talk about transcendentalist thought. We did not take any of these as literary works. Later, when I was teaching a course in eighteenth-century literature, I was embarrassed to discover that I was talking about the *Rambler* papers without considering them singly as essays. I stopped what I was doing, arbitrarily picked one of the *Rambler* papers, worked my way through it, and discovered that it had a wonderfully interesting plot (see "Ethical Argument in *Rambler* 154"). By and large, however, I've not been held to account in my professional work for nonfiction prose.

However, I have regularly held freshmen to account for essays in their readers and for their own essays. Ironically, in earlier days when I was not giving thought to nonfiction, I may, by reading freshman essays, thinking about them, and writing my own assignments with my students, have begun to learn a little about nonfiction and about essays. Then, along the way, I think I began to be motivated by discomfiture and embarrassed by the disjunction, holding freshmen to account for essays, but not being held to account myself. At any rate, I began to try to learn.

Among the matters that have plagued me in freshman composition classes, two questions have been especially nettlesome. Neither is new. Each requires to be considered, I think, as both a writer and a teacher of writing would ask and wonder: How does one proceed to write? How does one locate, reach for, and realize the blessed particular that we mostly say we want in writing? We've been looking to answer these questions for a long time, though they're not the only questions to ask or perhaps not the most significant, even if they're crucial enough, and we mostly know they won't be answered, except for now and then. How does one commence to write if advice is always diverse and sometimes contradictory, if one is disinclined or unprepared, if one is inexperienced or experienced but unready, if one has neither a genuine occasion for writing or a genuine belief in the value of or need for writing? How does one name and celebrate the particular if one is not

Jim W. Corder

in the habit of catching memory, if one has no special belief in the uses of memory, if one has not yet been given reason to expect that intimate experience can connect with public experience, if one is not on the way toward believing that the abstract and universally given incarnates itself if at all in the concrete and blessed particular?

The best answer I can give to my own questions is that I don't know. The answer I'll try, however, is that sustained practice in writing personal essays can be useful. That's scarcely a new message, though still, I think, worth attending to for a moment.

What I have called the *blessed particular* always belongs to someone. We believe that it can be given to someone else, shared in writing—given, offered, but not demanded, for no one of us is a measure for mankind. The observation and rendition of particulars, we know, will not necessarily yield certain universal truth. One moment isn't all of time, or one look a whole view, or one sense of things a revelation about all things. As I said a moment ago, advice about writing is always mixed. To demand our particular experience of another is arrogance and dogma, but to offer our particular experience to another is the only plenitude we have, and may be quite enough. The personal essayist and the biographer share more than a little. Each can take us to the lives of particular persons "not distinguished," Dr. Johnson remarked in Rambler 60, "by any striking or wonderful vicissitudes." Each can "lead the thoughts into domestic privacies, and display the minute details of daily life," reminding thus that "There are many invisible circumstances which . . . are more important than public occurrences" (111, 273).

Some years ago I tried to explain to anyone who would listen some of what I had learned the first time I wrote my own essay assignments for a semester along with my freshman composition students. Explanation quickly became confession, for much that I learned that semester was testimony to my own failures. I discovered, for example, that my wise classroom instruction and advice about writing was often not germane or useful while I was actually writing, and so was forced to

304

ignore myself. I found, too, that I often did precisely what I urged my students not to do when they were writing. I recognized that there often was no occasion or need for the writing at hand, and I had, besides, to acknowledge that I sometimes turned in rough drafts as if they were finished essays. But that was in 1975, and I don't want to linger there (See "What I Learned at School"). Since then, I have continued to write assignments—in the fall term each year, mostly personal essays—and I want to tell about some of what has happened. Some of the evidence that has accumulated is not pretty, but I continue in the fond hope that examining what has happened will tell a little about writing and the teaching of writing, about the two problems I commenced with, and about the relationship of personal essays to other kinds of writing. High hopes sometimes come with hard lessons.

Some hard lessons first.

I learned again that the received form, the "freshman essay," has few uses outside the freshman composition course, and none for most. The form works best, I expect, if one writes a lot and is already a weekly columnist for a newspaper or magazine. Otherwise, there is no waiting market for the prose we exact of freshmen. Consider, every once in a while, the annual *Writer's Market*: Some of the entries for general interest magazines attest that the editors of those magazines will not consider any essays except those submitted by agents, but some of the entries for literary agents attest that they will not consider essays for magazines. It's an interesting predicament, and not much interesting to freshmen, anyway.

I have become moderately adept at lying, cheating, showing off, and other classroom practices. In the earlier paper I have mentioned, I told about an advantage I had over my freshmen when we wrote. Since I am more or less accustomed to writing and expect to write hereafter, I keep a little notebook where I jot down words, phrases, paragraphs that I hope to make something of later. In addition, I frequently carry around folded napkins and wadded scraps with other scribblings. When it came time to write, then, I could often cash in something I had already scribbled about. That practice has continued in the years since the first paper—but it hasn't always been enough. Sometimes I have come up short of both ideas and time for writing. When that has happened, I have, of course, lied and cheated. I have recycled earlier papers and turned them in as new. I have taken parts of earlier papers, made more of them, and turned them in as new. I have rewritten rough drafts that I had submitted as finished essays in former semesters. Sometimes I like to imagine that in doing these things I was conducting my own private little writing workshop—trying things out, revising, working through writing projects. Mostly I was just deceiving. Sometimes I had the grace to tell my students what I had done. Sometimes I didn't. Despite everything, though, once in a while an essay worked out pretty well, and I knew when I turned such an essay in for my students to read that I was showing off. I have told myself that it's all right—early rhetors were expected periodically to make public speeches, testifying that they knew how to do what they taught, and we can reasonably expect that violin teachers will know how to fiddle. Still.

As I have written essays through these years, spent time talking to students about theirs, revised and worked through my own essays, I have come to be less and less sure of what composition textbooks are for. When you're caught up in a semester's work, living a life, maybe doing a little research, trying to read—and I'm talking about freshmen as much as about myself—and you're also trying to write eight or ten essays, then it's the *writing* that preoccupies and instructs, not the textbook, as, for example, when you write yourself into a muddle and then have to work your way out of it. In my own mind, textbooks have receded farther into the background until they are only reference works that we have in common to which we can point once in a while for help on particular questions. Perhaps everyone else already knew that.

See "showing off" above. Sometimes, when a piece of writing seemed to be going well, I found that the attention it required would distance me from the students. Wayne Booth described the behavior some years ago when he told what seems to happen when speakers (teachers) get too close to their subject or too close to their audience (See "The Rhetorical Stance"). Quite simply, I sometimes got to paying more attention to my own writing than to theirs. I got interested in my own performance. That's probably wrong for a teacher to do, but it's not all bad: I'd like my students to be intensely preoccupied with their own performance as writers. Wouldn't that be something—if they cared intensely about their essays? At any rate, if I had to choose between being preoccupied with my own writing and being preoccupied with the students, I'd choose the former. The latter, it seems to me, chiefly generates earnestness in the classroom, which is nice but not necessarily productive.

For two reasons I came gradually over the years to give more and more nonspecific assignments. One is decent. The other is selfish. The more I came to understand what I took *invention* to mean, the less likely I was to give specific assignments, reasoning that students needed room to invent and had responsibility, as writers, to invent. I think a reasonable case can be made for thinking and acting so. If so, my other reason for turning more to nonspecific assignments is considerably less noble: I sometimes didn't want to be boxed in by my own assignments, prevented from using notes, scribbles, ideas that were already lying around.

I became a poorer, or certainly more doubtful, grader. Looking at my own essays a last time before copying them for my students, I would sometimes mutter to myself, "I hope they see what I'm getting at" or "Surely they can understand why I put it together this way" or "God, I hope they realize how clever I've been" or "Well, it's the best I can do in the time I have." I came to imagine that these or similar questions were probably in the students' minds as they let go of their essays, and, reading them, found myself saying, "Well, given what it is, it's all right, I guess" or "I see what he/she is getting at— maybe we can work it out if we talk about what to do next." With my own doubts in my mind, I became more and more reluctant to give lower grades, however just they might have been. I didn't want to be graded; I wanted to be understood, appreciated, answered.

Jim W. Corder

I wanted to know how one proceeds to write and how one finds and renders the particular. I have believed and still do that a place to begin is with and in oneself, that the particulars of one's own life, if recalled, and cherished, are at least among the best, most vividly known particulars we're likely to encounter and perhaps own. But advice about writing is diverse, and I sometimes lost my belief, pulled away, for example, by that other advice telling us that what keeps a writer on target is the rigorous search for objectivity about the world "out there." And I often lost my place as student essays or my own sidetracked me. As a consequence, I don't much think that I match or in any way realize in my practice any of the current models for composition teachers or research in rhetoric. (A recent letter announcing a position said that "Familiarity and expertise in one or more of the current research paradigms would be a prime qualification for the position. . .") I don't much think I want to.

But while much that I have learned while writing essays over the years made me cringe, every once in a while I thought I learned something useful.

I learned, for example, that my essays as well as those of the students could sometimes be useful as occasions for teaching, as in the instance of this specimen:

CHEERIO

For a long time, until she came to suspect that my character was not susceptible of correction, my mother tried to get me to eat Raisin Bran for breakfast. I was young then, and she thought they were healthy, as such things go. But I couldn't face the dead bugs floating among the bran flakes in the milk—earlier my big brother had told me that the dark things in the raisin bread were dead bugs, too. I chose Post Toasties instead, imitating my brother, but after a while I realized that they were given to instant sogginess. Then for a long time I ate Wheaties, the Breakfast of Champions. I cannot recall whether or not I actually liked Wheaties, but the box had nifty baseball stories and pictures. But by and by, in the fullness of time, I lost all those pictures and discovered Cheerios.

But that was not until later, when I discovered that I had

children of my own. In the meantime, I had given up cereal for coffee and toast, usually cinnamon toast. But then, with my children, I found Cheerios. It wasn't easy: we spent a lot of time in the cereal aisle of the grocery store, looking at all the boxes, and we tried first one and then another. But we stayed with Cheerios a long time, though there was brief flirtation with Captain Crunch. I can't remember whether or not there was anything on the Cheerios' box that they saved, and I can't remember what the box itself looked like when they were young. I wish I could. I do remember that one of my daughters made a necklace of Cheerios, and my son played checkers with them, though it was a little hard to distinguish one side from the other. As they grew older, they mostly gave up cereal, and I went back to having coffee and toast, or coffee and a bagel, or coffee and a granola bar, or coffee and coffee.

The current Cheerios box is mostly yellow. The one on my desk is ten and three-quarters inches high, seven and a half inches across, and two and three-eighths inches deep. On what I think of as the front, there is a General Mills logo, and a big, black-print Cheerios, the i dotted with a Cheerio. Below that, this: Toasted Oat Cereal Made from the Grain Highest in Protein. Below that is a picture of a bowl of Cheerios and strawberries, and a sign that says Free Inside Two Hugga Bunch Easy-Paint Postcards (seems a long way from pictures of Joe DiMaggio and Dizzy Dean and Charley Gehringer), with pictures of Hugsy and Impkins (Oh, how far we've fallen). Two other signs betoken the dietary interests of the day. One says Only 1 Gram of Sugar Per Serving; the other says No Artificial Colors or Flavors Whole Grain—Good Source of Fiber. In the bottom left corner, I read Net Wt Oz (283 grams). On what I think of as the back of the box, there is a big display about the Hugga Bunch postcards, with notice that it is possible to collect twelve of them, if you eat fast and choose boxes cagily. One side of the box has testimony about why pediatricians recommend Cheerios for your toddler. The other side has a word about fiber nutrition information per serving, percentage of U.S. recommended daily allowances, and a list of ingredients: Whole oat flour, wheat starch, salt, sugar, calcium carbonate, trisodium phosphate, vitamin C (sodium ascorbate), niacin (a B vitamin), iron (a mineral), vitamin B2 (riboflavin), vitamin B1 (thiamin mononitrate), vitamin B12, and vitamin D. The bottom of the

Jim W. Corder

box has on it a logo again, another Cheerios, another notice of free Hugga Bunch postcards, and the mystical bar sign for the magic machine to read at the check-out stand. The top of the box has a Betty Crocker coupon, another Cheerios, and two last signs. The first says To Open Lift This Tab. The second says to Keep Your Cheerios Fresh, Refold Inner Bag on the top. Inside the box, there is a sealed white waxed paper bag. Inside the sealed paper bag there are approximately 2600 Cheerios. Inside there is also a lie: it is not Hugsy and Impkins that wait, but Bubbles and Chumley and Huggins with Hug-a-bye.

If there are indeed about 2600 Cheerios in the bag, then each single one must weigh something like 0.0038461 ounces or 0.1088461 grams. Each single Cheerio is an O in about the same way that each doughnut is O—that is to say, the individual Cheerios are O-like, but irregular. Diameters appear to range from about three-eighths of an inch to about one-half an inch; thickness seems to average at about three-sixteenths of an inch.

Any single Cheerio, then, seems to weigh in at about 0.0038+ ounces, to measure ⅜+ inches in diameter, about ³/₁₆ inches in thickness. Since I do not have a keen or an accurate sense of smell, I cannot report on the smell of Cheerios. The taste of a Cheerio, unadorned with either milk or strawberries, gives me a faint sense of walnuts mixed with a faint recollection from old days when I was a little boy. Sometimes, when my mother wasn't looking, I took a mouthful of uncooked oats (meant to be cooked and hot for morning cereal) and pretended it was chewing tobacco. The color is a sort of dun, verging on muckledy dun, verging on sand, verging on the color of soft buckskin, verging on the color of my hushpuppies, verging on the color of the horse Marshal Dillon rode on "Gunsmoke."

I doubt that I would ever have come to write about Cheerios were it not for a sorry episode in my freshman class, where we set each other dull subjects to write about. Now that it's happened, I find I don't mind. There's a little something to learn if you look closely at just about anything, and an archeologist friend once told me that he thought he could learn more about a culture by digging in a kitchen midden than by exploring a cathedral.

Hoping for Essays

Did I learn anything? Not much. I was reaffirmed in my present conviction that, after all, coffee and pipe tobacco make a better breakfast. I learned that in 1986 people pay more attention—or want to think they pay more attention—to diet and nutrition than they did in 1943 or in 1958. I learned that cereal makers, or at least the makers of Cheerios, aim their product at a much younger audience now than they did in 1938 or 1941, judging from the replacement of Charley Gehringer by the Hugga Bunch kids. I learned that almost anything, including Cheerios, can become a token setting off reverberations of other times, other places, and so I remembered the necklace my daughter made. I'm glad of that. But that's all for now. So long and cheerio.

I think that I was able to do a moderately good job with three points made through this essay: that an unpromising subject can become, not a silk purse, but at least a serviceable cotton pouch; that the personal can provide an occasion and context, a reason for writing about the nonpersonal when no other reason presents itself; and that the personal will sometimes open up possibilities and need for the impersonal and for research, raised in this case, for example, by the implicit question about whether or not advertising and target audiences have really changed or only seem to the speaker to have changed.

I learned that personal essays (and other kinds, if there are other kinds) may more commonly be exploratory than William Zeiger suggested (See "The Exploratory Essay: Enfranchising the Spirit of Inquiry in College Composition"), that the personal may entail exploration in one way or another, and that exploration will to some extent become self-revelatory. A personal essay doesn't require (though it may allow) any writer to reveal the hideous that may lurk inside, but it does require the sometimes chancy personal.

Trying to write personal essays provided over the years some need and occasion to try formulating suggestions about writing in language somewhat homelier than that of some textbooks and, homelier, more descriptive of what I thought I saw happening as I tried to write. The mostly personal nature

311

of the essays we were writing wanted, I think, to evoke a mostly personal mode, as in these "propositions for writers," none new or striking to teachers of composition:

a. Try to get good evidence, which is mostly in your own mind.
b. Try to look in the right direction and at the right distance.
c. Let readers know where you're going as soon as you know.
d. But you may need to ooch along for a while until you know.
e. Since you are a person, you might as well show what you're like and how you think.
f. We're apart (apologies to Burke), but we can be together for moments.
g. Nevertheless, you may have to go alone.
h. Tell some things, but show most.
i. Some subjects are just right, but others have to be made right.
j. Don't hide your motives or yourself.
k. You're always standing somewhere when you speak—try to know where it is.
l. You can't start from scratch.

These, I think, are at least not embarrassing versions of problems and practices in invention and sometimes have seemed to help with the first question I begin with. Once ooch is defined, item d, for example, offers a way into talking about essays that proceed not from a previously established thesis, but toward some discovery, however small, as in the "Cheerio" essay. Item g, for another example, can be a sometime corrective to our otherwise intelligent attention to audience. The list of proportions is small, but it grows—one might say that it ooches along.

I came to believe that the personal essay offers a way out of a nearly perpetual sorrow in human discourse. We often only announce ourselves to each other, declare our definitions to each other, write as authorities before or at each other, but don't give each other much time (see my little proposition). We can do otherwise. I think of Johnson in *Rambler* 154, seeming the very voice of authority, but in fact learning as he writes, in the second half of the essay tempering what he had said in the first, coming in the final paragraph to a wiser position than the attacking propositions of the opening could afford. The personal essay is not the exclusive place, but it is a place for us to begin to know ourselves and show ourselves to each other rather than confronting each other with definitions and theses, wanting (as some textbooks openly, others quietly, recommend) to be authoritative before or at each other. We seldom get it all to work out, but keep trying.

I wanted the students to value themselves, the world, and others enough to look closely, to pay attention, to see particularities, to know them, to know they mattered, and to show them to others, sharing them. I didn't want them to be imprisoned by their own particularities, as Richard Ohmann put it (See "Use Definite, Specific, Concrete Language"), and I don't think I believed that paying attention to particulars would inevitably yield clear and certain universal truths. We can't, as I've said, seize on one moment as all time, one feature of existence as if it were of all existence, a moment's perception as if it were a revelation. But paying attention to particulars will let us sometimes see and know the things, the places, the people among which we frail humans reside and have our woes and hopes, will let us know what Johnson called the incidents "of a volatile and evanescent kind, such as soon escape the memory, and are rarely transmitted by tradition."

I often couldn't get them to look, neither by saying nor by writing. They have to look and to pay attention, and a semester is never enough for that. As this fall term came to an end and I had once again failed, I could only tell them about miracles. They happen all the time. The trick is to notice.

I have learned that I don't know what a personal essay is or how it differs from other forms of writing, though some seem to know. We're never just writing about what we already know and are, but also about what we might unpredictably see and become. Every piece of writing is a personal essay.

Earlier, I said that the received form we know as the freshman essay had few uses. That's not true. The freshman essay is an exploratory and meditative form that gives us time to know, to accept, to understand selves, worlds, others, letting us rescue time. The world, of course, doesn't always want time in its discourses. It wants the quick memo, the rapid-fire

313

Jim W. Corder

electronic mail service, wants speed, efficiency, and economy
of motion, all goals that, when reached, have given the world
less than it wanted or needed. We can ask the world to want
otherwise, to want time for care, time to pay attention. There's
never enough.

Works Cited

Booth, Wayne C. "Rhetorical Stance." *College Composition and Communication* 14 (1963): 139–145. Rpt. in *Contemporary Rhetoric: A Conceptual Background with Readings.* Ed. Ross Winterowd. New York: Harcourt, 1975. 70–79.

Corder, Jim. W. "Ethical Argument in *Rambler* 154." *Quarterly Journal of Speech* 90 (1969): 352–56.

———. "Learning the Text: Little Notes About Interpretation, Harold Bloom, the *Topoi* and *Oratorio*." *College English* 48 (1986): 243–49.

———. "Rhetorical Analysis of Writing." *Teaching Composition: Ten Bibliographical Essays.* Ed. Gary Tate. Fort Worth: Texas Christian, 1975. 223–40.

———. "What I Learned at School." *College Composition and Communication* 26 (1975): 330–34.

Johnson, Samuel. *The Yale Edition of the Works of Samuel Johnson.* Ed. W. J. Bate and Albrecht B. Strauss. New Haven: Yale UP, 1969.

Ohmann, Richard. "Use Definite, Specific Concrete Language." *College English* 41 (1979): 390–97.

Zeiger, William. "The Exploratory Essay: Enfranchising the Spirit of Inquiry in College Composition." *College English* 37 (1985): 454–66.

17
ERROR, AMBIGUITY, AND THE PERIPHERAL

Teaching Lewis Thomas

Chris Anderson

Several quarters ago I used the writing of Lewis Thomas as an organizing theme and focus for Writing 222, a sophomore term paper writing course. In the first few weeks of the quarter I did a miniseminar in Thomas's writing to give my students practice in paraphrasing and summarizing texts and to generate material for the two research papers the course required, then drew on Thomas's essays for models of style the remainder of the term.

I also used a term paper textbook, of course—Jean Johnson's *The Bedford Guide to the Research Process*—complete with models of what the term paper should be. Taken in themselves Thomas's essays are too essayistic, I realized, too personal and exploratory, to be entirely useful as models in a class designed to teach students how to research and write papers for their other classes. I will admit that in some vague way I hoped these differences between the "essay" and the "article" might become a side issue as the quarter wore on, since I've never liked reading term papers and hoped I might be able to suggest more interesting approaches to writing about reading. But I didn't intend anything dramatic. I felt responsible for teaching the term paper as it is conventionally defined. I had chosen Thomas's essays as a focus mainly in the hope that some of his clarity and conciseness as a writer of sentences might rub off on my students as they wrote their term papers. And then there was the richness of Thomas's writing as a source of ideas for students to pursue in their research.

Chris Anderson

But as the course developed the tension between the essay and the article intensified, becoming more than a side issue, largely because Thomas himself kept emphasizing that conflict, pushing it into the foreground, in ways I hadn't anticipated when I was reading his essays for myself. In the classroom, under the pressures of a classroom, I began to see that the themes and structures of Thomas's essays ultimately force us to question the value of writing term papers at all.

For the first few weeks of the quarter I asked my students to freewrite daily about the reading in Thomas's *Medusa and the Snail* and *Late Night Thoughts on Listening to Mahler's Ninth Symphony*, recording impressions, asking questions, making connections, loosely summarizing and paraphrasing. I collected bits and pieces, gave quick feedback, used other pieces of freewriting as prompts for class discussion, and generally encouraged students to mine their journals for ideas and language leading to the first paper.

But almost immediately the ideas developing in our discussions of Thomas began to justify and empower freewriting as more than a reading tool. In his arguments for the limits of the scientific method and the validity of feeling and intuition, Thomas seemed to be making a claim for the value of freewriting, or something like it, over and against strictly rational forms of inquiry and presentation. Research, Thomas says in *The Youngest Science*—developing an idea that occurs repeatedly in all his essays—"is dependent on the human capacity for making predictions that are wrong, and on the even more human gift for bouncing back to try again." Far from proceeding unerringly from hypothesis to result, true research advances by means of "pure guesses." This is precisely what the public fails to understand about the functioning of science. In Thomas's view we need to make mistakes to learn about anything: "In order to get anything right, we are first obliged to get a great many things wrong." Science is no different. "Error is the mode" (YS 82).

Thomas devotes a long, technical essay, for example, to explaining how his unsuccessful research into the "Shwartz-

316

man reaction" to injected endoxtins led, "in the process of trying," to a better understanding of a number of unrelated phenomena "interesting enough in themselves, worth, as the Michelin travel guides say, a detour," including the action of enzymes released by damaged tissue cells (YS 154–56). Similarly, Thomas's digression as a researcher into the mechanisms of smell, an apparently trivial subject, becomes a way of better understanding how humans, like animals, may be biologically coded for relationship: we are attracted to our lovers because of their odor (LN 40–44). Nature itself is governed by error. "The capacity to blunder slightly is the real marvel of DNA," Thomas points out, since without mutations in genetic structure organisms cannot evolve in response to environment. Without this "wonderful mistake," "we would still be anaerobic bacteria and there would be no music" (MS 23).

In "On Thinking About Thinking" Thomas uses biochemical metaphors to describe the organic nature of thought processes. Our head is filled with molecules "leaving random, two-step tracks like paths of Brownian motion," "docking and locking," "the pairs coupling to pairs, aggregates forming" (MS 125). In a sense, thought functions like DNA, progressing through mutations, some abandoned, some useful. In "On Autonomy," taking a psychological tack, Thomas argues that we should let go, let our unconscious take over, rather than learning to gain more control over our bodily functions. "Couldn't we learn to disconnect altogether," he asks, "uncouple, detach, float free?" then concludes with a reference to Zen archery: "You learn, after long months of study under a master, to release the arrow without releasing it yourself. Your fingers must do the releasing on their own, remotely, like the opening of a flower" (LC 68).

For Thomas the world is full of mysteries which resist mechanical formulation, which always remain "unflattened by science" (LN 68). "Things that used to seem clear and rational, matters of absolute certainty," he says, "have slipped through our fingers, and we are left with a new set of gigantic puzzles, cosmic uncertainties, ambiguities." In biology in particular, "it

317

is one stupefaction after another" (LN 19). These mysteries delight Thomas. His stance is always one of wonder and amazement, of pleased astonishment. "The mind of a cat is an inscrutable mystery, beyond reach"; "Bees are filled with astonishments, confounding anyone who studies them" (LN 36, 38). The mitochondria inhabiting his own body are for him a breathtaking "mystery," unfathomable (LC 73). According to Thomas there's almost nothing we understand fully in our own experience, from DNA, to language, to music, to our own behavior, to the ecological symmetry of the whole earth, functioning somehow as giant cell, a "marvel" (LC 145). In the face of these wonders Thomas's stance can only be "erroneous" in his sense. "Illumination is the product sought," in science and in life, "but it comes in small bits, only from time to time, not ever in broad, bright flashes of public comprehension, and there can be no promise that we will ever emerge from the great depths of the mystery of being" (LN 27).

As I explained freewriting in class, I began to draw on these arguments for the limits of rational inquiry and the validity of intuition. It was not hard to show that in writing, too, "error is the mode." Thomas himself makes the connection, praising Montaigne for his capacity to "simply turn his mind loose and write whatever he feels like writing," celebrating the inherent ambiguity of all language, which inevitably "prevents us from sticking to the matter at hand" (MS 121, LC 95). Often Thomas sounds like Peter Elbow arguing for the importance of getting lost in order to discover material, of writing without first knowing where the essay is heading, of separating the critic and the creator. Indeed, in an essay on how he writes Thomas confesses that when he tried outlining in advance his essays were "dreadful." Instead he changed the method to "no method at all, picked out some suitable times late at night," and "wrote without outline or planning in advance, as fast as I could. This worked better, or at least was more fun" (YS 243).

What makes this notion of the scientific method and the writing process problematic in a term paper writing course is that its values seem to carry over into the written product.

Teaching Lewis Thomas

Thomas's writing everywhere bears the marks of apparent spontaneity. Whether in fact or for effect, the result is the same: he digresses, juxtaposes, revises as he goes, exclaims, changes his mind. The virtual simultaneity of the thinking and the writing seems very much at odds with the linear structure and subordination of the conventional term paper. "I will confess," Thomas says at the end of "Computers," that "I have no more sense of what goes on in the mind of mankind than I have for the mind of an ant. Come to think of it, this might be a good place to start" (LC 114). Or, in "Late Night Thoughts," he writes, "Now, with a pamphlet in front of me on a corner of my desk . . . an analysis of all the alternative strategies for the placement and protection of hundreds of these missiles . . . I cannot hear the same Mahler" (166). Our sense throughout the essay is that Thomas has put Mahler's Ninth on the stereo and is writing as he listens, letting the rises and falls of the music, the tonal changes, influence the rises and falls of his own moods and ideas. After recreating his experience watching beavers and otters at play at the Tucson Zoo, Thomas tells the story of his thinking as he reacted to their presence in front of him: "What was released? Behavior. And what behavior? Standing, swiveling flabbergasted, feeling exultation and a rush of friendship" (MS 7). Like freewriting, Thomas's essays capture the rush of his exultations, the flow of his questions, and perhaps even more to the point, they center on the kind of personal involvement with experience that freewriting sometimes makes possible.

Or to put this another way, Thomas writes in the tradition of the reflective/exploratory essay—the "essay" as opposed to the "article." His purpose is not primarily to convey information or argue a position but to recreate and then reflect on his own experience and ideas. Like Montaigne, Hazlitt, and E. B. White, he writes to tell the story of his thinking. "A personal essay," Edward Hoagland says, "is like the human voice talking, its order the mind's natural flow, instead of a systematic outline of ideas." The essay is thus fundamentally autobiographical—thus, by definition, more "wayward" and "informal," in Hoagland's terms, than an "article" or "treatise" (223).

319

Chris Anderson

"I have been trying to think of the earth as a kind of organism,"
Thomas says, "but it is no go. I cannot think of it this way. It
is too big, too complex, with too many working parts lacking
visible connections. The other night, driving through a hilly,
wooded part of southern New England, I wondered about
this. If not like an organism, what is it like, what is it *most* like?
Then satisfactorily for that moment, it came to me: it is *most*
like a single cell" (LC 5). Thomas is a located speaker, located
not only in a place and a time but in the now of the essay.
His writing issues from a self. It is a thinking through of an
important problem, much like freewriting, or like a journal
entry, or like a conversation. As Thomas says of reading Montaigne, "it is like the easiest of conversations with a very old
friend" (MS 122). Thomas doesn't have the answers. He is
searching as he writes, letting us into the drama of his thinking,
sharing with us its origins and uncertainty, engaging, in short,
in all the classic conventions of the genre of the essay. Ironically, the convention of the essay is apparent naturalness, a
lack of premeditation.

One day in class I went through "Out of the Corner of
the Eye" paragraph by paragraph to illustrate how Thomas
develops and organizes ideas (LN 12–17). As I pointed out to
my students, the essay is more tightly structured than much
of Thomas's writing, falling into three identifiable paragraph
blocs: two initial examples of peripheral vision, looking at stars
and listening to music; then a discussion of how computers
cannot account for language; then a long investigation of the
etymology of the word "earth"; then a concluding section
reflecting on the wonder of the universe and, finally, of our
own planet seen from space. The essay as a whole is easily
subordinate to the claim of the opening sentence that "there
are some things that human beings can only see out of the
corner of the eye."

But as we started going over the piece in class, I had to
admit that here, too, Thomas breaks too many rules—is too
essayistic—to be entirely useful as a model for what a term
paper is supposed to do. To begin with, Thomas is frankly
personal as he writes, recording his own reactions and the

progress of his reactions rather than remaining detached and "objective." He finds the limitations of computers a "relaxing thought" and the order of the universe a "miracle and a marvel," something "immensely pleasing." He feels "overwhelming astonishment" at the thought of the earth. His specific examples are imagistic and local rather than statistical or empirical. Rather than backing up a claim or proving a point, he evokes the image of children looking at stars, reminds us of listening to the music of Bach. Far from being neutral or generic, the language he uses to recreate these experiences is either down-to-earth and homey—"The niftiest example," "I used to worry," "mistakes can be fixed," "there is a deep hunch"—or textured, rich in detail, transluscent rather than transparent, as in his final description of the earth seen from space:

> We are only now beginning to appreciate how strange and splendid it is, how it catches the breath, the loveliest object afloat around the sun, enclosed in its own blue bubble of atmosphere, manufacturing and breathing its own oxygen, fixing its own nitrogen from the air into its own soil, generating its own weather at the surface of its rain forests, constructing its own carapace from living parts: chalk cliffs, coral reefs, old fossils from earlier forms of life now covered by layers of new life meshed together around the globe, Troy upon Troy. (LN 17)

The cumulative structure of this sentence suggests the spontaneous modification of the mind in the act of thinking, first fixing an image, then progressively refining and elaborating that image, unpacking it, in the ongoing addition of free modifiers.

Although more condensed and controlled than Thomas's obviously conversational essays, the whole structure of "Out of the Corner of the Eye" suggests the movement of the mind in the act of thinking. Thomas ends his reference to the inexplicability of music and then, without transition, moves to "I used to worry that computers would become so powerful," introducing a large bloc whose relevance to the initial thesis is not clear until several paragraphs later when he returns to the notion of ambiguity in language. Within that bloc he first records his initial worries about computers, then how his thinking changed. The movement is, in Burke's terms, qualitative rather than syllogistic, a set of free associations. The notion of the "peripheral" seems to suggest the notion of the "ambiguous" which then leads to the notion of the "surprising" and "astonishing" and finally the "inexplicable," but the words are not synonymous but overlapping, and they are enclosed within each paragraph bloc rather than featured in topic sentences.

A student shot up his hand: "Isn't the structure of this essay peripheral itself? I mean, doesn't Thomas in a sense do what he's talking about?" Yes. Form is the shape of a content here. The peripheral, ambiguous, inexplicable nature of the kind of experience Thomas is describing requires a peripheral, ambiguous structure. Ambiguity, Thomas says elsewhere, "seems to be an essential, indispensable element for the transfer of information from one place to another by words, where matters of real importance are concerned. It is often necessary, for meaning to come through, that there be an almost vague sense of strangeness and askewness" (LC 94). Thomas cannot describe straight on something in the corner of the eye. He must evoke that notion imagistically, concretely.

Or to put this still another way, implicit in the structure of Thomas's prose is a powerful model for reading. Thomas begins most of his essays by summarizing what he knows about an idea or phenomenon—say warts in "On Warts" or viruses in "On Disease" (MS 61–65, 75–82)—almost as if he is a student in a term paper course reporting what he's discovered in his research for the paper. But then always he goes on to connect that piece of information or that observation to the ideas and notions he really cares about. He sees the small in terms of the large, the factual in terms of the human. That is, he "reads" these things or events by applying them to who he is; he first learns, but then he asks, so what, who cares, why does this matter, how does this connect?

In this way warts, the biology of which he describes in some detail, eventually, as the essay "On Warts" proceeds, become another example of how the body regulates itself and functions as a self-sufficient, cooperating organism. "It is one of the great mystifications of science: warts can be ordered off the skin by hypnotic suggestions" (MS 62). Warts are not just warts but a way of gaining access to Thomas's persistent theme that we are too busy trying to control our lives when there are in fact all these wonders taking place around us. Or, in "On Disease," after several pages of term-paper-like information on the characteristics of the meningococcus, Thomas turns to reading the meningoccous as a metaphor for the symbiotic relationships always present in nature: "It is probably true that symbiotic relationships between bacteria and their metazoan hosts are much more common in nature than infectious disease" (MS 80). "Every creature," Thomas says in *The Lives of a Cell*, "is, in some sense, connected to and dependent on the rest." Microbes "live together in dense, interdependent communities"; bacteria "live by collaboration, accommodation, exchange, and barter"—are "social animals" (7). And human beings are part of this ecology, equally dependent upon other things, existing in various symbiotic relationships with microrganisms, animals, each other, the earth itself. Thomas's habit as an essayist is to read the behavior of all organisms—mitochondria, sea slugs and jelly fish, ants, bees, beavers and otters—as metaphors of relationship and cooperation.

This process of reading and interpretation can also move in the other direction. Having seen the individual in terms of the abstract, Thomas can also read past the abstraction to the concrete reality underneath it. At the end of "Late Night Thoughts" he describes a government official mouthing obscene generalizations about nuclear war. "If I were sixteen or seventeen years old," Thomas says, "and I had to listen to that, or read things like that, I would want to give up listening and speaking"—"I would be twisting and turning to rid myself of human language" (LN 168). This is the issue: the kinds of bureaucratic, resolutely impersonal phrases that often cover up the real experiences, the irreducible experiences, of people in the world. In effect Thomas takes the Orwellian demand for concreteness to its extreme. He is always making something like the "earnest proposal" of *The Lives of a Cell*, urging us to abandon political rhetoric about nuclear weapons until we first learn all we can about one small organism, say, the protozoan myxotricha paradoxa which inhabits the digestive tract of Australian termites (26–30). From this perspective, too, Thomas gives us a way of reading him and of reading anything else. He demands that we connect, that we ask why, that we do more than parrot information, that we resist the easy abstraction.

I don't mean to suggest that in Writing 222 I could not have used freewriting in the service of the term paper. Though freewriting tends toward the essayistic and autobiographical, as a heuristic it is applicable to all kinds of writing situations. Freewriting would not have been a problem in the class had Thomas' essays not at the same time been offering a compelling alternative to the stale, formulaic, disengaged, mechanical writing that in my experience term papers usually elicit. I don't mean to suggest that there is anything inherently subversive or unconventional in the structure of the essay. Thomas observes the conventions of reflective/exploratory writing as they have been practiced for several hundred years. The problem is simply that Writing 222 is designed to help students learn to write "articles" so that they can do well in their other courses on campus. It's a straightforward, practical demand, and not easy to shrug off, especially at a land grant institution where my colleagues in business and engineering and pharmacy are—rightly—complaining about the inability of their students to do the research and engage in the kind of formal academic inquiry, the kind of article writing, they must do to enter into those professional communities. No matter how much I liked getting carried away now and then by Thomas's essays, I couldn't escape the worry that I was perhaps indulging in a kind of "literariness" that was failing to teach my students what they needed to know.

There are various ways of healing the division I'm suggesting. It can be argued that we should teach the whole universe of discourse (Moffett), the expressive in addition to the transactional or referential (Britton and Kinneavy), or the reflective, informative, *and* deliberative (Beale). This is true, of course, and in my design for the class I tried to include a variety of assignments. The first, for example, was a hybrid of the reflective and the informative, asking students first to explain a theme in Thomas and then reflect on its significance. The second, larger paper I defined as more strictly a *term paper*, something purely deliberative or informative. In the same way I tried to distinguish between the kinds of personal engagement that go into freewriting and the more detached and analytical writing required in a finished product. On the second paper, furthermore, I gave students an option between what Winston Weathers calls the "A" style and the "B" style. Students had the choice of imitating the sample term papers in the textbook, or of experimenting with the more open-ended kind of writing modeled in Thomas's "On Warts" or "On Disease."

I was also careful to distinguish in class between Thomas's own more term-paper-like pieces, say, "Medical Lessons from History" (MS 132–46), and the clearly personal and reflective. Even in his more reflective pieces, there was much about paragraphing and development that Thomas could illustrate. It was not an either/or proposition. Because literary nonfiction is a hybrid form, it can be used to illustrate more than one kind of formal strategy or device. I was able to use a paragraph from Thomas's "On Medicine and the Bomb" (LN 114–19), for example, to illustrate Francis Christensen's notion of hierarchy and subordination in paragraphing. We simply diagrammed the paragraph rhetorically, representing its ebb and flow spatially on the page. In the same way I had the class reassemble a scrambled version of the paragraphs of Thomas's essay, "The Artificial Heart" (LN 64–67), as an exercise in understanding, from the inside out, his effective use of transitions and patterns of development.

In fact, it occurred to me in class one day that the paragraph and the organization of an entire theme are perfect examples of the kind of ecosystem Thomas celebrates in his essays. The sentences in a paragraph, and the paragraphs in an essay, are organically interdependent in the same way that organisms in the body and all living things are organically interdependent. Thomas even describes language itself as an

Chris Anderson

"active, motile organism," a system of living cells, a membrane admitting and releasing energy (LC 90). Surely the essay as a form is one of the more complex combinations of these cells of meaning, an ecosystem unto itself. On this level, in other words, the relationship between form and theme in Thomas worked effectively to organize our discussions of writing, providing metaphors for approaching the conventional concerns of producing clear prose. I was even able to use the metaphor of ecology and interdependence and collaboration to frame and justify thematically our in-class collaborative writing and discussion groups.

A second way to deal with the division between the article and the essay is to establish a sequence beginning with the reflective and extending into the argumentative and analytical (Moffet, Britton, Emig). I am skeptical about the capacity of cognitive psychology to justify any such sequence, but on a practical level it makes sense to me that students learn best by first writing about their own experience in more informal ways and then gradually moving to higher levels of abstraction. Thus I began with freewriting and moved to the first paper. The first paper was more personal and reflective, the second, full-length paper more detached.

Furthermore, though essay and article writing call on different strategies and thought processes, they both require directness, conciseness, and concreteness on the sentence level. This is the important implication of Ross Winterowd's recent "Dramatism in Themes and Poems," which argues that all good writing depends on a "dramatistic" movement in sentences. This is also the assumption of Joseph Williams's *Style: Ten Lessons in Clarity and Grace*, which I used in class to discuss conciseness and clarity. To put this another way, the same values of concreteness and directness, the same clear relationships between concrete subjects and active verbs, that Thomas illustrates so clearly in his reflective essays also make the sentences of the term paper readable and effective. It may even be—to return to the idea of sequence—that students can best learn about these stylistic qualities by writing reflectively first and then moving on to the article.

Teaching Lewis Thomas

For that matter, as the model student papers in my textbook showed, there are places in the term paper, particularly in the opening focusing event and in the conclusion, for the kind of narration and description of personal experience reflective writing requires, and for personal reflection on the meaning of information (see the student paper "Does Dowsing Work?" in Johnson, 244–55). Even classical rhetorical lore insists on the value of narration and description as ways of magnifying ethos and pathos in both the exordium and the peroration, and, furthermore, values the strategies of the poetic as ways of securing identification and creating presence.

But while all these compromises are valid and necessary, I think they finally tame the issues too much. The division, the tension, is real. Thomas, of course, has written hundreds of scientific articles, and he defends the scientific method even while recognizing its limitations. In his view the limitations are spurs to more activity and an argument for humility, not a reason for quietism and resignation. Yet it seems to me that Thomas is not final a rhetorical relativist. What I've been trying to suggest is that the themes of Thomas's essays ultimately justify and argue for the form of the essay itself. In addition to the organicism Thomas sees in nature, there is an organic relationship, a symbiosis, in the essays themselves between Thomas's notions of research and error and ambiguity and the style, the form, the movement of his prose. Read closely, Thomas's essays are an attack on the term paper.

As he says in his essay on the essay, the scientific papers he wrote earlier in his career were "composed in the relentlessly flat style required for absolute unambiguity in every word, hideous language as I read it today." Although the opportunity to write essays "worried" him a little, it also "raised his spirits" (YS 200). Given Thomas's facination with what can be seen "out of the corner of the eye," his faith in the ambiguity of language, his insistence that "matters of true importance" can only be expressed indirectly and concretely, it is inevitable that he would want to "break free" of the deadening prose of the narrowly scholarly paper.

Given his affection for the "full hairy complexity of

things" and his skepticism about computerized ways of thinking, it is obvious why Thomas thinks Montaigne is a "marvel," a source of "hope." The genius of Montaigne for Thomas is that he invented a form capable of embodying what it means, what it feels like, to be an "ordinary man." "On he goes," Thomas says, "page after page, giving away his thoughts without allowing himself to be constrained by any discipline of consistency." For Thomas this kind of self-dramatization has a moral force. "The greatest thing of the world," he approvingly quotes from Montaigne, "is for a man to know how to be his own" (MS 124).

In "On How to Fix the Premedical Curriculum," Thomas translates these implicit arguments for the essay into a program for education. The MCATs and the premed major should be abolished. Literature and languages should be at the center of premedical education. All future doctors should be made to read Greek and Latin. What we should be trying to produce is students "who are ready to be startled and excited by a totally new and unfamiliar body of knowledge, eager to learn, unpreoccupied by notions of relevance that are paralyzing the minds of today's first year medical students already so surfeited by science that they want to start practicing psychiatry in the first trimester of the first year" (MS 116). Students should be taught "error," in other words, trained and tested in ambiguity and the peripheral. What we should look for is "the free range of the student's mind, his tenacity and resolve, his innate capacity for the understanding of human beings, and his affection for the human condition" (MS 115). As William Zeiger has recently pointed out, these liberal and humanistic values are embodied in the open-endedness and concreteness of the essay as a form. The essay enables students to "test" their knowledge against their experience, exploring ideas rather than manufacturing false conclusions.

Another indication that the division between the term paper and the essay cannot be easily healed is that my students refused to accept my invitation to write essays. For the most part they chose to write in the "relentlessly flat style" required by their various majors. Not on the level of theory but in their own experience on my particular campus, the students in Writing 222 realized the danger, or the irrelevancy, of what I was giving them the option of doing. As one of my better students wrote in an evaluation, she appreciated the chance to write autobiographical pieces in my class and thought that such writing might even help her with her "real writing" later on. Like Thomas, my students are not rhetorical relativists. They realize, too, that form is ideology, and that despite the commonalities of style and strategy that extend across genre boundaries, there are choices to be made in a writing class just as there are in a college career.

My Writing 222 was not subversive or innovative in particular. It was a jumble. I hadn't understood the potential subversiveness of Thomas's writing, and I found myself often ignoring its invitations as I tried to do all the things that a teacher should do in a term paper writing course. We talked about thesis statements and research strategies. I forced my students to revise and attend to coherence and structure. In fact, in the last two weeks of the course I had to take my students to task for turning in sloppy and incoherent work. My thoughts about the ideology of the essay came as occasional asides, little epiphanies in the general blur of the quarter. There wasn't—and I think there can never be—methodological purity. At best there was a tension. When I could get my students to listen to what Thomas is really saying to them, all I could offer was my own category mistake.

Perhaps this is enough. Perhaps the tension itself is valuable. By making that an issue for part of the quarter, perhaps I was able to make the class interesting and important. After all, we *do* have a responsibility to our colleagues in other disciplines, and not just in a course like Writing 222. We may feel the pressures of practicality more strongly in a term paper writing class than in freshman or advanced composition, but all our classes are subject to the demands of relevance and usefulness, especially in a writing-across-the-curriculum program. From this perspective perhaps all we can ever do is identify the choices.

Chris Anderson

But as I've thought about my experience over the last few months, I've come to realize that Thomas won't let me or any of us off the hook so easily. As Elbow has recently argued, most excellent teachers are not "middling or fair," but passionate. We have an obligation to encourage our students yet we also have a responsibility to maintain the standards of our field; we must be positive with our students, bringing out, educing, what is inside of them, yet we must also grade and certify, making sure that our students have learned what they need to learn. This is a necessary "contrary," in Elbow's view. The opposition between "coaching" and "criticizing" is inherent in the teaching of writing, unavoidable. We must do both kinds of things, and each calls on different skills and habits of mind. Yet Elbow goes on to argue that good teachers, excellent teachers, emphasize one pole over another, even while keeping both elements in tension. Excellent teachers don't try to be two people at once. They "tend to be a bit passionate about supporting students or else passionate about serving and protecting the subject matter they love—and thus they tend to live more on one side or the other of some allegedly golden mean" (329).

Thomas makes the same demand for excellence. Obviously we need to teach our students a variety of rhetorical forms, including the forms of academic and technical writing. They cannot always write reflective essays. The question Thomas encourages us to ask is what the most important goals of a writing course should be. Ultimately he calls us to question again the subordination of the English Department to the practical demands of other disciplines. Yes, we have an obligation to teach our students how to write in the ways they will need to in other classes and out in the world, yet the implicit argument of Thomas's work is that we also have an obligation to teach students how to discover and test who they are in the process of writing, and that this, the second part of the contrary, is the pole we should be passionate about.

Even more than that, Thomas forces us to question the basic premises of those practical demands from other disciplines. If scientific research must proceed by error, motivated always by wonder, a sense of mystery, grounded always in the sensibilities of the inquiring subject, then the term paper as it is conventionally conceived is simply not useful, in any discipline. In both the form and the themes of his essays Thomas argues that there are no easy answers, in any field, that everything must be seen in terms of the self, that every self must be in constant interaction with other things in the world and other people, that writing is relationship and that all good writing captures the act of relating, the process of thinking about important things.

This is how Thomas's essays are "literary." It's not that in teaching Thomas as model we expect students to write up to a certain standard of stylistic excellence. One of the most compelling features of the essay as a form, particularly as it's practiced by writers like Thomas, is its unpretentiousness and humility. It is, by definition, an attempt, not a performance. The invitation is not, "watch me write," but "join me in thinking." Despite his grace and lyricism, Thomas writes in the voice of an amatuer. He is not a writer writing but a biochemist and doctor and person turning to the form of the essay to share his thinking. His essays are literary not because they are "good" in the elitist sense of displaying talent or genius (even though they *are* good in this sense) but because they look at the world in a literary way: because they recreate experiences and explore their significance, because they acknowledge the complexity of the image, the event, the idea. As a mode of inquiry this requires, not talent, but discipline and a shift in perspective. It is, as Thomas argues in "On How to Fix the Premedical Curriculum," exactly the way of thinking that young, inexperienced minds need to learn. Answers, abstractions, assertions come later, with experience and knowledge. Students first need to learn the discipline of exploring, of asking questions, of testing possibilities.

Our students seem to be wanting to twist and turn to rid themselves of language, because everywhere they see language unrelated to the things they care about, language in which individuals are absorbed and forgotten. All around them in the university language is seen simply as choice, not as value,

331

Chris Anderson

as corporate, not as individual. The challenge of Thomas's essays, and of all literary nonfiction, is a challenge to this kind of depersonalization and systematizing. It is the challenge of the humanities—a challenge that in my view rhetoric and composition as a discipline has yet to meet.

Works Cited

Beale, Walter. *Real Writing*. Glenview: Scott Foresman, 1982.
Britton, James, et al. *The Development of Writing Abilities* (11–18). London: Macmillan, 1975.
Christensen, Francis. "A Generative Rhetoric of the Sentence." *College Composition and Communications* 14 (1963): 155–61.
Elbow, Peter. *Writing With Power*. New York: Oxford, 1981.
———. "Embracing Contraries in the Teaching Process." *College English* 45 (1983): 327–39.
Emig, Janet. *The Composing Processes of Twelfth-Graders*. Urbana: NCTE, 1971.
Hoagland, Edward. "What I Think, What I Am." *Eight Modern Essayists*. Ed. William Smart. 4th ed. New York: St. Martins, 1985. 222–25.
Johnson, Jean. *The Bedford Guide to the Research Process*. New York: St. Martins', 1987.
Kinneavy, James L. *A Theory of Discourse*. Englewood Cliffs: Prentice-Hall, 1971; rpt. New York: Norton, 1980.
Moffett, James. *Teaching the Universe of Discourse*. Boston: Houghton Mifflin, 1968.
Thomas, Lewis. *The Lives of a Cell* (LC). New York: Viking 1974.
———. *The Medusa and the Snail* (MS). New York: Viking, 1979.
———. *The Youngest Science* (YS). New York: Bantam, 1983.
———. *Late Night Thoughts on Listening to Mahler's Ninth Symphony*. New York: Viking, 1983.
Weathers, Winston. *An Alternate Style*. Rochelle Park: Hayden, 1980.
Williams, Joseph M. *Style: Ten Lessons in Clarity and Grace*. 2nd edition. Glenview: Scott Foresman, 1985.
Winterowd, Ross. "Dramatism in Themes and Poems." *College English* 45 (1983): 581–88.
Zeiger, William. "The Exploratory Essay: Enfranchising the Spirit of Inquiry in College Composition." *College English* 47 (1985): 454–66.

NOTES ON CONTRIBUTORS

NOTES ON CONTRIBUTORS

Mark Allister teaches American literature and writing at St. Olaf College. He has published articles on Faulkner, James Agee, popular culture, and the teaching of literature and writing.

Suzanne Clark is Assistant Professor of English and Coordinator of English Education at Oregon State University. She has published articles and reviews in *The North Dakota Quarterly, The Minnesota Review, The MMLA Bulletin,* and *Technical Communication Working Papers.* Her work on Dillard is part of a long-term project on the questions of subjectivity for women writing.

John Clifford is Associate Professor of English at the University of North Carolina at Wilmington where he also directs the writing program. His most recent publications include essays on ideology and discourse in the *Journal of Advanced Composition,* on Kenneth Burke and democratic schooling in *Audits of Meaning,* and a critique of *Textual Power* in *College English.* He is currently editing a collection of essays on Louise Rosenblatt and writing a review of English studies in the eighties.

Jim W. Corder is Professor of English at Texas Christian University, where he has been a member of the faculty, sometime department chairman, sometime dean, since 1958. He is the author of *Contemporary Writing, Uses of Rhetoric, A Handbook of Current English, Lost in West Texas* (essays), and various pieces about rhetoric.

George L. Dillon is Professor of English at the University of Washington. He has written numerous books and articles on English language and the language of literature, on rhetorical and textual theory, most recently *Rhetoric as Social Interaction.*

Peter Elbow is Professor of English at the University of

Notes on Contributors

Massachusetts at Amherst. He is author of *Oppositions in Chaucer*, *Writing Without Teachers*, *Writing With Power*, and *Embracing Contraries in Learning and Teaching*, and numerous essays about writing, literature, and teaching. His essay "The Shifting Relationship between Speech and Writing" won the Braddock Award as the best 1985 article in *College Composition and Communication*.

Richard Filloy is Assistant Professor of English at the University of Oregon. His related previous publications have appeared in *The Quarterly Journal of Speech*, *The Writing Instructor*, *The Journal of Advanced Composition*, and (with Walter Fisher) *Advances in Argumentation Theory and Research*.

Phyllis Frus teaches American literature and nonfiction writing at Vanderbilt University. The author of articles in *College English, Genre, Biography*, and *Modern Language Studies*, she is completing a book entitled "The 'Other' American Literature: New Journalism and the Nonfiction Novel."

Douglas Hesse is Assistant Professor of English at Illinois State University, where he teaches writing, rhetorical theory, and narrative theory and directs the writing across the curriculum program. He is currently working on a book, "The Story in the Essay."

Pat C. Hoy II is Professor of English at the U.S. Military Academy, where he directs the freshman writing program and teaches British and American literature and composition. He has published articles and reviews in *South Atlantic Review*, *Twentieth Century Literature*, and *The Sewanee Review*. *Prose Pieces: Essays and Stories*, with Robert DiYanni, has just been published; *Women's Voices*, with DiYanni and Esther Schor, is forthcoming. He is also at work on *Writing Essays: A Persuasive Art*.

Carl H. Klaus is Professor of English at the University of Iowa, where he has also served as director of the advanced writing program and more recently as director of the NEH/Iowa Institute on Writing. Co-designer of the Primary Trait System for the assessment of writing, he is editor of *Style in English Prose*, co-author of *Elements of the Essay* and *Elements of Writing*, author of *Composing Adolescent Experience* and *Compos-*

Notes on Contributors

ing Childhood Experience, co-editor of *Fields of Writing: Readings Across the Disciplines* and *Courses for Change in Writing: A Selection from the NEH/Iowa Institute*, a co-winner of the Modern Language Association's Mina Shaughnessy Prize.

Jack Roundy is the Director of Academic and Career Advising at the University of Puget Sound.

Dennis Rygiel is Professor of English at Auburn University. He has published articles in *College Composition and Communication, College English, Neophilologus, Neuphilologische, Mitteilungen, Studies in Philology*, and *Style*.

John Schilb is Vice President of the Associated Colleges of the Midwest, a consortium of liberal arts colleges. His publications have addressed a range of subjects, including the history of rhetoric, the teaching of noncanonical literature, the relation of literary theory to composition theory, and women's studies.

Charles I. Schuster is Associate Professor of English and Coordinator of Composition and Proficiency Testing at the University of Wisconsin-Milwaukee. He has published articles in *College English, Rhetoric Review, College Composition and Communication, The Clearing House, Perspectives in Biology and Medicine,* and *Pennsylvania Medicine*. He is working on a freshman rhetoric and is general editor of a two-volume anthology of essays entitled "The Politics of Writing Instruction."

William Zeiger teaches rhetoric and composition at San Diego State University. He is the author of "The Exploratory Essay: Enfranchising the Spirit of Inquiry in College Composition."

337

Chris Anderson is Assistant Professor of English and Composition Coordinator at Oregon State University. He is the author of *Style as Argument: Contemporary American Nonfiction* (Southern Illinois UP, 1987).